Soldiers in a Rather Aimless War

Howard McGee MBE

Soldiers in a Rather Aimless War

Olympia Publishers

London

www.olympiapublishers.com

OLYMPIA PAPERBACK EDITION

A CIP catalogue record for this title is
available from the British Library.

ISBN: 978-1-78830-335-4

First Published in 2019

Olympia Publishers
60 Cannon Street
London
EC4N 6NP

Printed in Great Britain

Dedication

To my sons and their children — present and future, ultimately family is everything.

This book is dedicated to all those members of the British Armed Forces who never came home from our desert wars, those who carry the scars — both physical and mental — of our recent conflicts and all those who have served or still serve on *"Our city walls, so good citizens can sleep safe in their beds"*.

Acknowledgements

To "George" and Alex L for the kind use of their photographs, George and Mike in particular for their ongoing help and patience and to all my team, British and American alike, for their stoicism and unwavering support throughout our time together in Iraq.

For me personally, my road to the invasion of Iraq began in Eastern Europe — the last European conflict of the 20th Century to be precise — Kosovo 1999, a rather small Balkan province and previously unheard-of by most Westerners. That may surprise most people, but the perceived and often quoted "success" of NATO's 79-day air campaign gave rise and temporary credence to the practical military application of the New Labour concept of "Liberal Intervention" and (far more importantly) gave senior British politicians a taste for being world players. Military success is always rewarding for a collection of large political egos with a liking for basking in reflected glory, having streets named after you and the odd new-born babe christened in your honour. This perception of a "European victory" at little cost, combined with the UK's later highly effective (if on a far smaller scale) intervention in Sierra Leone further seemed to convince our leaders that we were virtually guaranteed success at a very low cost in both casualties and finances because of the "righteousness" (and undoubted technological superiority) of our cause, combined with the hugely mistaken belief that everyone ultimately desired our tolerant, increasingly liberal values and an overarching democratic society and, perhaps most of all, their self-perceived intellectual superiority when it came to great matters of statehood.

Later, in the wake of 9/11 and the swift and (initially at least) successful invasion of Afghanistan in 2001, a mixture of ignored military deficiencies and general political smugness from this highly successful but actually very small Balkan intervention (Kosovo is the roughly same size as Yorkshire in terms of land mass), combined with wholesale historical and cultural/social ignorance, together with an appalling lack of strategic planning, all combined to become major flaws during the Anglo/American Invasion of Iraq in 2003. These flaws would brutally expose our military deficiencies, lack of political vision and in many ways, Western naïveté when it came to dealing with the fractured, complex and occasionally medieval block that we so blandly refer to as "Islam". Then and now, we seem simply incapable of understanding the complexities, differences and ancient schisms that run across the Islamic world. One size does not fit all and liberal Western values are often seen as weak and despicable anathema rather than noble goals to aspire to.

The somewhat arrogant and repeated political mind-set of "Job done, move on to the next one" would also come back to haunt us with regard to Afghanistan, as Alexander the Great, Genghis Khan and both the British Army of the 19th century and the Red Army of the 20th would all testify to. Capturing Afghanistan was not that difficult in simple general war terms: Afghans may be rather mediocre, conventional soldiers, but prolonged and pitiless guerrilla warfare against foreign invaders is simply in their collective DNA. However, effectively holding onto Afghanistan proved to be yet another matter altogether, but none of our leaders appeared to have read any pre-1997 history, or perhaps they all naïvely thought it was just a large Balkans with a liberal dose of sand. The recent Afghanistan war and the bitter fighting in Helmand Province was, after all, Britain's fourth Afghan war. As someone once said "History is to politicians as sunlight is to vampires". That certainly applied to New Labour, at least from a British soldier's perspective.

Either way, by switching our focus to invading Iraq in 2003, we meanwhile allowed the Taliban all the time and space they so desperately needed to make a rather successful "come back", but that is another story and one well covered by a host of Helmand-based books. We Brits often talk about "*Afghanistan*" but by the end of that long and bitterly fought campaign, we actually controlled just three small districts within one single province, albeit a province almost the same size as England. Few people in the UK ever seemed to realise the sheer size of Helmand within a huge country by European standards. The British military never had a "national" footprint and quietly lost its "lead nation" status when the US Marines arrived en masse to bolster our gallant but failing efforts within Helmand Province in 2009, the second American military bail-out in less than 4 years, something which both our military and political leaders studiously ignore. Our troops, simply outstanding throughout the long years of attrition, were just never numerous enough to hold the ground they repeatedly fought over with incredible courage and determination, despite never being beaten at any time or anywhere in Helmand Province, or, indeed, Iraq. Modern asymmetric warfare is both complex and singularly resistant to a "quick fix", especially when you face ruthless enemies playing a very long game, who regard you simply as "the

Infidel" and appeal to medieval religious views using high-tech 21st Century social media and often don't particularly mind dying, which in itself is very much a "game changer". To paraphrase a Taliban leader, we may have had the watches, but they had the time and an exceedingly simple strategy of just outlasting us. Ultimately, they knew us far better than we ever knew them.

These collective flaws began in a wide variety of ways, the most glaring one being the enduring myth that air power alone had defeated the Serbian Armed Forces in Kosovo and forced them to withdraw. The air campaign over Kosovo itself (heavily wooded with numerous built up areas and quite mountainous in places) was remarkably ineffective, mainly resulting in moving large amounts of Balkan mud and the repeated destruction of numerous wooden dummies and an ingenious variety of associated decoys, much to the great amusement of the Serbian Army, who even held a victory parade, complete with a low level fly-past by Pristina-based Serbian Air Force MiG 21s despite our very best attempts to destroy them, when they finally left Pristina for "Mother Serbia". We had managed to destroy just over a dozen of the 350 Serbian armoured vehicles that had been active in Kosovo during the air campaign, not exactly a re-run of the Normandy campaign and a small detail that wasn't passed on to Western journalists, whilst our political leaders basked in the kudos of victory and ample photo opportunities with tens of thousands of extremely grateful Kosovars.

While the tactical campaign over Kosovo may have been of little real military value, the strategically effective bombing of immobile and large infrastructure targets, such as the Serbian equivalent of the BBC Head Quarters, all of Belgrade's power stations and a couple of "unhelpful" embassies was successful. Apparently accidently, but it did send a rather significant message in blunt diplomatic terms to those nations who hadn't supported our actions. The bombing of Belgrade and key national infrastructure, combined with Russian political pressure and fear of a NATO ground invasion of Kosovo duly brought the Serbs to the negotiating table. But the politicians of UK and NATO saw this as a shining example as a new age of "bloodless" warfare and totally ignored the numerous failures of the air campaign over Kosovo, except for the

Pentagon, who discreetly dispatched several "K MEAT" teams (Kosovo Munitions Effectiveness Analysis Team) to work out exactly why their best efforts had reaped such disappointing rewards and inflicted such embarrassingly minuscule damage to the Serbian Army and never seriously hampered their military operations within Kosovo. Meanwhile NATO's European Air Forces, including the RAF, went home for tea and medals and quietly ignored the boring fact that the Serbian air defences, whilst dented and battered, had never actually been broken. The US Air Force would soon actively display the collective results of these teams' findings when Iraq beckoned a later President in the aftermath of the Twin Towers and 9/11.

The land campaign meanwhile had exposed numerous problems in logistical and equipment terms for the British troops stationed in Macedonia, from personal clothing and tents to resupply and boots. However, the Treasury-driven "just enough, just in time" dispatch of armoured troops from nearby Bosnia and elements of the now defunct lightly equipped 5 Airborne Brigade from UK, together with most of the RAF's support helicopters combined, very successfully it has to be said, at the last safe moment to obscure these issues, and also looked very good on TV doing so. The overall result was that neither our political nor military leaders saw any reason to consider investing in any new equipment, despite all our major European allies (Italy, Germany and France) being both significantly better equipped and prepared for an operation of this nature. We had gradually committed, in total, some 40% of the Regular Army and withdrawn the vast majority as soon as possible, our equipment was barely adequate in several aspects and our organisation had rather creaked at times, but the now historical County Regimental System and remarkably well trained, led and motivated troops had enabled us, as always, to make it work.

But quietly, a lot of us were rather glad the surprisingly professional Serbian Army hadn't put us to the acid test against some of the best (in purely militarily terms) defensive terrain in Europe. Yes, we would very probably have won, but it could have been very costly. The Serbs may be viewed as xenophobic, bordering on racist in Western eyes, but they viewed themselves as patriots defending hallowed ground. Eastern

Europeans have a much keener view of their collective history (especially concerning the repeated Ottoman campaigns across the entire Balkans over several centuries) than their liberal Western neighbours who seem to view history as largely irrelevant. However, we didn't yet realise our "blood price" wasn't going to be paid in Europe, as large and enduring desert wars were not on our collective menu, but then neither did we realise our leaders had discreetly acquired a taste for ongoing military interventions, or that the Treasury simply did not wish to pay for these distant military ventures, so war on the cheap seemed to be the preferred option.

The Italians, to our great surprise, were remarkably well equipped to deal with the extremes of the Balkan climate. One Italian officer remarked that he had seen our tents before, on "MASH", (the American television satire set in the Korean War), while the French had some very impressive personal body armour and effective light armoured vehicles, the like of which we wouldn't see until around 2009. Everyone it seemed had far more reliable rifles than us and the Germans meanwhile had a complete brigade of tanks and armoured vehicles "prepositioned" in Macedonia and maintained in readiness for large-scale combat operations at very short notice, lacking crews only in effect. Meanwhile the Bundeswehr troops earmarked for Kosovo trained back home in Germany on a separate and dedicated training fleet of armoured vehicles, quite incredible to the British military mind set of doing more and more with less and less. We, the British military, had a deeply ingrained, ultra-positive "can do" attitude that would prove in the 21st Century to be a double-edged sword in many respects. Punching above your weight is a fine trait, but it can only stretch so far — as our Desert Wars would soon demonstrate in a pitiless manner — particularly when we returned to Afghanistan for our fourth Afghan war.

The Americans, who arrived quite late on this particular Balkan operation, had an obsession (or so we then thought) for force protection and AARs — after action reviews — something we Brits avoided as quite unnecessary after such a mutually satisfying success. We watched, in quiet and almost smug amusement, as the US Marines belatedly arrived in Kosovo. Even their supply vehicles were all mounted with heavy machine guns, grenade launchers and the like, while they, unlike ourselves, wore body armour and helmets continuously, courtesy of their Somalian experience as later made public by the *Black Hawk Down* film. The Americans, unlike the Europeans, faced up to mistakes and shortfalls and addressed them with both an enviable candour and remarkable vigour. As we would later learn in both Iraq and Afghanistan, the American Military learnt and adapted remarkably fast, whilst we had a collective hang-up over our much quoted Northern Ireland experience, though that admission would have to wait for a decade before we finally admitted that Basra and Helmand were not simply Belfast and South Armagh with sand.

As the conflict ended, numerous previously uninvolved nations sent thousands of troops as European nations from Scandinavia to the Baltic to Hungary and Greece literally flocked into Kosovo to eagerly assume peace keeping duties, allowing the UK to rapidly downsize its military presence: "Job done, go home," in effect. Simultaneously the major charities flooded en masse to provide timely and massive amounts of life-saving support to thousands of displaced Kosovars and assist in the rebuilding of Kosovo. Suddenly this small Balkan province was awash with white 4x4s from a plethora of organisations, almost fighting each other to distribute aid and support after months of sitting idle across the border in Macedonia.

Meanwhile the politicians seemed to take note of this as best practice for future operations and the immediate aftermath of conflict. However, no one mentioned the very strong influence of the Albanian Mafia amongst Kosovo's new leaders or the curious fact that an additional one million "refugees" had somehow "returned" to Kosovo, primarily from Albania, to massively boost its pre-war population. Simultaneously the Public Records Office in Pristina had mysteriously and rapidly burnt down, so no one could either prove, or disprove, property ownership and similar legal niceties, or indeed, the actual right of residence. Quite a useful "coincidence" for the conduct of large-scale and heavily armed criminal activity, which was quickly followed by wholesale land and house theft, armed and often brutal intimidation and widespread kidnapping. Such issues tend to rather take the gloss away from a successful liberal intervention operation. The media, as always, had by now moved on to newer stories in search of more happy endings. Kosovo had rapidly become yesterday's news, so the messy and violent aftermath was quietly ignored and the KLA, together with organised crime ruthlessly consolidated their power base to dominate post-conflict Kosovo.

So, like many other British soldiers, I came home with a grudging respect for the very determined and well-led Serbian Army and somewhat bemused that NATO had been the "Air Wing" for the Kosovo Liberation Army, who made the Provisional IRA look quite well-mannered in comparison. They were in effect almost the military arm of the Albanian Mafia and neither were too fussed about either human rights or basic democracy. We kept our distance from the KLA, partly by design and partly by choice. Many of us viewed them with mistrust and quiet disdain: their similarity towards our old enemy in Northern Ireland, especially in their methods and manner of dealing with collaborators or maintaining social discipline, was striking.

One conversation I now recall often, but then ignored as plain sour grapes, was a casual conversation with a Serbian Army Captain from Belgrade. Our advance into Kosovo frequently became mixed up with the Serbian withdrawal, so mixing with the enemy was not uncommon. He spoke fluent English and failed to comprehend how the Serbs and the English had come to be on the opposite sides of conflict. He reminded me of 1914 and "plucky little Serbia", the remnants of their defeated Army later being rescued from Albania by the Royal Navy to sanctuary in Corfu and our later support to the Partisans of World War 2, including a certain Randolph Churchill, amongst other British agents. Both his historical knowledge and respect for all things British was highly impressive.

Many Serbs apparently believed our PM had pushed for a conflict in order to make a name for himself on the world stage. He also bemoaned the use of the very high Muslim birth rate in Kosovo as a strategic generational weapon to alter the demographics of Kosovo itself dramatically over several decades. Serbs, he explained, unlike the local Kosovars and neighbouring Albanians (apparently), limit the number of children they raise to the number they can afford to raise and educate in order to have a better life than their parents. Kosovo itself was the first major battle between Christian knights against the invading Ottoman Empire in 1389 and so held a special place in the Serbian psyche, similar to Camelot in English myths and legends. He concluded by warning me against the joint perils of uncontrolled immigration and associated high birth rates, not for me but for future generations. Strong views indeed and proof to me that this part of the Balkans had almost physically deep memories of the long centuries of repeated Ottoman invasion and occupation. Back then I felt this totally irrelevant to us Western Europeans, along with his views over my own PM. I occasionally reflect on this conversation and quietly wonder to myself if his points are all so utterly irrelevant now.

I also had a nagging personal feeling that we Brits had "cuffed it" but ultimately got away with it, aided unconsciously by the media who, as ever, were very subjective and blessed with ultrashort attention spans, preferring dramatic images to boring facts. But as an army, we had done a very good job, undoubtedly saved thousands of lives and, I thought (rather optimistically as it transpired), we would, no doubt, learn all our lessons and quickly sort out the logistical problems and associated issues from what was essentially a rather small European conflict which had been relatively close to home. The geographic proximity had undoubtedly gone a very long way to the eventual and relatively painless happy ending, but this was also something we never gave much serious thought to. Western soldiers, Americans excepted, only really pay attention to logistics when the supply chain fails.

Little did I know that almost the complete reverse was true, and within less than 4 years' time we would be sent to invade Iraq almost as poorly prepared and equipped as our forerunners who had been so blithely dispatched to defend France in 1940. It rather appears, to me at least, that the political leaders of both periods quite liked sending the Army off to war in distant lands and the kudos thereof, but paying for it was an entirely different issue. Some things never change, it seems. However, overall Kosovo had been a "just little war". Whilst the much-reported genocide didn't seem to have actually taken place, many violent acts undoubtedly had and we, the British Army, had done an excellent job as enforcers of peace, as a "force for good" and felt exceedingly pleased with ourselves, proving yet again that we were, undoubtedly, the best army in the world.

Late 2002 was just another ordinary year in North Yorkshire to us all, another year nearly over and also a year since our regimental "Afghanistan Flap", when we had rushed to prepare for a deployment to Kabul in late 2001 that never actually happened. The invasion of Afghanistan had eventually been an "SF only" operation (Special Forces are normally referred to as SF within the British Armed Forces, although they have many more colloquial names, such as "the Blades" or simply "Hooligans") and this had been very much an SF affair, with some limited RAF involvement. The "Green Army", i.e. the conventional troops — Infantry, Armour and suchlike in Army slang — simply didn't have the right equipment to offer much to gainfully assist the American-dominated invasion and the RAF likewise didn't have the air transport capability to move us there anyway. Besides which, in military terms, the Americans didn't particularly need us and SF troops are very lightly equipped, and therefore quite a cheap but highly potent option to deploy in financial terms, which has always appealed to the Treasury in our recent conflicts.

Ironically, the main British contribution to Afghanistan from 2002-2006 was itself an SF task force, backed up by the now long-defunct RAF or Royal Navy Harriers, essentially a combined "SF playground" and a massive bombing range respectively for them both to discreetly "do their own thing". The rather small-scale deployment of my own brigade — 16 Air Assault — in 2006 to Helmand Province would act as a major insurgent rallying call and the Army would rapidly find itself in a world of pain, but that was far in the future and a conflict none of us could have then imagined in terms of ferocity, complexity and sheer bloody difficulty. We may not read our history books as a nation any more, but the Pashtun tribes in Southern Afghanistan still spoke of their various 19th Century wars against the hated British as if they took place last month, as we would find out to our cost in 2006.

So we prepared for Christmas and handing over our "High Readiness" status to a sister army aviation regiment based at Wattisham in East Anglia, yet another ex-RAF airfield taken over by the Army as the almost annual cuts to HM Armed Forces made ex-RAF airfields the home of choice for numerous army units steadily withdrawn from Germany, the main drawbacks being social and logistical, in that most of them were located in the middle of nowhere. The Americans had begun, rather publicly, moving men and equipment into Kuwait in very large amounts, but we paid little attention. Our then government showed no sign of the Army getting involved in terms of serious military preparation and Iraq had been bombed almost continuously since the first Gulf War of 1991, combined with various sanctions, so we didn't really see invasion as very likely, more like yet more sabre-rattling towards Saddam and his regime.

Most of the British public and the wider media have no real idea of the British Armed Forces' size and capability. "Bring in the Army" is a common cry for major problems like the foot and mouth outbreak or a potential firemen's strike, but the Army has steadily shrunk since 1991, the army of 2003 was already far different from the army that was sent to the first Gulf War of 1991 and the army of 2017 even more so in terms of both numbers and capability. The Army is not the bottomless pit of manpower and equipment that Joe Public seems to think it is: at the time of writing (2017) the British Army has quietly become a medium-sized European Defence Force with very little deployable "heavy" capability following the Afghanistan campaign. Ultimately you get what you pay for. People may not like that, but that is the stark reality of defence when the UK is cash-strapped and there are, to quote an ex-Defence Secretary, simply "no votes in defence" (or dead soldiers) in political terms. To put this in perspective, the entire Regular Army now fits very comfortably inside Wembley Stadium with several thousand seats to spare, whilst all of the Royal Navy (including the Royal Marines) accompanied by the entire RAF can do the same at Twickenham. The Americans are far too polite to comment publicly on the UK's lack of modern fighter bombers or serviceable tanks, but both Mr Putin and Islamic State have, no doubt, taken note accordingly.

Back in 1991, 2 of the 9 armoured brigades then stationed in Germany were deployed as a small, but very powerful UK armoured division containing massive firepower and a very noteworthy armoured punch while the RAF had an equally potent strike force which roamed at will, deep into central Iraq. The airborne and Commando forces had then been deemed just "too lightweight" and lacking any meaningful mobility and firepower for a major desert war: they had simply stayed at home, much to their mutual disgust and disappointment.

But the first cuts started as soon as Kuwait was re-taken and some units were informed of their disbandment whilst still in the desert waiting to come home, sadly quite typical of the future treatment to be given to the armed forces by all the successive PMs after the departure of Mrs Thatcher. She may have been controversial to some, but she took defence of the nation very seriously. Her male successors preferred the use of very selective media bites and the smoke and mirrors approach to defence, in effect maintaining the myth that we are a still "major player" militarily. So even back in 2002, the entire Army could raise only a single armoured brigade (7 Armoured Brigade) from its 3 remaining armoured brigades and the lightly equipped Air Assault Brigade into which had been placed the Army's elite airborne units. These units, combined with the Commando Brigade, would be sent to form a very ad hoc armoured division: in essence an armoured division with very little armour. As very few members of the public, journalists or defence correspondents actually have any significant depth of knowledge about matters military, these weaknesses were and are almost child's play to conceal from a public which, after decades of peace and security, tends to assume, as a default setting, that its armed forces remain both major players and a force to be reckoned with on the global stage.

Primarily and rather ironically compared to the 1991 war, these units were chosen because of their very light nature which could therefore could be deployed rapidly, shades of the "just enough, just in time" mentality which had proved so successful in Kosovo. It should be stated that the Army itself, in broad terms, fully understood the reason behind its significant downsizing: the Cold War was over, as was or at least it appeared that way then; the long and bitter Northern Ireland conflict, a unique "all British" affair also seemed to be finally drawing to a close after decades of strife. The PM of the day had loudly stated that his priority was "Education, Education, Education", along with the almost sacrosanct NHS and the eternally vote-catching and ever-growing welfare state apparatus, while the nation itself had little interest in defence and foreign wars and to be fair, why should it? So the Army did its best to reorganise accordingly. Unfortunately our foreign policy makers didn't appear to notice this at all, seemingly still believing we were a major and well-equipped military power with "global reach".

Meanwhile the RAF could fetch very little to the party also, a shadow of their former self compared to twelve years previously and would mainly limit their efforts to the Greater Basra area of southern Iraq. The US Air Force "K MEAT" teams following the American shock over at how *little* damage 79 days of air attack had actually done to the Serbian Army, had dissected their Balkan failures extremely well and the Americans simply didn't need anyone's help to rapidly demolish the Iraqi Integrated Air Defence System, a French-built, multi-billion-pound system named KARI, simply the French name for Iraq, spelt backwards.

At the time and because, militarily speaking, armoured units had totally dominated every aspect of desert warfare since the time of Rommel and Montgomery, it never crossed our mind that we would deploy as an air assault brigade with precious few helicopters and no serious parachuting capacity: in reality a 21st Century version of the wheeled infantry formation of the type sent to France in 1940, and comparably poorly equipped, in military terms of firepower, protection and mobility to conduct aggressive military operations in the 21st Century. So we went on leave in total unawareness of what was to come in early 2003. Our blissful ignorance was soon to be shattered as we moved inevitably towards the invasion of Iraq and the violent overthrow of Saddam Hussein's regime.

Personally, I was looking forward to Christmas leave for a number of reasons. Whilst lying in a shallow trench in Kosovo, a "shell scrape" in soldier parlance, just after we had liberated Pristina, I received some mail : an Officers' Mess bill and a posting order to N Ireland for 2 years, not quite morale-raising stuff, but that is all part of life in a Green suit. N

Ireland was to prove a long two years, placing a large strain on my marriage in the process. Separation is never easy an aspect of military life to deal with for all concerned: the Army's remarkably high divorce rate reflects this quite succinctly.

N Ireland was then in the slow evolution of the Peace Process, it was vastly different from the Ulster I had known in the early 1980's of the hunger strikes and regular atrocities by both Protestant and Catholic terrorists alike. After years of violence and sectarian conflict the Provisional Irish Republican Army (PIRA) had been forced onto its knees and finally asked for peace talks, the Good Friday agreement as it became known. The British Army and Royal Ulster Constabulary (RUC), having jointly forced its republican opponents reluctantly to the negotiating table, were in the process of winding down to some form of normality. As such, and following the Politicians orders, the Army was essentially confined to barracks, while the RUC tended to avoid the republican areas and PIRA was tactfully left to "maintain order" - normally with baseball bats and kneecappings, within its strongholds — a strange and confusing time to be "in the Province" as it was known to generations of British soldiers. Many soldiers, including myself, found the Politicians apparent eagerness to appease convicted terrorists quite distasteful — but orders are orders and the government obviously deemed it necessary. Accordingly collective lips were bitten, and the rest, as they say is history as our government, or so it seemed to us "little people", at least, rushed to ingratiate itself with both Sinn Fein and therefore its shadowy PIRA colleagues at almost any cost, it seemed: almost a living parody of the phrase "snatching defeat from the jaws of victory" in some ways.

Suffice it to say these were not two of the better years of my life and in late 2001, and with great relief, I was posted back to England for the final appointment of my career. Just one week later, I sat with my now ex-wife and we watched in shocked amazement, along with millions of other people around the globe, the tragedy of the Twin Towers attack unfold on live TV. I never for a single moment imagined the repercussions this would have on both my own life and indeed. the entire British Army and how this would lead to several hundred deaths and over ten thousand wounded, in pure army terms a battalion of dead soldiers and a division's worth of wounded, during over a decade of unrelenting desert combat in not one but two wars. Tragically sad figures which would grow on a weekly basis as the "Afghan campaign" unfolded: the British Army's fourth Afghan War, the Afghans had certainly not "forgotten us" and neither had the Iraqis, as I was shortly to learn. To many of them this was merely a continuation of previous conflicts following a lengthy intermission.

Having been commissioned from the ranks, I had transitioned, in 1997 after 22 years' service, from Corps RSM to a Short Service Commission of 6 years' duration, which was due to conclude in 2003. Incredibly, I was chosen, with a mere 18 months' "Colour Service" remaining in the Army, to play a key role in the introduction into front line service of the multi-million-pound Apache attack helicopter (AH). The upshot of my preoccupation with this game-changing weapon system was that in late 2002, I suddenly realised that I had a mere 6 months left in the Army to sort my life out before I became one of those strange people known as "civilians". A very frightening thought: leaving the British Army and the comfort zone of the "Green Machine" after joining as a young teenager decades earlier was simply terrifying to me. As many soldiers discover on encountering the realities of Civvy Street and 21st Century UK society, in direct comparison to the closed ranks of regimental life, it's a strange world. Having been a soldier for all of my adult life, like most career soldiers, I found the prospect daunting to say the least.

So as 2002 drew to a close and against the wider backdrop of American Sabre rattling and the domestic friction of repeated separation over the past 3 years, I was utterly preoccupied with the question of "what the fuck now then?" Unbeknown to me, Messrs Bush, Blair and Hussein were all to combine to answer that question on my behalf, and very, very shortly.

We returned back to our North Yorkshire barracks, following our Christmas leave, from various parts of the UK to rumour and counter rumour. Rumour control is, and always has been, one of the few growth industries within UK defence for generations of soldiers. Whilst no one had been recalled from leave, the Staff Officers in Regimental Head Quarters (RHQ) had been quite busy planning and replanning various options for war over Christmas. So, we did what professional soldiers always do at the behest of the politicians: "Hurry up and wait".

Our sister regiment in far-off Wattisham had, unbeknown to ourselves, had also been very busy over Christmas, reacting to various and often contradictory orders from "higher formation", as soldiers refer to their formation headquarters. Ultimately any British military deployment is driven by the Treasury, who approve or veto all aspects of the FET, the Force Equipment Table, which defines all aspects of the force composition, in infinite detail each and every piece of equipment, ammunition scales, manning levels, etc. All of these cost money, hence the ultimate authority of the Treasury who, like all our recent politicians, prefer to keep the cost down: understandable and laudable in pure spreadsheet terms. Unfortunately the cost for many British soldiers has been far more immediate and painful, as illustrated by the infamous "Snatch" Land Rovers. These vehicles were designed to cope with petrol bombs and bricks during riots in West Belfast and general urban patrolling in N Ireland, *totally* unsuited for any form of modern operations in either Iraq or Afghanistan and rapidly nicknamed the "Mobile Coffin" by soldiers. They were also abundant, quite redundant and most importantly, very cheap post N Ireland, but from the insurgent point of view in first Iraq and then Helmand Province, an extremely easy and very attractive "soft" target. Put bluntly, the crews of these vehicles all too often paid for this financially attractive option with their lives.

In fairness to our commanders, none of us anticipated the sheer levels of violence the insurgency would generate or indeed, that any significant insurgency would follow our invasion. Plus, we lacked suitable vehicles at this time: the mass purchase of American "M-RAP" (mine resistant, ambush protected) vehicles lay in the distant future as did the "IED War" which was equally unforeseen by all of us. In that respect we were all guilty of wishful thinking in terms of a grateful Iraqi population and no one really grasped the extent of the Sunni/Shia schism within Iraq, so our options were indeed limited. Neither did we imagine the later migration of IED technology from both Sunni insurgents and

Shia militias, across Iran (the world's only Shia nation) to the Wahabist dominated (Sunni) Taliban, an unthinkable act of information sharing pre-2003. Ironically, as the Army acquired better protected vehicles in Iraq, the Snatch vehicles were shipped to Afghanistan, just in time for the Taliban's switch of tactics to a massive IED campaign.

Following the hasty planning over Christmas, by very early January, the Individual Augmentee Bill had been finalised. In 2003 all Regular Army units had two establishments in manning terms, simply known as "Peace" and "War". The theory was that the extra soldiers for the War Establishment would be supplied by the Territorial Army (TA). The reality was that the TA, with the exception of some gifted individuals and a handful of specialist units, were then simply not fit for purpose: in effect a hobby in uniform and really a uniformed social club in 2003. Hopefully this may change with the advent of the future Army of 2020 but like most ex-regulars, I personally am far from convinced. I would argue a future major conflict or yet another foreign battlefield is not the time and place to discover that cost-cutting has gone too far, but the modern armed forces are dominated by budgets and spin doctors, not strategists and tacticians. So, for all major conflicts of recent times the Regular Army has historically backfilled the gaps by simply attaching regular soldiers to the deploying units from non-deploying units. The Iraq invasion (liberation is a term I would prefer to avoid) was no exception to this pattern: it had worked since 1945, so why not now?

The latest rumour was that approximately 60 or so personnel would be required, the vast majority of the regiment having loudly and persistently volunteered: me included. I had sat, as a young corporal, in County Tyrone in 1982 as the Task Force had sailed south to the Falklands and in Germany, as a Squadron Sergeant Major, in 1991 when Kuwait had been liberated with such consummate ease. I did not wish to miss this one, especially as this was my last chance. Prior to the Army's decade-plus of war and its very discreet, but growing weekly, casualty figures, which was all yet to come, just as all professional footballers yearn for a big Cup Final, so professional soldiers hoped for a war as the natural culmination of years of training and the ultimate test. That probably sounds very strange to anyone who has never served in the military, but that was how we felt. Following over ten years of hindsight and two expensive and fairly pointless foreign wars later, this is a classic case of "Be careful of what you wish for". But in 2003 that was all far in the future and people were liberally begging to go and be included on the FET, one of them being yours truly.

Much has now been made, in the political ground-shaping of Saddam's weapons of mass destruction (WMD) and the now infamous dossier, but then we were all very well aware of — and utterly believed — the WMD threat to be a clear and present danger. After all, why should we doubt the word of our democratically elected leaders? We, after all, were going into Iraq for the singular purpose of removing his threat from the region. It's hard to emphasise now, well over ten years later, how we simply and utterly *believed* our government without question. The mere idea that perhaps this has all been "sexed up" to facilitate regime change just did not occur to any of us, any more than recent ideas that New Labour's "open door" immigration policy was ultimately about changing the national voting demographics in a cynical bid to "grow" legions of new voters simply to remain in power: Power at all costs, in effect.

In old-fashioned terms, our cause was just and we had a mission to do, and we all, very badly, wanted to be part of that for our people and our nation. This may sound naïve but the UK's armed forces are patriotic by both nature and design. The MPs' expenses scandal, the long- term child grooming and abuse in Rotherham, Rochdale and several other towns, the Hillsborough disaster inquiry, Trojan Horse plots in UK schools, the then unpublished Chilcott Inquiry, plus the ongoing effects and social strains of over a decade of uncontrolled immigration on the UK and its population and the almost casual way in which we blundered into Afghanistan were all yet to come. In 2003 we little realised that "Telic 1" — the Ministry of Defence, or MOD, doesn't do "sexy" names for its operations — would, in many ways, herald a decade plus of war and thousands of quietly under-publicised casualties and ultimately massive defence cuts: a paradox in light of government's apparent eagerness for continual military intervention overseas and the overarching political desire to remain an enduring world player on a grand global stage.

Eventually it came to pass that, in traditional army fashion, we were all told one morning, "Take the morning off, pack your kit, the transport leaves at 4". That was it, time to go with the classic briefing of, "You'll find out what you are doing when you get there". British soldiers are supremely flexible, proactive, innovative and extremely well trained at all levels to provide solutions, not problems. They are not the unimaginative and often boorish characters often clumsily portrayed on TV. Those soldiers chosen to go quietly packed for war and the ones living in single accommodation boxed all their belongings: a standard procedure to make things tidier should the occupant fail to return due to death or serious wounding; after all, the Army has a significant experience of both, from Aden to Borneo and Korea to Northern Ireland, all long prior to our recent wars of "liberal intervention".

So, a few hours later goodbyes were said to loved ones, if you had any, personal weapons drawn from the armoury and a few people ensured last letters were safely deposited, just in case. Then, during the long and monotonous drive to East Anglia, the realisation dawned on all of us: "We are going to war", accompanied by the individually unspoken and subtly intrusive thought that, "I might not come back from this one". The Balkans had been a long slog for peace, but with a light casualty bill and the weekly casualty list from Northern Ireland's lengthy Troubles were long forgotten, but this was a major invasion of a large country with sizeable armed forces and chemical weapons and under the ruthless command of a despotic leader with few remaining options. So, to discount this possibility would be rather presumptuous, most of us believed, albeit in a quietly private manner.

Happy New Year to one and all. This could be one to remember for quite some time to come. None of us, as we sat quietly lost in our personal thoughts, remotely envisaged that this would be the swansong of the British Army as a major military force in terms of "State against State" conflict as it collectively and slowly haemorrhaged in terms of manpower, equipment and capability. Currently, politicians of various denominations, whilst they publicly espouse the somewhat weakly enforced soldier's covenant, and taking every possible opportunity to display uniformed personnel at large sports events or similar televised spectacles, are in effect utilising a modern and media-savvy mechanism to obscure the transition of the world's finest small army into a high calibre but ultimately medium-sized defence force from the general public.

Unfortunately for our politicians, both the various insurgents of Iraq and the Taliban and its allies were never going to be cooperative towards Western aspirations or willingly embrace a very forceful injection of Western democracy over their millennias-old tribal systems combined with ultra-conservative faith and traditional beliefs. Spin may work effectively in UK-based elections but these people were of a far more stoical and pragmatic nature, belonging to decidedly non-secular societies where human rights didn't exist and serious violence was remarkably commonplace, so lots of heavily armed non-Muslim foreigners would definitely prove to be fair game. But more importantly for the troops on the ground, we had yet to discover the true extent of the enormous cultural chasm which lies starkly between liberal Western Democracy and traditional Muslim Theocracy. After defeating the Sunni-dominated regime, we Brits would soon face the Shia militias, whilst the Americans would fight the Sunni insurgency and both our Special Forces would combine to hunt down Al Qaeda and its foreign fighters, in effect 3 separate but simultaneous wars in one country. If we had been told of that post-invasion scenario we would have simply laughed out loud at its very preposterousness.

What we collectively failed, in a singularly spectacular manner, was to understand the very complex and varied nature of modern Islam and how our liberal intervention would to some branches of Islam simply become a call to arms. Eventually, this would come home to Europe, including hundreds of UK Muslim residents eagerly flocking to become enthusiastic IS fighters, and this too was utterly unthinkable to us way back in 2003. The results of our actions, in many ways, would continue to echo far and wide beyond the forthcoming and fairly simplistic action of overthrowing Saddam and his regime.

Wattisham, as yet another an ex-RAF fighter base taken over by the Army, is a fairly remote site in Suffolk and hardly the best location to train for desert warfare. Luckily we had a cadre of personnel who had desert experience from Op Granby, as the first Gulf War was known within the military: however, this was to be a very different war. Now it is the home of the Army's Attack Helicopter Force in the form of two Apache Regiments (assuming there are no further defence cuts), then it was home to a force of mixed Lynx (armed) Anti-Tank and Gazelle (unarmed) reconnaissance helicopters: essentially exactly the same equipment as the 1991 war against Saddam. The years of Balkan Operations had changed little of any significance within the Army; in essence it was still the same Cold War beast and focused on armour-based operations in a European-style theatre. However, the discreet post-1991 disbandment of various units, combined with fairly stagnant military funding meant that in terms of spare parts and logistics, the Army was very limited in what it actually could send, support and above all *sustain* in terms of a large-scale desert war. Post Bosnia and Kosovo, the military — at the behest of the politicians — was driven by a logistical doctrine of "just enough, just in time" culture. However, war is by its nature a very unscripted activity and the enemy tends to not play by your rule set.

We arrived at the end of a prolonged period of fruitless Christmas planning. Initially the preferred option had been to invade Iraq from the north, through the overland route provided by Turkey. Unfortunately — and based on the old military maxim of assumption being the mother of all fuck-ups — the (rather major) assumption that the Turks wouldn't mind too much their country being used as a transit route for very large numbers of foreign troops in order to invade a fellow Muslim nation proved to be a somewhat overly optimistic one. The Turkish Government rather spoilt the party by their swift and overwhelming response of "no chance", so the operational urgency had rather petered out as the diplomats now sought clearance to send us by air through various Muslim nations' air spaces: Saudi Arabia in particular. Simultaneously the FET was changing almost daily as the Treasury sought to keep the cost of the operation to a minimum and any shipping for all our vehicles and equipment had yet to be hired from trade, it all rather smacked of the classic military doctrine of "hurry up and wait".

We, as augmentees, were divided up across the various squadrons by rank, trade and so forth, in essence scattered to the four winds to make up the manning gaps. I was sent to the Intelligence and NBC (Nuclear, Biological and Chemical) Cell, but my personal focus was to be the chemical warfare side of life (or death, depending on your perspective, really). Essentially, whilst I had to be fully aware of and advise on the Intelligence picture, I was tasked to develop our SOIs (Standard Operating Instructions) to ensure we were trained and ready to react effectively to any attack by chemical weapons (CW) and survive to fight with minimum losses or damage to unit cohesion. The "boys and girls" (as soldiers are often referred to by their immediate hierarchy) had a much more descriptive term for a CW attack: "being slimed". Based on the government's now famous dossier, this sliming was firmly believed by all concerned to be a simple question of *when, not if* and a prospect none of us relished in the slightest. To use the terminology of the period, I was to be the NBCD Officer (Nuclear, Biological and Chemical Defence). As the Iraqis had a very infamous general nicknamed "Chemical Ali" — so named for his penchant for using CW weapons during the Iran/Iraq war on several occasions and to quite devastating and ruthless effect — so the boys immediately christened me "Chemical Mac". I can think of much worse nicknames to labour under: all soldiers do tend to speak as they find ultimately.

I was shocked to discover the current SOIs was a mere 6 pages in length and totally unfit for any serious military purpose, especially fighting a major desert war over 3000 miles from home in a harsh and very demanding climate. But my aim was simple and quite focused: keep the guys and girls alive (or more realistically, minimise our casualties) and still able to fight effectively. After all, I figured, our forebears had managed to do so effectively amidst all the horrors of the First World War, so why couldn't we? Intelligence (aside from the well-known dossier) was, to say the least, vague on the nature and true extent of the threat Iraqi CW posed to us. However this wasn't something we could simply ignore, as indeed much as the majority of the Army and Royal Marines had done for years. We had firmly placed this particular form of warfare in the "too difficult" drawer and concentrated on the far sexier traditional stuff like large-scale armoured warfare and operations in built up areas (OBUA as it is known or FISH as the troops like to term it, their acronym standing for "Fighting In Some Fucker's House").

To put this in perspective, we weren't particularly bothered in 2003 at the prospect of fighting the Iraqi Army, or anyone else for that matter. We were, as the Americans referred to us, the "finest small army in the world". We were well led and well trained, morale was high, even if our equipment was quite average really, but that was accepted as traditional stuff for any British Army. Historically, no British Government liked to spend too much money on us, except in the unlikely event of a war of national survival, while our relationship with the British public was one of them being fondly distant towards its Army, as if we were a fairly large group of faraway second cousins in Australia, excepting the garrison towns on a Saturday night, of course. But this was immaterial to us, we were past masters at making do and making it work, it what was we did for a living.

We'd finally beaten our arch nemesis that was the Provisional IRA and enabled the UK Government to end that unpopular and seemingly endless conflict across the water and helped in a quite major way to bring peace to the very war-weary Balkans. Most importantly, we all believed in our cause, as corny that may sound with the luxurious benefit of hindsight: we were doing this for the nation and we were, after all, the Green Machine. None us then dreamt that while we may be going into Iraq like lions, we would later leave like lambs, even having to cut secretive deals with the local Shia militias for a trouble-free withdrawal from Basra City itself. The modern Army avoids mentioning its humiliating withdrawal from Iraq, in much the same way that the Army of the 1950s and 60s gave the utter debacle of Singapore in 1942 a damned good ignoring. The historical jury has yet to comment regarding the Helmand Province experience and politicians and journalists alike have exceedingly short memories, whilst the Chilcott Inquiry came and went with no significant or long-lasting fallout for any of the major players involved.

However, the looming spectre of chemical weapons (CW) being used against us and simultaneously having to fight in an extremely hostile desert environment with equipment designed primarily for the North German Plains was not one that flicked our collective switches. But, at least prior to the Iraq invasion and the subsequent casual national entry into the Afghan quagmire, failure was not an option for the British Army and my own singular focus was to provide pragmatic solutions to the CW threat, period. So I immersed myself in CW and its "higher form of killing" (as one German scientist of the 1930's chillingly termed his improvements in chemical warfare: the invention of nerve agent, to be precise) and the finer details of nerve, blister, choking and blood agents and their devastating effects — or hopefully not — on the human body and associated military equipment, without which we would be quite useless for offensive desert operations.

Essentially chemical weapons do no physical damage to buildings or property (unlike nuclear weapons). They do, however, do extremely nasty things to the human body, and effectively they "do what it says on the tin". The threat to ourselves and the Americans was, as best we knew, any combination of a broad variety of chemical agents and the Iraqis had used them repeatedly during their long and bloody war with Iran and also on the defenceless Kurdish population of Northern Iraq. For the uninitiated, CW falls into various categories, "Persistent" or "Non Persistent" in terms of the length of its effectiveness against the human body, from literally minutes to possibly days, depending on the type of agent, how accurately it was delivered, wind strength, weather conditions and the terrain. Blister agent (always persistent and referred to as mustard gas in the First World War and the cause of the evocative pictures of dozens of blinded soldiers holding on to each other) is deliberately designed to damage human beings by inflicting hugely painful and horrific injuries in both liquid and vapour form, rather than kill. Put simply, wounded soldiers (in large numbers) require major medical and logistical resources. Dead soldiers, equally simply, do not. Very callous perhaps, but also very true. We anticipated this would be the weapon of choice for the Iraqi commanders, hence the popular and fatalistic use of the term "sliming" by the troops.

The lethal threats ranged from nerve agent, incredibly lethal: a pinhead's worth in liquid form on exposed skin can rapidly kill a fit and healthy adult; it basically causes the central nervous system to break down and all bodily functions to simply fail in an extremely fast manner. We expected the Iraqis to reserve this mainly for "high value targets" once the blister agent had slowed us down with multiple casualties and badly contaminated vehicles along traffic-choked roads. Another popular choices was choking agent (chlorine based and heavier than air, so excellent against dug-in troops) which caused "dry land drowning": you simply drowned internally, not the best of deaths and commonly used by all sides amongst the occupants of the trenches on the Western Front. Lastly came blood agent, rapidly lethal and based on Hydrogen Cyanide (Zyklon B, the infamous agent used in the Nazi Concentration Camp "showers" was a blood agent), very short lived in duration and requiring a multiple rocket launch system for efficient battlefield delivery (being lighter than air, you have to rapidly saturate the target in order to kill lots of people, before the wind dissipates it), essentially it prevents its victims from utilising the oxygen within their bloodstream, so death is a rapid result. Not the most cheerful of topics for several thousand British soldiers to contemplate as a very serious possibility in the near term future.

So this was the cocktail we faced. You have to remember, at this time we had *no reason to doubt the word of* our own government and its highly publicised dossier: our job was simply to liberate Iraq. Our best estimate on exactly when and where CW would be launched against us was that Saddam himself would simply select a geographical feature and the Americans crossing that line would act as a "chemical tripwire". Exactly where this was situated was anyone's guess. The Iranians had been repeatedly attacked by all of these chemical agents, both individually and collectively during their long war against Saddam and suffered thousands of casualties accordingly, as indeed had the Kurds on a regular basis. (Ironically, we regularly used photographs of Iranian casualties who had received medical treatment in the UK to chillingly illustrate the physical effects of CW to our soldiers). The Iraqi Armed Forces were both uniquely placed and well experienced in this respect, the only recent example of the widespread employment of such chilling weapons for generations. Plus, we were reliably informed, Saddam had the intent and above all the will to use it against us: the equation was complete. Therefore the use of CW, in some manner, had become a distinct expectation on our part rather than a possibility.

Suffice it to say, all of the above focused my mind wonderfully. Like most professional soldiers I viewed being shot or blown up as just one of the risks of the job: a degrading, certainly painful and possibly long, torturous death following a good sliming did not appeal to me in the slightest. So I immersed myself into producing a Chemical Defence Plan that was robust, workable and would minimise our casualties (unlike most of society, any professional Army does not have the luxury of being risk averse: risk is accepted by default and therefore managed in order to minimise the inherent risks of warfare). My job was to manage the CW risk. I personally believed casualties were inevitable and unavoidable in the event of a CW attack: it's similar to chocolate cake at a child's birthday party in that "everyone gets a bit". As a popular Army saying goes, our mind-set in response to this problem was remarkably simple in nature: "Shit happens. Deal with it". That may not be politically correct, but anyone who thinks you can fight a modern war without casualties is either a dreamer or a fool, we'd been quite lucky in the Kosovo campaign and the later regime change operation in Libya would also prove to be exceedingly good bombing practice for a rapidly shrinking Royal Air Force against a third-rate and poorly equipped enemy, but these were military "blips". Iraq, in contrast to such easy victories would prove to be the warm-up for the bitter cauldron of Helmand Province and several thousand casualties over a long decade of war.

The enemy, as they say, has a vote and in both wars the locals used their vote quite well as we discovered the reality of prolonged asymmetric warfare against cunning and ruthless opponents, but this was all in the future, as was the amazing judicial view that UK Health and Safety law applies to a fast-moving and complex battlefield in exactly the same manner as a drunken argument or a factory site accident. But then our focus then was firmly on Saddam's weapons of mass destruction, in what now seems to so many UK Iraq Veterans a different era on behalf of a very different nation. To paraphrase a well- known

French Premier League football manager who said recently that when he arrived in England it was a logical nation, now it's an emotional one.

Our training during this period was haphazard at best, partly due to the ever changing FET, as the Treasury constantly tried to downsize troop and equipment numbers in order keep the cost down, partly due to a widespread lack of training materials, but also due to a major backlog of work in simply preparing our equipment for war. Our sister regiment had not had the luxury of Christmas leave and had worked tirelessly to prepare all their helicopters and associated specialist equipment for operational readiness, only to be ordered to transfer the bulk of them to the Commando Brigade. As the Royal Marines had been due to depart on an already planned exercise in early January and were diverted accordingly with minimum fuss, the decision was made to load our battle ready helicopters onto their shipping, as they would be the first troops into Kuwait. Accordingly the Naval-owned aircraft transferred over in a straight swop that required what could be politely termed as large amounts of TLC, all requiring hundreds of man hours to prepare them for sustained desert operations. Orders are ultimately orders so hours of overtime became the norm for a large percentage of the regiment.

Ammunition and range space were also in short supply and the aircrew needed to learn to fly by day and night on night vision goggles whilst wearing a bulky specialist respirator (the term "gas mask" has not been used in the armed forces since the 1950s): not an easy task whilst flying at ultra-low level over a featureless and pitch-black desert at night. So all in all, our training was at best disjointed and our intelligence regarding the Iraqi military remained quite poor. This was so unlike the Kosovo operation, I remember thinking, but it could only get better, or so I thought.

About 3 weeks into this chaos, a complete squadron was suddenly withdrawn from the FET. Someone, somewhere in the Treasury had decided that we really didn't need all these expensive helicopters for a major land war, so a quarter of the regiment suddenly found out that they weren't going. This was a major blow to our capability (these were the newer and more powerful Mark 9 Lynx, which though lacking a missile system and therefore unable to engage enemy tanks, gave us a greater lift capability in terms of troops, extracting wounded soldiers and general utility, such as moving senior personnel around or "Command and Control" platforms) and seriously dented morale within the unit. But this was the political direction, albeit obviously fiscally driven, so we reshuffled our plans accordingly. We had repeatedly asked for sand coloured paint for our vehicles, but were told we'd get the paint "in theatre", along with our desert clothing, body armour, ammunition and anything else we actually needed for a large-scale desert war. Some of us — the more experienced soldiers — began to think that this was all a major sabre-rattling exercise. Saddam after all was a master of brinkmanship with decades of experience of dealing with bellicose Western governments, and this could well explain the paucity of equipment and a general lack of support for our training being given to us by almost every government agency concerned.

Nevertheless, we had been warned off for war and the compulsory Anthrax jabs made us reconsider the situation. Surely they wouldn't give us jabs for no reason? I concentrated on my little world of a "higher form of killing" and how to survive to fight and win. Essentially, at the unit level (regiment or battalion) the key to survival was early warning, efficient "immediate action drills" (to stay alive), effective post-attack drills and good reporting at all levels. (There is far more to it than that but I don't wish to labour the point.) Well-trained troops can survive in a CW environment, albeit in a harsh, unforgiving environment and incredibly demanding in pure physical terms (but the British "Tommy" of 1914-1918 had managed to do so). My SOIs and Chemical Defence Plan would, I sincerely hoped, prove adequate and fit for its purpose: if not, then I would probably carry the deaths and maiming of literally scores of young soldiers on my conscience to my grave. A sobering thought.

Finally, after several weeks in and around the Wattisham area, we received our orders to deploy to Kuwait. War, it now seemed to us all, was now a matter of a few weeks away. This caused us all to reconsider our sabre-rattling beliefs and I, along with scores of others, quietly and sombrely wrote our last letters that night, marked to be opened "In the event of my death or being listed as missing in action, believed dead". Our collective destinies, it seemed, were all now firmly out of our hands.

Our helicopters and vehicles had at long last been loaded onto some merchant shipping that had finally been hired from trade at the Marchwood military port close to Southampton. The plan was to fly the troops out in advance and then reunite them with their "heavy kit" in Kuwait. Fair enough, we all thought. Whilst we were a bit bemused at the decision to move the helicopters by merchant ship (this hadn't been done since the Falklands War: normally they are moved by transport plane due to their quite fragile nature), we assumed it was simply to keep the costs down, although we later discovered only the helicopters that were permanently dedicated to supporting UK SF were flown out "into theatre" (even the RAF themselves had to send their helicopters by sea, so actually it was the perennial lack of transport aircraft that dictated this option), but it did mean some time off for most of us. A quick weekend at home for all concerned then off we all go to "do Iraq". Simple plans, in military terms at least, are always the best after all.

My final weekend in Lancashire was strained. My now ex-wife didn't really know what to say to me: "Have a nice war, dear and if it doesn't work out too well, I'll arrange a good funeral", doesn't quite cut it really. I didn't know what to say either, it was hardly the stuff of movies, more a case of a quiet and very strained last farewell. The Balkans and Northern Ireland had been nowhere near an aggressive operation on such a large scale, after all, nor quite so far away. My eldest son (now himself a battle-hardened young man after several gruelling tours in Helmand Province) was away, undergoing his basic army training in Yorkshire and my youngest son simply couldn't understand fully why his dad was going to fight a war in a desert so far away for such seemingly vague reasons. (With hindsight, he had a very good point really.)

Even now, well over ten years on, I vividly recall saying a very emotionally and mutually draining goodbye to him as he went off to school, visibly upset and utterly baffled by this turn of events, obviously convinced he'd never see me alive again, a life experience I wouldn't wish upon anyone. I desperately wanted to say something both memorable and meaningful to him, in the event I didn't return home. Sadly, I just didn't know what to say, and instead silently watched him depart for school with obvious tears in his eyes and mine too. A rather quiet and strained goodbye was then shared by my then wife and me. Once again words failed both of us, and it was, quite simply, time to go. I was both rather subdued and deeply miserable during my long lonely drive back to East Anglia and lost in myriad highly personal thoughts and raw emotions. Invading Iraq was a very long way from being top of my "to do" list.

We were all rather quiet when we reunited at Wattisham, the penny had finally dropped to us all that Saddam wasn't going to quietly relinquish power any time soon and Messers Bush and Blair were both equally utterly intent on violent and large-scale military action, which meant us. We packed our equipment, had our last-minute briefings — for what they were actually worth — and had an impromptu drunken "goodbye to England" evening as British soldiers have done for centuries past. It might be quite a while before we had our next drink, after all.

In traditional manner we assembled early for the coaches to South Cerney, the main transit and holding centre then used for troops leaving the country, on this occasion to invade Iraq and instigate regime change by rather violent means. We had been split into "chalks" for the flight to Kuwait, so we'd move as part of the brigade deployment plan over a period of several days. Meanwhile our vehicles would sail down in civilian "roll on roll off" shipping and arrive in a couple of weeks: that was the plan, at least.

On arrival at South Cerney the movement staff — "movers" as they are known — immediately went into their inimitable and hugely patronising style of briefings and management (it's not just civilians who get mucked around at airports). We formed orderly queues and the overzealous RAF check-in staff asked us questions such as, "Why are you carrying a knife in your hold baggage?" Again and again the boys answered, "because I am going to war and I might just need it to kill someone", or similar refrains. We grew increasingly impatient and each and every time, he or she had to plead their case to be allowed to take it with them. As all our Bergens and holdalls were going into the cargo

37

hold and the British Army wasn't particularly renowned for its appetite regarding aircraft hijacking , this was becoming increasingly annoying, petty bureaucracy at its military best. Eventually we found a "grown up" who explained to his staff that these were things the "Army blokes" might just need in time of war. Reluctantly the "light blue" Spanish Inquisition ceased.

Additionally anything that could be even remotely be construed as pornography (such as FHM and similar magazines) and any form of alcohol was confiscated, much to the annoyance of the troops: our first casualties of war, I suppose you could say. We had arrived to find the previous flight had not yet departed for Kuwait, and had also taken up all the existing accommodation in the process, as they too waited for the diplomats to obtain flight clearances with a variety of Middle Eastern countries.

We waited in the reception area, basically a small converted hangar with a communal TV area, a small cafeteria and a pool table: not a lot for well over 200 soldiers, really. Eventually it transpired that we would all just have to sleep there, so we found a bit of floor space and waited to be called forward for our food. There were simply too many soldiers for all of us to eat at once, so we ate in shifts, like a big modern-day U-boat crew. Some nice RAF bloke put several DVDs on a loop track to keep us entertained: *Saving Private Ryan*, *Platoon*, *Hamburger Hill*, *We Were Soldiers Once and Young* and *A Bridge Too Far*, amongst others in a totally military-dominated genre. Their single overriding common denominator was soldiers being killed and wounded in very large numbers, not the most tactful viewing for a lot of young men and women about to embark for a major land war in the 21st Century.

After 24 hours of almost nonstop military blood and gore, we asked the RAF if we could, perhaps, watch some comedy or similar movies. "Why, we thought you Army guys would like all this war stuff?" was the bemused response from the nice RAF bloke. Because, we replied, some of these guys may not be coming home and it might be a good idea to take their mind off things for a while. To be fair, the RAF changed the DVDs, which was just as well as we stayed there, in military limbo, for a total of 3 days, with no information and feeling like a bunch of camouflaged extras for the *Groundhog Day* film. Our main activity was finding, and retaining, an unoccupied piece of floor to sleep on. I and a couple of close friends found a particularly nice spot between the pool table and some radiators, a shining example of "RHIP" (Rank Has Its Privileges, a classic Army saying), or perhaps we were just grumpier than everyone else?

After many tedious hours of this, with very limited access to showers and most of our baggage (and therefore clothing) securely locked away and out of our reach, combined with eating in shifts and absolute boredom with the now tiresome DVD loop, morale was low. Everyone was quite short-tempered, frustrated and generally quite pissed off. Not the ideal preparation for troops about to fly into, start, fight and win a war, really.

Abruptly, another nice RAF person (the Army, Royal Marines and Navy alike view the RAF as the military wing of British Airways in terms of discipline, fitness and general warlike demeanour, or rather lack of: everyone appears to be on first names terms in the Air Force, something that any professional army would find quite unworkable if it wanted to be an effective one) announced that we were going back to East Anglia as our diplomatic clearance was unlikely to be given before Monday (this was now Friday morning), so we could go home for the weekend. We ("we" being the officers: the RAF don't really like talking to soldiers, who they tend to view as illiterate, modern day barbarians being both far too aggressive and military in nature, and quite beneath them) were informed that our chalk would have to return with all our kit late on Sunday afternoon. Fair enough, we thought, the married guys could at least see their families and the single guys could have one last night out.

So it was back on the bus and back to square one, with 4 days totally wasted. The general lack of progress made us all think that the war was off, it's just sabre-rattling again. Dejectedly we drove back to East Anglia. If nothing else, I thought, at least we can get a shower, a change of clothes and phone home. Hussein, Tony and George were now simply not on my personal radar. We arrived in a dark and fairly deserted Wattisham late on a Friday evening. The single guys were in a rush to get changed and head for the bright lights of Ipswich and the unexpected bonus of a night out. I settled for a carry-out of four cans of Fosters, a shower and a good night's sleep, an age thing obviously!

The next morning, after a nice English breakfast and a quiet start to the day, we were suddenly informed that Plan B had been introduced from out of nowhere and we were all required to be ready to move at midday to move to RAF Brize Norton and board a plane for Kuwait this evening. The general reaction was, "Fucking great". Some of the single guys had yet to return from their night out, the rest had hangovers from hell and the married guys had to again explain to their wives and kids that they had to leave some 24 hours earlier than planned: more tears all round. The consensus was that the Ministry of Defence (MOD) could not organise the proverbial piss-up in a brewery. What we didn't know was that this overarching incompetence would last for some while yet in terms of Iraq. Indeed, we were also unaware that we were embarking on what would prove to be over a decade of two major desert conflicts, during which our equipment shortcomings would be exposed (mainly to ourselves) in spades and the "blood price" that our then PM had so publicly said he was quite prepared to pay would certainly be paid in full by the British Army in its traditionally stoical nature. But no one can foresee the future and we still had absolute faith in our leaders: this was 2003, and in several ways, such a vastly different nation from the one we now live in less than a generation later.

Eventually we found or rounded up all our soldiers, be they sober, hungover or, in a few cases, still drunk and the frantic "recall" messages were finally passed to all and sundry. We paraded at the appointed time and place, to be told there had been a problem with the coaches (the Army uses civilian coaches, hard to acquire at short notice on the average Saturday for 200 + people), so come back at 6 and we'll try again. This was becoming the mother of all journeys and the troops were, by now, totally unimpressed. Hardly surprising, really.

As our weapons and heavy baggage were still at South Cerney, we just had our respirators and patrol packs (small rucksacks) to cart around. Most of us wandered off to find a TV or get some sleep. The way this journey was going, it could be a good move. A handful of diehards snuck off to find some alcohol (against orders, but they presumably thought,

"What are they going to do to me, send me to Iraq?") We discreetly pretended not to have noticed: what harm could it really do to our national war effort? A small part of me envied them. Life can be quite simple for a junior soldier and most of his thoughts concerned women, beer and occasionally sport (but mainly beer and women). I was growing increasingly concerned about this charade of a move to war and hoped our arrival would be better planned and executed. The PM's brave words were not presently being reflected by cohesive action, that was for sure, but the media, as always, seemed blissfully unaware. Defence, can be a boring topic in our multi-racial and utterly PC nation. Hugely inaccurate portrayal of British soldiers in Afghanistan would follow later, such as the ludicrous *Our Girl* and the banal *Bluestone 42* BBC TV series, which essentially demean both the harsh brutality of war itself and the demands placed on the soldiers concerned and bear no basis in reality to modern military service, not to mention their often bloody personal sacrifices on behalf of an mainly indifferent nation. This lack of interest, in turn, seems to maintain the illusion shared by the British public and media alike that we still have strong and powerful armed forces, when actually only our superb Special Forces and a handful of nuclear submarines ensure our place at the top table after the thorough decimation of the nation's armed forces conducted by the Coalition and then Tory Governments to balance the books after New Labour's financial incompetence. Irrespective of this, our politicians all continue to maintain the pretence of a major military capability in a very determined manner. Sadly, neither our enemies nor our allies have been taken in by this classic piece of political spin or posturing bluff.

Eventually the coaches arrived, people said muted farewells (again) and we, very sullenly and silently, drove to either war or some more major league sabre-rattling, we really weren't sure which one. We really had no idea what awaited us after the previous week's frustrations. The highlight of the trip was a stop at a motorway services at about 9 pm. Approximately 220 soldiers descended, a military plague of locusts, to buy anything and everything, memories of our 4-day epic still fresh in our minds. Everyone wanted to have some "survival rations" stuffed into their pockets, just in case the RAF wanted to test our endurance and survival skills again.

A pleasant (and quite moving) experience was a couple of families loudly wishing us, "All the best, boys. You all come home safe". You need to remember this was very much pre-Help for Heroes and the similar charitable initiatives established to support thousands of wounded personnel in lieu of any cohesive long-term governmental commitment for veterans, aside from populist, but rather empty words. Northern Ireland had been both a lengthy and very unpopular, dirty little war and British soldiers just weren't then used to their public being overly nice to them. Help for Heroes, parcels for the troops at Christmas and generally favourable media and public interest were all light years away in 2003, as indeed was the public and very brutal murder of a young British soldier in a busy Woolwich street in broad daylight by some of the very citizens the Army exists to defend. We mumbled our thanks in a politely embarrassed manner and quietly re-boarded our coaches to destiny. Unknowingly and unwittingly, those anonymous but very nice people had, with a mere handful of kind words to their army made us all suddenly think very seriously of what might just be coming next for all of us.

We duly arrived at RAF Brize Norton and its rather large "Gateway to Operations" sign at the main entrance. It didn't really enthuse us very much on a dark miserable February night, especially after having taking six days to get this far. Our weapons and Bergens had been transferred directly to the plane from South Cerney, so we thought the check-in would be mercifully swift this time: hopefully it would be a case of second time lucky.

At this point the RAF movers simply excelled themselves in dampening our remaining morale. We drove directly to a remote freight gate in our coach convoy and promptly parked in the darkness and waited. A very pompous and self-important young SAC (a private, in Army terms) eventually jumped on and told us to stay on the coach. *No one* was allowed off for *any* reason, he informed us in a rather abrupt manner, and without any further information or explanation jumped off again and left all of us literally sitting in the dark once more. He reappeared ten minutes later to give us the same message once again (being members of the British Army, our English was obviously quite poor, he seemed to think), *not* to get off the coach, in an even more curt, verging on downright rude manner, absolutely ignoring the fact there were officers and senior NCOs in abundance on all the coaches. God bless the Air Force, we all silently thought: who needs a rank system and its associated discipline in the military anyway? He was, as one of the soldiers rather loudly commented, obviously annoyed at either missing last orders in the pub on a Saturday night or he was on a promise: us going to war was quite trivial in comparison to his rather pressing social dilemmas. A good example of leadership and management this most certainly was not, I thought to myself.

Everyone, including myself, had expected the normal check-in system, which meant a last chance to go to the loo, grab a coffee, have a cigarette and (most importantly) make a last call to your loved ones before you go on a long boring flight to a possible war (we had been told to leave our mobile phones behind, for very valid reasons of operational security: OPSEC. If you didn't have a mobile phone, then the Iraqi spooks couldn't eavesdrop on it: a simple but highly effective philosophy). So, we waited and waited on our cold and dark coaches to be allowed to stretch our legs before boarding. Unfortunately for ourselves, either the RAF simply wanted to go home or some government official was desperate to get some more troops into Kuwait and abruptly the coaches jerked into action and drove a complete 300 yards forward, stopping alongside our long-awaited plane.

The now universally despised RAF SAC jumped self-importantly back on board and explained to us thick soldiers exactly how to board the plane (by means of steps, apparently. This guy really was annoying). We felt like cattle being transported to an abattoir, not the best of ways to leave your homeland en route to a major war. To be fair to the Air Force, they have made huge attempts since then to improve their customer relations, having now spent years taking the Army to and from its various wars on a weekly basis, but on this particular night they failed, totally and miserably.

In the coming years, however, the Air Force would more than make amends for this individual's failings in customer relations. The exceptional Aeromedical flights would prove — literally — a lifeline for thousands of wounded soldiers (especially the ubiquitous C 17s of 99 Squadron RAF, one of the many unsung heroes of a bitter war) as first Iraq, then Helmand Province, proved be a violent crucible for a generation of soldiers and marines, many straight from basic training. Ironically, whilst the Air Force itself is fast jet centred, for the Army the Chinook and transport fleets would be ever popular, the former to get you into (and out of) battle and proved superb at recovering the wounded within the now famous "golden hour" after wounding, whilst the transport fleet got you into theatre, and finally home to UK.

To our mild surprise it was an Air Iceland airliner we boarded: the RAF just didn't have enough transport planes in peacetime even back in 2003, so chartered aircraft were very common, we just hadn't expected to go to War by "Civair", as it's popularly known. The Air Iceland cabin crew were the exact opposite to the RAF movers: polite, helpful and cheerful, lots of smiles and a welcome change for the guys, who by now just wanted to go and get on with it. Once airborne, the trolley came around and a stewardess apologised to me and the two guys on my row for being unable to offer us alcohol. Surprised by this, we commented that we were used to "dry" flights in the military. She explained that on the last flight to Kuwait, the crew were all blissfully unaware of this MOD standing policy. As a result of this misunderstanding, when the drinks trolley came out at the rear of the aircraft — exactly where the boys tend to sit — they had promptly descended on it like a biblical plague. The officers, sitting further forward and blissfully unaware of this, were apparently quite shocked to hear loud and cheerful singing echoing down the aircraft. On inspection, they discovered an empty drinks trolley and a plane load of intoxicated soldiers who had "power drunk" their way to temporary happiness! Good for them, we commented, our own soldiers were simply jealous that the previous flight had managed to get one over the MOD and left them with a mundane choice of coffee, tea or squash?

The flight itself was duly boring (the MOD didn't stretch to in-flight movies back then) and utterly event free, with all of us preoccupied with our most personal thoughts. Even the guys who had done the previous Gulf War commented this one was different: last time it had been a measured and lengthy build-up of equipment, manpower and stores, with lots of comprehensive desert training; this was very much "lastminute.com" by comparison. Personally, my thoughts were divided between my own highly unsatisfactory goodbyes and the thought occurring to me that whilst the Iraqis hadn't fought particularly well to hold on to Kuwait in 1991, they may just feel differently about defending their own soil and homeland: after all they might view one (Western) man's "liberation" as a downright good old-fashioned invasion from their own perspective.

At long last the pilot announced that we would be landing shortly in Kuwait: it was shortly after dawn. Then, our flights into Kuwait were timed to avoid the eyes of the public and media alike, by landing at roughly 5.30 - 6 am. Ironically, for the following ten years or so we did the same on a weekly basis to discreetly recover our wounded from Afghanistan into Birmingham Airport (the Russians did the same for their own Afghan casualties, albeit into East German hospitals and by darkened early morning troop trains in the 1980s), which also helps to keep public and media awareness down with regard to the actual number of casualties incurred by British troops. I have to say it works very well in that context, even if I personally find it a very cynical ploy by successive governments to blur the true cost of modern war from the wider public. That said, I have to admit it achieved its aim in keeping the human cost out of the public domain whilst the Army, ever stoical, dealt with the steady stream of casualties and determinedly just got on with its given mission despite the lack of military hospitals and an NHS system that took several years to deal effectively with an unexpectedly large number of shattered young soldiers. After all, British soldiers are pragmatic, determined and loyal by nature and casualties are simply inevitable against determined enemies fighting on their own home ground during long and bitter guerrilla wars, irrespective of the political desires or wishes of a government with no knowledge or experience of military service or operations.

So, almost one week to the day since our journey commenced in now far-away East Anglia, we had finally arrived. Dressed in our European "temperate" green combats and black leather boots, we noticed the temperature the moment the cabin doors opened, despite the early hours. As always, we had parked well away from the passenger terminal — in our case we had steps to the tarmac — but with absolutely no sign of any transport. No problem, we all thought, we all needed to stretch our legs and the smokers (like me) were grateful for the chance of a quick cigarette, so all 240 of us found a piece of sand and just chilled. The Air Iceland staff (who did have transport), helpful to the end, came over and wished us all good luck and said they'd try and find us some transport. What really nice people to take you to war, we all thought. By now we were extremely good at waiting, which is exactly what we all commenced doing, but at least it wasn't raining, as some anonymous soldier wryly reminded us all.

As the sun quickly rose and therefore also the heat, some of the guys moved under the plane's wings for shade and we watched the local airport staff efficiently appear from nowhere, to clean and refuel it. Hardly gripping entertainment, but at least some activity to break up the tedium. Finally, a coach appeared and stopped close by, decorated with all manner of items hanging around the windscreen and windows, a typical "Jingly" coach as we called them. The driver, dressed in American Ray-Ban sunglasses, flip-flops and traditional Arab "dish dasha" robes slowly disembarked and casually strolled towards us.

Out of nowhere, a fast-moving American Humvee suddenly braked to a very noisy halt. Three rather burly American Military Policemen leapt out, wrestled our driver to the ground and handcuffed him. We watched incredulously as the struggling man was thrown unceremoniously into the vehicle and the MPs re-boarded the vehicle. The last American MP suddenly noticed 200+ Brits watching this piece of mini-theatre and in answer to our unspoken questions just shrugged his broad shoulders, merely saying, "Al Qaeda". With that they drove off at speed, leaving us sitting by our airliner in total bewilderment. We never did find out what happened to the guy, or why he was arrested in such dramatic fashion.

"Fucking hell," said one of the guys loudly. "What a nice fucking welcome to Kuwait, everyone!" Hardly Shakespeare at his best perhaps, but it summed things up rather nicely. So, we remained sat on the outer fringes of a busy international airport, a couple of hundred British soldiers all quietly thinking, "What the fuck is going on here?"

For about an hour we all tried to claim some shade under the wings and fuselage of the plane as the sun rose and we slowly began to melt, and this was only late February, what would a summer war be like out here, I thought to myself? The driver had kindly left his coach locked, so we couldn't even claim some heat sanctuary there or drive ourselves. Some water would have been nice, to say the least, but we were now beginning to wonder if anyone in Kuwait even knew we existed. This was becoming the perfect end to a perfect week; at this rate we wouldn't be physically fit to fight, assuming we ever actually got there, wherever "there" was, as we were all quite disorientated and thoroughly fed up by now.

A British Army Land Rover belatedly approached us (our vehicles were all painted green still, so stood out visibly from quite a distance) slowly growing larger in the heat haze and it proved to be a couple of Army "movers", always identifiable by the yellow "wagon wheel" symbol armbands they wore, the "wagon wheel of power" as it was termed across the Army. The "power" in question being the power to fuck us all about (you may have gathered by now movers are not generally held in high esteem by the average soldier). "What now?" we all thought suspiciously. This was rapidly becoming a military farce of epic proportions and this particular group of soldiers were no longer a bunch of happy teddies, all toys having been thrown forcibly out of the collective cot rather a long time ago.

A young lance corporal disembarked and loudly asked, of no one in particular, "Have you lot just flown in from Brize?" One of the officers, who had simply had enough by now, stood up and spoke for all of us.

"Corporal, of course we have just flown in from bloody Brize and we've been sat here for over two hours, with no driver, no water and not

47

a clue what's going on. So perhaps you could just arrange some transport please, instead of asking rather stupid questions, if that isn't too much to ask?"

Faced with a couple of hundred, obviously very pissed off troops, the young NCO decided not be pompous and officious: that really would have sparked a minor mutiny. Muttering something about how difficult life was, he jumped back into his vehicle and drove off, leaving us all alone again with our pet plane. This was not, I reflected, the ideal way to commence a major desert war. For all the haste to get us here, it rather appeared that Her Majesty's Forces in UK and Kuwait were not singing from the same song sheet at present. Eventually the surly movers came back, with an Arab passenger (apparently one whom the Americans didn't currently want to arrest) who was our new driver. The movers explained we would be shuttled to the other side of the runway, as this was the only coach they had. This was fast becoming a foretaste of the general organisation of our arrival, except we hadn't quite realised that yet.

So, following some six individual coach shuttle trips later, we were all finally, officially in Kuwait, in a small tented complex on the fringes of the airport terminal. But it had shade, seats and water, so we were fairly content while the movers gave us some "arrivals" briefings, which none of us listened to. Frankly, we just wanted our kit (which was still in the hold of our pet plane, along with our weapons) and a chance to chill. One of our Quartermasters (QM: each Army regiment has two, one to manage the equipment and technical stuff, the other to manage "life support", in the form of rations, bullets and clothing, etc) had arrived to meet us. He explained the advance party were in a remote desert site named Camp Eagle up towards the Iraqi border: apparently it was Spartan but essentially okay. He had bummed a lift, as no one had any transport: all the vehicles were still somewhere at sea and en route to Kuwait, so we had to wait for the movers to arrange some more Jingly buses, which simply wasn't going to happen for several hours apparently. By now no one was shocked at this news, it was all becoming par for the course.

We discovered, in idle conversation, that the government was quite desperate to get troops into Kuwait (known as "theatre" in Army speak) ASAP. The fact we had absolutely no equipment, vehicles or ammunition with which to actually *fight* (all of these being, literally, at sea) was deemed utterly immaterial. The omnipresent media needed to *see* soldiers going to Kuwait and the boring fact we were militarily impotent as a fighting force on arrival was quite irrelevant. It seemed as long as we *were seen* to be there on TV, this was 21st Century military bluff on a large scale. Luckily the American Military had simply taken over large chunks of Kuwait and they did have ammunition (in very, very large amounts), so they would protect us. How embarrassing, we all thought quietly. Here we were, in our capacity as the "world's finest small army" (as the Americans then used to refer to us) relying on someone else, albeit the US Marine Corps, to protect us. The QM — a veteran of several Bosnia tours and the previous Gulf War, named Andy — inquired whether we had all deployed with 3 days' rations in our Bergens (large rucksacks in civilian speak) as briefed back in UK. Yes, we replied. Why is that, we asked? It transpired one of the things Camp Eagle lacked was sufficient food. We had lots of bottled water there, but the food had yet to arrive so these rations were for us to live off until then. This just gets better and better, we thought.

As we had several hours to while away before we moved anywhere, most of the guys found a space and got their heads down to grab some sleep. I caught up on my caffeine intake and took stock of things so far (I think too much, not the best of traits at times in a professional soldier). "Just enough, just in time" had worked very well in Kosovo, I reflected, but that had been in mainland Europe and with the aid of several major NATO allies. This was just us and the Americans it seemed and our logistics were, to date, simply dreadful. Surely, I thought, things would improve very shortly. With hindsight, I marvel at my thought process. Three years later, in Afghanistan, 2006, I would almost have the same conversation with myself, but that is another story and one already told by many others. The sad fact is that no one has yet been taken to task for any of these repeated failings, or is ever likely to be. We just got on with making the best of it, it's what British soldiers do best, really. "Welcome to Kuwait," I said to myself quietly. I wouldn't forget this one for a while, that was for sure. Years later and now very much an ex-soldier, for once in my life, I proved myself 100% right about that particular thought.

Our onward journey continued rather abruptly. Someone had decided that we simply couldn't hang around Kuwait International Airport making the place look untidy, so we were moved to a transit camp which was much more out of sight of either the media or any interested civilians. We woke the troops up in order to move to Camp Centurion. "Who makes these names up?" was a question from the waking troops, but one we were unable to answer. There we found a similar, but larger, set-up in terms of general facilities. We were spared yet more briefings, but all of us were promptly given hundreds of cartoon-style leaflets, all with Arabic subtitles. These were for us to give to the expected thousands of Iraqi soldiers who would, we had been repeatedly informed, immediately surrender en masse once the American "shock and awe show" began. These were designed to reassure nervous Iraqi conscripts that we were nice guys, not really invading them at all: more benevolent liberators and very worthy of their trust and so on. The idea was we'd give them a leaflet and disarm them, expecting them to find their own way to the prisoner of war holding areas, therefore allowing us to crack on with invading/liberating Iraq. "Take as many as you want," some NCO told us. It seemed to me that we confidently expected almost the entire Iraqi Army and his dad to put their hands up as soon as we appeared. I sincerely hoped someone had informed the Iraqis of their support role in the coming war.

By now our kit had finally turned up and we went through the time-honoured Army tradition of sorting through several hundred identical pieces of baggage to find our own, always a good way to while away the time in someone else's desert for thousands of British soldiers since 2003. Our weapons were "bundled", which means 4 or 5 rifles were ensconced in a weapon roll (literally a canvas roll designed for carrying rifles and a two-man lift, ideally) so these were left for unpacking at Camp Eagle. We were all fed again by now and generally hung around waiting for the transport "up country", with most troops focusing on getting some more sleep. Soldiers on operations grab sleep whether tired or not, simply because they never really know where and when the next opportunity will arise.

We were actually quite lucky: later flights were ordered by the movement staff in UK to place their respirators, despite protests, in the aircraft hold. These soldiers then sat on arrival into Kuwait, minus their respirators, for up to three hours waiting for these precious items to be unloaded. Unfortunately, as Kuwaiti citizens hadn't forgotten Saddam's Scud missile offensive against Israel in the previous Gulf War, the black market was charging up to $1000 dollars for a British S10 respirator (then considered to be far superior to its American counterpart at the time). The result was wide-scale theft of respirators and spare canisters (the detachable filter which enables breathing) as the aircraft was unloaded at the airport and replacing these was a haphazard system which could take days or even weeks in some cases: not the best way of raising the morale of the individual (and temporarily defenceless) soldier concerned.

After dark the promised Jingly buses arrived, we all took a seat and, not having any clue as to where we were going to, merely passively awaited the journey with massive lack of interest: we had by now collectively regressed into sheep mode. I, like most of the officers and senior NCOs, sat with my respirator on my lap. The night is well suited for chemical warfare (CW) attacks for several reasons and the Iraqis were, after all, the only nation to use CW on a large scale for several decades. Temperatures are much lower at night, so any agent used in liquid form (such as blister) will not evaporate under the sun's rays and remain effective longer. The "bonus" is that come dawn, it will evaporate and become a highly toxic vapour, drift with the wind and cause yet more casualties. Additionally, the early hours are tailor-made for turning sleeping and/or tired personnel into mass casualties. Both the Kurds and Iranians can vouch for this tactic being very effective, especially if you don't have a respirator or protective equipment. Accordingly, my personal respirator was very much firmly to hand: after all, I reminded myself, the PM himself had sent us all here for this very reason.

We appeared to be taking the scenic route and the air conditioning didn't work on the bus, so it wasn't long before we had all become even more bored and begun to totally switch off. We slowed for what appeared

51

to be an American military checkpoint. As we got closer, the American soldier manning it was illuminated in someone's headlights. Suddenly it became obvious he was wearing a respirator. Shit, had we missed the warning alarm? "GAS, GAS, GAS!" Someone at the front shouted in a muffled voice (having first donned his respirator, as all UK personnel are taught). "Dozing troops woke with a dazed, "What the fuck?" look on their faces and promptly all scrambled for their respirators in a frenzy of rapid, panic-stricken movement. I had immediately donned mine: I could always ask questions later, which a dead man cannot do very well; seconds matter when you play this game. As the glass and metal of the coach would afford us some protection against any possible liquid agent, the dominant threat was therefore vapour (a good job really, as our "Noddy suits" — Individual Protective Equipment, to give our protective suits their full title, or IPE — were all packed firmly in our Bergens in the baggage hold). Feeling relatively safe, I looked around the bus.

Several people, all of whom were totally anonymous now, had rather wide and exceedingly white eyeballs visible through their respirator eye pieces. One soldier, having misplaced his respirator, had the brain wave of putting a plastic carrier bag over his head and holding his breath: not the most fool proof, or sustainable, of plans really but, I suppose you could argue, at least he was doing *something*. Another three soldiers, who had obviously ignored the briefing, had apparently put their respirators in the baggage hold and were now literally fighting each other to get down the vehicle aisle, off the bus and to the packed baggage hold below: all very futile if the attack was on target with a favourable wind to boot. (With CW you don't have to be precisely accurate: it's like cake at a wedding; everyone gets a piece). In a matter of mere seconds, a sleepy bus full of bored soldiers had become a madhouse within a very confined space. Suddenly the very bemused — and also totally unprotected — Arab driver stopped the bus and stood up to face us all, waving his hands and saying repeatedly in broken English, "Is okay, is okay," at which point the now suffocating soldier removed his plastic bag gratefully and the fight immediately ceased in the aisle. He must have thought these Brits were all raving mad, but unlike us he knew this was a nightly training drill for the American soldiers in this particular area, which no one had seen fit to tell us about.

"Ah well," I thought to myself, "at least perhaps now they'll listen to the briefings and take it seriously." There is always a bright side. The three soldiers who had provided the "in flight" aisle entertainment were all firmly told to sit down. Their pleas, along with that of "Bag Man", to stop the bus and be allowed to find their respirators were turned down. This may seem rather callous, but they had been repeatedly briefed and knew the threat fully. We needed to move on, our coach being part of a much larger convoy and this simply wasn't a game any more, they should have known better. Just ignoring orders, or perhaps simple laziness on their part, didn't evoke much sympathy from any of us. Either can get you killed in a conflict zone and there is no appeal process or human rights considerations once you're dead. To coin a phrase popular with soldiers, "Man up, Princess, and deal with it". I certainly had no sympathy: an army at war has no room for incompetent or uninterested passengers, military tourists or people who just "know better", all of whom tend to invariably get good people killed and wounded, usually unnecessarily.

Now all alert and fully awake, we moved on into the dark night of the encroaching desert having mentally made the transition from a long and mundane trip to that of the stark realisation of entering a war zone in a matter of seconds. The coach was a very quiet one for the remainder of the journey. Eventually we turned off the metalled road and halted at the end of a not-too-obvious track, to find ourselves in a very dark place on a very dark night. As no one appeared to be around to meet us, we made a "command decision" and unloaded our baggage, heading like lemmings towards a small chink of light, it appearing to be the only possible civilisation in this pitch blackness. We were each laden with a crammed Bergen, a large holdall and a smaller patrol pack and shuffled, rather than walked, towards the small light.

Out of the darkness a voice rang out, followed by a thin torch beam. We immediately recognised the voice as that of the RSM, possessed as he was of a strange-sounding quasi-Australian accent (he had lived there as a child: the boys' nickname for him, quite unsurprisingly, was therefore "Skippy"). He informed us to "close in" on the torch beam. We shuffled towards him accordingly, over one hundred men who frankly were just keen to arrive somewhere (anywhere would be nice by now) after such an epic trip from the UK. The RSM had a reputation for liking the sound of his own voice: he didn't disappoint us.

The short version, following a rather lengthy "Welcome to Kuwait" speech: he told us all to leave our bags where they lay and follow him. One of the officers, a pragmatic Yorkshireman named Andy, voiced all our thoughts by questioning the wisdom of leaving our (hundreds of) dark-coloured bags on a very dark desert floor under an equally dark night and wouldn't it perhaps wiser to take them with us? The RSM, obviously annoyed at his wisdom being publicly disputed, abruptly reaffirmed this and promptly walked off, leaving us with little option but to follow him and his torch beam. The lemmings had once again transformed into sheep, it appeared.

Clutching our respirators (all of us this time) we passed through a gap in the "berm" (a heaped, sloping sand wall about 15 feet in height). All our camps were surrounded by a berm as both protection against the effects of sand storms and a physical security measure in Kuwait. Inside the berm, we could dimly make out some very large tents in the darkness. Huddling round the RSM, he informed us this was Camp Eagle, and he waved vaguely in the darkness to indicate some other unseen camps nearby, which was quite meaningless really. He pointed out that this was the accommodation and we should get ourselves comfortable and we'd receive further briefings tomorrow and promptly walked off, his job done, it seemed. At this point we all, rather wearily, retraced our footsteps to the dark desert and attempted to find our dark bags on a dark desert floor under a dark night. Eventually we all simply grabbed everything, deciding to try and find our personal kit once inside the large, circus style tents, a perfect end to the perfect journey. Morale, once again, was low.

The sleeping occupants of the tents were quite unimpressed at over a hundred blokes spending the best part of an hour shuffling and swapping their kit around, unsurprisingly. Eventually we all found our sleeping bags and settled down to get some much-needed sleep. I learnt a hard lesson a few hours later when I awoke, shivering due to the bitter cold. I had now discovered how bloody cold the desert can be at night and a lightweight sleeping bag was a poor choice to cope with the piercing cold of a February night in Kuwait. Once again, I had to rummage through my Bergen to find a warm fleece before attempting, once more, to get some rest. What, I wondered, would come next? It had taken us a week to get here: no food, no ammunition and a totally avoidable fuck-around with the baggage. This really wasn't very confidence-inspiring.

The next morning we awoke to our new surroundings. Our large tents were of a civilian wedding marquee type, one or two of which were complete with a blue and white striped design, which, claimed some of the soldiers, just proved this entire operation was Billy Smart's Circus. I could sincerely empathise with his point of view, but I couldn't openly express that (officers aren't paid to undermine the cause in any army, let alone the British Army with its famously stoical traditions), so I simply said nothing.

We drifted outside to examine Camp Eagle in daylight. It was completely underwhelming in nature: essentially a square surrounded by a sand wall (the berm), with some Portaloos adjacent to the (empty) vehicle park. Several large and identical accommodation tents, a cookhouse tent (which lacked food), a recreation tent which was totally devoid of everything at this stage, so the name was fairly meaningless as we had remarkably little to "recreate" with. Finally, the operations and planning tented area, which had a few chairs, tables, a phone and a couple of large-scale maps of Basra and its surrounding oil fields (we referred to these as "GOSPs": gas oil separation plants). Otherwise the shower blocks were inbound (along with everything else, it seemed). That was, in summary, about it.

Nothing was planned for us, it seemed, so we carried out our ablutions, as the Army terms washing and shaving, etc and made a brew and some breakfast from our rations. We had to eat these before we were permitted to use the cookhouse: rations were, it seemed, in that short supply. Our rifles had been unloaded and placed in one of the emptier tents for us to collect. Okay, we thought, we can pass some time by giving them a good clean after the epic journey. In a desert, soldiers become obsessed with trying to keep their rifles (and any other weapon for that matter) clean and sand free, it helps when you have the confidence that your rifle will work when required. The model of assault rifle then in use, (the SA 80 A1, as it was known), had a very poor reputation for reliability amongst the soldiers and did not cope with sand very well at all, so we really didn't have that confidence, which made people even more obsessed with weapon cleaning. It took the MOD two major upgrades of the SA 80 weapon system over several years — at the cost of tens of millions of pounds — to make it fit for purpose. Our opponents ironically had far more reliable weapons with their far older, but reliable, AK 47s and RPGs: this in turn eventually also caused the quiet "off-the-shelf" mass purchase of various light machine guns, rifles, pistols and other weapons by the MOD to provide us with trustworthy weapons as our desert wars dragged on.

We arrived to find some rather disgruntled troops. After our mother of all journey's, fate played another little trick on us, as we discovered, to our disgust, someone at Brize Norton had loaded the wrong rifles onto the plane in UK, so we had, to a man, the wrong rifles. Amazing, you just could not make this up! We cleaned the weapons anyway and awaited the solution to this new problem. Contrary to popular cinematic myth, you don't just pick up a weapon and shoot accurately. Professional armies spend a lot of time and effort to ensure each personal weapon is correctly zeroed to the firer. Sight alignment (better known as aiming) is, with the traditional iron sights we had then (the MOD later bought optic sights for all personnel), a four-point relationship between the eye, the rear sight, fore sight and the target. Add the personal height, eye relief and build of the firer and every individual has a very different "sight picture", so in order to hit a man-size target both quickly and accurately at, let's say, 300 metres, the weapon needs to be fully zeroed to its nominated "owner". This takes time, effort, and ammunition, coupled with adequate range time (if you don't use it you lose it, they say: shooting is no different in that respect) to fully achieve confidence, competence and proficiency.

Now all of that had been wasted. We had no idea where any rounds fired from these weapons would land. Bear in mind that unlike Europe, in the desert you tended to have few if any obstacles blocking your line of sight, so weapons engagement could take place at far greater ranges. We were told to keep hold of whatever weapons we had currently until this could be sorted. Oh well, at least we now had weapons, at least it was a start, we thought quietly. Luckily another flight from our regiment arrived within 48 hours or so, complete with our weapons (we had their rifles, by sheer fluke), so following a mass quick swop everything was as it should be, albeit we still had no ammunition in sight.

By now I had managed to get an overall situation from the Regimental Signals Officer (RSO), another veteran of the previous Gulf War and various Balkan tours, named Mike. He had arrived earlier and witnessed the UK build-up (or rather lack of) and had a good handle on the bigger picture. In simple terms, Saddam was holding his elite Republican Guard "up north" for the defence of Baghdad — the very heart of his regime — and it came as absolutely no surprise to learn that he was saving his best equipped and most loyal troops for the final battle. Our Commando Brigade had arrived by sea some weeks earlier and had the luxury of bringing all their equipment with them as they had their own shipping, courtesy of the Royal Fleet Auxiliaries and Royal Navy assault ships. That said, they were, like the Army's Air Assault Brigade in which we served, very lightly equipped, but unlike us they were boosted by 2000 US Marines, some SEAL teams and, much more importantly, dozens of US Marine F 18 fast jets and Sea Cobra attack helicopters, all supported by the massive firepower of the US Navy (our Navy were very much bit players, which was fine as the Iraqi Navy had ceased to exist a long time ago during the first Gulf War). They faced, we believed, mainly Iraqi Army units, a large number of regular troops, in the Al Faw Peninsula. Frankly, we had little interest in the Al Faw and our Marines: that was their war as the "right flank" brigade of the British Division and anyway the Royal Marines didn't much like us and that was a mutual feeling.

The centre brigade would be 7th Armoured (when they eventually turned up) with the British Army's combat-ready armour in its entirety:

two regiments of Challenger 2 tanks, with armoured infantry, artillery and engineer units, small fry by American standards, but this was by far and away our national "main effort" with *all* our nation's available heavy metal and firepower (it's rather less now as the Coalition Government have now essentially transformed the Army into a very lightly equipped and far smaller force). They would be tasked to capture Basra, Iraq's third city of some 1 million inhabitants, a very big ask in many ways. They would face a mixture of the Iraqi Army and the Fedayeen, literally the sons of Saddam, composed primarily of the orphaned sons of murdered Iraqis and then callously raised by the state to worship Saddam as a benign father figure. The Fedayeen were an unknown quantity to us, probably fanatical, but how well equipped were they and would they fight? In the Basra area, besides Iraqi infantry and tanks, was both light and heavy Iraqi artillery, including both Canadian-made Howitzer artillery and Serbian-made multi launch rocket systems, excellent weapon systems in their own right and capable of accurate fire at long ranges, which we fully expected to slime us once the chemical tripwire was reached, wherever Saddam had decreed that was.

As the left flank brigade and by far the most lightly equipped one, an air assault brigade with no means of air assaulting in essence, lacking any transport helicopters and having no planes to parachute from, we were basically an elite and very well trained "lorried infantry brigade" significantly *less* well equipped than most of the weaker Iraqi divisions we faced and having similar fire power and mobility of a similar British brigade of the 1940 era, that is to say very poor in all respects. Unsurprisingly, the US Marines (our UK 1st Armoured Division was part of the American MEF — Marine Expeditionary Force: essentially, we were all commanded by a US Marine General ultimately) rapidly decided our offensive capability as a division was rather limited, essentially a very polite way of saying we would actually hinder, rather than aid their operations towards Baghdad. Accordingly, our own mission would be merely to protect the American Main Supply Route (MSR) and defend the southern oil fields once captured by US Forces. We had no significant offensive mission allocated to us, in effect we would support the US Marines by providing security to their logistic efforts. Reluctantly I couldn't really disagree with them from a purely professional point of view: we were exceedingly lightweight for a war of this nature. But we were also all the UK had to send, and the government had elected to send us "ready or not". This was turning out to be very much a "come as you are" war.

Eventually all the troops arrived from UK over the next few days and we duly settled into life in Camp Eagle. All around us were several identical camps, one for each regiment or battalion in the brigade essentially. Viewed from the air, they would have been seen as a number of walled squares containing about 3500-4000 extremely highly trained Air Assault and Airborne soldiers. What any aerial observer wouldn't have been able to ascertain was our lack of food, ammunition, desert clothing and just about everything else we needed to fight. Morale was, unsurprisingly, fairly fragile, albeit quietly amongst the soldiers. Why, they asked each other, were we so short of everything? This was a common question amongst them. They had a very good point, I thought to myself, we seemed to be more of a large-scale public relations exercise than a serious act of war. By stark contrast we were acutely aware of the massive and overwhelming American military presence: their large and well equipped footprint in the small country of Kuwait was geared for one singular purpose and one purpose only; war. They were confident without being arrogant, purposeful and very well disciplined. Our doubts were slowly overcome by their overriding sense of mission. They simply didn't need us in pure military terms and whether we privately admitted it or not, we would most definitely not want to be on the receiving end of their awesome firepower, but they viewed us Brits as their number one ally and were patently glad for our support.

By contrast to our rather ramshackle logistical efforts, the Americans had been moving massive amounts of supplies and equipment into Kuwait since November, to the extent that they now gave us food daily: Meals Ready to Eat (MREs, or Meals Rejected by Ethiopians as the US Marines referred to them). Each day several hundred MREs were unceremoniously dumped in the middle of the camp and each man grabbed one quick while a chance remained to actually get a menu you liked. Any late arrivals simply had to take what was left, or go hungry.

This was our lunch meal and helped see you through the day as breakfast and evening meal in the cookhouse tent were rather minimalistic in terms of both portion size and choice. About this time, to our deep embarrassment, the American Military came to refer to the British Army collectively as "The Borrowers". Luckily for all of us Brits, because they both liked us and simultaneously felt very sorry for us, they were overly helpful: their generosity was total and utterly one way in nature (we had nothing to offer in return).

As we also had so few vehicles in Kuwait, for the vast majority of us, our initial life was one long and repetitive Groundhog Day in Camp Eagle. We had no equipment to train with, no maps, no facilities and no showers so after any PT (Physical Training) a strip wash (once a wash bowl became free) was the limit of our personal hygiene. One enterprising QM who did get down to the American Camps by KC (Kuwait City, strictly out of bounds to all of us), cheekily asked the US Marines for 20 camp cots (camp beds). In a typically generous American response, they gave him 20 pallets of camp cots (about 400) which enabled all of us to sleep off the floor, a major upgrade to our lifestyles. God Bless America!

Our ships finally arrived after almost 2 weeks of our military version of Groundhog Day, and the unloading of these vessels gave people something to do. Most of the vehicles were quickly collected and driven up to Camp Eagle while the helicopters went to the Ali Al Salem Airbase on the outskirts of KC for reassembly and critical maintenance work. We were slowly beginning to look like some form of a military unit.

I had bumped into three soldiers from my own squadron back in UK, led by a very competent corporal named Glenn. They were now attached to 3 Commando Brigade and living in the unsurprisingly named Camp Commando. They were passing through for a couple of days. Unlike us, they were all dressed in desert combats and they seemed quite annoyed that "their officer" was sweating profusely in his European green combats. I explained that desert clothing was very scarce in 16 Brigade at the moment. Muttering something about, "We'll sort it, sir", they all wandered off.

The next day, Glenn and his two partners in crime found me and asked if I could come with them as they had something that needed a quiet word. I duly went along to their tent and to my amazement, they presented me with not only 2 sets of desert clothing but a precious pair of desert boots in my size also! Brilliant! I simply couldn't thank them enough, now I could just sweat profusely on a daily basis instead of melting. First a camp cot and now this. Life was certainly improving, I thought: at this rate we might even get some bullets to fight with next!

We had now commenced daily morning and evening briefings for all the key players, of which I was one, being the Chemical Weapons Guru, part of the Intelligence Cell and now the Training Officer also. I was undecided if this was a good or bad development as we still had absolutely nothing to actually train *with*. Part of the brief was on security and the RSM announced that there had been a number of thefts in one of the neighbouring camps: the Royal Signals had discovered one of their washing lines (we all did our own washing by hand, irrespective of rank: quite a socialist concept, which would have pleased some of our then political masters no doubt) had been comprehensively raided and some desert clothing stolen. In addition, several pairs of desert boots had also gone missing from their stores. I kept a straight face, nodded sternly and agreed that this was totally unacceptable behaviour. He went on to say that the guys should have faith in the supply chain: people (apparently) were working flat out in the UK to resolve our problems. Bollocks, I thought, we haven't even got enough food to go around and absolutely no ammunition, how basic is that for any professional army?

About this time, the shower blocks were finally completed, much to the initial joy of the troops. However, the RSM had grave concerns that we might use too much water if this facility was abused by all these sweaty and dusty personnel. No one else actually shared these concerns, but the British Army only defends democracy, it doesn't actually practise it. Accordingly, the shower times were tightly controlled and opening times issued, furthermore an ad hoc "shower police" unit was formed by the RSM to enforce "ship's routine" (Ship? What fucking ship? thought the troops. We are in the Kuwaiti desert!) Apparently, the Royal Navy had a rule (somewhere) that no one could spend more than two minutes in the shower in a submarine, so we would follow suit. To say this had a quite major impact on the troops' new-found morale was an understatement. However, he had made a very public statement and to contradict him would undermine his key position, so the Royal Navy tradition of "ship's routine" came to pass in the arid Kuwaiti desert in the form of 400-plus rather bemused soldiers showering against a stop watch under the watchful gaze of the RSM and seemingly omnipresent Shower Police. The keys to the showers were subject to a similar amount of security to the crown jewels, so we all became accustomed and resigned to queuing patiently for a shower and then being timed accordingly, once we finally made it to the key to our personal hygiene.

Some ammunition actually turned up. Apparently the Royal Marines had donated a small amount to us to help us check zero our rifles, which was quietly appreciated: no professional soldier ever likes to give away ammunition, after all. It worked out at 20 rounds each, not much, but better than nothing and it gave the troops something to do, as the travel time to the ranges was significant and transport still in short supply. This, fitness training, assorted briefings and vehicle maintenance tasks were now all combining to give people a sense of purpose. Concurrently the helicopters were being reassembled in Ali Al Salem Air Base, close to KC. Desert clothing and food were still both relatively scarce but at least we had begun to resemble a modern, if fairly poorly equipped army and we had become used to doing a lot with a little.

We had a minor wake up call in the form of a locally employed civilian (LEC as they are known colloquially) being arrested at Camp Commando. He had been found stealing soldiers' discarded letters from rubbish bags. His aim had been to compile a list of parents' and loved ones' addresses and send them to the (then embryonic) jihadist extremist movements in UK as targets for violent revenge attacks against them and therefore, by association, us. Not a pretty thought, but quite a chilling one. After this incident, all letters from home, once read, were duly burnt. We were slowly realising exactly what 21st Century asymmetric warfare consisted of, and the fact that this was not just about a single frontline here in the desert. Quite a minor incident in the grand scheme of things, but it certainly helped people to concentrate their minds on exactly why we were here and the task in hand, and the fact that not everyone agreed with our presence in Kuwait.

About this time a (single) TV was installed in the recreation tent, which became permanently tuned to Sky News, our main source of any view of the outside world. We had also been issued phone cards, which entitled us to a 15-minute call, once a week, to the UK. All calls had to be booked on a slot system and we soon learnt that if you were late for your slot to call home, then you would simply lose your slot. This may sound harsh, but with several hundred people and only two phones, you had to be prompt or be disappointed. Additionally, you had to accept that the strong likelihood of several intelligence services (including our own) listening, and possibly recording your brief words to your family and loved ones was a simple fact of life. No doubt someone, somewhere, will loudly proclaim "This is a breach of your basic human rights", but war, by and large, is exactly that and most soldiers have a more pragmatic view of basic human rights than seems to be so prevalent in modern UK. Continuing to practise unaided and long-term breathing and coming home in (hopefully) one piece is the key concern of most soldiers about to embark on inevitably violent combat operations.

The killing fields of Helmand, with their fields of seemingly mass produced Improvised Explosive Devices (IEDs, so inaccurately named roadside bombs by the media) were far, far in the future, but their origins would lie in post-occupation Iraqi ingenuity and the subsequent migration to Afghanistan, to be embraced on an almost industrial scale by the Taliban, both insurgencies being healthily aided by shadowy Iranian agencies, though the innovative Afghan addition of human excrement liberally smeared over the IED, in order to immediately and massively infect the resulting casualties' bloodstreams and various internal organs gives a fair idea of our future opposition's attitude towards human rights and Western soldiers in general. But we were still, on the eve of war in 2003, quite naïve of all this, in many ways a classic case of "what you don't know won't hurt you". Essentially, we were all still "intervention virgins".

That Army, of only fifteen or so years ago, is virtually unrecognisable from the one now routinely seen at most major sporting events or in recruiting adverts for the Army Reserve as the government seeks to avoid spending money on defence post-Afghanistan. In terms of clothing, communication systems, personal weapons and personal equipment, major and quite impressive improvements have been made in all respects but nothing is free in life, so the Army is also far smaller and primarily geared for very limited counter insurgency operations, rather than larger-scale "State on State" warfare in terms of its vehicles, the heavier "crew served" weapons, major equipment types and overall organisation. All of which probably explain why Mr Putin isn't too concerned by any deployment of the remaining units of the British Army into the Baltic regions or indeed why Islamic State aren't losing any sleep over the possibility of the Brits arriving en masse. But this is an ongoing Western European tendency in military terms and what the overwhelming majority of European voters want, in a way slightly reminiscent of the popular mood of the 1930s democracies, you could argue, perhaps. But that is the very point of Democracy after all and the overwhelming majority of modern politicians are populist for reasons of political survival.

One unforeseen result of our intervention was then undreamt-of actions of a group of former (Sunni) Iraqi Army officers, whilst held in American captivity post-invasion, of both brainstorming and planning the concept of Islamic State post-Western occupation. In effect they turned their captivity into an asymmetric staff college and they did it very well, sadly. This would have been dismissed as ridiculous fantasy by any of us until very recently indeed and any army has to rapidly adapt to new enemies and unforeseen battlefields. the British Army in 1914-1918 or the Americans in their Pacific Island-hopping campaigns are classic examples of having to fight wars in a new and novel manner previously beyond everyone's imagination. Again, the all-predominant British Army of 1918 had precious little in common with the one of 1914 and the massive American amphibious forces assembled to recapture various Pacific Islands were on a scale simply undreamt-of by friend and foe alike at the time of the attack on Pearl Harbour in 1941.

Armies, like many large and conservative organisations, like to stay in their comfort zones, which is why "fighting the last war" is such a common and recurring theme across military history, in our case we Brits tended to quickly default to the Northern Ireland "internal security" setting in military terms, whilst our politicians did exactly the same with the Good Friday Agreement often being spoken of wistfully, if naïvely, as a shining example of peace and reconciliation for all to emulate. Regrettably, neither is remotely fit for purpose to transfer across to, or even begin to, address the cultural chasms of the bitterly divided Islamic Sunni/Shia conflict, ancient tribal rivalries and very numerous well-armed, fanatical and often barbaric medieval Jihadists who are ultimately self-perceived "Holy Warriors", quite a different species from Western European terrorists in so many ways. After all, the last people both we and the Americans had fought who possessed the utter ruthlessness, enduring stoical willingness to die for their cause without hesitation and such overriding contempt for infidels and outsiders as currently ISIS/Daesh do, was the Imperial Japanese Army, very much a historical and little-known episode for the current generation. Sadly, the mistakes and failures of your history, as we soon discovered to our cost, does have a nasty habit of repeating itself should you fail to heed its hard-won lessons.

It had slowly become obvious to all of us that, ongoing and large-scale logistical shortfalls or not, we were going across the border and whilst we may not be a very effective fighting force in the traditional military sense of previous wars, this mattered not at all. It was increasingly obvious that Her Majesty's Government was quite adamant on the invasion taking place: "simple as", to use a soldier's phrase. Little things like the lack of ammunition, key equipment and mission-critical spare parts were just utterly irrelevant in the grand scheme of things, at least it seemed that way to us. Luckily for all of us, the Americans were still giving us our daily bread and seemed to view us with widespread and wholescale sympathy, verging on feeling quite sorry for us, which made obtaining stuff fairly easy for us, the singular exception being all the American PXs (military shops) in the KC area: we Brits were banned from shopping in all such establishments by the American authorities as in a modern impersonation of a biblical plague of locusts, British soldiers were simply buying everything. Much to the major annoyance of our

American allies they had discovered row upon row of empty shelves following the Brits passing through, credit cards in hand, in an attempt to better equip themselves for the forthcoming war. Ironically, these had been "rear area" units rather than the fighting troops stationed much closer to the border regions, so they gained relatively little of war value from this brief commercial outlet except feeling much better for their pseudo-military purchases.

I managed to make one of my very few escapes from the isolation of Camp Eagle and hitch a ride to Ali Al Salem with the Regimental 2IC, a highly experienced desert veteran major named Peter and very much the brains behind the operation, being imbued with both a keen intellect and a major dose of common sense. He was very much an occupant of the real world, unlike some of our current leaders, it seemed to me. Essentially the trip was to find out how the re-assembly of our post-sea voyage, battered and dented helicopters was progressing. The Air Base was home to several dozen US Marine and US Navy helicopters and the resident RAF Tornado Squadron, who had been discreetly bombing Iraq continuously since 1991 and now seemed fairly upset at the sudden arrival of all these sweaty soldiers. Most of our technicians and aircrew were living in the Spartan remains of several bombed-out hardened aircraft shelters, German-built and, quite ironically rapidly destroyed by the American and British Air Forces in the first Gulf War. The reinforced concrete shelters had been literally blown away with, it still seemed even 12 years after the event, rather consummate ease. These impressively solid structures had been utterly devastated by some quite awesome destructive forces of a man-made nature. The Kuwaitis, for reasons best known to themselves, had made absolutely no attempt to reconstruct or repair any of these buildings. The entire effect was one of living in some very authentic Hollywood film set, but minus all the associated amenities.

Our officers had approached the RAF and politely inquired if it might be possible to arrange for the use of their showers once a day, with a promise that the showers would be left spotless and only used at "off peak" times. The RAF explained that, as a "long term resident unit in Kuwait", it wasn't their policy to share amenities with any "non-resident units" in any respect and especially with the trivial issue of a major land war looming. The RAF, it seemed, viewed Kuwait as their personal stomping ground and didn't seem too pleased at all these "Pongos" turning up and rather lowering the tone of their weekly bombing practices over southern Iraq. RAF fast jet personnel tend to view their main role as adding a touch of class to an otherwise rather vulgar battlefield thousands of feet beneath them and many of their officers still cling stubbornly to the ongoing myth that modern war can be won from the air alone. Accordingly, their favourite topic of conversation tends to be themselves, essentially very much a case of, "That's enough about you, let's talk about me". Oh well, back to the strip wash and patiently queuing up for a wash basin, obviously sharing a nationality and a common cause didn't count for much with the "Fast Jet" crowd, who were somewhat infamous for both their oversized egos even amongst the wider RAF itself. Our guys' point of view was mainly disbelief that asking for a shower was beyond the ability of our "Light Blue Brethren" to oblige us, especially in the run-up to a major conflict and disappointment that such a petty attitude could be displayed by our own countrymen. This little incident did little for the enhancement of inter-service relations. "Well, at least we still have the US Marines on our side", seemed to be the prevalent attitude amongst our soldiers.

Although we still had serious clothing, equipment, ammunition and food shortfalls, rumour had it that we'd be getting body armour soon and the vehicles had all been unloaded without too much hassle. The only issue was that our shipping, having arrived so late to this particular party, had to anchor offshore until the Americans gave up a berthing slot for unloading, as virtually all of KC's docks had been booked up in advance by the huge American merchant fleet busily involved in moving large chunks of American might and enormous amounts of supplies across the world's ocean. Hence most of our soldiers had to accomplish this between midnight and five in the morning, which didn't exactly please the troops, but we now had lots of green vehicles at least: the promised sand-coloured paint had still yet to be purchased apparently. By now this was quite unsurprising to any of us, we were after all The Borrowers within this coalition of allies. Hardly the stuff of military legend, or a memorable nickname to stir regimental pride within a professional army with such a rich history and valiant traditions as ours, but we learned to live with it. In any case the Army didn't lack self-belief and we were very accustomed to making do with whatever we had, it was, after all, simply how we did things, was our unspoken collective mindset.

On returning to Camp Eagle, we passed a huge purpose-built desert airstrip, newly built by the American Army's Corps of Engineers, the Americans simply did — and still do — logistics in a manner and scale that no European Army could remotely compete with. On this strip was parked some several hundred US Army helicopters of all shapes and sizes, from large Chinook transports and the smaller Blackhawks (made so famous by the *Blackhawk Down* movie), to highly lethal-looking Apache attack helicopters. This was in addition to the US Navy and Marine helicopters we had just seen in their dozens at Ali Al Salem, it rather put our two squadrons' worth of 30-year-old helicopters into perspective, I quietly thought to myself. We were definitely the junior partner for this operation by far.

A wise (military) man, now a serving major general, once told me that, "War is ultimately all about getting there first with the most". The Americans obviously intended to do exactly that, on a very large scale and in the very near future. I suddenly realised at this point that this was not mere sabre-rattling. The post-9/11 American Military was simply waiting to be unleashed by its President, and no power on this Earth, let alone the Iraqi Army and Republican Guard, was remotely capable of stopping them. After all, someone had touched America, and now the US Military was very keen to "reach out and touch people" in return, only with massive compound interest: shock and awe, in simple terms. Whilst not quite an epiphany moment, nevertheless it was a singular moment of clarity. America had obviously made its decision weeks, if not months, earlier regarding the fate of Saddam Hussein and by default, the entire Iraqi nation itself. We Brits, despite being late arrivals, had simply no choice but to adhere to the American timetable, ready or not.

I rode back in a pensive silence for the rest of the journey, contemplating the coming war and what training I could realistically organise in the remaining time before we crossed the border, given our ongoing lack of ammunition and key equipment. Ironically, for the liberation of Kosovo, a rather small-scale European piece of aggressive peace keeping in comparison, we'd had ammunition literally thrown at us. Now, on the verge of a major desert war, ammunition was as rare as the proverbial rocking horse shit, to coin a highly popular Army term, as were several other crucial items, from common-or-garden wound dressings to body armour and key items for protection against the well-publicised chemical weapons of dossier fame. What the hell was going on back in Whitehall, I pondered? Soldiers tend to believe that words are rather cheap and actions are what really matter. I was just beginning to realise that in the age of professional politicians, exactly the opposite was true. Substance had definitely been replaced by style, or rather spin with a capital S: we, it seemed, were just a collection of commodities to be used as they saw fit, at least that is the way we were beginning to suspect. Luckily none of us had any idea of the Army's demanding future, which still lay ahead of us and our concerns were very much focused on the immediate future.

My professional responsibilities were rarely far from the top of my daily thoughts. Unlike the vast majority of modern professions, complacency or mistakes in a conflict zone both normally tend to cost people dearly, from shattered limbs and lives to multiple deaths. It really is that black and white at the end of the day and whilst coroners and lawyers have the enormous cushions of perfect hindsight, time and distance to dissect and criticise each and every decision made on a 21st Century battlefield, soldiers and their commanders have to make split-second decisions, often under enormous and life-threatening pressures the like of which is almost incomprehensible to the vast majority of the UK's population. War is not merely some form of bizarre and large-scale industrial accident in a far-off place and the enemy can often be ingenious, cunning, ruthless or just plain lucky. Neither do they remotely adhere to the Western popular concept of tolerance and fairness or any aspect of any human rights protocol, all of which seems to be just too plain and simple for some sections of UK society to comprehend. Demanding fairness on a modern battlefield is at best naïve, at worst a life-ending expectation and our current enemies are utterly ruthless in the manner in which they wage war, to say the least.

My personal piece of the pie was to attempt, as best I could, to prepare the guys and girls for the forthcoming war. I was also hugely conscious that the enemy has a vote too and this particular one might be expressed in a variety of ways, including the large and violent delivery of an incredibly toxic collection of chemicals, the like of which the British Army hadn't seen since 1918. After all, no less a person than our own Prime Minister in person had repeatedly told both us and our nation so, or why else were we all here? Our American allies were visibly on their starting blocks, it was our turn next, and after all, there were no other significant allies in this somewhat narrow coalition of nations. So, I reminded myself, very forcibly, to shake off these negative thoughts and just concentrate on fulfilling my own piece of the mission. Time was now becoming a rather short commodity, after all.

The Americans would launch their offensive at a time of their choosing and we Brits would be expected to go with them, any delays or excuses on our part regarding our incredibly poor logistic support or lack of serviceable equipment would fall on deaf transatlantic ears and find no sympathy or patience, it seemed. Time, ultimately is just another resource to a professional military, so we Brits would have to dance to an American tune and very soon, it seemed.

At a fairly recent reunion dinner (ironically to mark the 10th anniversary of the Iraq invasion), our former Commanding Officer admitted to those who attended that he had been informed in October 2002, that "The Regiment will be going", by a senior officer. The caveat added was that, "You can't prepare anything. Just plan". It surprised me that the political and military decision was made several months before any of us knew and, far more importantly, no one made any discernible effort at all to prepare our armed forces for large-scale war against a major nation state. I remember thinking, no wonder it was such a shambles, with a mindset of that nature as the foundation for the violent overthrow of such a well-entrenched and all-encompassing regime as that of Saddam Hussein.

This subsequent and rather frantic planning bout was all done on the overarching assumption of an overland northern invasion route, via Turkey, so even this limited planning period was ultimately a fruitless effort as no one had seen fit to actually discuss this aspiration with the Turkish authorities. They in turn (and unsurprisingly) strongly objected to being used as a springboard for Western troops to violently invade a neighbouring Muslim nation, even one ruled by such an infamous dictator as Saddam. At the time this was unknown to the vast majority of us, we were all just personally fixated on making the best of it in a variety of isolated locations in the Kuwaiti desert.

As we scrambled to get our equipment together and combat ready, plus squeeze in some worthwhile training, our "embedded media" arrived in Camp Eagle, fresh from the relative luxuries of UK. Every unit was given a handful of journalists by the MOD. We received a former royal photographer who had been around a few wars of his own already, a very young and inexperienced local news reporter from East Anglia and a national daily reporter with quite left-wing views, quite a varied mixture all in all. Like most soldiers, we simply didn't trust the press, they just want to sell papers ultimately and don't get the military mindset with its emphasis on selfless teamwork, honour, loyalty, courage, mutual respect and other "ancient values" in 21st Century UK. Soldiers view the media as "self-licking lollipops" with the BBC as market leaders in that field, frankly, but in the age of immediate media access and highly polished spin, whilst we would have preferred more ammunition, we had absolutely no choice in this particular matter.

But they were here for the duration, so we quietly vowed to give it a go and be ultra-careful what we actually said in front of them, for fear of a personal opinion expressed in quiet confidence to a seemingly friendly journalist rapidly becoming an "unnamed MOD source" within an article in a major newspaper. The MOD work extremely hard and very successfully, it must be said, to ensure they have full control over the lines to take with regard to all information given to the media, which explains why the British public, when august bodies such as the BBC really just report the party line in all matters military, and seem to believe that large-scale involvement in the Syrian Civil War, or similar very large-scale operations remain well within our remaining military capability, when in reality anything other than small stuff is patently way beyond our drastically downsized, albeit still exceedingly high calibre armed forces.

Almost immediately an embedded journalist from a now-defunct Sunday newspaper was sent home for allegedly offering large sums of money to young soldiers of another regiment in exchange for any "kiss and tell" stories centred around a theme of "sex in the desert" between the ranks, the more lurid the better. The forthcoming invasion of Iraq, it seemed, was of little apparent concern to him, but it was hardly an auspicious beginning. In their defence UK journalists are (unlike their American counterparts) subject to strict censorship, which they simply have to adhere to if they wish to retain their embedded status with HM Forces. I assume this explains the BBC's eternal tendency to unquestioningly repeat the MOD party line, especially when it comes to casualty figures. Incredibly, on the 10th anniversary of the Iraq war, the BBC gave the unbelievably small figure of 456 wounded personnel during the Iraq War and subsequent occupation. Most soldiers who served there would contest that as ludicrously low by a factor of 8 to 10, but then, I ask myself, after over a decade of war who cares anyway, apart from the soldiers and their families? That may sound cynical, but it's a very common theme amongst military veterans.

From somewhere a single wide screen TV had arrived in the "Rec tent", which gave us all a chance to discover what was happening in the world courtesy of non-stop Sky News, singularly aided by the simple fact we couldn't actually change channels, merely turn the TV off and on. But it was somewhere to go and try and discover a little more information, accurate or not. We still had very little in the way of either resources or equipment, but at least we had something to watch and a reason to congregate socially. It was progress of sorts after all.

To my personal (and enduring) embarrassment, I had to send the RSM away to inspect some American-owned weapon ranges for possible air-to-ground gunnery training. Our three Lynx Mark 9 helicopters each had a door gunner manning a 7.62mm machine gun for close-in self-defence of the aircraft. We badly needed to ensure the gunners were current and competent in all respects for the forthcoming conflict (once the ammunition arrived). However, the range complex in question was quite some way from us and I could hardly just point vaguely at the desert and say, "It's somewhere over there, RSM," and then let him wander aimlessly around the featureless desert for a couple of days. My problem was promptly resolved by a US Marine Captain who dropped in to discuss some issues with our HQ. He left his map unattended on the table and after some quiet internal wrangling with my conscience, I figured it was for the greater good and the US Marines were probably awash with maps of Kuwait, unlike ourselves. So, to my eternal shame, I was reduced to covertly "liberating" it in order to safely dispatch the RSM on his cross-desert mission. To that nameless US Marine officer, in the unlikely event you ever wind up in South Lancashire, I'll buy the beers all night long and beg your forgiveness. Though I strongly suspect it didn't affect the overall combat performance of the United States Marine Corps. Nevertheless, as a British soldier and then an officer with over 25 years' service in the Army, I was, to my great personal embarrassment, reduced to "relocation of assets" due to our utter lack of basic military essentials. How pathetic on my part and sad in respect of an army with a reputation second to none.

The camp had filled up by now with a mixture of units. The brigade's armour, which was a squadron from the Household Cavalry Regiment (HCR) with just over a dozen combat vehicle reconnaissance (tracked) or CVR (T) for short: not really a tank at all, they were thinly armoured vehicles and nearly 50 years old, but it was all we had and we were pleased to see them. The Pathfinder Platoon had also arrived with their stripped-down Land Rovers with machine gun fits, very warlike and pleasingly photogenic, but they would be cruelly exposed by Taliban IEDs in 2006 as utterly vulnerable and completely unfit for purpose in such a deeply hostile environment (the Army's Reserve units now operate these vehicles, their part time crews probably totally unaware of the huge relief of the regular Army in getting rid of these obsolete vehicles). They were known colloquially as PFPL and consisted of some very highly trained soldiers who would be operating deep behind Iraqi lines, but they were tough, confident troops, essentially one step down from Special Forces and one of the few British units capable of working alongside the Americans in both equipment and long-range communications compatibility terms. For reasons of operational security or OPSEC, they kept their distance from the rest of us, which is fairly common practice for anyone in the SF world and similar units within that orbit.

Lastly came some elements of the (now disbanded) NBC Defence Regiment, most of them being deployed along the border with their various sensor systems, just in case Saddam went for a pre-emptive strike against the American build-up to buy himself some time. In terms of capacity, the camp was full and around us lay the various camps of the Infantry Battalions — 2 from the Parachute Regiment, out-and-out assault troops who were the Army's "Rottweilers" — and the Royal Irish Regiment with their flamboyant ex-SF CO, Colonel Tim Collins, who would later make his world-famous eve-of-battle speech, so widely reported by the world's media. Lastly was Brigade HQ, the Airborne 7 Royal Horse Artillery with its light guns and the logistic and support units of the REME, Logistic and Medical Corps. We were now balanced, as the military saying goes, and ready to shake out for war.

We embarked on a number of "shake out" exercises, which mainly consisted of rehearsing our very simple plan. As we were to secure the southern oil fields and protect the GOSPs from any acts of sabotage, once captured by our American big brothers, whilst also protecting the Americans Main Supply Route (MSR), essentially, we would just follow the US Marines into Iraq. They would rapidly push north and we would be a large glorified security force due to our sheer lack of mobility and firepower. In order to get the Iraqi border guards conditioned to the sight of large-scale British movement we drove up to the border en masse several times and we also got accustomed to large-scale night moves in the pitch darkness of the desert night. Doing so in a major sand storm was an experience, when visibility dropped down to metres and the sand penetrated into the vehicle cabs, with the results that crew members had to wrap a shemagh in true Arab style around their head, mouth and nose and don goggles *inside* the vehicle to be able to operate. As we all followed the convoy light of the darkened vehicle in front (a small dim light under the rear axle), these exercises became known as "mass crashes" as shunts and bumps became the norm. As we had no Global Positioning Systems or Night Vision systems either at this stage, daylight normally brought the sight of dozens of scattered vehicles all over the desert. It would have been a familiar scene to any old Eighth Army veteran really, quite traditional stuff in many ways.

On one occasion, we introduced a notional ("pretend" in plain English) large-scale and accurate Iraqi chemical attack into the "war gaming" phase. As we were going to drive en masse down a single Iraqi-built main road, it rather made sense to assume the Iraqi Artillery would know the ground down to an accuracy of mere metres. Essentially it was rather like our own artillery being tasked to target the M25 in concept and would therefore, it was reasonable to assume, hit us quite effectively. After our estimated casualties in the lead unit rose past 40% and the route became blocked by dozens of notionally chemically contaminated vehicles (blister agent sticks to most things very well, not just human beings) and hundreds of "notional" wounded as a result, we simply cancelled this phase of the exercise as "too difficult". This worried me massively, as it demonstrated our serious inability to effectively extract and provide medical treatment to our wounded or even decontaminate our vehicles. Equally worrying was this also exposed the amazing fact that we didn't have enough spare IPE suits (Noddy suits, as the troops called them) to go around if soldiers were contaminated by liquid CW, POL products (which seriously downgraded the suits efficiency) or simply accidently tore their suits open. In all our Germany-based exercises during the past decades, each and every single soldier always had 3 sets: one with him/her, one held at squadron or company level and a third at regimental level (with thousands more in reserve at various military warehouses), as we firmly believed the Russians, in the form of the Red Army, would routinely use massive amounts of CW as a standard offensive practice. Most guys in Kuwait had one suit only. Why, I thought to myself, is this such a problem, when we have been doing this for decades in Germany? Yet another of life's great unanswered questions for me and part of our numerous and repeated major logistical failures, which to this day remains unanswered by anyone.

After this little debacle we retired to sort the vehicles out and prepare for the big day. As we all chilled one night in the Rec tent, to our utter amazement the Million-person March was shown by Sky News. All conversation stopped and everyone, irrespective of rank or unit, surrounded the TV. No one spoke as we beheld the sheer size of the anti-war demonstration. We were literally speechless: our people — the British nation that we existed to defend — had "voted with its feet" in a quite overwhelming fashion. Stunned is probably the best word I can think of to describe the collective reaction of us all. On this, the very eve of a major war and all the conflicting emotions that unique and life-changing experiences like this generate, our own people seemed to be making their feelings clear on a massive scale. We were simply flabbergasted and I would venture that all of us were affected in some manner by this overwhelmingly large-scale example of British democracy in action.

Over twelve years later, with fully a third of the population of the nation's capital now being immigrants, with approximately another three million-plus immigrants across the remainder of England, all of whom hold little or no interest in such distant political/military ventures and even less interest regarding the British Army itself, the NHS, access to UK's well financed education system and our rather generous welfare benefits are all a far greater "pull" than the distant exploits of a fairly small and, to the vast majority of our immigrants, a very "foreign" army. British Muslims have never joined the Army in anything other than small numbers, initially due to adverse social pressures within their community, but it's much simpler now, you just run the risk of abduction and an Internet beheading by doing so, plus possible violence towards your family, so it takes a remarkably brave young British Muslim male to join HM Forces in the 21st Century. As recent events have tragically shown, some people are literally violently hostile towards both the police and HM Forces as a result of our recent wars, with the British passport itself viewed by some "citizens" as a mere "travel document", with hundreds of others actively fighting for the so-called Islamic State.

All of these were unthinkable at the time of the invasion, as was the long-term enduring chaos about to be unleashed, which was also then simply unimaginable to us, as were the massive, politically enabled, demographic changes that would take place within the population of the society we were all pledged to defend. It is probably doubtful if a march of this magnitude would ever take place again in UK post the ill-thought "open borders" immigration policies since 2003 and multiple associated failures regarding key aspects of social and racial integration, all of which have been given an ongoing and enduring "damned good ignoring" by our professional political classes, but back then, albeit briefly, our little world in the Kuwait sand had been well and truly rocked.

To be honest, this wasn't much discussed amongst us, but not because we didn't care, rather we just didn't know *what to say* about this massive outpouring of anti-war feeling by the British people. This wasn't a handful of left wing pseudo intellectuals or traditional CND-type sympathisers. These had been Mr and Mrs Joe Public and in their hundreds of thousands, who obviously agreed neither with our cause or our government's foreign policy. Quite a few people openly expressed the opinion, "That's it, we won't be going. There is simply no way the PM can ignore that", but of course, he surely could and promptly did, as we shortly found out.

I cannot speak for anyone else, but I went to my sleeping bag a very troubled man that evening. It would appear that both our cause and faith in the judgement of our elected leadership were none too well supported at home. My thoughts centred upon, "So if we weren't going to fight for our people and our nation, then exactly who and what were we going to fight for?" I had a job to do and soldiers to lead and look after, but far more importantly, soldiers to take home in one piece. I expected them to follow their orders to the best of their ability as I would mine and I'd strive to lead them by example. There is no ultimately other way of leading in the British Army and I couldn't afford for them to become confused by this significant and, for us in the Kuwait desert at least, utterly unexpected turn of events. But conversely, here I was becoming rather confused myself, albeit silently and privately. I decided to banish these troubling doubts to a faraway corner of my mind until I was safely back home in the UK, with my soldiers all hopefully still alive and preferably all in one piece. For a professional career soldier on the very eve of war, thoughts of this nature verge on heresy.

Thereafter I worked rather hard to banish them to a distant corner of my mind and keep them safely confined there, but they certainly resurfaced later in my life. To be honest, as is the nature of the beast for professional soldiers, once the time came to cross the border and rock Saddam's world, we forgot about the march in all respects and got on with the job in hand. Soldiers who don't want to get involved in the real thing are relatively few in number in any professional army and they tend to be rather discreet for obvious reasons. That said, every army also has its "war dodgers" who like the uniform but not the harsh and dirty reality of what soldiers are ultimately trained (and paid) for. Luckily for us, the vast majority of our brigade were enthusiastically "up for it". At that time in Kuwait, none of us were particularly careful in what we wished for, but then hindsight is, and always has been, a truly classless, multicultural and universal enduring aspect of adulthood.

Our morale was raised considerably by the sight of several British Challenger 2 Main battle tanks (MBTs) driving past Camp Eagle: finally the long-awaited heavy metal had arrived from Germany and they were a very pleasing sight to all of us. No offence to the Royal Marines or the Paras, as proud and as fit they undoubtedly are, but fundamentally they are simply extremely well trained amphibious and airborne light infantry in pure military terms and no match for anyone with a large force of MBTs and Armoured Fighting Vehicles (AFVs). Ultimately courage and fitness simply don't overcome significant amounts of firepower and thick armour plate in large quantities, the battle of Arnhem being a tragic, if exceedingly gallant example of that particular imbalanced military equation. To be fair, we the (theoretically) Air Assault troops also lacked armour and firepower and both our own and the Commando Brigade's Artillery Regiment'slight guns had a maximum range of 16 kilometres, firing quite a fairly small 105mm shell in the process, which the Iraqi Army simply outranged and outgunned, on paper at least. In terms of simple movement ability, we all lacked mobility in terms of large scale desert warfare where "manoeuvre" would be king, along with the logistical support required to enable us to simply keep moving. Logistics was a glaring and repeated weakness in the British Army of 2003 (this was a major reason why the drive to Baghdad was an all-American affair: we simply couldn't keep up with the Americans essentially).

Our Armoured Division was now complete, although unlike our American brethren, it wasn't very armoured: one amphibious brigade and one air assault brigade, both of which lacked tanks or heavy artillery and the sole armoured brigade the army could muster. Just to further complicate the matter, none of the three brigades had any experience of working together, again unlike our American counterparts and the way they trained together. In essence we were neither equipped nor trained to be an expeditionary force; our recent experience in the Balkans had been relatively close to home and a fairly small-scale affair with a decent local infrastructure and all the warring factions concerned were both tired and very war-weary, whilst Kosovo had centred upon a state equivalent in size to Yorkshire. Our successful operations in Sierra Leone had been on a rather smaller scale involving very lightly equipped elite troops against an opposition of essentially heavily armed criminal gangs. Subsequently our initial intervention into Afghanistan 2001/02 had been very much an "SF only" affair. None of these operations was on anything remotely approaching the same scale as this rapid and very large-scale deployment to the desert, which had painfully exposed our weaknesses and unlike the first Gulf War, we wouldn't have several months' grace to consolidate ourselves. In essence this was a "come as you are" war, which we were very ill-prepared for, although we all confidently expected this to be resolved before we went into action.

So, the arrival of British Panzers was a welcome, reassuring and morale-boosting "happening" for all of us "Borrowers" in Camp Eagle. One of my other jobs was Intelligence Officer, so I was very well aware of the number of tanks, other armoured vehicles, medium and heavy artillery the Iraqis possessed in Southern Iraq. I also knew that along with the "Chally 2's" as they were commonly known, came a single AS 90 Heavy Artillery Regiment (real artillery, as our feisty little ex-SF Brigade Commander referred to them) and a couple of armoured infantry battalions in their Warrior Infantry Fighting Vehicles — another potent weapon system that demanded respect. At last I thought to myself, we have finally got some *real* military hardware into Kuwait.

The unit we had seen was the Royal Scots Dragoon Guards — "Scotland's Cavalry" — universally known as the SDGs across the Army. One of our (Scottish) officers had a brother serving with them and loudly told us "English bastards" that we could all relax now as the SDGs were accompanied by the Black Watch in their Warriors and there was absolutely *no way* the Iraqis could stand up to this combination of Scotland's finest. Personally I didn't care who drove the Panzers or Warriors, I was just so glad we had some around. After all we were an elite air assault brigade, with no real means of air assaulting anything, now operating in the "lorried infantry" role of 1940 troops, (although no one would actually say that openly for reasons of military etiquette and general politeness), whilst the Royal Marines didn't really fetch a lot in heavy equipment terms to the party either, so we badly needed these guys.

The Challenger 2 was and is simply an awesome beast, the other MBT Regiment was the second Royal Tank Regiment (2RTR) and quite simply back then it could easily cope with any other MBT or armoured vehicle in the world. However, our MBT Force has been notably neglected over the past decade, but they also cost money and the post-Afghanistan British Army can't really afford much heavy armour, so only 3 Regiments of MBT now remain, none of which have any form of upgrade since the Iraq invasion, putting them years behind their counterparts. Post various defence cuts 2 RTR having been disbanded along with a couple of dozen other regiments since the Iraq invasion and Scotland's cavalry being re-equipped with large reconnaissance Jeeps as the Army is forced to make use of the various specialist vehicles hurriedly bought for the lengthy counter insurgency war in Helmand Province. This family of vehicles, "M-RAP" as the Americans refer to them (Mine Resistant, Ambush Protected) are not designed to fight other armoured vehicles on a major battlefield. There is a simply massive capability gap between armoured *fighting* vehicles and armour *protected* vehicles, people lacking any military experience tend to fail to see these differences. However, any future enemy tank commander knows an armoured truck when he sees one through his weapon sights and will view it as an easy kill, frankly.

If these vehicles are totally unsuited to high tempo operations in NW Europe, or indeed, fighting a conventional army, then, "Unlucky, mate", as the saying goes. Indeed, it could be said that the Iraq invasion was the last throw of the dice for the British Army in many ways. The current tranche of professional politicians may speak wistfully of military intervention in Syria or similar vicious conflicts, but the harsh truth is that the UK doesn't really have much of note to intervene with after its decimation of the Army and large-scale cull of the RAF's fast jet fleet, except perhaps as a modest little token force sheltering under the American military blanket.

We still have the world's finest Special Forces (albeit within a much reduced recruiting pool) and a handful of nuclear armed submarines guarantee our place at the "top table" but we offer precious little else, particularly in the eyes of the Americans, as I would discover 5 years later in Afghanistan when I spent 6 months on attachment to their SF. On a battlefield, the truth can literally hurt and bellicose statements by far-away professional politicians do not change the stark reality of a lack of military capability. The subsequent years of neglect towards our tank fleet would mean that when Mr Putin rattled his sabre in Eastern Europe, the post-Afghan Army would struggle to field a few dozen battle-worthy tanks: less than a single regiment, shades of a hollow force essentially, whilst the RAF's aging Tornado Force had similar issues in maintaining a single squadron to contribute in the campaign against Islamic State: an incredible contrast to the military of 2003 when our PM speaks of military power post the murderous outrages in Paris and other European locations.

Back in 2003, the general feeling was that if our tanks had finally arrived then the invasion couldn't be too far away and the seemingly mythical ammunition ship was due in at Kuwait Docks soon (apparently), so we'd very soon even be able to shoot at the Iraqis, always useful in the average war zone: besides which, most of us were quite keen to be able to defend ourselves if necessary. By now, I was busy compiling a training programme for the troops once we had finally sorted the equipment out. Our REME (Royal Electrical and Mechanical Engineers, the part of the Army that fixes everything when it gets broken, in simple terms) technicians were working past themselves to try and make all the helicopters airworthy. Helicopters are basically a mass of whirring and rotating parts and the omnipresent desert sand has an incredibly negative effect on all things mechanical: rotor blades in particular suffer from a "brillo pad" effect of rapid motion meeting highly abrasive sand and grit. Likewise, the vehicles had been trapped in a ship for several weeks and demanded a lot of man hours to prepare them for a war of manoeuvre in a hostile and unforgiving environment: breaking down is not a desired option in this part of the world (and the AA will definitely not come to your rescue). So the boys and girls were busy in preparing the vehicles, which was good as it kept their minds off things yet to come.

I was trying to keep an eye on the Iraqi dispositions. The pending invasion was hardly a well-kept secret by now and a pre-emptive chemical strike was not an option we could ignore. Whilst Saddam's Air Force would have to be simply suicidal to take on the USAF (we were blissfully unaware he had literally buried his Air Force to save it for post-war operations against his own people, even at this stage he obviously thought he could strike some kind of deal with Tony and George) whilst their artillery in Basra had the range and the delivery systems to cause us serious problems. Our intelligence still indicated the strong likelihood of several chemical agents being stored in various locations in the Basra area, but types and quantities were totally unknown. Personally I wasn't concerned about biological weapons: we had a massive supply of bottled water (one of the few things we had a surplus of) and a secure food supply (our operational food was all vacuum packed and sealed), so it would be very difficult for them to deliver a bio agent effectively against a large and mobile force. Traditionally water reservoirs or air conditioning systems are much more "user friendly". As the Israeli Air Force had kindly taken out Saddam's nuclear programme for us way back in the 1980s, CW was by a long way the main threat to us in terms of WMD.

Rumours were circulating about low morale within the army units opposing us. Desertion was on the rise, so the Iraqi regime introduced their version of a Ba'athist disciplinary three strikes system: the first time a deserter was caught his left ear was cut off so his crime and punishment were visible to all; the second time, a large "X" was crudely carved into his forehead, which made the crime difficult to hide for the rest of your days and with "strike three" he was promptly executed in front of all his comrades. Simple plans are the best, they do say.

By contrast the Fedayeen were loudly proclaiming their desire for martyrdom in Saddam's name, a sort of modern day Hitler Youth organisation: we didn't really take them too seriously at this stage. Essentially they appeared to us as ill-disciplined, lightly equipped and poorly trained militia. Even if they were keen to die in the near future, we could help them out in quite a big way with their aspirations, was the general consensus of opinion within the brigade.

All in all we were now a busy little brigade: the Paras were busy "beasting" themselves physically in a modern day version of Spartans preparing for battle (the Paras don't really do "hearts and minds", they are, after all, the Army's Rottweilers). The crack Pathfinder Platoon, who were going deep into Iraqi territory had quietly withdrawn into "mission isolation" to plan their very own 21st Century "Long Range Desert Group" campaign, while the Royal Irish, quietly extremely confident, seemed to just do their own thing in a very professional and typically Irish, laid back manner. Meanwhile the planners in Brigade HQ had suddenly gone off on a complete tangent, and were busy working on a plan to jump onto a deserted Iraqi Airfield, which concentrated the minds of various Parachute Regiment Officers splendidly but left most other units firmly on the military fringes of this airborne wish.

This little planning frenzy had been sparked by the discovery of over a thousand parachutes, which had somehow been "packed in error" by the Paras on leaving Colchester, so if the nice Americans would just lend us a couple of dozen transport planes (as we didn't have any of our own available) the first British combat jump since Suez could take place, which we all thought was absolutely a waste of valuable time and utter bollocks in tactical terms, essentially a mere PR stunt by the Paras. Luckily so did the British Divisional Commander, but that had wasted several days of higher level planning and left us mere "hats" (as the Parachute Regiment refer to everyone who isn't "Para Reg" as hats, except for the Royal Marines, who are termed "Sea Hats" instead) very much lacking direction and working on self-drive during this period. I recall thinking that, "I bet the US Marines don't have this problem". I proved myself right: they proved to have a unity and impressively collective sense of purpose and most importantly, large scale and efficient logistics to both support and sustain them once the show began.

By contrast, in an attempt to make up for our logistic shambles, the UK had hired local truck drivers to transport shipping containers (universally known as ISOs within the British Armed Forces) from the docks and move them forward for delivery to our waiting units. However, in an attempt to enthuse them, they were paid by the ISO. In turn, on reaching the desert and well out of sight of prying eyes, many drivers simply dumped them in the desert in order to move more ISOs and therefore earn more cash. This practice was discovered by sheer fluke by some of our troops out on desert driver training. Our QM, like many others, was then reduced to searching the Kuwaiti desert for missing equipment. By luck rather than planning and at the last safe moment, we managed to find a vital batch of missing tail rotor blades, without which we'd have a Helicopter Regiment that was unable to fly. A significant amount of equipment was quickly "liberated" by British regiments (from other British regiments), all equally desperate for equipment and the feeling was that anything was better than nothing. What a way to go to war, I remember thinking.

Two things occurred at this time which left a deep impression on me as a person. One was immensely public in media terms and the second quite extraordinarily discreet. The first I found quite uplifting (if well-rehearsed and scripted) and the second both depressing and disappointing in a significantly personal manner.

We were informed that the majority of the regiment (less most of the REME guys who were still trying tirelessly to get the aircraft ready for war, as most of our mission-critical spares had been "misplaced") would be bussed to 7 Bde for a pep talk from our overall boss, a US Marine General who commanded the "MEF" (Marine Expeditionary Force: the bulk of the US Marine Corps, in effect a rather large army in its own right). Feelings were mixed over this order: many of the guys felt we had become "rent-a-crowd"; others were critical of the event and resented being lectured by a Yank. Nevertheless, the British Army obeys its orders, irrespective of its feelings towards them, an oddity in 21st Century Britain many readers may think in an age when even the police appear to be very risk averse, politicised and lacking discipline at times. But you don't get the job done on a battlefield by encouraging debate and asking for personal opinions from everyone concerned, so we duly drove to a dusty location of 7 Bde's choosing.

As our own transport was insufficient at the time, a series of trucks from the Royal Logistic Corps collected us and we sullenly sat on the bare freight floor for three hours, becoming more and more dust-covered as each bumpy mile passed by. Our morale was not high, especially as no water was available. As one of the soldiers expressed to no one in particular, "All this shit for some fucking Yank General to tell *us* how *good* they are". Not too eloquent, but many of us shared that particular sympathy at that time and place.

On arrival we were met, to our great collective surprise, by a scene directly from a Hollywood movie, a cross between *Saving Private Ryan* and *the Battle of the Bulge*; on either side of our pedestrian route, dozens of Challenger 2s had been arranged to line our route, each with its imposing barrel cranked up to maximum elevation. An even larger number of Warrior Infantry Fighting Vehicles, (a highly effective and potent vehicle: "White Death" as the various warring Balkan militias had called them when they first appeared in that conflict in white UN Colours), again with their lethal-looking cannons pointing skyward, extended this avenue of armour. At the base of this spectacle were some Armoured Engineer Bridge Layers, massive vehicles, each carrying a bridge capable of supporting a Main Battle Tank's weight with ease, their bridges had been raised to form what appeared to me a huge military parody of a Mc Donald's "M" symbol. Either side of them were some AS 90s, the hulking Self-Propelled Armoured Howitzers of the Royal Artillery, again with their enormous gun barrels raised towards the ever-present desert sun.

This was a serious display of British armoured fighting power, in effect a modern day (but democratic) offering to the very God of War himself and making a singular statement of focused intent to all and sundry. After all, I thought to myself, "didn't Josef Stalin say that artillery was the God of War?" This was impressive and had obviously taken hours to prepare, and the press simply loved it, they were almost wetting themselves in taking dozens of photos, which no doubt was precisely why the British Military had taken such pains to arrange the vehicles in such a dramatic manner. Unfortunately, none of the British press seemed to realise was that this display was virtually all we had in military terms, a fairly thin veneer of armoured might in global strategic terms, but very photogenic and a great press pleaser nevertheless.

The more experienced officers and senior NCOs recalled how we had stripped 3 entire Armoured Divisions bare of gearboxes, engines, main armament barrels and so on to field just two armoured brigades in 1991. When you fight, you also have to be able to maintain and sustain operations so ironically, whilst we could replace human casualties very easily, armoured vehicle casualties would be far more difficult for us to replace, but we weren't going to tell the UK press that. The phrase "Hollow Force" hadn't then entered the military vocabulary, but if it had been then, that would have been a fairly apt description of our "Armoured" Division and its capability. But back then, before the multiple failures of Iraq, Afghanistan and Libya, neither we nor the press around us could see past the excitement of an impending major war, let alone consider the long-term ramifications of our pending violent regime change, especially in terms of the Iraqi nation, its people and many of Iraq's neighbours.

We duly assembled by units, our light blue berets alongside the maroon of the Parachute Regiment with the tam o'shanters of the Black Watch and the grey berets of the RSDGs, all waiting patiently for the arrival of our very own US Marine General. To our collective surprise, unlike our own generals, who always preferred to be fashionably late, he was punctual to the minute, as we discovered when a thick Scottish accent called us all to attention over a public address system. We assumed this was the RSM of the Black Watch and we duly managed to interpret his outrageous "Billy Connelly on steroids" Scottish accent. All silent now and frankly rather curious as to what he had to say, we focused onto the roof of an armoured vehicle which was front and centre of the assembled military throng.

A stocky, shaven-headed American, dressed in US Marine pattern desert combats (which was very different in style from that of their army) climbed some steps on the vehicle and took up position behind a pre-positioned microphone. He paused and looked us over: we returned his gaze, all inquisitive by now at the sight of our overall commander. British soldiers don't traditionally take kindly to being commanded by foreign officers.

He addresses us in a loud, clear transatlantic accent. He began by explaining that there had been a time in American history when mothers used to frighten their unruly children into domestic submission by telling them that if they were naughty the Redcoats would come and take them away. He went on to say that our two great democracies, since that "little misunderstanding" had stood side by side to defend the free world for almost a century and America owed Great Britain a huge debt of thanks for being its most steadfast and greatest ally.

Now he had our attention, you could hear a pin drop from the assembled soldiers, our faces upturned towards him. He knew how to grab and hold a crowd's attention. I had to give him that. I remember thinking he was most definitely a soldier's officer (in British parlance a "down looker": an officer who doesn't take his soldiers for granted, as a pose to an "uplooker" who focuses purely on his superiors for career advancement purposes, and the British Army has a lot of those. Military organisations also breed ambitious self-publicists.). He continued to tell us that it was his great personal privilege to command British soldiers and expanded on the enormous respect that the entire American Military had for such a famous and professional organisation. We were unashamedly hooked. As I looked around at our enraptured soldiers, I remember thinking, "This man is obviously a very good leader", and a highly capable professional soldier: a wise choice, I thought personally.

He shifted his attention to the forthcoming conflict and our Iraqi counterparts. He encouraged us to show compassion towards those Iraqi soldiers who saw sense and surrendered to us. We were instructed to disarm them and "pat them on their sorry and raggedy little ass" and point them towards the rear to go and give themselves up en masse, but above all, continue with the advance into Iraq. Should they be foolish enough to resist us, then we were to consign them to oblivion swiftly and efficiently: they had had their one and only chance. At this the entire Parachute Regiment contingent nodded enthusiastically, the Army's attack dogs straining impatiently at their collective leashes, I thought, smiling to myself. Well, life is after all, about choices, living or dying being quite a major one of them, I suppose.

As a prelude to the big finale he described a ten thousand-strong Iraqi Infantry Division located at the major town of An Nasirayah, and its strategic crossroads, as a mere "speed bump" to the allied advance yet to come. Only an American General could say that and get away with it! He then explained that his own Marines brought a lot to the party also, at which point — and timed to utter perfection — four US Marine F 18 fighter bombers, two from our left and two from our right, screamed over our heads at a height of twenty or so feet, noisy and bloody impressive!

As the noise died down, he pointed that the US Marines also had a "few helicopters" and, right on cue, four fully "bombed up" Sea Cobra attack helicopter gunships, this time two from the front and two from the rear, repeated the move but flying slightly lower before climbing steeply to bank hard and break away into the surrounding desert, looking for all the world like airborne sharks on the prowl for prey. Smiling broadly, he bade us all good fortune and good luck as he knew that come what may, he and all his Marines knew, with utter certainty, that the British Army would, true to all its traditions, *never* fail in carrying out its duty, as the past three hundred and fifty years had amply shown to its friends and enemies alike. With that he saluted us and was gone.

The troops simply loved it, in essence their mood was now one of, "General, where do you want us to go, when and who do you want us to fight?" The pep talk, the dramatically staged fly past and the immaculately presented armour had completely won everyone, including myself, over, our swift victory was both assured and inevitable, it was that blindingly obvious and we, the British Army, were going to be a major part of this.

I walked back to the transport with a quiet smile on my face, thinking how effective the use of fighters and helicopter gunships had been on the assembled cap badges: we had done the exact same in Germany when facing our old friends the Soviet 3rd Shock Army, then to impress their visiting generals with just how superbly professional and well trained the British Army of the Rhine (BAOR) was in pure military terms. We wanted them to go back to East Germany thinking, "Those Brits are going to be a hard fight — it will cost us an awful lot to get through them". The trick was lots and lots of rehearsals combined with efficient, discreet communications, and we rehearsed an awful lot in Germany.

But this wasn't Germany and we were a long way from its dark but friendly woods and our well-stocked supply depots, but still our collective morale was now inordinately high and the next day's newspapers in UK had all the glossy war photographs their editors (and no doubt our politicians too) could wish for. The modern world is founded on media-driven perceptions and image, rather than hard facts and balanced debate: this was being seriously applied to the military now and these images portrayed to the public back in UK a sense of a powerful military machine, no doubt, which was rather a long way from our current reality as we sat in Kuwait awaiting the green light from our political masters.

Sadly, this routine would be repeated again and again, especially when we made our entry on a "reconstruction mission" into Helmand Province 3 years later, based on rather fanciful political ambitions and historical ignorance combined with a blind eye being applied to any and all "negative" intelligence reports. Essentially the Ministry of Defence was slowly becoming the Ministry of Good News to cover yet more shortcomings at all levels. Still, we drove back to Camp Eagle in fine heart: the US Marine General had rapidly inspired the troops after several weeks in the military doldrums. A mere five years later in Afghanistan, an American Special Forces Colonel would tell me that, whilst the Brits were admired and trusted by the American Military, our government "wrote cheques it couldn't cash". We were their most trustworthy allies by far, he informed me, but we simply brought less and less to the party and never seemed to stay the course. How things had changed in a few short years, I had reflected on being told this by such an experienced operator.

To our great amusement we discovered that we had "lost" several soldiers on our return to Camp Eagle, they had boarded the wrong truck and ended up spending the night in a distant RLC camp, minus beds, etc, but some nice man took pity on them and gave them some food. They had made the mistake of asking a Ghurkha driver if he was going to Camp Eagle. In true Ghurkha manner he merely smiled back at them and nodded enthusiastically, not having the slightest clue what the Brits had said, but we got them back eventually. Most British soldiers feel the Ghurkhas are simply disbandment proof, purely for political reasons: as 21st Century soldiers go they are not quite the little brown supermen of popular legend, but they do have Joanna Lumley and no politician is going to cross swords with such a popular celebrity. Meanwhile the Scottish Regiments, in the era of a newly powerful SNP and possible independence for Scotland, seem to be spared the axe for reasons of pure politics, while the English and Welsh units have no such defenders, so all of them can be slashed at will, it seems (we have no spare Irish Regiments left to get rid of after the past few decades).

So now we had all been enthused American style, it was back to the final preparations for the destruction of Saddam's regime and the associated Ba'ath Party apparatus. Intelligence was still quite poor; although we were fairly sure the SAS had covertly "snurgled" their way into Basra already and we suspected the remaining SF hoods ("the Blades" as they are popularly referred to within the Army) were located somewhere in Jordan waiting to move into Western Iraq and its remote desert expanses, which was an ideal area to hide things, like missiles and CW warheads, for example. Otherwise we could easily get stuff about Baghdad from the Americans, it was hardly a secret they were all going there soon, but we didn't appear to have an awful lot on the Basra area. No matter, we all thought, we'll do the job anyway, a typical "can do" British Army approach. Then again, the British Army was well accustomed to punching above its weight. Sadly, in many ways this also proved to be a two-edged sword in the years following the invasion itself.

I spent my time studying the various intelligence reports, weighing up the chemical options from the Iraqi perspective, essentially where and when would I hit the Brits to cause the maximum possible casualties, damage and overall disruption. After all the Iraqis had stopped the Iranian "human wave" attacks in the Basra area, with devasting effects, in the mid to late 1980s by this very means, so it made sense that some of their officers from that era were still serving in their military, by now as very senior commanders. After all, when it comes to the crunch, people will fight with the weapons they *have*, no one can fight with weapons they'd *like* to have. You could argue that suicide bombers (or martyr bombers, depending on your ideological view point) are a poor man's cruise missile when you lack both technology and funds. Whatever you may think of that particular statement, these human weapon systems are now a cause for major concern in any serious Western military or police mind over ten years down the road from the Iraq invasion. So I stayed focused on us inevitably being seriously slimed, while trying to limit our casualties to a minimum in the process and just accepting that it would all become very messy.

As I worked on a training programme to get the rust off the troops' military skills before the big day finally arrived (less any range work, as we still had no training ammunition available to us so firing of any form of weapon was simply out of the question), all the officers were summoned to the HQ tent for a quick briefing. We duly assembled and received the latest military direction from Brigade Headquarters, listened to the progress on equipment availability and the political overview of the situation in Iraq as Whitehall saw it. All useful stuff really. At the end of the briefing the CO (the CO always has the last word for obvious reasons) informed us that the leader of the opposition, Ian Duncan Smith or "IDS", as he was known, would be visiting the troops in Kuwait shortly.

Fair enough, I thought, the Conservatives had after all backed the government in sending us all to Kuwait for probable military action, so he had a right to see the Army and its associated preparations for a major war, really. He was also the only major politician to make the effort, the rest seemed to prefer waiting for a better photo opportunity with the troops, preferably in Baghdad, I presume. The CO then announced that if IDS came to visit us during his visit, on no account was *anyone* to mention *any* of our equipment problems of logistic shortfalls to him. If asked by him, we were all to tell him that we had more than enough of everything we needed in all aspects of supplies and equipment, our morale was very high and all the boys and girls were raring to go, period.

This bothered me greatly in moral terms, to say the least. I was, like most soldiers, firmly apolitical, in my case because I believed (and still do) that the Army's role was to defend our democracy and unlike numerous South American Juntas, there was simply no place for politics within Britain's Armed Forces. One of our officers asked where this directive had originated from. "The top level, back in the UK", was the simple response, which indicated to me that this order had political, rather than military origins. To me personally, this was not British Democracy in action: I personally viewed this as simply telling lies to cover someone's wholesale ineptitude, indifference and incompetence.

Many of us were extremely unhappy at the prospect of forcing our stoical and ultra-loyal soldiers to remain silent over so many issues and pondered how best to achieve this whilst not betraying the trust of our young soldiers and perhaps, for the younger officers, seriously damage their future career prospects. Thankfully, in some respects at least, this quandary resolved itself in that IDS never got to us, he apparently spent his time in far off Divisional HQ being briefed on the big picture and never came to our brigade, so our shortages, frustrations and any possible outbreaks of honesty were all kept neatly in house. Rightly or wrongly, we never mentioned this to the troops: the last thing they needed was to witness their officers openly questioning or contradicting official government policy on the very verge of war. Sowing seeds of doubt with regard to the cause is not the way of the British Military. Ultimately our army existed to "Defend Democracy, not practise it", in the words of many an RSM, and ultimately for professional soldiers orders are orders, period.

Personally, this particular episode left a very bad taste in my mouth and for the first time *ever* since joining the British Army in 1975 as a teenage soldier from the Labour stronghold of North West England, this caused me to inwardly question the motives, values and judgement of those people who were our elected leaders, on whose collective behalf we were all prepared to fight and possibly die. Put simply, my faith in the cause and my leaders was now seriously in question. Soldiers aren't mindless beings, and they suffer ethical dilemmas and have to address serious moral questions just like many other professions. However, I dutifully hid these doubts and focused on keeping British soldiers alive, first and foremost. I had my duty to carry out, however old-fashioned and quaint a concept that may seem to many people in the 21st Century. Duty may be just another four-letter word to most people within the UK, but it also weighs very, very heavily when people trust you with their lives. In many ways it is the longest single word in the English language and often carries with it a great personal cost.

Now everything suddenly seemed to change up a gear, as if all concerned tacitly accepted that any pretence of a peaceful solution had finally and irrevocably evaporated. The now almost legendary ammunition ship was still inbound and we remained very reliant on the Americans for food, but we all knew that we would succeed with whatever task we were given and we'd simply make it work. This was our forte as British soldiers and why we were the finest small army in the world: simultaneously our greatest strength and biggest weakness in many ways and the launch pad for our politicians to demand that we do "ever more with ever less" for the next decade or so, without any clear strategic aims or consistent direction on their part. Essentially this very ethos would became a self-inflicted wound in blunt old-fashioned military terms as a small volunteer army became bitterly entrenched in ever more vicious fighting in distant but complex lands whilst the political intent changed on a regular and seemingly random basis.

Our training now centred largely on prisoner handling, as we confidently expected literally tens of thousands of Iraqi soldiers to simply give themselves up in the same manner as the 1991 Gulf War and we were duty bound to treat them in full accordance with the Geneva Convention. After all we came as liberators to free the Iraqi people from an oppressive regime, not invaders. Sadly, and shamefully, as subsequent events would later display in the immediate post-war period in Basra, a handful of British soldiers would prove to be not nearly so conscientious with regard to the treatment of suspected insurgents, but that was a minuscule number of soldiers in comparison to the volume or troops who would ultimately serve in this troubled land. I was also very aware that, duty and sheer morality aside, we would badly need the majority of the Iraqi population to fully support us, "hearts and minds", as it's popularly known, so our behaviour needed to be beyond reproach, otherwise it might just get messy on a rather large scale across an equally rather large country as we were just beginning to realise. Iraq, (like Afghanistan, as we later found) is a very large country.

I was also quietly aware that we ourselves had created modern Iraq after the fall of the Ottoman Empire in 1918 and duly occupied it and within two years both Sunni and Shia, in a rare show of unity, violently rose up against the British Army and "Infidel Rule", which after a short but rather bloody rebellion we ruthlessly supressed and installed a puppet ruler of our choosing. Hopefully the Iraqis had forgotten this little "disagreement" between us (and their pro-German 1941 uprising, too). But there and then we were totally confident that the vast majority of Iraqis would welcome us with open arms. Strange as it may now seem, we were totally oblivious of any religious connotation. This aspect of the invasion was, to us at least, absolutely irrelevant: our enemies were Saddam's (armed) followers, not Islam itself in any context at all, be that Sunni or Shia Muslims alike. That said, our cultural awareness, like Helmand to follow, was almost entirely non-existent, my own consisting entirely of quickly buying a few books on the wider aspects of the Islamic religion from WH Smith before leaving UK.

Additionally, we carried out lots of first aid training. Casualties are simply expected in the military during kinetic (a more refined and less descriptive word for very violent) operations. The enemy has a vote after all and advance notice of "shit happening" tends not to be given by the bad guys, so British soldiers just deal with it rather than look for someone to blame or complain loudly that their human rights have been significantly breached. Rank and status do not prevent you being killed, wounded or maimed when it's for real (as Afghanistan has repeatedly shown) so this extended to all ranks and it helped to remind everyone that this was not a drill, as the Americans say. As we lacked sufficient protective (in chemical warfare terms) "Noddy" suits to train with, our CW training was mainly theoretical rather than practical in nature. It's extremely difficult to replicate the claustrophobic effect of being fully "suited up" and rapidly dehydrating and therefore overheating physically in a desert climate. Add the lack of tactility for any form of technical work, the muffling of verbal communications, lack of peripheral vision and the sudden anonymity of everyone and the net result is that everything takes at least twice as long to achieve, on a good day. I was constantly amazed that our forefathers in the First World War had coped with it all: they must have been one tough generation of soldiers. I was also very aware the Iraqis had successfully and repeatedly managed the same feat in the 1980s during their long, bloody and bitter war with Iran.

We also received orders to commence taking NAPs — Nerve Agent Pre-treatment tablets, looking remarkably similar to the contraceptive pill and to be taken three times a day by all personnel. The aim of NAPs is to build up a limited resistance to nerve agent poisoning. To be honest, it's only effective against very small doses and you'd probably still be badly incapacitated, but hopefully you'd live and fully recover (with the emphasis very much on hopefully). NAP has a variety of side effects: some people feel sick, some vomit, others lose their appetite or have diarrhoea attacks and many feel fine, but it's not a popular pastime with the troops, so Commanders have to physically check the boys and girls take their tablets every 8 hours (which includes waking them up to do so if necessary), otherwise no resistance is ever built up and it's all quite a nugatory effort all round.

However this was also a singularly major signal of intent, the order to take NAPs had only been given once before in my then 28-year military career and that had been prior to the first Gulf War in 1991, so we were definitely getting rather serious. By now we all carried our respirators everywhere and at all times, this was sheer second nature to everyone except our embedded journalists, so we introduced a strict penalty of numerous press-ups every time they forgot, which sounds a bit harsh, but it's far less painful and infinitely less final than dying horribly. In the end they got the message or perhaps just bored with being made to do yet more press-ups by the "nasty soldiers". Either way, it worked.

As the big day grew closer, pre-match nerves increased accordingly. Our key equipment types were finally coming on line, though critical spares for the helicopters were still a major issue and a cause for concern. Our senior engineering officer, named Bradley, being by far the most stressed officer in the battle group as he attempted a modern equivalent of "loaves and fishes" with a small fleet of helicopters in an extremely difficult environment, while my lifelong friend Al (another career soldier who finished his lengthy career as a major) as the senior REME Warrant Officer and a soft-spoken, proud Scot encouraged, coaxed and cajoled our technicians to daily work small engineering miracles, working almost 24/7 to do so, but aircraft ultimately need spare parts and not just wishful thinking in order to fly. The REME were, as always, the unsung heroes in their ongoing efforts to keep the equipment serviceable in such harsh conditions and with a dreadfully poor supply chain that was never fit for purpose and notoriously unreliable.

Intelligencewise, the various Iraqi units in the Basra area seemed quite disorganised and the elite Republican Guard was way up north waiting for the big showdown with the Americans, an event which we all knew would have absolutely nothing to do with us. Meanwhile the Iraqi Air Force had simply disappeared en masse, which slightly baffled us at the time. At the risk of repeating myself, it never crossed anyone's minds that Saddam had actually *buried* his entire air force for post war operations against his own people. Hiding your warplanes are one thing, but literally burying them in a remote region of the desert is not something Western air forces tend to practise much.

Our training had pretty much come to an end, the major concern being lack of range time and therefore weapon proficiency due to the ongoing ammunition shortage, but hopefully the US Marines we were following would have disposed of the majority of hostile Iraqis as our mission was essentially to guard the GOSPs and provide security for the American supply routes: not a sexy task but orders are orders after all. Our main threat was therefore stay behind Iraqi SF, any Iraqi stragglers with "attitude", assorted sabotage attempts and the still fairly unknown

Fedayeen, all with the overarching CW spectre and their relatively large amount of artillery. We wrote off any offensive moves by Iraqi tanks: we doubted their army had much of a taste for attacking us, or indeed the training to do so effectively.

We learned that the RAF would be primarily supporting 7 Bde and UKSF operations, the Commandos had both US Navy and US Marine "fast air" and their helicopters in large numbers supporting them, while we would get the sum total of 2 RAF Puma helicopters in support to us and nothing else, which just made us feel even more like a modern day "forgotten legion". Moreover our brigade's area of operations (AO) had recently been designated a "dump zone" for returning US jets to drop any unused bombs prior to landing at base or onto a carrier at sea. That particular nugget made us feel very unimportant in the grand scheme of things: we were obviously not going to be anywhere near centre stage for this little scrap.

By now, nerves were apparent across the board. Our first little piece of collective stage fright was triggered by an anonymous US reconnaissance aircraft dumping excess fuel, probably flying at high altitude and just inside Kuwaiti airspace, in effect looking into Iraq electronically. Aviation fuel can trigger CW sensors, especially when it becomes an aerosol as it falls thousands of feet through the air, which is exactly what happened on an otherwise normal day. I recall it clearly, because I was comfortably sat on a Portaloo (having just taken my NAPs) and I was quite surprised to hear the chemical attack alarm sounding (an air horn) and also feeling rather helpless and literally, exposed. The chaos outside, even in purely audible terms, seemed rather frantic, the lack of any form of intelligence warning added to the sheer authenticity of the event. I cautiously emerged from the Portaloo, looking around nervously with my own respirator duly donned and thinking the timeless and eternally classic military phrase, "What the fuck?" I found an utterly deserted and empty vehicle park, where moments previously the usual lengthy queues of dozens of soldiers had formed, patiently waiting for the loos. Now I was eerily alone: everyone had taken shelter in the nearest tent or in some cases, a vehicle; standard procedure is to seek shelter of some kind until the attack ceases and also to avoid as much of any possible liquid contamination as possible.

I hurriedly ran straight to the Operations Tent to try and find out what was happening. Confusion reigned there and worthwhile, accurate information of any form was precisely nil. Some hours later we finally found out the cause of it all, but it served as a wake-up call to all of us in terms of how quickly things *could* happen. This happened on two or three more occasions for various reasons, but it also served us well in getting the troops mentally focused, though personally I was quietly concerned over our inability to *de-contaminate* if and when it happened for real. In 2003 all we had was a collection of hand-powered stirrup pumps connected by a rubber hose to a brush (very 1950s stuff, they were named DAPs — Decontamination Apparatus Portable, the MOD is hardly renowned for its prosaic language after all). The other problem was that our basic decontamination agent was bleach based, which would simply corrode or actually damage our helicopters, communications and other fragile equipment types, plus in addition it would eventually also rot our protective suits in the process, as we also lacked protective oversuits which in any case would have acted as a microwave for the unfortunate wearers in this climate, but it was yet another annoying logistics failure. Unlike major armoured formations that could quickly close the hatches and simply move to a clean area, we were not well placed to function well after any major CW attack, or effectively even look after our own wounded under these conditions.

Equally our superbly trained Airborne and Air Assault Infantry, in their new found "lorried" role were even worse off, as it was quite a poorly kept secret that we would follow the obvious main road to the southern GOSPs centred around Rumaila. Most Iraqi artillerymen could fairly easily hit several hundred slowly moving wheeled vehicles spread over 20-30 miles of their own road system, I thought, and trucks with canvas sides would afford less protection than the average London bus when exposed to shrapnel and high explosive. Effectively we placed out faith in 7 Bde to occupy them fully and the Iraqi fear of American air power to limit their ambitions, we didn't have much option really. It was another example of our very limited capability, but the troops accepted this in their usual stoical manner. As one of our sergeant majors succinctly put it in discussion with his US Marine counterpart, "They're British soldiers, so they don't expect too much".

A US Marine Corps "ANGLICO" team joined us (Air and Naval Gunfire Liaison and Coordination), commanded by a totally laid back dude US Marines Captain aptly named Wolf (short for Wolfgang apparently). These were West Coast Marines (apparently East Coast Marines are the "high and tight" ones of movie fame) and surprisingly laid back, but very professional soldiers, all of whom were quite shocked by our lack of key equipment, but also very impressed by our "can do" attitude. One of the things I then discovered about the American concept of war was the Blue Force Tracker: essentially an aircraft-style transponder in each fighting vehicle, which enabled their commanders to electronically "see" their location, direction of travel and so forth. We Brits had the grand total of *none* between us in the entire Division, which they found simply amazing. The Americans were in several respects such a long, long way ahead of us, or any other army in the world, for that matter, at that time.

We consoled ourselves that we had extensive recent operational experience in the Balkans and our 30 years' worth of N Ireland's "troubles", a card which our own generals played for far, far too long, to the extent that by 2008 it had become something of a long-playing joke amongst the American Military about the British Generals' obsession with our N Ireland experience. It didn't really cut it in the killing fields of either the infamous Sangin Valley or the Musa Quala Wadi, as we would later discover in a very brutal manner. But in 2003 they lacked our experience and were keen to learn from us at all levels, but as we would soon discover, Americans learn remarkably fast, adapt well and embrace change far more readily than our own high-level military leadership.

The ANGLICO guys were particularly impressed by our skills with regards to dealing with mines, booby traps and IEDs. We had a long acquaintance with IEDs in particular, courtesy of the IRA, who after all were market leaders for decades in that field, and the Balkans had been simply awash with mines of all shapes and sizes. It simply never occurred to any of us that the Iraqis would rapidly surpass the IRA's best efforts in technological terms and sheer ingenuity (albeit discreetly aided by some of Iran's best minds) or that the Taliban would later turn IED-laying into a thriving cottage industry on a scale never before experienced by any Western Army.

As the invasion became more imminent, a Royal Engineer Mine Warfare Training Team did the rounds to provide realistic and thought-provoking training to us all. Our US Marine colleagues were hugely impressed by this, stating loudly that this was the best training of this type they had ever seen. For us Brits it was more like post-Balkans revision, but with lots of sand added: however, no professional soldier likes the prospect of exploding sand beneath his (or her) feet; mines and IEDs alike are both infinitely blessed with patience, after all. This training and the news that after having been in Kuwait for several weeks, the MOD had finally purchased lots of sand-coloured paint for our vehicles were combat indicators that war was closer than ever. Unlike the Americans, we seemed to be working on our money-saving "just enough, just in time" principle to the very last possible moment.

The rehearsals ended. The Iraqis knew we were coming, as did the entire world, it seemed. All thoughts of the million-person march were mentally parked, we had a job to do and then we could go home. It was, after all, that simple, as no doubt it has been for generations of soldiers over the centuries. None of us felt the remotest trace of hatred for our Iraqi opponents, this was just a job to be done. War is arguably the ultimate in team games and the British Army, at that time anyway, did not have a reputation for losing. Ammunition was still a concern, with the singular exception of TOW (TOW being Tube launched, Optically tracked, Wire guided) anti-tank missiles mounted on our Lynx helicopters. As the Apache would shortly enter into British service and TOW was therefore being phased out of service, we were given the Army's entire stock to "fire off", which sounds very impressive. However, in the coming weeks we would discover that one in three of our missiles failed to function. Post-war, no one cared, but at the time quite a few of our aircrews were unimpressed, especially as most of these targets had a consistently rather boring tendency to shoot back.

Aside from the increasingly frenzied logistical preparations, my little world of nasty ways to die was thrown somewhat by a sudden change of emphasis from on high. Essentially, less mention was now made of the Iraqi CW threat to us and, from nowhere came the term "ROTA": Release Other Than Attack; in plain English a major industrial accident resulting in the release of large-scale toxic substances. Basra was a major city of over one million inhabitants and home to some large-scale industrial activities, but after literally months of hype over WMD, for this to quietly change from an issue worthy of large-scale war to an industrial accident caused by military activity (such as bombing, shelling or a desperate act of sabotage by defeated troops) was very much a major sea change. Accordingly we were all issued facelets, of the type worn by Chinese citizens in their more polluted cities, which we would wear whilst sleeping in an attempt to raise our personal protection levels when essentially defenceless. I kept my own counsel, but I was baffled by this sudden watering down of the threat after weeks, if not months, of constant emphasis on Saddam's WMD being a major threat to the region and the now infamous dossier. To this day I wonder if I should have questioned this, but I didn't. Rightly or wrongly I followed my orders and the party line. To make things slightly more confused, the officer who had so enthusiastically spread the word about ROTA then had a nervous breakdown whilst serving in Brigade HQ and was discreetly and quickly flown back to UK. In the British Army, officers are simply not supposed to have breakdowns.

We had a minor faux pas over the repainting of our vehicles. In order to be discreet (God knows why, as most of the globe already knew we were about to invade in the very near future), the decision was made to paint all our vehicles under the cover of darkness in order to maintain OPSEC (operational secrecy). The Kuwaiti Marines had a barracks close by and had kindly agreed to lend us their parade ground for this very purpose. We dispatched a senior major to discuss timings and so forth. Unfortunately, our CO thereby ignored Arab social sensitivity, as the Kuwaiti CO took massive umbrage at our colonel's absence and being expected to deal with an officer junior in both rank and therefore social status to him. So our Major was politely sent home and nothing was agreed, thereby stopping our long-awaited painting programme before it even began.

Our CO was old school, a top public school product and very much upper crust, who found talking to the troops awkward at the best of times, so he only spoke to them when it was absolutely necessary. Over 10 years of combat later, seven hundred dead soldiers and close to ten thousand wounded, that old-fashioned style of leadership is now a much more rare beast to encounter (though it does still exist: for some military people a decade plus of war has changed absolutely nothing) which pleases me immensely, personally. I am not a particularly great fan of the "born to rule" philosophy. So we had to wait until the CO swallowed his pride and deigned to meet his Kuwaiti opposite number for tea and then we could *finally* paint our several hundred vehicles and trailers. I was left with the nagging thought that if this is how we view and treat our hosts, their officers and friendly locals, how are we going to interact with the Iraqis?

Eventually we managed to paint our vehicles under cover of night and in a very rushed manner. Better late than never, though I singularly failed to see why this had been such a difficult problem to overcome for one of the world's richest nations, but then again I was just a mere captain in the grand scheme of things, one of the countless small people so far away from the powers that be and their ego-dominated world. Even the long-awaited ammunition had finally arrived, but in nowhere near the amounts we had expected, so we now had to prioritise how much ammunition each individual soldier received according to their role. The crews of vehicles fitted with "secure" (encrypted) radios got 4 full magazines each. Essentially this was to buy time, so that the vehicle and its vital communications equipment could be destroyed rather than fall into the hands of the enemy (or perhaps the nearby Iranians).

Simultaneously the drivers of HGV and other non-FFR (Fitted for Radio) vehicles received on average ten rounds, but some received a mere 5 rounds (a whole five bullets to go to war with, not quite what we had expected in the 21st Century). Even our pistol-armed aircrew only received 5 rounds, which meant that capture would be almost guaranteed should they be shot down in the wrong piece of desert. Suffice it to say this was not too good for morale and the source of angry and repeated discussion amongst our long-suffering troops. They had an extremely valid point and were rightfully indignant, verging on anger. After all, most people do logically tend to associate war fighting with various types of ammunition being fired around the place in large and liberal amounts. But the infantry rightly had priority and if it came to it, it seemed we'd all cross the border with just a sharp knife each and some pointed sticks between us if deemed necessary from our government's distant perspective. It appeared to us that, as long as both the media and the British public were blissfully unaware of this minor issue, this key and possibly life-threatening shortage seemed to be quite acceptable within the corridors of power in Whitehall. I personally felt our young men and women deserved far, far better than this disdainful and cavalier treatment and was quietly disgusted by this sheer negligence and complete incompetence, but orders are orders, so invade we would, and very shortly, it seemed.

In stark contrast I sat on the berm surrounding our camp that night, looking at the myriad stars you can see in the clear desert night sky, having a cigarette and thinking of home and events yet to come. I watched the seemingly endless procession of amber flashing warning lights of scores of American tank transporters moving their Abram's main battle tanks and other armoured fighting vehicles to their desert assembly areas in final preparation for the land phase of the imminent American "shock and awe" campaign. I went back there seven hours later, en route to breakfast, to see this movement of armoured fighting vehicles still happening. When America takes the proverbial gloves off it's truly quite an awesome sight to behold. Meanwhile we had British soldiers going to war with just 5 rounds and numerous major equipment shortages. So much for saving money with a "just enough, just in time" supply policy. That said, no one was ever called to account for this and other failures and I am quite sure no one ever will be, the Iraq war is after all just another lost war in the grand scheme of things now and somehow it was all simply no one's fault, be they a politician, a senior civil servant or a general.

Shortly after this, we all watched an incredible cloud formation high in the atmosphere, a swirling, massive spiral, which appeared to slowly grow and spread across the brilliant azure blue desert sky. This lasted for most of the day, until it grew to seemingly fill the entire sky and simply fascinated us all. One of the locally employed civilians explained that this normally preceded an event of major importance: a "sign", in effect. We took this as good news as we were all about to make sure that important event happened in the very, very near future.

That night, however, saw the mother of all sand storms. I had decided to walk to the next tent where most of the junior ranks from my own regiment were accommodated in order to ensure they were fully briefed on what was happening and to brief them on our latest intelligence regarding the enemy. Sometimes British soldiers are subjected to the "mushroom syndrome" by their officers (kept in the dark and fed shit) and I was personally very keen to ensure my blokes went to war fully briefed. The storm was so fierce, with visibility down to feet rather than metres, that I missed the large tent completely and overshot by some distance. Luckily the berm wall prevented me wandering off into the desert, and eventually I stumbled rather dramatically into their tent, having taken well over an hour to cover 30 metres from tent to tent, a good reminder for me that the Desert is a harsh, dangerous and unforgiving mistress. Despite being totally covered up from head to toe, including hood, goggles, shemagh and 3 layers of clothing, sand was between my toes, in my navel and each and every other possible contour of my body. I was well sand blasted and deeply uncomfortable. At least it had happened before we crossed the border, as a storm of that magnitude would immediately stop both us and the Americans dead in our tracks, a stark reminder of the overwhelming power of nature.

We began to draft the final orders for crossing the border. My piece was primarily the chemical threat, the one thing that frightened us frankly and the one thing that could, literally, stop us in a rapid and painful manner. The orders process is a standard format across the Army and designed to be used alongside our NATO allies and it works well. However this event became bigger than Ben Hur as the CO, conscious of this being centre stage in a history-making event, decided the orders process would be photographed in its entirety for future posterity. Accordingly, rehearsals were mandatory and several changes were made to make the event more photogenic and pleasing to the eye. I had never experienced this before or since, but this wasn't my own regiment and we had a war to fight, so I bit my lip and got on with it. As the saying goes, "If you can't take a joke, you shouldn't have joined".

Two bizarre incidents stand out from this period of the build-up. Following one of our daily "O" Groups the RSM informed us solemnly that a serious incident in the showers had come to his attention. Apparently two junior NCOs from the Military Police — one male, one female — had been cavorting in the showers. This raised two issues, namely unauthorised access to the showers when they were out of bounds (and therefore should have been locked) and the prospect that "intimacy" had taken place. We were all dumbstruck. Here we were on the verge of a major land war, lacking just about everything we needed, possibly about to suffer significant casualties and we were discussing two young people possibly having a quick knee-trembler as a matter of operational priority? However, we all listened politely and promptly, if discreetly, ignored this apparently major breach of military discipline. The majority of us believed we had a few more pressing issues to attend to, such as invading a very large sovereign state, defeating its armed forces and overthrowing its entire government at the express behest of our Prime Minister.

About the same time, the Iraqi General who had specialised in the "imaginative" and effective use of CW against the Iranians took over the forthcoming defence of Basra, which drew the comment, "Another quiet day in the AO", from our Intelligence Cell. I was quietly furious: this was very significant; he wasn't named "Chemical Ali" for nothing, this was an utter lack of awareness of a major combat indicator. I pointed out that Chemical Ali was a ruthless and trusted confidant of Saddam himself and hailed from the same tribe. Moreover, he had both slaughtered defenceless Kurdish villagers in their thousands and masterminded the defence of the Al Faw peninsula against the Iranians (for several years in the 1980s the Al Faw had been one of the most fought-over pieces of land on the planet). He had hit the Iranian supply lines with blister agent to both cause mass casualties and clog up the main supply route (MSR), caused chaos in their rear and command areas with simultaneous nerve agent attacks whilst using blood agent on the Iranian front line. Blood agent is highly lethal but very short lived in its effects, which enabled the elite Republican Guard to attack "unmasked" and slice through the surviving Iranian defenders to recapture vital ground with ease after months of bitter conventional fighting. I strongly suggested this was an extremely significant event and a major cause for concern for all of us. I made my point rather aggressively, (I suspect I lost a few friends within the Int Cell) but this was not a game and personal egos simply couldn't be allowed to come ahead of soldiers' lives, so I didn't lose any sleep at all over this little rant of mine.

Come the day, we delivered the orders to a very sombre audience of the battle groups' commanders. Going to war is traditionally a serious venture after all, but the photographer, at least, was enjoying himself. It was surreal in the fact that while most of the players with "speaking parts" were taking it (the war) seriously, whilst some key players seemed to think this was still just some kind of Salisbury Plain with sand, but unlike Wiltshire war games, people could rather easily get killed on this little venture. The CO duly insisted on lots of photographs for his personal speaking part, amazingly complete with a large and very up-to-date top-secret map as the backdrop. I recall thinking, "Thank fuck the Paras can't see this, we'd never hear the last of it!" Meanwhile, and totally unbeknown to us, the world's media was reporting the now famous stirring (and exceedingly well rehearsed) "Eve of Battle" speech from Colonel Collins. Our own eve-of-battle pep talk was somewhat less inspiring in its nature, as our colonel still didn't much enjoy talking to soldiers and most of us couldn't actually hear his words due to a strong and persistent desert breeze. In a way this was immaterial, we all knew our jobs and what we had to do: besides, we were all very aware this was turning out to be a "come as you are" war and accordingly, no one really expected too much any more.

My last major task before we crossed the border was to brief the troops over our route into Iraq and the strong likelihood that we may be "slimed" in the aftermath of the American armour rapidly smashing through ahead of us. This was a golden opportunity for the Iraqi artillerymen: our route would be known, we would be bunched along the obvious major road and in range of various weapon systems well hidden in a large built-up area and therefore difficult to both spot and neutralise; they would not get a better chance. If the roles had been reversed, our artillery would have rubbed their hands with collective glee at such a large and vulnerable "target array" of soft-skinned vehicles: easy meat and ideal for high explosive mayhem, frankly.

Accordingly, my little team of NBC gurus (bearing in mind no one in the British Army had done this for real since 1918) of myself and 3 very high quality Senior NCOs made a very large-scale model of Northern Kuwait, Southern Iraq, the outer fringes of Basra City, the border-crossing points, our route and our objectives (the GOSPs of Iraq's southern oil fields). Using models is standard practice in the British Army, even in this high-tech age it is the ideal method of ensuring everyone can relate to the ground, enemy/friendly locations, key areas of interest, where and when to carry out various actions and so forth. The audience was surprisingly large and attentive, approximately three hundred very quiet and pensive soldiers. Obviously such local offerings as blister, choking and nerve agents have this attention-grabbing effect on people, I thought. To say the mood was sombre would be an understatement of huge proportions.

For my part, I was extremely conscious that my next words were hugely important. I had to get the chilling facts of the assorted threats across in a manner everyone understood, but also avoid terrifying them. Concurrently I had to convince them that we could get through this with minimum casualties, but it wouldn't be easy and also that our individual protective equipment was the best in the world, providing we all knew, understood and applied our drills rapidly and effectively: the price for not doing so would be swift, agonisingly painful and potentially lethal. I drew a deep breath, it was simply critical that I gave an image of quietly professional confidence to all present and ensured they walked away fully briefed about the challenges we faced and also, how we would survive to fight and be successful in our allocated mission.

So I got a grip of myself and walked, hopefully with apparent confidence and purpose, slowly out to the centre of the hollow square of attentive soldiers, hugely conscious that, with the singular exception of the birth of my two sons, this was possibly the defining moment of my life. My next words would be hung upon by all and sundry. British soldiers accept, almost as a matter of course, being shot at or blown up and the risk of wounding or death, like the omnipresent IEDs of Helmand Province, but chemical weapons were something quite different psychologically and frighteningly inhumane in nature by comparison. As usual in the Army, I asked the troops to listen in. (American soldiers "listen up", British ones simply do not use this phrase, contrary to recent TV dramas). I explained the layout of the model, with a very capable SNCO named Stew simultaneously pointing out the geographical features, including our perceived ranges of the Iraqi artillery systems, essentially visually displaying when and where our "sliming" could occur. The assembled audience was quiet and gave me their undivided attention: no one wants to die an agonising death thousands of miles from home and become the victim of unseen but rapidly lethal assailants against your central nervous system, being painfully blinded by blister agent or slowly choking to death internally.

I explained the CW agents we believed the Iraqis had available to them and where I believed which agents would be used, the effects the enemy sought to achieve and how we could best defend ourselves by a mixture of our alarm systems, vigilance and effective warning and reporting etc. It was all very sombre and sobering stuff, I was hardly a bundle of joy, but "spin" here was simply unacceptable, these British soldiers, the first of thousands who would put their lives literally on the line on behalf of our nation for the next decade-plus, deserved the whole truth, "warts and all" and besides, I was a professional soldier, not a professional politician merely seeking to be popular with the masses and therefore highly unfashionable words such as duty, loyalty, trust and if necessary, self-sacrifice were the code that I — and they — both believed in and lived by. I tried to finish on a high in concluding that this would be a demanding phase of the operation and whilst we may well take casualties, we could minimise the effects of any and all CW attacks by remembering all our recent training, individual and collective drills whilst working together as a professional team and for each other (the "Buddy-buddy" system, as soldiers refer to looking after one another): lastly I reminded them we had the finest individual protection equipment in the world, so have faith in your kit, remember your drills and stay switched on, were the key messages essentially.

I paused and looked around. This was deliberately an early morning brief before the sun got too high and also to give them the maximum possible time to sort out their equipment and any last-minute issues before we crossed the border. "Are there any questions, guys?" I asked. British soldiers are not renowned for being PC, they have a habit of being extremely direct and bluntly to the point, war at the lower levels simply doesn't suit political correctness, just as our enemies don't encourage democracy or secularism or any form of recognition for the Geneva Convention, or indeed basic humanity in terms of IS and other jihadist groups. I expected some blunt questions: instead all were silent, seemingly pondering the information; the usual banter was decidedly absent. "Shit," I thought. Had I just baffled or frightened them?

"Sir," a young corporal spoke from the front rank.

"What's your question, Corporal?" I replied.

"What's the likelihood of us being slimed?" He voiced everyone's thoughts succinctly.

I glanced around. All eyes were on me. "No pressure, then," I thought. I explained that from all our intelligence (sparse as that was), the precedent had been set of use of CW by the Iraqi military, they had the means, shortly the opportunity and we would be travelling down an obvious route, which was well known to them. I had to conclude it was probable rather than possible. However I pointed out that the key Iraqi Artillery OP (observation post) on top of Safwan Hill, a geological oddity that rose some 300 feet out of the otherwise sandy billiard table that was the topography of southern Iraq and therefore dominated our approach routes would be "lowered" by 10 feet, courtesy of the United States Air Force before we deployed, in a singularly highly explosive manner. That made them smile, soldiers like to know the threat is being neutralised, which is something the American Military do extremely well, and they will literally move heaven and earth to protect their people.

He looked at me and quietly considered my answer, before replying simply, "Okay, sir. Thank you." No fuss, well-mannered and quietly stoical in his acceptance of the threat, typical of the British military ethos and so radically different from our often celebrity-obsessed and sometimes superficial social values of modern Britain and its ongoing acceptance of spin rather than substance from its political classes, at least from my own personal point of view.

Another NCO asked when would any attack be most likely. Probably during the night or close to dawn, I replied: sleeping troops are obviously more vulnerable and the night temperatures would prevent any rapid evaporation of liquid agents (which are a "contact" hazard: they stick to exposed flesh, feet, clothes, vehicles, metal surfaces and so forth; a very "democratic" agent really) and at dawn they would evaporate as the sun rose and be spread by any passing desert breeze in a vapour form, so you get two shots in effect. He just nodded in response, as if discussing the weather over the garden fence. I was quietly amazed at their calm response, no fuss, no melodrama, just a professional acceptance of that being the way it was. A very common saying within the Army is, "Shit happens. Deal with it", which was exactly what they were doing. How would I ever explain a stoical mindset like this to anyone in a pub back home as our society became dominated by an ever-growing Nanny State, whilst its diminishing number of soldiers were quietly dispatched to ever more savage conflicts for vague and ill-defined reasons? I suppose you just had to be there. For my part, I was immensely proud to be merely associated with people like this. We may have looked like military tramps in comparison to our American counterparts, drive pretty old vehicles and have little or no ammunition to fight with, but we were going to do our job and do it well. Of that I was utterly certain.

Shortly afterwards and after a few more questions of a similar nature, they all quietly drifted off, to write solemn last letters to loved ones, check their equipment for the last time and try to get some sleep. I was tremendously relieved: they had listened attentively and I had received the ultimate accolade from a collection of seasoned senior

NCOs in the British Army by one of the sergeant majors saying, "That was good, Boss, nice one." It simply doesn't get better than that in terms of military compliments, British soldiers don't gush with their praises, so I was content that I had done my level best for the troops. Now the die was well and truly cast, it was almost time to go, and there was simply nothing further to be said.

I lay dozing on Kuwaiti soil, for the very last time in our communal tent and erstwhile home of several weeks, my head resting on my body armour, rifle and respirator, as always, immediately to hand, eyes closed and my thoughts vainly trying to avoid the coming war and failing quite miserably. All of us had been very subdued, each person alone with his or her thoughts, no doubt re-running their own life to date and wishing they had done things differently, regretting saying — or not, in my own case — something to their loved ones: I know I did. Sleep was highly elusive that evening. Anyone who ever tells you, "I wasn't scared", at the prospect of war and the possibility of violent death or serious injury is either a liar or perhaps just an utter fool. The stark truth is that it focuses the mind wonderfully and puts the trivia and shallowness of modern life into a clear perspective, which probably explains why soldiers who have faced this reality (essentially the entire British Army and the Corps of Royal Marines over the past decade or so) often find the 21st Century civilian mindset very "precious" in many ways and remarkably obsessed with trivial, normally self-centred, "What's in it for me?" issues and the ongoing escapades of so-called celebrities most of the time, with frank and honest non-PC communication being just so difficult at times.

The surprising fact of the matter is that the Army is basically a very foreign beast in nature to its general public (at the 2012 Olympics 75% of people surveyed said they had never met or known a soldier prior to the Games: a rather telling statistic). An army, after all, is meant to reflect the society that it defends, however in many ways the Army has become just another little, if slightly strange "ethnic minority" within the UK in the 21st Century, admittedly one of which the majority of the population are very proud in a distant but friendly manner, but also a very stoical and loyal one, which in turn makes it just so much easier for a generation of professional politicians, lacking any experience of conflict, physical risk or hardship, to use and abuse the Army as they see fit. Words, after all, are the cheapest of modern political commodities and there are no perceived votes in defence, as recent events have consistently displayed, with a former Defence Secretary actually verbalising this thought prior to a recent general election: shades of "do as I say" rather than "do as I do", at least in the eyes of several thousand former soldiers.

I looked at my watch and its dimly lit numerals. Almost time to go, but time for one last cigarette outside our shared home of several weeks before we went through the breach. (Saddam had built a rather large sand wall along the entire length of the Kuwaiti border, so the engineers literally had to knock a breach in it for us to drive through. It was much more symbolic than warlike, but it had a very martial ring to it nevertheless). I glanced around at the dim figures dotting the floor, all quietly waiting for the word to go: essentially lots of very normal people from average backgrounds in a highly abnormal situation.

The pace of preparation was now slowly heading to its natural conclusion of events all around the darkened camp: more and more shadowy figures, all burdened with their personal equipment, slowly and quietly but inexorably heading towards their vehicles. This was not a time for lengthy debates, noble speeches or poor attempts at humour. Our time had finally come. I moved back inside towards my "bed space" as it's termed in the Army, rolled up my sleeping mat and attached it to my Bergen, my kit now neatly stacked and patiently waiting to migrate with me into Iraq.

I walked across to our embedded journalists. It wouldn't do for them to miss the war, after all the British public was relying on them to keep them fully informed. Sadly, over the next few years few of their profession would seem to be very diligent in fulfilling this role: the majority seemed content to merely repeat the party line, but I naïvely then expected them and the likes of the BBC to actually do their job and report things accurately (like most military or ex-military types, I have been, in the main, disappointed on a regular basis). I gently shook the young East Anglian journalist awake. He looked at me drowsily as if to say, "Do you know what fucking time it is?" I wasn't really in the mood for a chat, so I quietly told him, "It's show time. We have to go now."

He just nodded in response. I walked away to gather my kit and then meet my waiting crew for our trip north. Unbeknown to me, he would later repeat my words verbatim and refer to me as a "grizzled Balkan veteran" in his newspaper article. I'm not sure if that was meant as a compliment or not, but it amused me anyway.

By now it seemed like everyone was up and about, heading like a sizable human stream of desert-coloured lemmings towards their allocated vehicles, all neatly lined up in their "packets" — the pre-designated Order of March for large-scale vehicle moves. We had been practising this sort of thing for decades, so it was actually very well-organised chaos. My crew were already at the vehicle (it's not the "done thing" for the officers to arrive first, for several good reasons). Mike, a lance corporal, the only southerner in the crew and my driver — a quiet, utterly reliable and highly competent junior NCO — would prove to be simply indispensable to me in the weeks to come, my confidant and also the recipient of my moods when I was frustrated by the policies (or rather, the apparent total lack of any policy worthy of the name) of the UK Government or more locally, a sanguine attitude towards events.

The two senior NCOs were quietly muttering things to each other: Nelly, a stocky veteran of the 1st Gulf War and a seemingly irascible Yorkshireman with a quick dry wit and both very competent and confident in his role as an Assistant Intelligence Officer or "A10" as it was termed. Next to him was "Bird" (as in Big Bird of *The Muppet Show* fame), at 6'4" an apt nickname for a big paratrooper and a very voluble Scotsman, but also my assistant NBC Plotter. His main, and very important, role would be work out the likely spread of the CW hazard and contamination limits when we eventually got slimed. A good crew overall and all of us augmentees to the Regiment: "us and them" was always a problem for this operation. Soldiers are human after all and not everyone gets on with everyone all the time, but soldiers aren't paid to like each other, simply getting the job done is enough ultimately. But so what, I thought, I personally couldn't have asked for a better mix of talent, skills and temperament. I trusted these guys implicitly and in the military, you can't ask for more than that.

We were quite blessed by the gods in the fact that we all had bullets, due solely to our secure radio fit. We also had a sole red phosphorous or "red phos" grenade, not for use against the enemy, but to deny our vehicle: rapidly destroying it by simply throwing it inside the wagon and then running away very quickly. All a red phos grenade (the Americans called their own equivalent "thermite" grenades) would leave behind would be the engine block essentially: it totally does what it says on the tin. Otherwise, we had lots of water, "Boil in a bag" rations, our personal gear and the usual paraphernalia of war. Liberally applied to both the vehicle and trailer were little blue squares of one colour detector paper, low-tech but reliable and our first line of defence against "sliming". It turns a distinct dark blue when touched by liquid chemical agent, an immediate, "soldier proof" and obvious visible warning. Conversation was limited: we knew where we were going and what our mission was, it was time for us to go and earn our pay as previous generations had so often done in the name of the British nation and its people.

All around us our comrades were bound for different parts of the brigade. From my own regiment, Keith, our "Essex Boy" was bound for the Pathfinders, a strange job as he had basically our standard farmer's Land Rover, while the Pathfinders had stripped down WIMIKs bristling with machine guns ("Pinkies" as they were commonly referred to) all very sexy looking, but not too great at all against IEDs or any form of high explosive in general, as we'd later discover in Afghanistan. Andy, the frank-speaking Yorkshireman and self-styled scourge of the RSM had been detached to become "our man" in Brigade HQ, knee deep in thrusting and ambitious young staff officers, all eager to catch the boss's eye: some things just don't change in terms of any large organisation. I had made these two solemnly promise to attend my soldier son's pass-off parade, due later in the year at Harrogate, should I not return from this little venture of ours. War is after all a rather large game of chance in so many ways. The rest of the guys were with their nominated packets, all with defined "set in stone" timings, some with different routes, all deliberately planned in order to avoid congestion, present as difficult a target as possible for the enemy to engage but remain a cohesive, orderly formation and arrive in the correct sequence to conduct our business.

The guys were ready to go, just awaiting my arrival and the nod to go; there were no last-minute pep talks or similar: this was our chosen profession; all of us had taken the Queen's shilling; we were all career soldiers. The Army doesn't recruit many drama queens, just as well really as we all tended to major in cynicism (apart from Mike, but he was still young and impressionable then). I stashed my kit on to the wagon, we shared a few words: I don't remember what exactly, it was dark, very early and we stood on the precipice of a major war; our minds were focused on what was coming next.

Overhead, in the darkness we could hear the constant sound of jets flying north: the Americans with lots of high explosive "hellos" en route to their various target areas inside Iraq. During my time in the now long-disbanded Air Mobile Brigade, we Brits regularly spoke about SEAD — the *suppression* of enemy air defences — which enabled large-scale helicopter movements to take place fairly safely during a specific time period within hostile airspace. The Americans were earnestly engaged in DEAD, the *destruction* of the enemy air defences: the multi-billion pounds French-designed and built KARI Iraqi Air Defence system had been systematically overwhelmed and simply destroyed by waves of US Aircraft over the past 48-72 hours. we knew the American SF had been inserted, over previous weeks, deep into Iraq by means of lengthy helicopter night flights: the skies of Iraq were totally American-owned. Several years later, the Americans would briefly repeat this over Libya, purely to enable Europe's Air Forces to then support another regime change safely, in a rather more leisurely and small-scale manner, over several months, without any fear of credible opposition. by then the RAF would bring even less to the military table and our aircraft carriers had been collectively earmarked for conversion to razor blades. Tonight, however, our attention was firmly on Mr Saddam H of Tikrit and his rapidly decreasing circle of friends.

Our vehicle packet consisted of several Land Rovers and trailers, small in comparison to other packets and the overall number of vehicles on the move that evening. Planning, coordinating and physically moving several thousand darkened vehicles, in the pitch black of a desert night, is a very complex and literally mobile jigsaw. The planners did their jobs very well on this particular evening. We looked at our watches, all synchronised in the best military tradition. Timings in the military are not to be trifled with. Around us, other packets had begun to depart, vague and indistinct slowly-moving black lumps in a sea of blackness. Somewhere out at sea the Royal Marines were no doubt doing their amphibious equivalent and looking at a dark sea, at least before that unique capability too became eroded by our politicians desperately trying to save money and pretend cuts were, in fact, merely "changes", but on the battlefield you get what you pay for, ultimately.

We were the last vehicle in our line-up, drivers were carrying out last minute checks. No one wanted to break down on the way to war, after all. I was redundant until we moved off, my role was navigation (by old-fashioned time and distance: you cannot map read at night in the desert and the much-promised GPS had yet to arrive, like most things we had been assured were en route from UK) and monitoring the radio net. The latter was a non-job really, as the entire division was on strictly enforced radio silence, so barring a military disaster, that should remain as quiet as the proverbial mouse until the big kick-off, I thought. With two minutes to go, our vehicles all simultaneously started their engines — despite our safe location in Kuwait, old habits die hard and this was done to minimise our thermal "signature" — which in the old days of the massive Soviet Air threat had been standard practice. We had simply kept the habit as a good practice.

I climbed into the vehicle and donned my headset, fussing around with maps, ensuring my torch was to hand whilst my rifle and respirator were securely stowed next to me. Everyone seemed to be closing their vehicle doors as quietly as possible, me included (in hindsight it's rather doubtful the Iraqi Army would have heard us if we had slammed the doors). Mike patiently endured this busy intrusion into "his" vehicle and we sat quietly waiting for the now long-awaited "GO". Meanwhile, thousands of British soldiers spread across the Kuwaiti desert and beyond them our American counterparts undoubtedly did likewise.

At the time allocated to us, we slowly moved forward, playing "follow the leader", each darkened vehicle following the small convoy light of the vehicle in front — a discreetly dim white light close to the rear axle, and you simply stayed close and followed the light in front of you — very traditional stuff really. This was 2003. Whilst most American soldiers had helmet mounted night vision goggles (NVG as they are known), the absolute reverse was true for the British Army: Special Forces and aircrew had them, regular units in the main, did not. NVG aren't cheap and would not become general issue for several years yet. I imagined a night move in the era of El Alamein or the Korean War would have been remarkably similar in both concept and method: only our tanks and Warrior armoured fighting vehicles had any serious night-fighting capability at the time. We left Camp Eagle, our home of so many frustrating weeks, behind us and headed north, across country, towards our eventual TAA (Tactical Assembly Area). Each had a code name, ours being "Gryphon": all were in reality simply bits of desert where we would meet up and shake out, ready for the next phase of the invasion.

Without any ambient light, not even the moon, it was extremely dark, although I was well aware that all around me, thousands of troops and their vehicles were moving across the Kuwaiti Desert, but it seemed as if our entire world consisted of one small dim light in an overwhelming sea of utter blackness. Mike and I hardly spoke. He was totally focused on the small light ahead, I on my compass, occasionally asking him how far we had travelled in order to mentally plot our progress on the map I held across my knee (we finally had some: not many, but enough for "government work" as the saying goes). The Iraq/Kuwait desert region is nothing like the shifting sand dunes of Beau Geste fame. It is flat and featureless, in places it seems never-ending, stretching from horizon to horizon, a very sand-coloured billiards table, as it was commonly referred to by the troops.

British Army convoys do not travel by kilometres per hour, but kilometres in the hour, so our rate of advance was fixed at 20 kilometres in the hour. Essentially it is a traffic control measure: if the commander feels he is advancing too fast, he either slows down, or stops, to stay within this direction. Chaos tends to ensue when two large groups of darkened vehicles become mixed up, all with little or no visible means of identification, as had happened during our night driving training, when various units discovered at dawn's first light they had both lost their own and gained other units' vehicles with rather boring regularity.

The light in front became suddenly rather close and then completely stationery. We stopped also, safe in the knowledge that as the last vehicle, we wouldn't suddenly get rear-ended in the darkness. Obviously, I thought, we had been travelling too fast, made sense to stop for five minutes. Mike was leant over the steering wheel, resting his eyes, obviously not in the mood for idle chit chat. I sat back, suddenly thinking of home, wondering if my marriage would survive, picturing my sons when I'd last seen them, the possibility of dying fairly soon. All of these were at the forefront of my mind, when I heard a distinctly non-battlefield noise: the unmistakable sound of adult males snoring. My two trusty senior NCOs, cooped up in the kit-laden rear of the vehicle had obviously (and quickly) thought, "if in doubt, get your head down" and were both snoring impressively loudly, as if trying to out-snore each other as if it was a personal point of military honour. British soldiers learn, very early in their careers, to get sleep wherever and whenever possible. These two were obviously highly qualified instructors in this crucial subject.

"So here I am," I thought to myself, "in a dark place, on a dark night, going to war and I can't even talk to my own crew. F****g charming!" I looked out of the side window in disgust and something caught my eye: a straight line object squarely in my eye line, strangely out of place in the barren desert. I stared at it, trying to comprehend what the shape was, to no avail. Finally I thought I had better check it out, if only for personal curiosity reasons. I quietly told Mike, still resting his head on the steering wheel, not to leave without me (tired and bored soldiers do strange things sometimes) and got out of the Land Rover to investigate. I glanced to my right. I could see the next vehicle along, but none of the others. Using a torch would be massively unprofessional, so I walked softly over to the offending object. As I got closer I discovered it was a household fridge, abandoned out here by the Iraqi border, but not alone: to my surprise I discovered a settee and two armchairs neatly arranged around the fridge, a bizarre land mark along the way to war. I looked around. For some random reason, I almost had a picture of some bored soldiers playing a childish practical joke on me, all lying close by in the darkness and giggling quietly like schoolgirls in desert camouflage clothing. But the reality was the Kuwaiti Desert was strewn with dozens of such mundane items, all simply dumped and abandoned by their owners. The environment was not too high on the "to do" list in that part of the world in 2003.

I hastened back to the vehicle, just in time as our progress abruptly continued. Mike didn't even ask where I had been, I suppose he assumed the boss needed to answer a call of nature. I didn't enlighten him. Officers, even ones with northern accents, have a certain "street cred" to maintain, especially en route to a quite large war!

We edged forward into the pitch black, the snoring now drowned out by the engine, thankfully, with the fridge left to carry on its lonely vigil in the desert and Iraq becoming ever closer. We passed by several long-abandoned defensive positions: trenches, coils of barbed wire and the like. I assumed these were relics of 1991 when the Iraqi Army had been decimated with such ease by the large multinational and American-led coalition. The thought also occurred to me that, unlike the brief and one-sided conflict of 12 years later, we now had a coalition of just two nations this time around. Once we had taken Iraq from Saddam then, hopefully, like Kosovo I thought, they will all quickly appear after the action is complete — I hoped so anyway — I personally didn't perceive two countries as much of a coalition in terms of global perception.

We quite suddenly came to a fairly abrupt halt, dispelling any further pondering over world politics. I turned to Mike as if to say "What the fuck?" Before I could ask, he shrugged and said, "They just stopped. Don't know why." Ignoring our two sleeping beauties in the back of the wagon, I got out, immediately seeing one person, lying underneath the halted vehicle and using a shielded torch to obviously inspect something. Another shadowy figure appeared next to me: it was our "Guns", Johnny, an Artillery Officer who was attached to us to spot for the guns, calling in artillery fire as targets presented themselves for his personal high explosive attention. He was an ultra-fit guy, quietly very professional and totally chilled.

"We've got barbed wire wrapped around the prop shaft. It's all a bit noisy, really," he announced quietly.

I simply nodded, not being much of a prop shaft barbed wire removal specialist by nature. A second gunner was now under the vehicle. I showed willing by having a brief look and saw the wire had firmly wrapped itself around the entire length of the prop shaft, no wonder it was noisy. The guys were obviously having trouble removing this major souvenir of a past conflict. We were equipped (at least theoretically) for war, not a Kwik Fit job. I was very conscious that the other vehicles had obviously cracked on: apparently they hadn't even noticed we were adrift, and they were getting further away by each and every minute. Johnny and I had a hurried chat. We agreed that my vehicle should catch up and brief the packet commander. They would follow on as soon as possible: our little Guns Team was a very important asset within the battle group. All soldiers simply adore firepower, and these guys existed to generate that particular currency in large amounts on our behalf. Airpower is far "sexier" with a much greater range (and looks terrific on TV whilst you are enjoying your dinner at home), but old-fashioned artillery has much greater 24/7 stamina and is virtually weatherproof, combined with a huge degree of very responsive flexibility in comparison, being a superb "on call" quick reaction asset across the battlefield. All professional soldiers like the thought of being tucked beneath a friendly artillery umbrella: we needed them and their vehicle-borne specialist communications fit badly, in order to have that nice warm, high explosive-based glow. This wasn't a good start at all.

Leaving them to hack away at their rather sturdy problem, with the ubiquitous 21st Century tool of the modern British soldier, namely their Leatherman tools, we drove off in an attempt to reconnect with our comrades (colleagues is not a very apt term for soldiers going to war), I rapidly working our distances and compass bearings by torchlight from the map on my knees, Mike desperately searching for that comforting little white light in a sea of blackness.

"Shit," I quietly thought to myself, no bullets, not enough desert kit to go around all the troops, the Americans taking the piss for weeks out of their "Borrower" allies from UK and now no bloody artillery support on the very eve of the war. "What next, then?" I thought.

We found our packet fairly quickly, mainly by lots of good luck to be honest, but for about 20 rather concerned minutes I had quietly nursed a recurring vision of just the four of us invading Iraq once the dawn rapidly arrived: a single, rather sad little Land Rover in quite a large desert gainfully doing its duty, much to the total bewilderment of any Iraqi defenders we might by chance encounter along the way. Thankfully, at least we were now guaranteed some company I thought, albeit quietly, to myself once the elusive "little white light" actually became a confirmed reality in the midst of our all-encompassing and oppressive sea of darkness. Mike and I were both massively relieved to rejoin the camouflaged fold. British soldiers are, ultimately, very tribal by nature, plus, I thought, rather morbidly, no one really wants to die alone. Words are very cheap indeed when the likelihood of meeting your chosen god in the very near future becomes a distinct possibility.

True to form, Nelly and Bird never stirred once, oblivious to such a minor little event as the invasion of quite a sizeable sovereign nation state and the now increasingly imminent forceful regime change of a rather major regional power and whatever form of chaotic aftermath that would inevitably bring along with it. Their (now fully synchronised) snoring added some rather inconsistent, if fairly unique, sound effects to my little lonely panic in the front of the vehicle, hardly *Ride of the Valkyries* but in quite mellow hindsight over ten years on, probably far more apt in many ways for the war in which we were about to engage in the next few hours. All our concerns about no ammunition, exceedingly poor equipment, lack of desert clothing and all the other varied logistical and planning incompetencies during our build-up to war faded away to nothing: we were British soldiers with a job to do, and we were now completely and singularly committed and everything else was utterly immaterial. "Simple as", to use a soldier's expression.

We became aware of the sudden appearance of dark shapes, black blobs really, randomly dotted around the featureless desert, which signified to us that we had rejoined our unit. These were in fact darkened and camouflaged vehicles of several shapes and sizes and irregularly spaced so as to minimise the rather painful effects of any possible incoming artillery fire. The lead vehicle had now been met by our guides, who slowly led us, at a sedate walking pace, into our designated parking areas just as we had practised countless times. It was paying dividends now and, more importantly, avoided potential confusion and therefore minimised the need for the use of torches or any unnecessary movement or sound. I knew that, close by in the surrounding darkness, were over a hundred vehicles and close to 500 soldiers, nearly all motionless, ultra-silent and no doubt all quite thoughtful over events yet to unfold.

The sudden change of the engine note must have triggered some long-dormant primeval instinct in Bird, who finally stirred in the back of the vehicle to call over the radios and assorted cascade of assorted equipment to inquire, "Where the fuck are we, Boss?"

I replied, "Just arriving in the Regimental Assembly Area," to which he enthusiastically responded, "Great, I've got a bladder the size of a bloody space hopper, just bursting for a piss!" Not quite geo-politics or stuff that would make Her Majesty inordinately proud, I thought, but at least he's awake now, at which point Nelly interjected with, "Keep the fucking noise down, some of us are trying to get some fucking sleep here, you know." Well, if it came to it, once our collective handful of bullets rapidly ran out, we could always challenge the enemy to a team sleeping competition, then I felt sure our victory was ultimately assured: nothing the Iraqis had could muster between them could remotely match the utterly awesome combined "gonking power" of these militarily outstanding members of my crew, I silently reflected to myself.

Once we had been marshalled into our designated piece of flat, featureless desert, we immediately started to "cam up", that is, pulling our camouflage net over and across the entire vehicle. You may ask, on a dark night in a dark place, why bother? Apart from breaking up the "square" outline of any vehicle, it obscures detail and shadow and helps vehicles merge into their background, especially in forested areas (which this clearly was not), all of which makes it much more difficult for any observer, human or technical, to first find, and then accurately identify, the equipment type, which in turn helps to disguise the type and nature of the unit. Plus, in a desert climate, it provides very badly needed shade when the sun rises and temperatures soar. This was another well-rehearsed skill, one of several which the Army would lose as it moved from general war to one long, relentless and costly desert Counter Insurgency (COIN) campaign and living in fixed, albeit fortified and relatively comfortable locations, but right then, in the border region of Kuwait, none of this was imaginable. Our focus was on purely on the rapid and total defeat of the armed forces of Iraq.

Neither did any of us remotely suspect that within 10 short years, the British Army would have paid the then PM's blood price for him in a very significant manner, be reorganised and rebranded almost beyond recognition and that this would become our last involvement in "State on State" warfare as it transformed into a medium-sized and quite lightly equipped defence force, due to desperate cost-cutting and an obsession with downsizing. Then, our enemies, both real and potential, viewed us with a wary respect. Now, they still recognise the British Army as both highly professional and well trained and led, but also lacking the numbers and sheer "combat power" to be militarily relevant, despite the regular belligerent noises made by our foremost politicians. "You reap as you sow", as the saying goes.

An anonymous soldier appeared and told us, "Just cam up, don't dig," (noise travels a long way in the desert at night) and he asked for me by name. It was far too dark to make out each other's faces.

I said, "That's me." He explained that the CO was having one last "O Group" before we went through the breach at daylight (O = Orders, in civilian speak a senior management meeting) and a vehicle would be here in 30 minutes to pick me and two other "heads of shed" to take us there: another little way of minimising movement and general activity. I got my kit together and slowly made my way to the nominated pick-up point, which was, unsurprisingly, a dark piece of sand on a rather dark night. I blundered into the other two guys along the way, which gave me a sense of being in the right place and also one of great relief, it was far too easy to literally disappear into the blackness around here, I thought to myself. We made some military small talk as we waited for the inevitable Land Rover: we'd hear it long before we'd be able to actually see its dark shape. The main topics of conversation were, as usual, our appalling lack of ammunition, no first aid equipment worth the name and when/where would we get slimed? All part of the rich fabric of military life in a war zone, really. As an afterthought we idly wondered what the CO wanted to say. The plans had been made and the orders given, tens of thousands of soldiers were now on the move as a result, so what had changed?

The Land Rover duly appeared and we boarded, festooned with all the paraphernalia of war, which made space somewhat of a premium. We slowly drove the mile and something to Battle Group HQ, past dim lumps of vehicles and the occasional subdued sign of human activity. All very surreal but also very sobering. We had passed the point of no return, in effect. We finally reached our destination, I remember it was bloody cold and thinking, "So much for desert war". It felt more like a German winter in faraway Westphalia or even the infamous Hohne Ranges in winter. But back to business. As usual we left all our non-essential equipment in a neat pile outside the large tent — space inside was always a commodity in short supply at these gatherings — and filed silently in to receive our last words of wisdom before we crossed the international border and then whatever fate decreed for us all.

We were the last to arrive. After a brief hello to our missing gunners, who had already caught up, we received a (for once) to the point and concise brief: coalition troops had already crossed the border; contact had been made (which meant someone on our side was, as the troops say, "swopping rounds" with the enemy); and all was going to plan. We would cross into Iraq after first light (dawn) and move into our designated assembly areas and then advance to our objective on orders. We got the usual, "Make sure your vehicles have full fuel tanks/troops are briefed/all are fed and watered/have all your kit sorted", military reminder. Radios crackled in the background, too faint to actually understand, but a sure sign fighting had commenced: it was the only permitted reason to break radio silence, after all. The only bad news was that, currently, we only had one squadron's worth of helicopters ready to go, due to the yet-again late arrival of critical spares to make them airworthy, so our second squadron would be employed in fairly unique alternative roles, if necessary as a prisoner handling unit (we still expected mass Iraqi surrenders, quite naïvely as it transpired), with a secondary role of chemical decontamination of "dirty" equipment should the chemical trip wire be close to the international border and Saddam slime us much earlier than anyone expected. Not really a military textbook use of an Army aviation unit, but needs must, war isn't an exact art, plus the enemy do have a really annoying and persistent habit of using their vote by doing their own thing, and you just make the best of it. No one had any questions, it was way past question time. The atmosphere was rather subdued all round.

The intelligence update had been very sobering: the Second Royal Tank Regiment (it's just the Royal Tank Regiment now, as in singular) had been already engaged by both American Marine Cobra attack helicopters and US tanks, a friendly fire "Blue on Blue". It was unclear if any casualties had been taken by 2 RTR, but thought to be highly likely. Shit. Our Challenger tanks were our most potent and best protected weapon system. That got our attention. Our SF, plus the Polish SF (what the fuck were they doing here? was our collective unspoken thought) had captured some off shore oil rig and, rather unsurprisingly, killed quite a few Iraqis in doing so, but 6 Royal Marines had also been killed in a separate helicopter crash. This was the moment of grim realisation. This wasn't a game any more, despite what the politicians may wish for. People inevitably die when you engage in ground combat, but these people were ours and that made all the difference, to us at least.

I stayed behind for five minutes to get any further intelligence, especially on the whereabouts of the Iraqi heavy artillery and any associated equipment, but no news was forthcoming. We had SF in Basra itself "snurgling" around (as SF are want to do), plus lots of surveillance assets dotted about the sky, so this was slightly reassuring. For the Iraqi artillery to hit us with CW, they had to first expose themselves from their hiding places, at which point we'd rapidly destroy them in an extremely violent manner. Simple plans are always popular with soldiers. On leaving the dimly lit tent for the desert blackness, I was annoyed to find my promised lift had buggered off into the pitch-black night. I was now totally disorientated and simply didn't have a clue where my own vehicle was. This could be rather embarrassing for me, I thought. I desperately tried to work out my bearings, but I really was stuck. I would have to go back into the tent and ask, which all the soldiers would discreetly find hilarious and by dawn the senior NCOs would be seriously taking the mick. Bollocks, I figured, I can't just stand here like a prat for several hours.

Just as I was about to admit defeat, a figure appeared. As it came closer, I realised it was Bernie, a highly competent and old school corporal. "You need a lift, sir?"

There is a god after all, I smiled to myself. "That would be much appreciated, Bernie," I immediately replied. To this day I am not sure if he was being polite and discreet regarding my geographically embarrassed situation or it was just plain good fortune, but my credibility remained intact, for that night, at least. We drove slowly to my vehicle — wherever that was — and we chewed the fat informally en route past dozens of black lumps, all waiting to move north into Iraq. Regiments are like large extended families and you almost literally grow up with people, it is actually a living, breathing and very close-knit team. The rather mindless and brainwashed Army so badly portrayed by BBC dramas just doesn't exist. It's quite normal to have a laugh and a joke with your troops. They also know when it's time to put their serious heads on. Bernie was reliable, professional and very competent, plus, unlike me, he knew where he was going, for which I was very thankful.

I gratefully climbed out of the vehicle, gave my thanks to Bernie and he promptly disappeared back into the all-pervading blackness. I glanced at my watch and decided I needed to get some rest. Soldiers sleep whenever possible, purely because they never quite know when the next opportunity will arise, and this was a classic, rather notable example. I fought my way through the camouflage net, trying hard not to snag my kit as I moved inside the net and decided to have a tactical cigarette and then get some sleep. Nellie came over as I smoked covertly in between the vehicle and trailer. We were, I was informed, doing "1 on 3 off" now (our guard stags: 1 hour on duty, 3 hours off, everyone does their share irrespective of rank. Quite democratic really) until we moved again. I briefed him on the war so far. In turn he informed me the vehicle had been refuelled, everyone had eaten something, all was quiet and the other two were asleep in the vehicle. It seemed to me we were set, we just awaited the main event now. I just curled up on the desert floor and closed my eyes: no point in worrying about anything now, events far larger than I were unfolding around me. All I could do was roll with it.

Seemingly five minutes later, Mike woke me. I realised two things immediately: firstly, it was almost daylight and secondly, he was offering me a brew. What a good bloke! "Boss, we move in half an hour." As I was fully dressed already it didn't take long to get ready to go. The cam net was quickly stowed, kit thrown inside and we were good to go. I glanced at the surrounding vehicles. Small groups of soldiers were carrying out exactly the same activity, but then, we all had the same destination after all. I learned that in my slumber I had missed our first casualty of war. A young soldier had woken from his deep fatigue-induced sleep to wipe an itch away from his eyelash, but the itch refused to go away. He had reopened his eyes to vaguely focus on a black line across his line of vision. Baffled, he had wiped at it, to find it was actually the leg of a large "thing" attached to his forehead. In a panic he knocked it away and illuminated it with his torch, just in time to see a large and bloated camel spider scuttle away under his equipment. He raised his hand to his forehead to discover a blooded, rather deep wound, roughly the size of a 50 pence piece where the camel spider had been feasting on him (after injecting him with its own anaesthetic, its very own party piece), which raised some panicked screams from him and quite a lot of resulting activity before everyone realised we had actually been attacked by a lone and hungry camel spider. These ferocious and dirty sand-coloured creatures were to plague us as the weather improved: they were not afraid of man and seemed to view anything and everything with a pulse as simply potential prey. Charming creatures to share a cold desert floor with, all in all.

The MTO, Dave, whose brother was in the RSDGs, "Scotland's Cavalry", was up and about, ensuring all the vehicles were ready to go and in their right order of movement, etc. I asked him if the Ammunition Fairy had magically delivered any more ammunition during the night. No, he replied, we'd just have to go with what we had. Five or ten rounds only if you were a young private soldier. "What would the great British public say about this if they knew?" we wondered. I also asked if permission had been given for us to "suit up", that is, wear our protective suits as we moved into Iraq. As the NBC Defence Officer, I knew that would give us protection against liquid agents and all we'd have to do is don respirators, instead of having to find your Bergen, open it up, unwrap your vacuum-packed suit and frantically put it on, all whilst trying to stay alive. Again the answer had been no, we had too few suits to risk them being damaged, apparently. Obviously us being damaged instead was acceptable, I thought quite bitterly. Some regiments chose to just ignore this order and look after their troops instead, such as the Black Watch and Royal Irish, but we didn't, in the main, an attitude I personally found both rather negligent and exceedingly complacent, a leftover from the Salisbury Plain mentality in some ways.

We rolled forward and, much to my surprise, within 15 minutes we were at the breach, complete with numerous signposts that preceding units had left in their wake, mainly American, but, as would become the norm, the Royal Irish had also left their mark. Much to the chagrin of the Paras they were consistently quicker off the mark then the rest of the brigade, always one of the tell-tale signs of an ex-Special Forces Commanding Officer.

We halted next to a large ex-United Nations border post, looking for the entire world like a large military car park, with lots of American Military Police vehicles clustered around it. We assumed it had been commandeered accordingly as a traffic control post. All around us, as far as the eye could see was the stuff of war, patiently waiting to cross into Iraq and "do its business". Eventually we edged slowly forward, it was M25 stuff, single lane and nose to tail movement, all at walking pace.

I just took in the view. The radio was quiet, no need to map read, just follow the crowd to war. Simple stuff after 28 years of waiting for this day. Mike and I exchanged subdued small talk: his girlfriend, my family, what we'd do after the war; standard soldier stuff to the core, really. Nelly and Bird had the back door open, for both fresh air and to "watch the war". It was all very surreal. Eventually we shuffled through the breach and got our first sight of Iraq, the same sandy billiards table and some distant oil refinery infrastructure on the horizon, hardly the stuff of military legend.

To our right was the Iraqi border post, a small single-storey and rather innocuous building, with a fence and some sandbags surrounding it. It could have been any border post anywhere, frankly. As we edged closer it became obvious that it had been, literally, shot to pieces by the Americans as they simply drove straight through and at some speed. We later discovered that all the Iraqi border guards had been ordered to stay at their posts to act as a human trip wire and notify Baghdad, by telephone, the instant we crossed the border. Land line telephones, as we had discovered in Kosovo, were impossible to jam and exceedingly difficult to eavesdrop in comparison to mobile phones or radio transmissions. They had all obediently complied and promptly died at their posts to a man, as to not do so would have meant the arrest and immediate execution of all their extended families by Saddam's regime. A rather more serious breach of your human rights than the average daily British interpretation, I would suggest, but outside the EU human rights seems to be of little real importance, with Islamic State becoming market leaders in a calculated reversion to medieval barbarity in the Iraq we would eventually simply abandon.

We came to yet another halt directly opposite the Iraqi border post. Off to our right were several dead border guards. I recall thinking, "I bet they never even got a round off". The entire area was just so badly shot up, it had obviously been a rather one-sided contest. They hadn't been dead for too long, rigor mortis didn't appear to have set in, although they had stopped bleeding. We didn't feel anything, they were just a bunch of dead blokes, to all intents and purposes. That may seem callous, but this wasn't an average day in an average British high street, the world isn't always a nice place and being fair on a battlefield doesn't happen. This wasn't a video game, after all and, as we had already discovered, the good guys die too.

Mike nudged me, "Boss, look at that." He indicated to his right. I leaned forward to get a better view. In between the side of the building and the fence was a sandbagged entrance, slightly in shade from the rising sun. In this gap lay three very dead Iraqi border guards. I struggled for a moment to comprehend some movement in the shade. As my eyes focused, I realised it was several very mangy and obviously feral dogs, all violently tearing at the bodies of some dead Iraqi soldiers. It was like a scene from the *Resident Evil* video game and one which I felt somehow strangely compelled to watch. One of the dogs broke away from his companions and trotted away from the concentration of traffic and therefore living humans, heading towards open desert to no doubt feast alone on his bounty. As he trotted away, I tried to focus on a familiar, yet indistinct, object protruding from both sides of its mouth which seemed to bounce up and down, in a direct rhythm with the dog's gait.

He broke into a patch of sunlight and halted, looking over his shoulder to ensure he wasn't being pursued by either the rest of the pack or us humans. As he did so I realised his "dinner" was a blooded, grisly and still partially clothed human forearm, and the movement which had caught my eye and intrigued me so, had in fact been the dead soldier's hand "waving" to me. Mike looked at me grimly and said quietly, "Welcome to Iraq, boss."

The traffic finally edged slowly out of the major bottleneck that was the ex-Iraqi border post (a building full of freshly dead people can only be termed as "ex" really), and we drove north, close to the infamous the Basra road, the scene of utter carnage 12 years previously when the thoroughly thrashed and totally demoralised retreating Iraqi Army had been ruthlessly devastated by the repeated and exceedingly violent attentions of massive American air power. It seemed as if the Iraqis had simply pushed the scores, if not hundreds, of burnt, blackened and twisted vehicle carcasses to one side and just left them there to quietly rust, like some massive and macabre "Death From Above" theme park. It was an extraordinarily strange sight to behold and most probably one most Iraqi citizens were strictly banned from ever gazing upon: it certainly wasn't a "victorious" vision from Saddam's perspective.

Our previously well-enforced tactical vehicle spacing had now gone to pot in a military holiday atmosphere, there were just so many British and American vehicles all urgently wishing to go somewhere. In addition, we all knew there was absolutely no air threat for us to be concerned over (unless the Iraqi Air Force had a secret Kamikaze

Squadron ticked away somewhere, which was, to say the least, highly unlikely in those distant pre-ISIS days) but from an artillery perspective, it was a potential desert turkey shoot. Fortunately no one on their side seemed interested in the slightest, or we could have joined the destroyed vehicle theme park in considerable numbers. However, I wasn't prepared to actually voice that opinion in public, that would be the military equivalent of "bah humbug" after all in the midst of such massed military (and no doubt political) euphoria.

We were headed for our next pit stop, an assembly area named "Gryphon" as in the mythical beast, essentially because we couldn't occupy our designated future positions until they had been cleared of booby traps and other nasty exploding things and then secured by the infantry, the Royal Irish as usual in our particular case. The GOSPs, as it later transpired, weren't too badly sabotaged by the Iraqis, apparently because Saddam fully expected to reoccupy them after some mythical diplomatic agreement he patently expected to happen, just like the 1991 war in effect. He had, however, seriously misjudged American intent this time. All the same, various devices had been left behind to hinder us: one American bomb disposal operator lost his life accordingly, as we would later learn when we finally moved into the GOSPs. It was a singular and stark warning to the troops to leave stuff alone in case it abruptly explodes on you. British soldiers sometimes have a habit of suffering from "shiny kit syndrome": in polite terms, this translates to "liberating" ("proffing" as it commonly is referred to by soldiers) items they feel may be useful to them in carrying out their mission, or perhaps just looking good on the bedroom wall back home.

In the mean time we would occupy various assembly areas, in line with the Army's long established "echelon" system and patiently await our orders to move forward. These areas were simply pre-designated pieces of desert and we would form a big box with hundreds of vehicles in each area, lined up in pre-planned order. It may look to any passer-by like mass chaos, but actually it made good military sense and was remarkably easy to control. By now it was early morning and quite a nice day for a war, much better than fighting uphill in the rain anyway. Our assembly area was a mixture of Royal Irish, REME, RLC, Royal Signals and some other assorted odds and sods, essentially all non-fighting elements, commanded by us, as we had our CO with us: rank rules in any Army, after all.

We were among the last to arrive and I noticed on the route in, most of the vehicles were some form of stores or supply trucks, nearly all towing large trailers and there was a distinct shortage of machine guns or other "good to have" weapons with which we could mount any form of decent defence against anything remotely approaching a determined onslaught. Eventually, albeit several years later, some form of machine gun or grenade launcher would indeed be mounted on each and every one of our supply vehicles and for very good, if entirely insurgent-driven, reasons, but for now it was very much war on the cheap, so we cracked on accordingly. Everyone was busy digging by the side of their respective vehicles, the ubiquitous "shell scrape", deep enough for two to four soldiers to lie down in and seek lifesaving cover within Mother Earth should high explosive begin to rain down. Highly unlikely, we all thought, but we were now in Iraq proper and most people do tend to get slightly pissed off when you invade their country. You could also fight from these scrapes, but the chances of a determined ground attack against us were slimmer still, though we might have major problems with shooting back, as still no one to our knowledge had yet been visited by the mythical Ammunition Fairy during the night.

Hopefully all those nasty, but ever so well-armed, Americans in front of us had scared all the Iraqis away seemed to be most people's best solution to this ongoing shortage, which we were under orders *not* to divulge to our embedded journalists. This was fairly pointless as they all had quite healthy ears and could easily listen to our soldiers constantly complaining about the lack of most things you'd like for a decent-sized war, but democracy after all was what we defended rather than practised. Unlike the American Military, we diligently vet our journalist's reports and uncooperative journalists do tend not to retain their "approved" status for too long.

Most of the troops now had an air of "let's just fucking get on with it" attitude about them. British soldiers are by nature loyal, innately patient and long suffering, which is just as well as successive PMs and governments have had, at best, rather vague and changeable long term war strategies and little real interest in the recent human cost of 21st Century desert wars to these soldiers. It was now warming up in temperature terms and digging a shell scrape was becoming sweaty work. The Iraqi desert is soft sand for the first 6 or 8 inches and easy digging, then its consistency tends to turn rock hard and it becomes traditional pickaxe work. Some things in life remain best dealt with by simple, if low-tech, means. I left this joyous little activity to my crew, as I was summoned to the CO's vehicle as we had assumed control of the assembly area and I was required in my joint chemical defence and intelligence capacity. I didn't expect to have to do much, except watch the war pass us by in the form of the seemingly endless American military machine.

We were situated close to a power line, which ran northwards into Iraq. Predatory-looking US Marine Cobra attack helicopters were obviously using it as a navigational "hand rail" and every seven minutes or so, they flew by in formations of 2 pairs of aircraft heading either north or south, which gave several hundred extremely bored British soldiers something to watch at least. On the left-hand side, closest to us, flew the "bombed up" Cobras, we could clearly see they carried Hellfire missiles on their port weapon pylons, TOW missiles (the much older type we then used) on their starboard ones. On the opposite side of the pylons flew the returning Cobras, their mission over for now: rather ominously for persons unknown to us, with totally empty weapon pylons. In the language of soldiers, someone, somewhere had very recently got "the good news". I was one of the few guys present, at the time, who was familiar with the superb capability of the Hellfire missile, now a very common weapon system which was in almost daily use in Helmand Province by British forces since 2006 and also now well known, and reported in the media accordingly, for its "Drone Strike" capability in Pakistan and Yemen as part of the ongoing War on Terror. The thought occurred to me that while they — the Americans — were fighting a 21st Century war with 21st Century weapons and equipment, we Brits were firmly stuck in the 20th Century by comparison. It was probably all for the best that we had a very secondary supporting role this time around, I reflected quietly to myself, as we'd just get in their way. We simply weren't geared logistically or equipped with sufficient armoured fighting vehicles to participate in any serious military capacity or add "mass" for their drive on Baghdad: embarrassing but sadly true in 2003; over a decade later we are worse placed still for "State on State" warfare, but all armies ultimately are as well-equipped as their political masters wish them to be, or not, as the case may be.

To shatter that discreet reflection, somewhere in the mass of vehicles, a tired driver leant forward onto his steering wheel and unwittingly sounded his vehicle horn several times, shattering the quiet routine of the location. This "non-battlefield noise" was one of the standard British Army alarms to be used in the event of any chemical attack and well drilled into all the troops. Immediately a frenzy of human activity erupted across the area as panicked soldiers reacted and, just like fear, panic is also decidedly infectious. I was listening in to the Command Combat Radio Net at the time, therefore, I was very well aware that no one had yet reported any hint of CW release by Saddam's regime, plus no one was anywhere near Baghdad yet, so he had no logical reason to do so either. But tired and nervous young soldiers don't often think logically and right now it was somewhat of a fiasco as people ran around like headless chickens, ransacking their kit for respirators, leaping under vehicles to find some form of shelter or frantically winding up vehicle windows and so forth. This was not the stuff of British military legends and glory: unseen, deadly and invisible enemies have a very forceful psychological impact on the mind, and at that point in time and space, the general perception was "it's started" and perception is an awfully powerful tool sometimes, as the media and modern politicians are well aware in our daily lives.

I asked Alan, the more senior captain present, if he could cover the radios while I attempted to sort this shambles out. We were listening to two radio nets: our own, now very dispersed battle group and the brigade net. He agreed, as did the CO, who was sitting quietly in the front of the Land Rover and not really saying much. We stood outside the vehicle surveying the chaos. Grabbing my rifle and kit, I reverted to type (being an ex-ranker) and walked around loudly shouting, "False alarm, unmask," and grabbing a few NCOs en route to "cut about" and pass the word around. Eventually we restored order to the situation, but it was clear the troops were both nervous and rattled. Our position was rather exposed in every sense of the word and many of them had seen precious little sleep for quite a while.

Being composed of several disparate units, we lacked a clearly defined command structure and in many cases we simply didn't know each other, but the Army excels at "all arms" operations so I got hold of one of our better NCOs and briefed him to literally go round, find the senior man from each unit and ask them to report to our CP (Command Post) ASAP. Hopefully this could be achieved before the next false alarm made the troops jump through pointless hoops again. I noticed nearby one of our embedded journalists, a rather left wing and usually very confident female reporter, normally one who had an awful lot to say about anything and everything. She was remarkably subdued now, huddled in a shell scrape with a couple of young officers, bereft of makeup and wrapped in body armour and ill-fitting helmet, looking very sorry for herself. War is a very big social equaliser and cares nothing for anyone's perceived sense of self-importance. I sat down and shared a few words with the officers and quietly asked her if she was okay, patiently briefing her to simply "copy what the soldiers do and do what they do when they do it". To be honest, I am not a very great fan of journalists in conflict zones. Too many of them appear to be rather self-important and do it purely for some form of fame with ultimately self-seeking reasons, often ignoring humdrum, if accurate, facts and truth for more opinionated, preferably emotive drama, not for any sense of noble quest for the truth on behalf of the people. Then again, I also didn't want to see anyone hurt unnecessarily and she was a long, long way from her comfort zone right now.

By now, several warrant officers and senior NCOs had arrived at the CP. Few people are better placed to quickly grip British soldiers than their sergeant majors, after all. I got to the point as time was definitely pressing: we in the CP had the communications and therefore the big picture. We all needed to get a grip of the troops. I proposed we get everyone who was non-essential moved into cover to avoid any more confusion and everyone brief their respective troops that the indirect fire (IDF — artillery, rockets, etc) attack alarm would be an air horn (like the ones used at school sports days or fetes). Additionally, the local CW alarm would be metal banged against metal and followed by everyone's traditional favourite of the words, "Gas, Gas, Gas!" being shouted loudly. In the desert heat we were at pains to avoid any unnecessary donning of protective gear due the rapid physical degradation effects which quickly followed. Soldiers react best to clear, unambiguous direction and keeping it simple always works best for tired or frightened troops, especially in confusing and/or rapidly changing circumstances. I'd also do my best to update people by means of a "runner", literally a trustworthy soldier who runs to key posts and verbally passes on a message word for word (a rather famous example being the then Corporal Adolph Hitler in WW1), old-fashioned perhaps, but it still works in this increasingly high-tech era of ours. To my relief, everyone agreed this made sense and was fairly "soldier proof" (few things in military life actually are soldier proof), plus, to paraphrase the Duke of Wellington, the very last thing we needed right now was "Order and counter order, resulting in complete disorder".

With that settled, everyone went back to their respective soldiers to ensure this was briefed down to the lowest soldier as rapidly as possible; one thing all soldiers passionately despise is "mushroom syndrome": that is to say, being kept in the dark and fed shit. Soldiers respect honesty and integrity. Much as they don't welcome the prospect of another Operation Certain Death (of which there have been several since 2003, to say the least), at least they know the score and aren't being bluffed or just plain lied to in order to keep them quiet. Personally, if you expect to ask someone to literally put their life on the line on your personal say-so (and very probably not for the first time), I would argue that the very least you can do is be totally honest with them, a very old-fashioned concept in the current era of "spin" in which we all live, I know, but then the well-paid spin doctors and their high powered clients — or indeed their sons and daughters — never actually go to war in person.

We went back to our routine, with the majority of people sat in, or on, their respective shell scrapes, the more dedicated soldiers doing some minor "home improvements" with pick or shovel in relays: this was a marathon after all and not a sprint. To our great surprise at the CP, we received an urgent Strike Warning Red message. This meant an Iraqi missile launch of some description, definitely not what we expected. Minor panic immediately set in, we passed the word for everyone to immediately take cover and between Alan and I, urgently tried to fathom this one out. I voiced an opinion that it couldn't possibly be the very well known Scud type missiles as they had all been destroyed years ago. He promptly and laconically replied, "It really doesn't fucking matter as they all go fucking bang." A very pragmatic attitude really and a singularly good point exceedingly well made, I thought quietly.

Strike Warning Red was meant to give us between 6 to 8 minutes' warning of any possible impact, but as it took time to pass the message down the various and numerous layers of command, those of us at the bottom of this military food chain ended up with 1 to 2 minutes' notice of likely impact. Someone had to man the radios, so Alan and I decided to accept the inevitable and just have a cigarette and wait for its arrival. Besides, we had no shell scrape to go to and absolutely no idea where this thing would actually land. All was deathly quiet around us and not a single person could be seen above ground. Very apocalyptic, I thought to myself, even the American Cobras had ceased their fly-by antics, by sheer coincidence admittedly, so we didn't even have anything to look at now. The CO still quietly sat in the front of the vehicle, he didn't much like to mix with soldiers, very much a class thing really for him, so we all waited around the Land Rover for our very own piece of "good news" to arrive. However, as it was also supersonic, so we knew that we wouldn't even hear it coming. As many veterans from our wars, both past and present, will testify, you simply don't hear the one that hits you.

After what seemed like a long, pregnant pause, the sand in between us and the electricity pylons erupted into a small geyser of a dirty yellow consistency. Not a very impressive movie style explosion, but an explosion nevertheless. I estimated the detonation range at approximately between 600 to 800 metres away; not a long distance for artillery at all. The wind direction was on our side and almost immediately began to blow the small dust cloud, several metres tall by now, away from us. Not a bad first shot though from quite some distance away. I thought, "Now what?" All of a sudden the ongoing and previously amusing American paranoia over members of the Iraqi Republican Guard SF being "Goatherds with satellite phones" and acting as stay-behind "spies and artillery spotters" in effect seemed quite relevant to our situation.

Around us, numerous helmeted heads cautiously appeared above the lips of their assorted shell scrapes like a large pack of lemmings, the human being's natural curiosity overcoming the inbuilt sense of self-preservation, I thought. It was in some ways almost comical to behold, but the more serious business of where exactly had that been fired from and where the next one would land were more pressing issues. We reported the impact to "higher formation", asking their opinion over this unexpected missile attack and promptly received the response of "Roger wait out", which meant they didn't have a bloody clue either.

A young soldier appeared at the front of the vehicle, wearing his respirator. Obviously he had decided not to take any chances at all with his personal well-being, highly commendable but also totally unnecessary. I moved towards him to show him we weren't being slimed and tell him to remove it, before everyone decided to put their masks on, which quite defeated the object after all. Before I could do so, the CO suddenly launched into a rather loud tirade along the lines of, "Get that soldier to take his mask off now!" British soldiers aren't accustomed to their officers shouting loudly, let alone senior ones, they (rightly) expect their officers to be calm, decisive and collected, so this type of behaviour tends to unsettle them frankly and makes them feel it's all going wrong. I assured the CO that it was "being sorted, sir" and explained to the soldier that as I was (obviously) neither dead or in the process of dying, perhaps he could take his respirator off and just follow instructions? He sheepishly did so. He was actually one of our own soldiers, for some unknown reason wandering aimlessly around the location. As we were about to discuss something, Alan announced "Strike Warning Red" again. The soldier was nowhere near any vacant shell scrapes, so I elected to throw him under our vehicle trailer. This might sound harsh, but it did give him some form of cover and also stopped the place looking untidy.

The air horn was duly sounded and all the lemmings went rapidly back below ground and sure enough, a second explosion occurred within seconds, but slightly further away this time. Again in military terms, quite ineffectual, but it served to remind us, someone, somewhere was making an attempt to kill us. They could only improve with practise, after all. About this time, the CO suddenly decided to speak on the radio and rally the physically dispersed troops of our battle group with a rather long and rambling Churchillian-style transmission. Unfortunately for all concerned, in all the confusion, his radio was somehow accidently switched to "Intercom" which meant that Alan and I were the sole recipients of this lengthy outburst of military wisdom. Meanwhile we concentrated on keeping the guys under cover until we had worked out exactly what the overall threat was and also keeping abreast of other units' locations and what they were experiencing in their areas.

Three more times we received Strike Warning Red and each time the impact moved steadily away from us. The Iraqis, wherever they were located, were now obviously firing blind and it all became little more than a nuisance. It later transpired that the missiles used were actually Chinese-made coastal defence truck-mounted missiles, designed to engage our warships rather than our trucks. They just "cranked it up" and fired on fixed bearings really, but I had to admit we hadn't considered this possibility at all in our planning, in hindsight an early indicator of the asymmetric wars to come and proof that ultimately people will fight with what they have, including, as we'd soon discover, the human version of cruise missiles: literally a one-shot weapon, but one which posed very serious problems for us and our American allies to defend against. It was also a valid reminder of the wise old military maxim that "the enemy has a vote too". I wondered where, when and how would they choose to vote next?

Shortly after the last anti-shipping missile had been launched in our general direction, we received orders to advance further into Iraq. Shell scrapes were filled in, kit packed and everyone prepared to move. The Army employs various standard phrases to pass crystal clear meaning and avoid possible misunderstandings amongst tired soldiers in a possibly high-pressure environment. It may seem unimaginative but it works well and has done so successfully for countless generations of British troops. It's a bit like football, you need to do the simple things consistently well before you do the fancy stuff and the British Army, for all its perceived faults by its various critics, trains its officers and soldiers exceedingly well. It has to, really, in order to make up for its perennial equipment shortcomings accompanied by a series of mediocre defence politicians and eternally unrealistic military ambitions.

I rejoined my crew, who unsurprisingly had been mainly engaged in sleeping. However the wagon was already prepared to go, everyone aware that we were now about to drive, in a rather large convoy, along a very straight and major road to the GOSPs in broad daylight, a totally untactical formation after all our years of training for a major European war. But as we were little more than flank protection for the Americans it seemed that this hardly mattered, so we'd better just concentrate on getting used to guarding things as our main role in this war. Well, I thought, if the Iraqis really want to have a pop at us, now is the time in this billiards table landscape. They built this road, after all, so I imagined they knew quite well where it is and we provided a rather target-rich environment. But again, there was nothing, it seemed as if the Iraqi Armed Forces had just melted away in the face of the huge American armoured juggernaut, plus they were painfully aware of what would happen to them should they remain in the open and tried to stand and fight. After all, the visible evidence of 12 years previously and the lethal results of massed US airpower still littered the road to Basra and, no doubt, many Iraqi officers and soldiers hadn't forgotten all that "death from above" courtesy of the American taxpayer in 1991.

The move to the GOSPs had an almost joyous atmosphere: soldiers like little better than to be advancing relatively unopposed and "taking (someone else's) ground"; as a species most of us want/need to be part of something bigger than ourselves and "belong". UK's national obsession with Premier League Football is a classic example: the "Opium of the masses" as Karl Marx once observed. Being part of a (quite) large, physically challenging, superbly trained, patriotic and well-motivated team ticks the boxes for many young men and women from less fortunate backgrounds in the UK, then add some travel, variety and adventure and you have all the perennial cornerstones for Army recruitment. Certainly, I personally had left my native North West for many of those self-same reasons, and like most professional soldiers "ours is not to reason why" had been an eternal maxim for many soldiers (including myself) of those years. I never realised as we all happily drove north that Iraq would cause me, at length, to question that very reason. Previously N Ireland had been us against one of our longer-term traditional foes and in direct support of the police force, and Northern Ireland is an integral part of the UK after all. Then the Balkans had then seen us deployed very much as a "force for good" into that war-weary and bitterly divided region. Iraq and latterly Afghanistan would radically change all that, along with the very Army itself.

We saw some flames and smoke in the distance, some burning crude oil geysers, as later advertised in the national media, quite obviously deliberate and caused by the retreating Iraqis some hours earlier, but that aside, it was remarkably peaceful, mainly due to our American "big brothers" in front of us, no doubt. Somewhere off to the east 7 Armoured Brigade were in the process of isolating Iraq's second city of Basra prior to capturing it: a "big ask" in military terms for a single brigade of approximately 5000+ troops. It had a population of just over a million with some highly determined defenders and large urban areas tended to just soak up troops in very large numbers, as the Germans famously discovered at Stalingrad. I was full of admiration for the Desert Rats, as they style themselves: they fought a patient, thoughtful, intelligent campaign and worked extremely hard to avoid both collateral damage and avoidable civilian casualties in a very complex and difficult environment. Their ultimately successful efforts have totally faded from the collective military memory now in terms of current military interest, all overshadowed by the national debacle that Iraq would later become and the growth of media interest in the military quagmire that was Helmand Province, but the eventual capture of Basra was, nevertheless, one of the few noteworthy large-scale successes of purely British arms in recent times. That said, it is doubtful if it is a feat that could be repeated for a decade or two by the much shrunken post-Afghanistan Army.

Further east still, in the Al Faw peninsula, 3 Commando Brigade, with very significant British Army and US Marine support was facing some stiff resistance from Iraqi regulars and Fedayeen alike. Al Faw had once been a rallying call for the Iraqi people in their long and bitter war against Iran:a war much ignored by the West but a million people had died, hardly a small scale "local skirmish" by anyone's standards. Meaningless to the Western world, Al Faw had once been a rallying call to the entire Iraqi nation and was burnt in the collective memory of the Iraqi population in a similar manner to that of the bloodier names of several First World War battles for ourselves. The ferocious Iraqi resistance to keep hold of this bloody peninsula had ultimately involved a massive and well-coordinated use of chemical weapons against the poorly protected, but courageous (to the point of almost suicidal) Iranian attackers, with hardly any comment from the West. The well-equipped and highly motivated Republican Guard had then smashed the dazed and battered Iranians. A lot of Iraqi schools we found later had large and colourful wall murals relating to this event. This form of history teaching was not something our National Union of Teachers would probably condone with any form of enthusiasm, I would suggest, but then all aspects of Iraq's society were simply dominated by the personality cult of Saddam up until 2003.

As we drove north, all the GOSPs we passed had been given a code name (for use over the radio), nearly all of which were based on the London to Glasgow railway line, so we slowly passed Rugby, Stafford and Crewe, etc. I dutifully relayed our progress to the, for once, wide awake SNCOs in the rear in a sort of, "Sing when you are winning" style, due to our slow convoy speed, they also had the door open a lot to admire the view, such as it was. But in their defence, we had all been waiting a while for this event and also travelled quite a distance to be part of this little piece of history. We were headed for St Helens, (very ironic for me personally, as my own home was only 4 miles away from that small, and incredibly Rugby League-focused Lancashire town) but that was in the real world, not this sandy-coloured one we were driving through en masse. At the time we failed to realise that "someone else's desert" would become for tens of thousands of British soldiers, our collective home in a wide variety of bases, some fairly plush and quite safe, with others verging on the primitive and highly dangerous for the next 10 years, but back then ignorance was quite blissful in so many ways.

We saw very few Iraqis en route, a couple of captured Fedayeen who, as we soon discovered, had a rather large stockpile of navy blue motorcycles in the area. We never did work out why they were that colour, an unusual choice of paint scheme in the desert. The Fedayeen had been captured by a platoon of R Irish who had quietly been guarding a crossroads when the motorbikes came tearing around a corner, apparently to warn people that the British were coming. Faced with thirty-plus British rifles all pointed their way, they rapidly decided Saddam wasn't actually worth dying for after all. The two young men now sat dejectedly by the roadside, their war over before it even began, but no doubt they later made very fine insurgents for one of the various militias who rapidly sprang up against us and the Americans. I do wonder occasionally whether they actually survived to watch us leave within a few short years, in vastly different circumstances or who they fight for now as Iraq continues to self-destruct. I'll never know, of course, the answer to that question, which is probably just as well for all concerned.

The only civilians we witnessed were the occasional Bedu, silently watching us impassively from a safe distance (we tend to use the term Bedouin in the West): nomadic desert dwellers, who paid no heed to either national boundaries or politics. Their country was the desert and their people were the extended family and the tribe. They did not, as we later discovered, actually class themselves as Iraqis, or indeed, any nationality for that matter. Every time Saddam's regime had tried to integrate them into the Ba'ath fold, they had simply retreated further into the desert, navigating by the sun and stars as they had done for millennia. The Bedu were regarded as untrustworthy scavengers by the Iraqis, but also recognised as superb camel breeders (camels are still rather important in this part of the globe), and scavenging was exactly what they were doing as we drove by: they had quickly noted the total lack of any form of authority due to a war in which they had absolutely no interest, but seized the opportunity to acquire things. We Brits were universally ambivalent to them, they were no threat to us and we were also highly amused by the quite haughty manner in which they gave literally thousands of foreign troops a "damn good ignoring". Besides which, the stuff they were busy acquiring was, in our Western eyes, mere junk. In a strange way, I was slightly envious of their simple life style and the ageless black and white values which they happily lived by, very literally a world away from that of the world we invaders belonged to.

Abandoned T55

Ali Al Salem Destroyed Shelter

Ammunition Hoard

Assembly Area Gryphon

Wall Art - Ayatollah

Camel Train

Camel Herder

Camel Train

Camp Eagle

Cheftain Trophy

Cimic Team

Burning Oilfields

Crossing the Border

Desert Village Cimic Team

Destroyed T55

Dockside LYNX

Flooded School

Flooding

Food Drop

Food Drop - George

The border area had little apart from the southern Iraqi oil fields in the way of infrastructure or buildings, just the Russian-built gas oil separation plants and an interlinking road network, which was at best in the minor "A" road class by British standards, but we were advancing and therefore quite happy. Soldiers don't particularly dwell on geo-political implications or social upheavals, they just get on with it, but as our wars progressed in time, ferocity and location, many soldiers would be simply concentrating on staying alive as our deployments widened to involve the Army in its entirety. Overall it was peaceful, even pleasant as we drove past a series of GOSPs, the odd collection of British troops and the distant Bedu while sun shone down on us all: almost military bliss really. One minor nagging concern I had was the almost total lack of Iraqi prisoners of war. Apart from the two young Fedayeen we had seen, this figure was currently precisely zero, a far cry from the literally thousands of prisoners we had been told to expect to receive. So, I thought to myself, if they didn't want to give themselves up or fight us, then where had they all gone?

We finally arrived at our next location, situated on the fringes of Rumaila, the hub of southern Iraq's oil production and the first significant town as such en route north. Quite uninspiring in appearance and very 1970s in terms of visible infrastructure, hardly a modern-day Camelot to inspire us all to deeds of martial glory, more one of sad urban decay. Even the sand was discoloured, numerous large oil patches had literally seeped to the surface so black areas abounded everywhere we looked. It took me a while to realise that the value of this black sand and what lay beneath must have been a mind-boggling figure to anyone in the financial know, but at the time, a hot drink and stretching my cramped legs was far more pressing. Occasionally we had spotted timid-looking Iraqi civilians peeking at us from a distance, and withdrawing into the shadows when they realised we had seen them. Saddam's regime had repeatedly warned them that we would steal everything, kill the men, rape the women and leave all their children as homeless orphans: after all, the regime had controlled literally every aspect of their lives for decades and most Iraqis had never even seen a Westerner. As this state control fully included all aspects of the media, this simplistic propaganda carried some weight with a lot of Iraqis, so to say they were cautious in welcoming us at this early stage of our armed intervention was an understatement in itself.

As we approached the entrance to the location we had a short pause while vehicles were shown their parking spots and all the other information such as the "track plan" for vehicle movement, sentry locations and all the other traditional military stuff were briefed to the guys in front of us. We sat in our vehicle, patiently waiting to be called forward and a bit tired, to be truthful. Conversation had long since dried up, we just wanted to get on with it, get a brief and get some food accompanied by a hot drink (scoff and a brew as the Army calls it, scran and a wet if you are a Royal Marine). I really wasn't paying much attention, my thoughts were back in England and exactly how I was going to work out how to resolve my marriage and its associated problems, just like thousands of other British soldiers have done so since then. It tends to go with the 21st Century territory during our recent wars, after all.

Mike disturbed my thought pattern by pointing out two small drab-coloured finch-type birds sitting on our spare wheel admiring the view. "You know what that means, Boss?" he asked me. I just looked blank in reply. He smiled and said fairly triumphantly, "No nerve agent!" I have to admit he had a good point: coal miners had used canaries as an early warning system effectively for generations. I was both pleased he was so switched on to the threat and quietly embarrassed that I patently wasn't. Also, he inadvertently reminded me that none of us had yet been issued our promised "Combo Pens", large spring-operated pen type syringes, containing Atropine, an antidote to nerve agent poisoning, if self-injected (the spring was to enable the rather large needle to penetrate several layers of clothing) in its very early stages at least. The actor Nicholas Cage had "advertised" this on the film *The Rock*, but unlike him we were trained to kneel down and inject ourselves in the thigh muscle, not the heart, movies are just movies after all. Apparently we had "refrigeration issues", so we would be issued these as and when, which I personally took as government shorthand for we didn't have enough to go around everyone and would be issued after the event to the fortunate survivors.

Luckily the troops either hadn't noticed or simply didn't bother to ask. They were, after all, now accustomed to a lack of most war fighting materials and simply couldn't be bothered complaining any more really: the collective mindset appeared to be "What's the point"?

As we drove into the location, which was criss-crossed with minor earth (or rather sand) works, I fleetingly saw some Iraqi soldiers running away into a fairly large industrial complex and disappearing from view just as I brought my rifle into the aim, these guys were candidates for the Iraqi national sprinting team. Some of our guys had taken cover and were obviously awaiting orders. I jumped out and asked what was going on and why hadn't anyone engaged them? It transpired the senior warrant officer present had told the guys not to fire as they were running away, and no threat to us therefore.

The senior corporal present reported between 20 and 30 fully-equipped Iraqi soldiers, all with AK 47s and at least 2 carrying RPGs, a very effective weapon against people, helicopters and unarmoured vehicles (like our Land Rovers especially). I was quietly incandescent with rage: why the fuck hadn't we opened fire? They may not be a threat now, but later today or tomorrow, when they get organised, we may well badly regret this act of misguided compassion, I ventured. The warrant officer protested, I quite rudely interrupted and pointed out that we were at war with these people, not pissing about on Salisbury Plain any more and our first and overriding responsibility was the lives of our soldiers, not the enemies, especially one who appears quite well armed and knows the area a damn sight better than we do and has just been allowed to quickly bugger off in order to do whatever they now please. Hardly an ideal start, perhaps?

This was a classic case of our engrained years of the "Yellow Card" rules of engagement mentality, which (rightly) seriously limited our rules of engagement in Northern Ireland and to a lesser degree, the Balkans. However, this was now a general war situation, but some of the older and theoretically more experienced soldiers hadn't made the mental jump in terms of aggressive action and this was a classic example. Ironically, as a Black Watch Warrant Officer told me shortly after this incident, his eighteen and nineteen-year-old jocks, unencumbered by this military baggage and often straight from their training depots, professionally and calmly killed the enemy without any hesitation whatsoever, much to the great surprise of the older soldiers from the Northern Ireland generation. After all, it was exactly what they were trained to do, so they did precisely that and to great effect. Unlike Islamic State and its barbaric medieval doctrine, the British Army doesn't dehumanise its enemies, it kills purely and simply because it is what the job requires. It's a professional requirement, and not a religiously-driven barbarous murder or racially-driven state-sponsored genocide. Ultimately, killing is the elementary base essence of war, once stripped of the various layers which 21st century philosophers, politicians or academics attempt to wrap around violent military activities for their own diverse reasons. Given the right circumstances or motivation, the vast majority of the human race are very easily capable of this action. As much as we would all loudly deny it, it's simply well hidden under a surprisingly thin veneer of civilisation.

It was an embarrassingly large mistake, one which hopefully wouldn't return to haunt us all very soon and in a physically painful manner. The warrant officer looked sheepish, and the soldiers were all very quiet after my little outburst. It had happened very quickly, as things do in a conflict area. Events have a tendency to unfold incredibly quickly in these situations. The British Army trains itself extremely well, but ultimately, even in our increasingly high-tech world, everything still boils down to the soldier on the spot and his/her decision or actions, or not as the case may be. I forced myself to calm down and praised everyone for their reactions and forcing the enemy to (literally) run away and then had a quiet word with all the NCOs present, saying essentially, "Next time, open fire, hit a few. Once they fall over the majority will rapidly surrender and then the threat to us will have been neutralised". They all nodded: point taken. That possibly sounds blunt and callous to some people, but I would argue that vigorous and liberal democratic discussion over relative points of view is not a realistic option in these "unusual" circumstances. As Islamic State (in particular) and the Taliban have recently proved in abundance, the liberal Western concept of "fairness" doesn't exist on a middle eastern (or indeed any) battlefield in the 21st Century.

The very next day, less than a kilometre away, in a fairly remote area, we discovered what had become of our (actually nearer 40 in number), "fugitive" Iraqi soldiers. Neatly laid out, almost parade style, were their Soviet-style steel helmets, drab-coloured uniforms, boots and belts. What bothered me was the total absence of any of their weapons at all. They may have just "gone home" in preference to either fighting us or surrendering, but they had taken their weapons with them to a man. I found this ominous, to say the least. Iraq had a large standing army, far larger than the entire British Army and the vast majority of the Iraqi adult male population had some form of military experience. If it wasn't giving itself up and instead, large numbers of them had apparently just chosen instead to simply go home, and do so fully armed — possibly to await further orders — then I thought we may have some quite serious problems once Saddam and his regime finally went. The relevance of this small incident would soon echo in the grand scheme of our occupation.

I quietly and fervently hoped that we, the UK, had a detailed, very robust and timely plan to prevent any post-war power vacuum and therefore lack of effective governance, which in turn meant law and order, because this population was beginning to look both heavily armed and possibly reasonably well trained, so any displays of public dissent or dissatisfaction could, perhaps, be quite attention-grabbing compared to our recent experiences. In more practical and possibly personal terms, in turn this scenario could prove quite emotional for all concerned, but I thought it wouldn't come to that and I was quietly confident that someone, somewhere back in the UK political centre of power had surely anticipated all these issues.

Our battle group was all now firmly established in its allocated positions, as usual dispersed geographically into pre-ordained tactical groupings. Each sub unit (as a company or squadron-sized body of troops is known) was self-sufficient in terms of defence, communications, life support, and transport and so on. Now, the Army, when deployed on operations, is very heavily reliant on civilian contractors for many of the non-combat functions, such as catering, bulk fuel supply and vehicle repairs, for example, but then, it was a self-contained entity and fully able to operate and sustain itself to conduct mobile operations 24/7 in an austere environment several thousand miles away from home, a core requirement for a professional army engaged in modern, large scale 21st Century warfare. Our fiery Brigade Commander had decreed the chefs were all to be left behind in Kuwait and that each and every officer or soldier could cook for him or herself, irrespective of rank: nothing that any of us weren't used to and anyway, as we had neither access to fresh rations or the means to store them, it simply wasn't that significant in the grand scheme of things. It just meant we had to be self-reliant and survive from our Operational Ration Packs (ORP) the field "boil in a bag" ration packs, as the Army then ate, each individual soldier being issued with new ORP every 3 days or so.

Our site was basically the usual (rock hard) sun-baked sand, with numerous little berms running across the entire area, which gave good cover for fire positions as they were waist high and several feet thick, very solid and sun-baked natural walls in effect. We erected various tents, mainly for use as part of the Battle Group HQ. They were joined together to form a small tented complex encompassing all the various disciplines required to plan and conduct modern warfare, in all its operational aspects. Smaller ones were used for some accommodation: I was fortunate enough to find a bed space in one of these, it made a nice change from "bashas"; essentially a poncho lean-to of some description and a desert floor bed, so I viewed myself as a very fortunate individual indeed.

We rapidly settled into a routine. Soldiers like routines and big organisations engaged in mounting very large scale 24/7 operations need to be fully "on the same song sheet". My own shift pattern was 12 on, 12 off. I had the night shift, along with Bird, primarily because was this period was the most likely time of day for any form of CW to be used against us. Doubtless the Iraqis knew at least our general positions: their land line telephone system was still functioning, plus we couldn't simply "lock down" the entire civilian population, we were, after all, here in the role of liberators, not conquerors (at least in the very early stages), so good relationships were very important to us. The locals, at this stage, were composed of two opposing tribes, essentially oil workers and railway line workers. They didn't trust or like each other and each referred to the other as "Ali Babas", a bunch of thieves in plain English. Ali Baba is not seen as some glamorous Robin Hood character in Iraq but a mere common-or-garden thief. This was compounded by their lack of faith in us in terms of sheer staying power. I had been rather surprised by Nellie on our arrival in this area. "I've been here before," he suddenly announced to the rest of us. It transpired that, as a younger man, when he had served here during Gulf War One in 1991, he had then driven an armoured vehicle as part of a UK liaison team attached to the American Army. They had liberated this area, albeit briefly and to mass popular adulation, but then promptly retired en masse to Kuwait, at which point Saddam's (Sunni-dominated) forces quickly and violently reoccupied the area, promptly killing several thousand people and forcibly relocating thousands more. The local population had definitely not forgotten being utterly abandoned by the West 12 years earlier, or the very bloody human price they had paid in the immediate aftermath of Saddam's military humiliation in Kuwait.

My little tent had the added advantage of the two of us being on different shifts, which meant that each of us could use the other bloke's empty camp bed to get our kit off the floor: a huge bonus as the local scorpions, ants and camel spiders all seemed to like occupying our Bergens, boots and generally most things we owned, during the night. It seemed to us that none of Iraq's crawling, creeping or flying creatures had any understanding of the word "timid" and they all had a tendency to bite us, sting us or try and quietly eat pieces of us during our sleep, so getting "off the floor" was highly desirable all round. I was one of the lucky ones in this context. Small things matter in these exotic countries that Her Majesty's various recent governments seem to like the armed forces to visit so much, whether invited or not by their occupants, and normally without any form of long-term strategy or forward planning. The Devil, after all, normally lies in the detail.

We discovered the joys of the local "black sand" quite rapidly. One of our Artillery guys was boiling some water for a brew in their little tent in the main HQ complex, which was directly opposite our INT/NBC cell, as they were then termed by the Army. As we sat there at early o'clock on the night shift, listening to whatever radio traffic was going on — or not on a quiet shift — all of us fighting off the eternal enemy of utter boredom, the sand underneath the cooker suddenly burst into flames, which broke up the monotony somewhat. Reacting quickly, one of the guys kicked some sand onto the flames which, to be fair, in most parts of the world would be a highly effective course of action. However, the sand itself merely acted as more fuel and the fire suddenly went from being a minor and rather entertaining distraction to the classic, "Fuck — the tent's on fire!" Various soldiers tried to stamp out the flames or find enough water to make a difference, all quite farcical and amusing in hindsight, but on a serious note, our escape routes were rather few in number and cluttered by the odds and sods of equipment any military HQ needs to function on a 24/7/365 basis. Not really the stuff of Health and Safety Executive dreams, but then again, they don't tend to visit active war zones very often. However, the fire was confined to one small part of the complex and a fire extinguisher was duly produced from somewhere to great and satisfying effect. So we resolved, along the lines of traditionally sound military advice such as "never eat yellow snow", also not to light open fires anywhere near black sand: lesson learnt, as they always say.

Shortly after this dramatic little fire safety lesson, the rains came and they came and then came some more, in effect a desert deluge, which surprised us, to say the least, but we were Brits and quite accustomed to rain so we just shrugged our collective shoulders and carried on "normal jogging" as the saying goes within the Army (it means the normal routine in effect). However, this very unseasonal, rain quickly became something of an unseasonal, unexpected and very major Arabian Monsoon in nature and our rock-hard, sun-baked surroundings became something akin to the Somme on a very bad day. Our vehicles were soon bogged past their axles and foot movement became a minor physical challenge all of its own.

One of the less exciting aspects of expeditionary warfare is the lack of any and all forms of facilities people just take for granted in their everyday life, which includes the most basic form of toilets, therefore everyone had to conduct "shovel recces" to answer the call of nature. Whilst we briefed repeatedly on the need to ensure that you dig deep, for obvious reasons of both health and hygiene, human beings are by and large intrinsically lazy creatures, especially if they are accustomed to a fairly senior management position/high social status or just plain "pampered Westerners", depending on your point of view. So it came to pass that as I was lying on my camp cot, fast asleep in my nice, warm sleeping bag, I was oblivious to the fast rising water levels around the location as the rains angrily lashed over our (no longer) desert location.

I awoke to find the complete tent floor literally awash, to a depth of several inches, but fortunately all my kit was off the floor and therefore bone dry, over which I felt rather childishly smug and pleased. However, my cheerful self-satisfaction came to an abrupt halt when I noticed a small whirlpool which had formed between the partially closed entrance flaps. My smugness was shattered by the sight of several chunks of human excrement swirling lazily around within the whirlpool, a disgusting sight to wake up to and quite medieval in concept. Suffice it to say that this forced me into a prompt reaction in cleansing the interior of my tent. I later discovered I was not the only recipient of poor hygiene courtesy of some very lazy and rather selfish people. We later had an area-wide cleansing operation, followed by a rather large waste-burning session. Historically, armies suffer far more casualties from disease then actual fighting: this little episode was a stark reminder of how and why that had been possible so often over previous centuries of warfare. For the rest of our time in Iraq, the building or digging of latrines was conducted with far greater attention to detail and enforced enthusiasm. We had been extremely fortunate to avoid a large scale outbreak of non-battlefield casualties once: we didn't care to risk it twice. Not to mention the sheer embarrassment factor: at least being shot or blown up has certain credibility within military circles; being incapacitated by quite easily avoidable diseases, especially in a highly technologically advanced Western Army in the 21st Century, certainly does not.

Unsurprisingly, quite a few of us, myself included, had what can politely be described as upset stomachs after this disgusting little episode, but we all just thought "that's life in a green suit" and our austere diet, plus the large amounts of bottled water we were all drinking, soon saw us back to rights. At this stage, none of us were remotely aware that our anticipated "war of liberation" would soon see the entire British Army embroiled in two distinctly different wars, which would become one long and painful campaign, so enthusiasm and belief in our cause was still extremely high. Fortunately the future is ultimately unknown to all of us, even those who aim to shape it in accordance with their own personal ambitions or political designs. I went back to my 12-hour night shift, ever mindful of the possibility of an Iraqi CW attack. What did Saddam have to lose anyway? I thought to myself. The world and its dog knew he couldn't win or talk himself out of utter defeat on this occasion. Our PM himself had stated he had the undoubted capability to do so, so if absolute defeat was a certainty, then why not take a lot of us with him? I have to be honest, if I had been in his shoes and staring bleakly at oblivion, I would have found it a rather tempting idea.

I gave nightly (at midnight) intelligence updates over our Combat Net Radio (CNR), the now completely obsolete "CLANSMAN" radio system, reliable 1980s technology in itself, but rather limited in its range over a featureless desert environment. Like most of our equipment, it had been designed and procured with a major European land war in mind. So I read aloud, like some BBC World War 2 presenter of old, albeit with a distinctly Northern accent, focusing on the latest situation at the front. This included all the British Brigade's current situation and also that of the neighbouring American Marines, whose supply lines, after all, we protected. Nightly I spoke about previously unknown towns such as Az Zubayr, Al Qurnah, Ad Dayr and An Nasirayah, encompassing the various actions, casualties and allied movements across these areas, not to mention the Al Faw and Basra. To avoid giving the Iraqi Artillery direction finders an easy target, I spoke in short bursts, giving outlying sub units the opportunity to question or confirm any detail in between my transmissions, which they inevitably did. It was very time consuming, but all we had there and then. Our American exchange officer was horrified, he was used to far more advanced methods and equipment. "Fighting the Stone Age way" was a term he often used in amazement. Unlike us, the American Government had invested wisely in its military forces since the previous Gulf War and also taken on board the harsh lessons they had learned from their painful Somalian experience.

Very early in the land campaign I had a sharp introduction to the true meaning of the term "the fog of war". We were told, around 7pm that two Royal Engineer soldiers from 7 Armoured Brigade (7 Bde) were missing following an ambush on two British vehicles in a heavily built-up area. This was very bad news; no one wanted to be captured by the Iraqis. We all knew, courtesy of *Tornado Down* and *Bravo Two Zero* from the first Gulf War that our treatment would be harsh and painful if captured, to say the least. In my "Resistance to Interrogation" guise, I also knew from some personal intelligence sources in UK (but had been told to keep it to myself by Regimental HQ, for reasons of morale apparently) that Saddam, well aware of the bargaining power that any Western hostages would afford him, had given detailed orders prior to hostilities commencing for all Western prisoners to be kept isolated and alone. They were to be kept in a number of designated safe houses, rather than the prisons our intelligence services knew of very well. Schools, municipal buildings, cellars and the like were all to be used to hold prisoners secretly by a dedicated branch of the Iraqi Secret Service. Callous but cunning, I had to admit. It would make locating, let alone rescuing personnel virtually impossible. No matter how good our Special Forces were at the tremendously difficult art of hostage rescue within an extremely hostile environment, if you can't actually locate hostages accurately, then you can't rescue them either. Islamic State have moved these goalposts by some way now, and it's pretty impossible to train troops to resist beheading or being burned alive. That may sound incredibly cynical but it's also a truism that UK's "Prone to Capture" troops simply have to face up to as an accepted part of their job, and our media regularly talk of "heroic performances" by Premier League footballers: an overused media term if ever there was one.

For two British soldiers to be taken captive so early, and especially by what appeared to be a local militia, rather than the Iraqi Army, was a huge shock to all of us. It had apparently been a very close quarter ambush in a fairly small town. They were the driver and commander of a radio-equipped Land Rover, hit by RPGs and AK 47s at extremely close range. initially they were believed to be dead, but when a platoon of Black Watch were sent to ensure the secure radio had been destroyed (we didn't want it to end up in nearby Iran), they got close enough to report "no bodies present" before being beaten back by the sheer volume of fire coming their way. This was shock number two: a full strength, aggressive and highly trained British Infantry platoon (approximately 32 - 34 soldiers) had not been forced back from anywhere since 1982 and the Falklands War.

A period of silence then followed. This wasn't part of the script, after all. A transmission then came through from our own Brigade HQ: both soldiers had been found by a Military Police patrol, having escaped their captors and evaded them across the desert. We were ecstatic! This was real *Bravo Two Zero* stuff: brilliant, we all thought! Shortly afterwards a very experienced and highly respected major (a Falklands veteran, who had taken part in bayonet charges for real: a rarity in 2003,but now quite a commonplace qualification in 2017 for a lot of serving and recently retired British soldiers) who had just returned from HQ and dropped in to ask what was happening. I repeated the report to him. He replied in essence, "That isn't what I was briefed. Please keep me informed". Of course I responded, he was a good friend of mine, but his rather unenthusiastic attitude to this news perplexed me somewhat. Frankly, I was both puzzled and mildly concerned.

Early in the wee small hours of the morning, the truth abruptly came out over our CNR: both soldiers were indeed dead. Another, unconfirmed report hinted they had been forced to dig their own graves prior to being shot. This eventually turned out to be a mere rumour and a very inaccurate one — one of the very first victims of War is the truth, after all — but I do remember feeling physically sick at the news. Two soldiers had indeed escaped the ambush: one young soldier, having first hidden his wounded comrade and then promptly hijacked a passing car at gunpoint to enable their joint escape from the "killing zone" as ambush sites are very aptly known (the clue is in the title). These were the two soldiers we had been made aware of via our CNR. We all badly, indeed desperately, wanted to hear good news, so this supposition was rapidly passed on to us, in a well meant but inaccurate manner and to our great and short-lived delight. In essence, we had all confused the two pairs of soldiers and their widely differing fates. The harsh and bitter reality was that two brave young men had died alone a very long, long way from home.

Sadly since 2003, with the sole exception of two SAS soldiers being very forcefully rescued by the Army from the custody of our Iraqi Police allies in Basra City itself, no British soldier has survived being taken prisoner by either Iraqi insurgents or the Taliban for much more than a few minutes, not a subject the MOD is particularly keen to discuss but the stark reality of the brutal nature of our recent conflicts. Our enemies, both real and potential, have precious little time for human rights. Our soldiers are only too aware of this: any thoughts of surrender or being captured have quite simply ceased to be an option in either Iraq or Afghanistan (and will doubtless remain so for any foreseeable future conflicts, as Islamic State have made brutally and abundantly clear on repeated and widely publicised occasions) for any UK personnel from 2003 onwards. International accords such as the Geneva Conventions and their ilk now only apply to Western armies in real conflict terms and no amount of political rhetoric or liberal, multicultural debate in a nice warm, safe TV studio, or verbose statements by rather well-paid human rights lawyers can deflect from that reality for any young British soldiers or Marines now serving in harm's way on our nation's behalf.

My generation of soldiers, in the era of the Red Army, the first Gulf War, the Balkans and the Falklands Conflict were understandably quite concerned at the prospect of being captured and interrogated with the ever-present threat of liberally applied, systematic and very one-way violence. For the current generation of soldiers, however, their rather stoical viewpoint is really quite simple and very much to the point. They don't want to talk to us, just kill us.

The routine continued and was tweaked to further fine-tune our "Battle Rhythm", as we simultaneously strived to enhance our rather Spartan surroundings. Soldiers like a routine and as war is a 24/7 activity, establishing and maintaining the Battle Rhythm at all levels is simply key to effectively and successfully sustaining large military operations.

Fictional military films and programmes, from the classics such as *Saving Private Ryan* to the singularly inaccurate, banal and vacuous Afghanistan TV offerings that are *Bluestone 42* or *Our Girl*, all of which fail to convey the numerous boring activities soldiers need to do; such as eat, sleep, clean themselves, inspect and maintain their equipment, carry out never-ending guard or fatigue duties and myriad other associated tasks. None of these functions have much in the way of dramatic content, so the viewing public will remain convinced war is either all just nonstop action or, in classic BBC drama terms, mainly "having a laugh" or bonding with Western democratic-leaning and highly empathetic locals, all of whom speak surprisingly good English, whilst in reality much of it is quite mundane and boring in nature with the odd large dose of adrenaline. But all of these are also rather critical activities in the shrinking but highly professional organisation that is the British Army in the 21st Century. As the saying goes, "You're only as good as your kit": another way of saying if you don't look after your equipment, it won't look after you, normally when it matters most.

The seemingly distant war continued and Saddam's regime was gradually shrinking by the day. Basra was almost completely isolated, several major Iraqi towns had already fallen to the American advance and the Kurds in the north of the country had risen in open revolt, albeit discreetly aided by numerous American SF personnel and the omnipresent threat of American air power. There had been some minor setbacks here and there: UKSF had inserted a Squadron of SBS mounted in WIMIKS (the "sexy" Land Rover variant with machine guns fitted). They had been compromised (discovered, in plain English) almost immediately after commencing their mission, which had then rapidly evolved into a running fire fight in the dark across the Northern Iraqi Desert as more and more Iraqi units flocked to join the fight against the invaders. After several hours of nonstop, if highly mobile, fighting, someone, somewhere made the difficult decision to extract the SBS totally and "deny" all the vehicles: destruction by means of a US Air Force C130 gunship with its massive firepower. Most of the UK personnel were safely recovered, except two guys left behind in the chaos, who simply opted to make their way to Syria, a massive and daunting challenge for most mere mortals, but these are simply exceptional men by any yardstick, and duly they succeeded in the finest UKSF traditions, only to be then captured by the Syrian military after a fierce gun battle. They were later released post conflict, when an American general (allegedly) told the Syrians to give them back or he wouldn't tell his tanks to stop at the Syrian border. Probably totally untrue, but a hugely popular story at the time. Not all the UKSF vehicles had been destroyed, however, and these trophies of war were proudly displayed in the city centre of Mosul: useful propaganda for the regime no doubt, but in the grand scheme of things it changed absolutely nothing regarding the ultimate fate of Saddam and his Ba'ath Party apparatus. It also made us think somewhat: the SBS are one of the world's finest SF units and for a complete squadron of them to be forced to "extract" was not something we would never have imagined in our wildest dreams frankly. There was obviously some fight in quite a few of the Iraqis yet was the conclusion we quietly drew.

Meanwhile the American Army launched a deep raid with a regiment's worth of Apache attack helicopters (more than the British Army holds in total), the aim being to strike deep into Iraq and destroy major military installations and key Iraqi resources. These ultra-lethal weapon systems crossed Iraq at ultra-low level, during the pitch dark of night in two waves, aiming to unleash mayhem and havoc at their appointed destination. The Apache is superbly suited to the environment of darkness with its impressive sensors and optical systems, as the Taliban could later bitterly testify to their cost following eight years of UK Apache operations in Helmand Province. In an early indication of the years of "asymmetric" warfare which were to follow the invasion of Iraq, the Ba'ath Party posted "noise sentries" on the outskirts of sizeable towns, their task being to simply listen for the noise of approaching helicopters and warn the local regime. Rather low-tech by Western standards but effective nevertheless, and also quite impossible to either jam or detect.

These noise sentries duly alerted the local Ba'ath Party, who, having first armed the entire population (Western Europeans simply have absolutely no comprehension of just how heavily armed the populations of Iraq, Afghanistan and similar nations are: a couple of assault rifles are just merely standard family possessions, with the odd RPG as a status symbol here and there for the more well-to-do citizens). The regime then ordered the said population (essentially anyone big enough to carry an AK 47, male and female, young and old alike) to quickly go out into the streets and, on a given signal, just "spray the sky with bullets". All Ba'ath Party buildings also tended to have some form of anti-aircraft artillery (AAA) on the roof or close by at least and these, normally rapid firing cannons, joined in the communal spirit for defiance against the invaders. Western militaries can't really train for random events like these, it isn't normal behaviour in the urban areas of Western Europe or North America and you cannot envisage every bizarre possibility irrespective of the opinions of the legions of "after the event" armchair TV experts our media seems to produce in increasingly prodigious numbers. Nevertheless the Apache crews flew through literally one hail of bullets after another in pressing on stoically towards the target. "Flying through multiple reverse hailstorms" was one pithy description. The next town was alerted to the incoming American presence by the simple measure of the town currently doing the shooting turning its entire electrical power grid on and off rapidly: a massive torch signal in effect. The American crews all took varying levels of damage in this repeated and increasingly gruelling process and some badly damaged aircraft had to abort, while others were forced to change their route by the sheer weight of repeated small arms fire coming their way again and again and again, so the well-planned "deep raid" gradually became fairly ad hoc in nature, with very limited results at the objective end of the mission.

One Apache ran out of fuel on its way home and Saddam's propaganda department (every government has a very large one after all, we just call it "spin" in the UK) who rapidly claimed it had been shot down by a lone old man with his hunting rifle, who was quietly tending to his flock of goats when the invader came along in his state-of-the-art attack helicopter, so he promptly brought it crashing down to earth with a couple of shots from his trusty bolt action rifle: incredible! But under Saddam's rule the entire population was inclined to react enthusiastically to such statements and in the desired manner and instantly, if only for pure survival reasons.

We all felt deep sympathy and concern for the two American aviators whom we knew had been rapidly captured. We later found out they had been very badly beaten (as expected) but both ultimately survived the conflict in one piece. I was the sole qualified Resistance to Interrogation Instructor in our unit, having myself completed this physically demanding, exhausting and (deliberately) degrading training myself and I was very well aware of Iraqi interrogation methods. It's specifically designed for "Prone to Capture" troops, such as SF and aircrew to experience the shock of capture and harsh treatment in a controlled manner, but however realistic it's designed to be, you cannot replicate torture or beheadings, a brutal fact of recent life in 21st Century military interventions. These Americans pilots were hugely fortunate in comparison to the fate of some of their Marine and Army counterparts. Events later unfolded elsewhere in Iraq and Afghanistan too for some unfortunate NATO soldiers.

We spent one fairly boring afternoon watching, by means of our local friendly surveillance radar, three Iraqi field gun positions vigorously firing rather large shells at each for most of the afternoon. It was rather like the old 1970s Space Invaders game, but played by adults with high explosives. We didn't know why at the time this "artillery duel" was being conducted (and I still don't to this day). We therefore assumed they were local army factions that were for and against Saddam and the "for" faction appeared to win. This bizarre duel varied from a two-way shoot to a three-way shoot and finally back to two positions firing at one lone site, which eventually was "neutralised". Watching unknown people die electronically is so easy to do when death is so remote, I remember thinking quietly to myself. A few of the guys were disappointed by the result as it lasted long enough for a small sweepstake to take place and after all we had absolutely nothing to spend our US dollars on anyway. Boredom and the need for patience are very fearful enemies for Westerners who are so accustomed to having everything at our finger tips and having them now. Later Mullah Omar (the late one-eyed leader of the Afghan Taliban) would make a telling, but accurate, comment in 2008, aimed at NATO's intervention in Afghanistan, essentially saying ,"You have the watches, but we have the time". He was right, the Taliban never had to defeat Western troops in order for us to leave, merely outlast us at whatever cost to their fighters which, to be fair, is exactly what they achieved. A stark reminder that, no matter what you may wish for in political or military terms, the enemy tend not to play be your rules and definitely will not "play fair".

About the same time lots of varied elements of the British Army started to track quite a surprisingly clever ploy by some anonymous but obviously very intelligent and singularly determined Iraqi Officer: approximately a dozen T55 tanks in small groups of lone vehicles, pairs and occasionally trios of tanks were slowly sneaking through Basra towards UK Forces. Moving only at night and keeping to darkened side streets, all hiding in warehouses or similar large buildings during the day, sometimes making mere hundreds of metres on some days. They were slowly, but inexorably heading towards a pre-designated point, as yet unknown to us, where we presumed they would join together to mount a deliberate and aggressive attack against us. None of us had expected this, but they had been spotted very early, probably by our SF guys in Basra, who were doing their usual SF stuff in style and having fun along the way, no doubt.

Various plans were now being made to destroy them once they finally assembled as a unit. They were now, I thought as I charted their cautious progress across Basra, merely forty-plus brave men unknowingly going slowly to an inevitable and violent end, "dead men driving" in effect. All that really remained to be decided now was the where, when and how they actually died, it was that simple. Against a "second division" military, such as the Iranians (at that time), they would probably have succeeded with this audacious surprise attack and succeeded very well, but against a first rate European or North American Army, it was always going to end in tears. Nevertheless we developed a sneaking admiration for their ongoing quiet determination and patience, neither of which were ever quite good enough to defeat our assorted high-tech surveillance assets, of which they were totally oblivious to the bitter end. Unknown to them, we were keenly following their nightly progress with ever-growing interest as they all moved in blissful unawareness towards certain death.

About this time, our Signals Officer invited me to accompany him on a "mail run" to his rebroadcast stations. In simple terms, our "Clansman" radio system was an old system and only had an effective range of about 30 kilometres. In order for us to communicate with our forward troops, we had to establish a "rebroadcast ladder". Essentially these small 3-man teams manned the radios which received the various transmissions and then "hurled them" forward (or backwards as the case may be), an electronic ladder in effect. This was Korean War stuff in comparison to our American allies, but without reliable communications you can't fight an effective campaign anywhere, let alone in a rather large and very empty desert. The single most powerful weapon on a modern battlefield is a radio, after all. This mail run, which included water and rations replenishment for the troops (but not ammunition or any form of medical equipment, we still didn't have much of either commodity) would give me an excellent opportunity to see the ground and hopefully get a much better picture of the actual "state of play" up at the sharp end of our increasingly isolated little war, so I accepted Mike's offer with alacrity.

We drove in a small convoy (a vehicle packet in Army parlance) of Land Rovers towards the North Hammar Canal, a major water feature which was in effect the beginning of the front line in our AO. The Paras held the main bridge over the canal which, I discovered to my surprise, was a major and impressive piece of civil engineering, being well in excess of 400 metres wide with tall, vertical concrete banks and very much a major obstacle to major military movement. Despite some serious damage from failed Iraqi attempts to blow up the bridge, it was quite navigable by light to medium weight vehicles and well defended by "dug in" Para WIMIKS, except these were the MILAN anti-tank missile equipped variant, a good indication just how important this bridge was to us, plus the fact we had little to cope with any form of determined counter attack. Luckily this wasn't particularly high on the Iraqis' to do list.

On crossing the bridge, we found ourselves in a remarkably flat landscape but criss-crossed by dozens of irrigation ditches of widely varying depth and width running basically parallel with the canal itself: that is, across our required direction of travel towards the enemy. Additionally, all the tracks capable of carrying vehicles were raised above the landscape, a simple civil anti-flood measure by the Iraqis. However, this was now a major boost for any defender watching us as we were rapidly obvious in movement terms, coupled with the unavoidable dust trail that inevitably accompanies any and all movement in the desert. Now I realised exactly why the Iraqis seemed to have so many motor bikes and just how useful these were for getting rapidly around a landscape such as this: discreet, reliable and highly mobile — especially when you knew your way around — a classic example of local knowledge overcoming a technological inferiority. In contrast our infantry either used "transport left, transport right" — walking in old English — or used the larger tracks with vehicles and thereby invited a high explosive response.

We reached the first rebroadcast site ("Rebro" for short): essentially a lone Land Rover plus tent in the middle of nowhere with 3 soldiers manning the radios 24/7. I was shocked: the site had no form of defences at all, not even a roll of razor wire, the guys had 30 rounds each and little else. We were simply taking a big gamble the enemy wouldn't have the will to attack them. If we had done this a mere three years later in Helmand Province, then I would have been visiting headless bodies and a well-looted position, complete with a burnt-out vehicle. Luckily our "warm welcome" from the Taliban precluded any thoughts of being so stupid by the local commanders. The troops were pleased to see us, they had been isolated for days at a time with a basic routine of work, eat, sleep and absolutely no creature comforts of any kind. In effect they had no idea what was happening anywhere other than their own little three-person world.

Simple conversation with someone else was almost a joy to them and they eagerly sought any form of news — the war, regimental gossip, sport — anything at all. They took the water gratefully, the rations in a matter-of-fact fashion. We all did that: bread, fruit, potatoes and the other food staples so taken for granted back in UK, had long since become a memory; we just ate because we had to, in effect. Some guys had mail, other didn't and were obviously disappointed, a fact of military life, sadly. Some guys passed their mail around as a gesture of "mateship", some didn't; each to their own, really. At this stage of the Army's decade-plus of war and for several years to come, it cost a small fortune to post food parcels from UK to British soldiers at war. The Royal Mail was rather slower than their American equivalent to forego any possible source of profit, so it was airmail letters (blues, as they are universally known) or nothing for all of us. Occasionally there was the odd snippet of intelligence. One NCO named Ben, locally famous for being an exceptional runner, had seen several armed men very early one morning on the opposite bank of one of the smaller, but still quite wide and deep, canals that irrigated the area. In the half light of early morning twilight, he had waved at what he assumed to be the Paras on patrol. They looked his way, but they didn't wave back to him, which he found strange. On my return I followed this up. It transpired that the men he had seen were neither Paras nor indeed British. That canal, I thought, had probably helped to save three British lives simply by being there and thereby acting as a serious obstacle to the unknown armed Iraqis who didn't feel too inclined to wave back to Ben that early in the morning.

We repeated this process several times, heading closer to the most advanced call sign, our small Tactical HQ element embedded amongst the Infantry Battalion HQ in the form of a liaison officer and his signallers. We found them in a small man-made dip in the ground, not large enough to be termed a gulley, but it gave then cover from view if nothing else. Again, they were glad to see faces from their own regiment. Cap badge is simply all in the British Army, it's what the troops fight for, along with looking after their mates, but that has been lost to a large degree on the powers that be in the MOD, who seem to view unit affiliation at the same personal value level as that of holding a Tesco club card. I had a long chat with a young NCO named Curtis, another soldier who had made the long trip from North Yorkshire to Southern Iraq. I hadn't seen him since Kuwait and he had both lost weight and visibly matured since then. He explained that the Iraqis had quite a very good

DF (Direction Finding, in terms of radio transmissions) system, combined with rather active motorcycle scouts, so they been shelled several times and had rapidly become very good at packing up and moving quickly, all of which he said with big smile on his face, I noted. We then spoke of mundane stuff like Yorkshire weather and how jealous certain characters we knew would be for not having been there. As we spoke a languid Household Cavalry Officer strolled past dressed in desert boots, football shorts and a tank crewman's helmet only: hardly the elegant Guards Officer of public imagination, I thought to myself. As we spoke he clambered into his CVR (T) turret, I watched him plug his helmet into the intercom system and disappear out of sight into his vehicle, rapidly emerging to loudly proclaim, "They've found us again!"

Curtis looked at me and simply said, "You need to move now, Boss, there will be incoming in a few minutes. Good to see you again." With that, he quickly turned away to pack everything up and move his vehicle. I just stood there for a few seconds, taking in how quickly the situation had changed, as I did so Mike appeared, complete with Land Rover and shouted, "Jump in, we're off," and then we were, as fast as we could go: the trailing dust cloud mattered little now. Once we had made some distance from the location we pulled over to look back. Our vehicles were moving quickly, but in an orderly manner to a pre-arranged emergency rendezvous point (ERV) for an ultra-rapid head check and reorganisation and then on to a pre-nominated alternative location to set everything up again and simply carry on, as drilled into us by years of exercising in Germany. As the last vehicle cleared the location Iraqi artillery rounds began to pound the now-empty desert sands in an accurate and lethal high explosive fashion, a reminder that the enemy can and does use his vote too on occasion. This was definitely not safe spectator sport material, so we hastily drove back towards the relative safety of the southern bank of the canal.

Our drive back to the outskirts of Royal Irish Town was a quiet one, all of us realising yet again that the old military adage of "There is always someone, somewhere worse off than you are" is a very true one. I just didn't realise there and then that thousands of British soldiers would actually live this adage over the years to come, and in much worse places under ever more violent and often dire circumstances.

Shortly after the tragic incident of the executions of the two Royal Engineers, we moved forward by a matter of mere kilometres to a fairly urban location within the oil fields. The weather had improved by now, so everything was dry and baked rock hard again. We had been told, in no uncertain terms, not to tell the soldiers about the very recent murders, again for alleged reasons of morale. I personally strongly disagreed with this policy, believing that all our soldiers had the right to know what the score was should the risk of capture be imminent. They were, after all was said and done, adults and volunteers without exception, not immature little children. As it transpired, the news inevitably leaked out: any regiment is essentially a large extended family by nature and British soldiers are simply superb at both overhearing hushed conversations by their commanders or "sniffing things out", irrespective of the environment or the orders themselves at times. It did however bring it home to all of us that, whilst we all knew that our victory was absolutely assured (we had the Americans on our side after all), life in a war zone can be an incredibly fragile possession, dying is not too difficult a pastime frankly, and situations can change incredibly fast and, unlike the movies, not necessarily always in your favour.

So, we dutifully arrived at the new location and went through the usual routine of each and every vehicle being shown into its specified location. I was summoned to the "step up" headquarters, so named as all British Army units keep "one foot on the ground" whilst moving to ensure continuity of command at all times. The second in command, a relaxed and unflappable guy at the best — or indeed the worst — of times, explained to me that one of our ARPs (Aviation Reconnaissance Patrols) in the form of two Gazelles was receiving sporadic but quite inaccurate artillery fire and asked my opinion of this new tactic. My view was simple: the Iraqis, being no strangers to war, were using their artillery as an improvised anti-aircraft weapon; the Argentinians had done much the same in the Falklands War with mortars, thereby keeping our armed helicopters at arm's length. It prevented them from doing their job effectively. Indeed, it seemed logical that the Iraqis were now doing the same, to prevent us approaching to within our own possible maximum missile engagement ranges to actually shoot at them (3750 metres for our TOW armed Lynx anti-tank helicopters).

The fact the totally unarmed Gazelles flew literally feet off the desert floor, in effect just meant they were a rather small, very nimble and quite fast-moving target to the unseen and distant Iraqi gunners. Everyone seemed content with that and I ventured an opinion the guns were probably D30s, a common and typically reliable towed artillery piece of Soviet origin within the Iraqi Army's units. The Republican Guard had much more modern self-propelled artillery, but we knew they were absolutely nowhere near Southern Iraq, ensconced much further north and faithfully waiting to go and meet the approaching American juggernaut on Saddam's personal orders. A task none of us, if we were honest, envied them: it could only end in tears on their part after all. But we didn't doubt for one minute that they would give it a go when their time came: they were elite troops, battle-hardened and undoubtedly determined, but it wasn't a real concern of ours except in terms of pure professional military curiosity, plus we already knew the inevitable result already of that one-sided contest.

No one seemed too excited about a few random shells being lobbed around the desert expanses and the crews seemed very calm, from the placid tone of their transmissions. We were trying to ascertain the exact locations of the Iraqi Army to the north of the GOSPs: you can't fight someone unless you know where they physically are after all and this was well prior to the British procurement of any sort of unmanned aerial vehicles (UAVs or "drones" as the media likes to call them).

This was still very early days inside Iraq. To date the main tasks we had conducted had fallen to our Lynx aircrew in the Basra area. Ever mindful of collateral damage and literally hundreds of thousands of civilians in the area, they had been used as a "pinpoint strike" asset. TOW was old even in 2003, but it was, and remains (it's still in use by the Americans, mainly for firing into caves, always quite a useful trait in Afghanistan) surprisingly accurate and its warhead, whilst small compared to the current Hellfire missile, is highly effective in confined spaces and against Soviet era armoured vehicles. Accordingly, our first mission, unofficially named "Certain Death" had seen a lone Lynx taking off in bad weather on a pitch-black night to grope its way over a series of rather tall power lines (which were not marked on any of our maps) in the darkness and then hover right over the front line in a highly built-up urban area. The target was an Iraqi observation post on the top floor of a block of inhabited flats, which also had a bird's eye view of British troops. Not exactly the easiest of first missions: even more so as it wasn't on behalf of our own brigade. But we were the weapon system of choice in order to avoid possible civilian casualties, something the British Army consistently take great pains to guard against at all levels despite repeated media claims to the contrary. The crew groped their way to a firing position over what previous generations would term "no man's land" to hover in the darkness as they confirmed their small target was the correct one. Urban areas in Iraq can be quite uniform in nature. The senior NCO in question, nicknamed "Kev", and his co-pilot promptly put a couple of missiles directly through the enemy's window (literally) and the Iraqi OP was immediately "effectively neutralised" as the military like to say. No doubt a rather major and hugely memorable wake-up call (literally) for the Iraqi occupants in question, who doubtless felt rather safely hidden in the early morning hours, or at least anyone who actually survived the attack may have thought so.

Our armoured comrades in 7 Bde seemed somewhat pleased with this and began to request our services on a more regular basis. Our own Bde meanwhile was firmly "Para Centric" and was slowly becoming almost desperate to unleash some airborne fury against the Iraqi Army, the Fedayeen or just anyone with a decent sun tan and a foreign accent really. Unfortunately Basra was very much an armoured war and for the Royal Marines to ask for assistance from the Paras would be almost a hanging offence for any individual concerned, that was never going to happen. So, the Iraqis, in our area of operations (AO as it's known), whilst keen to avoid a major fight, also used their artillery and tanks, all neatly tucked away within built-up and populated areas for good cover and concealment reasons, to keep us at arm's length. All in all, a rather frustrating affair for several thousand well trained and aggressive troops, but we lacked mobility (no one walks to war in the desert). We were, in all respects, essentially a "lorried" 1940s style infantry brigade, and our firepower was quite limited. The Iraqis had significantly more artillery with greater range than we did, even if our own gunners were by far better trained and motivated, plus they had tanks, whilst all our armour was busy in Basra. When you don't have any, a tank (or a couple of dozen tanks in this case), indeed *any* tank, even if it is 40 years old, is very much a showstopper for lightly armed troops, especially when you are already desperately short of ammunition before any serious fighting even begins and have no dedicated air support.

No doubt our feisty ex SF Brigade Commander was aware of this increasing frustration, but almost alone within the Anglo-American coalition we had a completely defensive task, despite having several thousand of the Army's finest and most aggressive infantry, elite troops by anyone's measure, anywhere on the globe. But, limited by our poor equipment and ongoing lack of logistical support, attacking anyone was simply not a realistically feasible option for us and the Iraqis we faced were content to maintain the status quo. They knew as well as we did exactly what the outcome of this war was ordained to be and seemed extremely keen to remain alive to witness that outcome.

Slowly it was dawning on our brigade that we offered both quite rapid mobility and effective anti-armour firepower with our helicopters, essentially a highly flexible combination despite our reduced (cost saving) numbers in lacking a third squadron. Ironically the true value of helicopters in modern counter insurgency warfare wouldn't sink truly home into the UK military mindset until the desperate battles of 2006/7 in Helmand Province when the UK Government would almost absentmindedly send a small and, yet again, very ill-equipped force into ferocious action against the Taliban with some vague and ill-defined notions of "provincial reconstruction" against all historical experience or extant intelligence data, but that was yet to come. All of which was ironic in light of our much-vaunted and oft repeated Northern Ireland experience (which would prove so utterly tiresome to our American allies, as our generals repeatedly threw this in their faces) when movement around South Armagh had been virtually impossible without some form of helicopter support for decades, but we had managed to forget that little fact. Yesterday's war is soon forgotten by all concerned, especially those at the higher levels. So, the two brigades had a minor ownership tug-of-war competition over us and we all sat sipping a brew in the morning sunshine and listening to our ARP calmly discussing the "fall of shot" from the enemy's artillery rounds in an almost conversational manner.

Whilst we were listening to the war, a report came in that one of our patrols had just captured three Iraqi fighting age males (FAMs as they were also referred to) by a sizeable and well-hidden arms cache. At the time I was still a qualified interrogator, so I volunteered to go and conduct some tactical questioning. People, when captured, go through a wide range of emotions, commonly known as the "shock of capture" amongst the military. This is an ideal time to gain information from a prisoner who is mentally "off balance" (a normal person suddenly thrust into a highly abnormal situation in quite basic terms) and trying to come to terms with this rapid and unexpected change of their personal fortunes. So, exploiting the shock of capture is a standard military practice and well recommended as a critical course of action in gaining useful and timely intelligence. As nothing much was happening in the war, the threat of CW attack had receded and the wide spread belief now abounded that Baghdad itself was the chemical trip wire. Against that context we were quite relaxed, so permission was given for me to go and have a quick "chat" with our newly-found friends.

The three prisoners/FAMs had been captured a few kilometres away by an alert Para patrol. Though unarmed when captured, they had been caught in the act of actively uncovering a very well camouflaged arms cache located in a dried-up irrigation channel, the area was criss-crossed with scores of these large ditches. Dressed in well-worn civilian clothes, they had pleaded total ignorance about what they had found: several modern rocket propelled grenades: not the famous RPG 7, but the far more up to date and compact, extendable one-shot Russian made disposable variant modelled on the American 66-millimetre Light Anti-Tank Weapon, complete with instruction manuals in Cyrillic and Arabic. Additionally, a slack handful of grenades, some AK assault rifles with folding stocks, numerous rifle magazines, plentiful ammunition and similar warlike items. Not the average bunch of farming tools really.

The young corporal in charge informed me they had taken the prisoners completely by surprise and they had offered no resistance. Now sitting forlornly in the open, they were playing the innocent peasant card for all it was worth. All fit men with no excess fat on them, well-fed and clean-shaven, but sticking determinedly to "the script" that they had just been idly wandering around looking for scrap metal and they had chanced upon these strange objects, which they had been innocently examining out of simple curiosity, nothing more sinister, when suddenly they had been arrested and for no legitimate reason, their apparent leader added indignantly. For a bunch of illiterate peasants recently arrested at gunpoint they were remarkably composed, which itself smacked of being fairly abnormal: the majority of civilians by and large react quite differently when several guns are suddenly pointed at them by a lot of large aggressive strangers who don't even share their language.

One by one, I inspected their hands: not a single callus between them, quite strange for men who "worked the land" (and Iraq is not a green and pleasant land to work by any stretch of the imagination). I duly told them to open their mouths and checked out their teeth. All of them had good, well cared-for teeth. Saddam invested heavily in ensuring the dental and medical fitness of his elite Republican Guard troops and devoted and ultra-loyal Fedayeen militia, unlike his people. One of the main purposes of tactical questioning is to quickly decide who has an intelligence value and therefore requires further questioning (formal and detailed interrogation conducted by specialist personnel from all 3 services) and who doesn't, especially when you take very large numbers of prisoners, as we had done in 1991 and fully expected to do so again. Irrespective of the fact that these were our first three prisoners, the fact they had been captured behind our lines in the act of retrieving weapons from a significant arms cache made this decision very easy: they were obviously at the very least some form of "stay behind" party, either Fedayeen (most likely at the time) or SF troops with hostile ambitions and intentions against our supply lines. So off they all went to be interrogated. "You win some, you lose some," I thought as they were taken away. None of them seemed too happy at the prospect, unsurprisingly enough. I had absolutely zero sympathy: their singular aim had been to cause significant British casualties and maximum destruction and realistically speaking, they still had their lives so they could count their blessings several times over and it was very much a far cry from the murderous treatment our own prisoners had so recently received.

As I look back on this minor incident, so many years later, the question has repeatedly crossed my mind as to whether any of these fighters received financial compensation from the UK Government for their detention following the aggressive marketing campaign mounted by several UK-based human rights lawyers in Iraq to drum up clients. At the other end of the spectrum, no one actively sought out the several thousand British soldiers later wounded in Iraq to offer them their services. The civic freedoms of liberal Western Democracy often follow rather strange courses.

I drove back to the Walled Garden, only to find a complete change of atmosphere during the brief period of time I have been absent. A Household Cavalry Regiment (HCR) patrol had been chasing a couple of "technicals", the ubiquitous pickup truck with a large machine gun mounted on the rear of the pickup, as regularly seen in Libya, Syria and so forth on various UK news channels in the wake of the much vaunted "Arab Spring" and its complete failure to bring any recognisable form of democracy to the Middle East. The HCR, had given chase in their lightly armoured CVR (T) Reconnaissance vehicles to the technicals, both firing at each other as the chase developed into a running fire fight over the flat desert. However, everything rapidly changed when the HCR were suddenly engaged by well-hidden Iraqi T55 main battle tanks and artillery fire. They had been lured into a well prepared "L" shaped ambush which allows the ambusher(s) to shot at the "ambushee(s)" from 2 directions at once, which makes life for the people inside the L quite unpleasant, to say the least.

Outnumbered and badly outgunned, two things happened. our Lynx were rapidly dispatched to assist the HCR whilst an urgent request for air support was made. Tragically, the two passing American A 10 ground attack aircraft, who were quickly tasked to support the HCR, mistook them for the enemy. Their vehicles were quickly destroyed and numerous British casualties taken. A very young HCR trooper showed uncommon valour in repeatedly clambering onto burning vehicles to rescue badly wounded and trapped comrades, all the while under heavy and accurate fire, both Iraqi and that of the heavily armed A 10 ground attack aircraft. For this amazing act of selfless courage, he was later awarded the George Cross for his unselfish gallantry that day and deservedly so: incredible heroism for a young man barely out of his teens.

However, this tragedy merely emboldened the Iraqis, who rapidly committed more assets, a mixture of tanks, artillery and other armoured vehicles into the action, which was now becoming somewhat of a rescue mission to extract the surviving crew members, including their wounded. All around this scene Lynx helicopters were rapidly manoeuvring to engage the enemy armoured vehicles, whilst the unarmed Gazelles attempted to seek out their locations, all the while under increasingly accurate and heavy enemy artillery fire. It became a swirling and very fast-moving fight across the barren desert floor, the British using speed and movement whilst jockeying for fire positions, the Iraqis using old-fashioned high explosive to try and bring them down. The battlefield became increasingly obscured by sand as this vicious little skirmish escalated, as the Iraqi shells hurled large sand "geysers" into the air, whilst the low-flying British helicopters left a series of sandtrails in their wake, not to mention the smoke from burning vehicles from both sides. Fresh helicopters were dispatched to conduct a "relief in place" so that the Iraqis could be contained whilst one of our two RAF (unarmed) Pumas was dispatched to collect the wounded and fly them to medical aid.

When the RAF was initially attached to our battle group there had been the usual jokes of, "The RAF don't dig in, they check in". (The RAF are renowned within the armed forces for staying in hotels whenever possible), but as the battle swirled around them and the Iraqi Artillery homed inexorably towards their stationery aircraft the crew refused to "pull power" until the last casualty was safely on board: a badly wounded Iraqi casualty, as it happened. They lifted just prior to the Artillery finally zeroing in on their position. Following this, we had nothing but major league respect for our own RAF detachment and wouldn't hear any hint of criticism over our personal "Blue Jobs". Okay they do things very, very differently to the Army, but these particular "Crabs" (as they are referred to by the Army and Navy) also had extra-large gonads and saved the lives of several British soldiers. Around them the Lynx, flying at ultra-low levels, had repeatedly engaged T 55s tanks and other Iraqi armoured vehicles, hitting around a dozen of them in the process, despite a third of all the missiles fired that day being "rogues": that is, they flew skyward, utterly out of control, to harmlessly engage the azure blue desert sky and the omnipresent blazing sun overhead. A mere 3 years later, a single British Apache could have rapidly devastated the Iraqi armour, without even being seen by them, all on its own and annihilated them in a very brief and one-sided period of time, such was the quantum leap forward in sheer firepower, weaponry and sensors, but the UK's Apaches were still in the trials stage and all ultimately destined for Helmand Province. But, just like the Iraqis and later, the various insurgents we would face, our crews fought with what they had there and then, much as our enemies now routinely utilise suicide bombers as "human cruise missiles" and liberally sow the ground with incredibly well-hidden IEDs (occasionally covering them in human excrement, a quaint medieval touch to 21st Century warfare). "If only" is a pointless irrelevance on a battlefield ultimately: hypothetical whims, a plea for a fair fight and liberal aspirations just won't keep you alive. We live in a highly regulated "Nanny State" in the UK of the 21st Century, so it is difficult to grasp that "fairness" simply doesn't exist as a concept within the confines of conflicts such as these. That may sound harsh, but it is also an eternal truism of warfare at the sharp end of the spear.

I had arrived back in the Walled Garden just as the Puma crew were about to launch, bumping into a grim-faced Bird, stomping directly towards the aircraft. "Where are you going?" I had asked him. Drawing himself up to his full height (I'm 6 foot tall and he just towered over me) and replied aggressively, "Sir, I am a fully-trained paramedic and I am getting on that fucking helicopter, *right now*, because there are wounded British soldiers out there." I noticed he was carrying his well-stocked medical pack with him. I thought to myself, he's right, this really isn't a time for asking permission or getting authority. "All right, Bird. Just don't get yourself killed, okay?" I replied. He smiled and nodded, "Aye, sir", and with that he was gone. I couldn't fault him for his initiative, albeit verging on downright insubordination in the traditional military sense, but let's recover the wounded first and we'll sort the all bullshit stuff later, I thought to myself.

I debriefed some of the crews on their return, after the CO had given them all a well-deserved and hard-earned collective "well done". They looked like a modern-day version of Bomber Command crews: tired but euphoric, sweaty and unkempt but highly professional and all of them simply running on adrenaline. The stories they told were remarkable: an Australian Pilot, serving in the British Army, had hit a T 55 and immobilised it by hitting the tracks and drive sprocket area (an M or Mobility kill in Army speak). He was about to deliver the coup de grace when he spotted the Iraqi crew bailing out of their disabled tank. Accordingly, he deliberately held his fire until they were all clear, not willing to kill them in cold blood: their fight was over, after all. His next missile left the tube and immediately soared gracefully upwards, another complete "rogue" missile on that day. Before he could re-engage the target, he came under quite accurate artillery fire as his aircraft was showered in sand by a near miss and had to change position rapidly. Having dodged around the desert at low level, he finally shook off the unwanted artillery attention and moved to re-engage and "kill" in order to upgrade the hit to a "K" kill — a fully destroyed target in all respects — the stranded T 55. As he was just about to launch his last missile, to his horror, the tanks turret swung around to point its rather large main gun directly at his aircraft. The Iraqi crew had climbed back into their tank while he was dodging their artillery, not an event he had expected. The split second he launched his missile, the T 55 also fired a 100mm round directly at him. He instantly chopped the guidance wire and climbed to avoid the incoming round. He calmly stated, "It felt just like a freight train drove underneath me". That had been his fourth and last missile (rather than the normal eight carried in European-based operations: a weight constraint imposed by the searing desert heat).

A Gazelle pilot, a "diamond geezer" South Londoner, who was busy around the fringes of the main fight attempting to locate and identify more Iraqi targets, suddenly noticed movement, in the form of a lot of people on foot on an elevated sand berm. Worried it was enemy infantry, he looked at them through his roof-mounted observation sight. It was in actual fact thirty to forty Iraqi women, all dressed in the traditional black burka from head to toe, not what he had expected to find by a battlefield and a surprising sight for him to behold. He was about to dismiss them as "no threat" when they all suddenly stopped in an extended line formation and turned to face him and the aircraft, like a bizarre group of fringe activity war spectators. He obviously found this a very strange and highly unusual movement for women in a "hot" combat zone to carry out as a rather well organised group activity. As he looked again, three of the "women" suddenly produced RPG 7s from underneath their burkas, knelt down and fired at him and his aircraft. He dodged them by some quick manoeuvring and when he looked again, the women were busy shuffling themselves around, thereby making it impossible to accurately identify the firers. "Like a herd of penguins at a disco", was how he described the sight to me. The crew immediately put some distance between themselves and the "penguins". Even if the aircraft had been armed (the crew actually had a pistol each, complete with a whole five 9mm rounds each between them as the sum total of their "firepower"), there was absolutely no way on Earth they would have engaged a bunch of women, despite the well-disguised soldiers hidden in their midst.

The only slight down side to our collective euphoria — we had after all given the Iraqis a rather bloody nose, despite them having executed a very professional and obviously well-planned ambush — was that, unlike us, once nightfall came, they could recover and probably repair any damaged vehicles. That small battlefield was still dominated by them, not ourselves. However, never again did they venture out to engage us in such numbers or with such aggression. Until the end of the war they were content to "stay safe" and you simply don't win wars by staying safe and thereby handing the initiative completely to your enemy. Sadly, this simple concept has never been understood by a generation of professional politicians with no military service between them, as our later hasty withdrawal from Iraq would do exactly this, much to the great pleasure and satisfaction of all the insurgents concerned.

Two of our guys were later awarded Distinguished Flying Crosses (DFC) for their actions that day. We felt it should have been significantly more, but much more important, by far, was the fact everyone came back in one piece. If an aircraft had been shot down, all each crew member had was a pistol and five rounds, with minimal escape or survival gear (like most things they had yet to arrive) and our unarmed RAF Puma aside, we totally lacked any form of combat rescue (or emergency medical evacuation) backup, so almost immediate capture seemed a very likely prospect. Although, to be fair, we honestly expected fairly decent treatment from the Iraqi Army, or at least we strongly hoped that would be the case.

On later reflection, it occurred to me that had we been an American unit, this little skirmish would be seen as potentially good box office material, it had so many aspects to it: "action" and the "thrill of the chase" euphoria rapidly changing into tragedy and possible disaster; uncommon gallantry and a successful rescue mission despite being outnumbered and outgunned. In the early days of the 21st Century, our 1980s helicopters had fought 1960s tanks with 1970s missiles on a well-prepared ground of the enemy's choosing and been repeatedly engaged by tanks, artillery, mortars and armoured personnel carriers, not to mention "women" suddenly firing rocket propelled grenades from within a group of "Penguins at a disco". It was in some ways very much a "throwback" in military terms of tactics and equipment, but you fight with what you have and we did it very well and in an old-fashioned, but very British understated manner.

But we are British and being so absolutely politically correct in the 21st Century, such matters wouldn't do, as it might just upset somebody. Whilst the Americans make gritty realistic series such as the Iraq-based *Over There* TV series, with several major league films about both the Iraq and Afghanistan conflicts, all our TV moguls can produce is a hugely inaccurate "Afghanistan comedy" about a "hilarious" bomb disposal team and the far-fetched offering of *Our Girl*. In comparison to the realistic and well-researched American offerings, all are simply rather ill-informed and banal twaddle, verging on the insulting for the thousands of UK personnel who have actually served in our desert wars and made by people with utterly no concept, even remotely, of the true nature and demands of modern war. Just another stereotypical and inaccurate representation of the UK military, combined with immensely large applications of artistic license. But then again, it probably simply reflects the almost complete lack of comprehension of the military and all things associated with the armed forces that is such a wide gulf spread across modern British society. An ever-decreasing handful of professional soldiers fighting remote and ill-defined wars on behalf of a very comfortable, increasingly self-centred and relatively prosperous society, literally a world away from the collective and national experiences of our fathers and grandfathers, after all.

This is perhaps a good indication in a quite visible manner of the differing attitudes of the two nations, and their respective feelings towards the military and recent conflicts in several ways. Many former British soldiers, myself included, openly envy our American counterparts in that respect. In UK the military covenant is, in the main, only a populist and politically-based catch phrase. Yes, it is slowly getting better (after over 12 years of war), but we have a long, long way to go compared to American society and the superb support given to both their serving and veteran personnel alike.

Post debrief, I bumped into Bird, he had just returned from the field hospital and he looked very tired. "Well done, Bird, you did a good job today," I said.

"Actually, Boss I might be in the shit," he responded. I asked him to expand. Essentially, when they landed at the hospital with a helicopter full of badly wounded men, some of them seriously burned, with blood literally running out of the doors, one of the first people to the scene was a UK tabloid newspaper photographer. He was about to take several close-up photos of men in great suffering, burns, blood and all, when a big Scottish hand suddenly reached out and grabbed his lens, pulling him forward to find Bird waiting at the other end of his camera for him. Bird, in essence, had then quite loudly and aggressively suggested to him that he go away NOW, in short, sharp jerky movements, or he would shove his camera somewhere where the sun doesn't ever shine. He also mentioned something about "Blood money for low-life ghouls who weren't fit to clean a British soldier's boots". As a piece de resistance he somehow forgot to give him his camera back until all the wounded were safely in the hands of the waiting medical staff. Suffice it to say that the photographer in question didn't get any "action snaps" that day. No doubt our media colleague was rather upset at our total ignorance of press freedoms. I can't say we lost any sleep over his total loss of images, or income.

I had problems keeping a straight face. Luckily it was dark, so I tried to play the serious officer card. "Did you actually punch him then?" No, he said, mainly as he felt it might kill him apparently (he was one of Scotland's larger sons after all). "Don't worry, I'll sort any fallout," I said. Looking after your soldiers is bread and butter stuff in the Army and anyway I totally (if discreetly) agreed with him and his actions. Whilst I was mildly surprised and pleased he hadn't actually damaged the photographer in any serious life-changing way: remarkable restraint for Bird in full flow, all in all. Plus, on a purely personal note, I didn't particularly want to have to explain to the CO how one of my SNCOs had hospitalised an authorised member of Britain's media: not a conversation that really appealed to me, frankly. "Get some sleep," I said. "Tomorrow's another day." As he disappeared into the darkness I quietly wondered to myself, after a day like today, what exactly will tomorrow bring?

Our new location was quickly named "the Walled Garden" by the troops, somewhat of a misnomer, as while the entire location (600 x 600 metres roughly) was surrounded by an eight to ten feet high wall, with only one entrance gateway, but there was absolutely no garden. We did however have a large semi-ornamental fountain in front of the only building in the compound, which was large enough for several soldiers to sit on the edges of it and dangle their feet in the water: quite a luxury in many ways. We also discovered a recently abandoned large yellow JCB digger. We viewed this major windfall as a nice little gift to us from a "grateful Iraqi nation". This extremely useful "gift" was quickly brought it into British military service, digging trenches and some minor defensive earthworks and thereby saving literally hours of physical labour for the vast majority of us. Shortly afterwards it was discreetly "transformed" into a British military vehicle by the liberal application of sand-coloured paint and some homemade military number plates. It then stayed with us for the remainder of our time in Iraq, eventually being quietly left at the quayside of Kuwait City's docks after providing a sterling and very useful service to its new owners. Presumably it was then re-liberated by either Kuwaiti dockers or other troops. We neither knew nor cared, it had done its work for us and, far more importantly, UK beckoned at that stage.

As our newly-found asset was put to work digging our trenches, I became the Force Protection Officer, in addition to my other "day job". This essentially encompasses all aspects of physical security to personnel, infrastructure, key equipment and suchlike. Orders are orders, so I just got on with it and together with Mike, established a Force Protection Office in a rather plush (in that it had no significant holes in either the roof or any of its walls) abandoned building we quietly commandeered. This job had come as a somewhat of a surprise, but the Army expects its officers to be extremely diverse and adaptable in their skill set. Besides which, I had been a soldier for my entire adult life and soldiers are very accustomed to the ethos of "fast balls".

The key focus was now on protecting our newly acquired oil fields from sabotage or indeed any form of attack by Iraqi SF, intentional "stay behind" troops, totally committed Fedayeen or any isolated pockets of still enthusiastic stragglers. A lesser, but important, concern was theft of major assets by the ever present Bedu who were sheer market leaders at "acquiring things", and were still paying remarkably little heed to our war. The irrelevant manner with which they just dismissed and frankly blithely ignored our fairly major invasion never ceased to impress me during our time in Iraq. They continued to view the entire war and the ensuing disruption as both nothing to do with them and a significantly major window of opportunity to "do some business".

We reorganised our little team in light of the fairly diminished CW threat and our new-found real estate. Mike and I would run the office — booking vehicles and personnel in and out, keeping track of their progress and suchlike — whilst ensuring everyone received a full "threat brief" so no one wandered innocently into avoidable high-risk areas. We had a secure field telephone installed which allowed us to talk to other units around the area (an old, but reliable and proven system called Ptarmigan) and link in with our local Intelligence Corps gurus as necessary. Nellie was quickly added to the FP team, which in turn gave me a certain amount of freedom to visit other units and face to face with them over any issues. Local knowledge is always invaluable, indeed priceless, in any country and all forms of conflict from a military perspective. Bird was back to "stagging on" with his night shifts — we hadn't given up on Saddam and his perceived CW threat totally: for all his well-known faults, you couldn't really accuse him of lacking either determination or perseverance, plus a large amount of cunning combined with total and proven amoral ruthlessness in even larger amounts.

I took the opportunity to visit Brigade HQ and ask for an update regarding the local population, the likely threat(s) to us and suchlike. Threatwise, nothing had changed really and our front line was fairly static in nature, mainly regular bouts of small artillery duels and a lot of inconclusive foot patrolling by us, not much of a war really in comparison to the massive armoured thrust by the Americans or 7 Brigade's ongoing large-scale scrap down in Basra. As for the locals, we knew next to nothing about anything at all, which did rather surprise me. After all, we had been sitting on our hands in Kuwait for weeks waiting for our vehicles and equipment to finally arrive from the UK, so why hadn't we bothered to find out anything of interest about the local population and the surrounding area which we knew, well in advance, that we would both capture and hold? After over 3 bloody decades in Northern Ireland in order to finally force the IRA to their knees and force them to ask the British Government for peace talks, we, of all people — the world's self- proclaimed Counter Insurgency experts — should have realised the immense value of local knowledge in terms of population sympathies, where the "hard areas" were in relation to the population centres, figures of influence and religious divisions and so on ad infinitum. But it rather appeared that we had rapidly forgotten all these hard-earned lessons with consummate ease. We had invaded Iraq, after all, being rather publicly advertised as "liberators, not conquerors".

I was quietly speechless. The best a young and well-meaning Intelligence Corps NCO could do was to inform me that "There are a lot of Marsh Arabs around". I said thank you to him out of pure manners, but my mind was concurrently saying, "No shit, Sherlock?" I suppose our mindsets had been severely influenced by comfortable and quite recent memories of the tens of thousands of Iraqi soldiers, who had surrendered so easily in 1991, but then they had been defending Kuwait, not their own soil, and Saddam had given them a simply impossible task in military terms. The resulting ease of the coalition's swift victory against battered and demoralised defenders is very well recorded. But this was Iraq itself, not the "lost province" of Kuwait and our collective lack of knowledge and intelligence, to me at least, was frankly quite shocking.

I wandered off in a somewhat disillusioned, but unsurprised, manner in an attempt to find Andy for a brew. He was still attached to Bde HQ and living somewhere in the large compound they had commandeered, acting as our Liaison Officer, which meant he was our eyes and ears amongst the staff. A job that was always good for picking up some snippets of real intelligence, or at least a bit of interesting military gossip over "cunning plans" and the ever-present desire of the Paras to "jump in" anywhere and for any reason at all, irrespective of any form of military logic it seemed to the rest of us. Some things never change in life. I tracked him down to a small office which he had commandeered as his digs and where, he proudly proclaimed, he had sole and personal use of the only working flush toilet in the entire Brigade HQ, a little gem he kept (understandably) literally to himself. I was impressed, for a mere captain this was a coup almost on a par with annexing a small Balkan nation, though being sworn to secrecy over its very existence was possibly somewhat melodramatic.

We chewed the fat over our little war so far. Bde HQ had managed to enhance their force protection in a major manner by finding a forlorn troop of three US Marine Abram's Main battle tanks, who had been left behind after running out of fuel in the American haste to drive on and capture Baghdad. The Brits had offered them food, shelter and water if they agreed to act as force protection for the HQ location and provide a massive (if static) deterrent to any would-be Iraqi attackers. The US Marines in question were now patiently waiting for someone in the USMC to actually notice they were missing. Unbeknown to them, we Brits were taking our time in actually mentioning their presence to the American chain of command as three large and friendly tanks were simply rather nice and reassuring to have around. Quite a coup, really, as we had nothing in our brigade that could remotely match them for sheer firepower, and the locals far less so. I told Andy about our recent little battle, which apparently had seriously annoyed the Paras, purely because it was a fight (any fight would do in 2003) and they hadn't been invited, which hadn't gone down too well with them, unsurprisingly. The Paras' chance for some major league combat would duly arrive in 2006 during the Army's optimistic entry to Helmand Province on the now infamously ill-defined and poorly resourced reconstruction tasks, as 3 Para's tour rapidly then become the sheer stuff of military legend, often consisting of isolated and vicious, desperate fights verging on bitterly contested last stands, when they would gain the absolute respect of the entire Army (and even the Royal Marines would acknowledge this, albeit quietly). The sheer desperation of the fighting became rapidly well known, despite the MOD's repeated attempts to impose a total media ban as the "reconstruction task" instead became the fiercest fighting since the Korean War (no doubt 3 Para themselves would have preferred some major reinforcements), but in 2003 their frustration was markedly palpable.

Meanwhile the Royal Irish had discreetly taken over the oil town of Rumaila and in effect turned it into what everyone now commonly referred to as "Royal Irish Town". Having been brought up in the midst of the long decades of the troubles in Northern Ireland, they were ideally suited in maintaining security and understood intuitively the "hearts and minds" aspects of running a small town with a divided population of two tribes. Not a long way from the Falls Road/Shankhill Road divide in some ways, I mused, but rather lacking in pubs and drinking clubs by comparison. Yet again they had been sharper and more proactive than other units: a theme had developed and they had also been rather active in arresting any and all suspected Saddam loyalists in the bargain, often led in person by their now rather media-famous Commanding Officer. Between the Royal Irish and our borrowed US Marine Panzers the chances of any violent mischief happening locally was rather remote and quite probably an almost certainly suicidal venture in the bargain.

I also learnt that the Black Watch had carried out a highly successful night raid to capture the Ba'ath Party leader who, we believed, had ordered the murder of the captured Royal Engineers, in the process killing a large number of his fighters and effectively destroying organised resistance in that area. He would, I was informed, be brought to justice accordingly. At the time we were ecstatic, but now I suppose it means he became a free man the moment we withdrew from Iraq. The American or Israeli Governments would simply never give up in a quest for justice, of any kind, frankly. If a similar event happened to their soldiers, then their killers would then have to look over their shoulders fearfully for the rest of their days on this earth. But we all quietly knew that our own government didn't have the same view point regarding British soldiers' lives: after all, we had already made covert deals to pardon, or issued "no prosecution" letters to hundreds of convicted Irish Republican murderers well before 2003. This is now publicly well known, so the precedent had been set by our politicians, albeit discreetly, that the lives of British soldiers (and Northern Irish police and prison officers alike) were of small value from their lofty perspective. Strong words are, after all, just sound bites which soon become just worthless noise if they aren't capable of being backed up by robust action, especially when you are dealing with very violent and often absolutely ruthless men.

Andy had a very good overview of the wider situation across Iraq, essentially that the Americans were regularly meeting some major resistance, but almost solely in built-up areas, mainly from fanatical Fedayeen fighters. As the Vietnamese had discovered a generation ago, when fighting Americans it's best to "grab them by the belt" and get in very close to them, in order to avoid their overwhelming firepower being used against you effectively. Large built-up areas were simply ideal in that respect and the Iraqis were neither military fools or suicidal fighters.

The Iraqi Army had developed a tendency to quietly melt away when the massive American armoured juggernaut appeared on the horizon and meanwhile the Republican Guard was still waiting for the inevitable final showdown, probably somewhere on the approaches to Baghdad, whilst the American Air Force simply bombed Iraq at will, the Iraqi nation's air defences having been simply obliterated with singular ease, which made me wonder if Saddam would ask the French for his £2 billion plus back, as it really didn't appear to be money particularly well spent. A new addition to our coalition force, in the form of the Australian SAS had now joined in the fun too: Iraq was quickly becoming a large SF play ground in some respects and 7 Bde were busy strengthening their hold over Basra to the extent that a city of over one million people was almost cut off from the rest of the country. Our Royal Marine chums were in the process of capturing Um Qasr, Iraq's sole major port and our own Pathfinders had long since been launched deep into Iraqi territory in a modern-day Long Range Desert Group role, a role well suited to them and one they were no doubt enjoying immensely.

Otherwise our infantry were dominating "no man's land" by aggressive patrolling and the Iraqis stayed in the built-up areas they held, plugging any gaps with artillery fire or tank main armament, but not coming out to fight, much to the chagrin of our infantry, who knew their colleagues in Basra were "doing the business". What made things even worse for our Paras was the fact that these were mere county regiments, "hats" in airborne parlance (county regiments don't exist any more as the Army is no longer big enough to justify them and the steady process of enforced amalgamations — mainly to reduce manpower and thereby save money — has finally defeated over 300 years of these units being the epitome of the very backbone of the British Army). The Black Watch in particular had achieved a major psychological domination over the Iraqis, who had never, in their wildest dreams, dreamt of meeting adrenaline-fuelled screaming Jocks at close quarters, complete with fixed bayonets. Meanwhile highly accurate Light Infantry (now the Rifles) snipers were something else the Iraqis had never encountered before and lethally paralysed daylight movement accordingly: not for nothing are well-trained and disciplined snipers greatly feared for their discreet and covert ability to "reach out and touch people". Not to be outdone, the Fusiliers had been busy capturing bridges and approach routes into Basra and the two Challenger 2 Regiments (the entire British Army now has only three regiments of tanks) were simply terrifying the enemy's forces and must have appeared seemingly invincible to the Iraqi defenders.

On the "plus" and bigger picture side, the Iraqis had been pushed far away from both the American Main Supply Route (MSR) together with the oil fields and just lacked either the military capability or the sheer will to seriously attempt to disrupt either of these key facilities in any major way. As these were our two main tasks as a brigade, this was a highly successful "result" for us, so the US Marines were accordingly content with our efforts, despite our own infanteers' increasing desperation to find, or simply make, a worthwhile scrap with anyone, anywhere and any time. Our next task was to get the oil fields working again as soon as possible and to ensure no one interfered with this task. This surprised me as we were still in the process of capturing Basra and the Americans still had quite some way to go in terms of "liberating" Baghdad, but apparently this had the "highest sanction from Whitehall", so our job, as always, was to simply "make this so". Quite how we actually achieved this was something we weren't too sure about as none of our soldiers were "oil field reactivation qualified": this wasn't a skill much in demand within our regimental system.

The guided tour of the flush loo over and having no wish to again listen to the brigade staff's ongoing machinations to "jump in" somewhere/anywhere and for any reason, no matter how bizarre or simply unwarranted, I drove back to the Walled Garden through a very friendly and peaceful Royal Irish Town. At each junction we were besieged by local kids loudly asking for sweets or chocolate from us: British soldiers are very much a soft touch for kids, and these kids knew that fact extremely well. Soon afterwards, we were all banned from the practice of throwing gifts to the kids as we drove past when a small boy, utterly desperate for a few squares of chocolate, blindly ran out into the road and was run over and sadly killed by one of our vehicles. I doubt if his tragic and pointless death was ever even noticed by anyone outside his immediate family and a handful of soldiers. In a bizarre way this could be construed almost as a microcosm of our efforts in Iraq: well-meaning on our part but with totally unforeseen and unintended consequences for the population.

Surprisingly, this didn't cause any particular animosity between us and the local population, the general reaction was one of a stoical "Inshallah" — God's will be done in effect — an attitude and mindset I would become increasingly familiar with when I would later regularly meet the Iraqi people at very close quarters and also, a view of life that was, in so many ways, completely utterly at odds with the commonplace values held by the majority of Western people in the 21st Century.

But this small tragedy aside, we were utterly in control and the local population seemed fairly pleased to see us in the main, albeit in a very reserved manner. We may have been on the fringes of the war in pure military terms, but our mission had been quickly and relatively smoothly achieved while the Iraqi Army seemed very content to keep its distance, so life wasn't too bad overall. Bearing in mind the ill-equipped way in which we had launched our piece of the invasion, we, as usual, were making things work in a typically British military manner and neither our allies nor our enemies had realised just how short we were of "mission-critical" equipment and basic supplies such as ammunition. Our bluff, it seemed, was working fortunately for all of us.

All the same, we were in essence quietly content with our war so far and we confidently expected our numerous logistic issues to be resolved — or at least we fervently hoped so. It was becoming apparent to even the most junior soldiers that we were increasingly bluffing our case. In the meanwhile, we constantly strived to conceal all our logistical shortcomings and military weaknesses from the Iraqis. It was, after all, in our best interests for them to remain blissfully ignorant of these matters.

We had some minor excitement the following day when a member of the QM's staff, whilst clearing out a small abandoned building, found a large number of documents, including an old-fashioned, quite large and rather bulky ledger. On inspection these documents were all in Cyrillic and the ledger contained various personal details of some two dozen or so

Russian nationals, including passport photographs and numerous other details which we could only guess at as none of us could read the Cyrillic writing. The fact that these had been, or so it was assumed, hastily hidden from view in light of our imminent and uninvited arrival, merely added to the little mystery. What were Russians doing here? This was the basic question bandied around by the troops.

Our local Counter Intelligence Section duly hotfooted it across to our location, no doubt excited with grand visions of nefarious activity by the FSB or some such similar shady Russian Intelligence Agencies and subsequent pats on the back all round from number 10 Downing Street et al. Sadly they were all to be rather disappointed. Once the documents were translated, as it became rapidly obvious that these people had actually been the key engineering staff who had maintained the Russian-installed pumping equipment and the large ledger was actually merely an old-fashioned record of their individual salaries and expenses. They had, it seemed from the documents, maintained oil production across the GOSPs until the last safe moment, leaving only when our invasion seemed a certainty and a mere question of when, not if. Then they had quickly driven to Baghdad and a discreet flight back to Mother Russia. Not quite the international spy ring or covert military advisors our intelligence people had been hoping for. Oh well, we all thought, back to WMD and chemical weapons all over again.

With the local excitement over, I went back to my day job of force protection and my little empire was growing in a singularly expediential fashion. We had now been given 2 FUCHS vehicles, lightly armoured and quite large 6 wheeled German-made (and therefore Teutonically reliable) vehicles, whose normal job was to provide early detection and warning of chemical and biological agents being used on the battlefield. Each came with a 3-man RTR crew and a 7.62mm machine gun fitted, a useful addition (they even had some ammunition, a rather pleasant change for us all). Their warning role was now considered superfluous by our hierarchy, which struck me as fairly strange, bearing in mind the yet unlocated WMD was the stated reason for our invasion. Never mind, I thought, you have now some light armour to play with, so make the most of it before someone notices and demands them back.

In addition, I was now in sole charge of tasking the two Pumas to deploy lightly equipped troops to do helicopter-borne "Eagle VCPs" (vehicle check points, a technique used a lot by us in N Ireland) short in duration and very unpredictable to any observer, especially from any potential insurgent perspective. This was an ideal delivery means for conducting snap inspections of traffic along the main routes in our AO. The RAF guys were happy to do whatever was asked of them as long as they could fly most days, so now I had a very small, but proactive, Air Force too: more boys' toys, my life was on the up, I concluded. To complete my force protection empire, the Royal Artillery Air Defence Troop, having no actual Iraqi Air Force planes around to shoot down, were now employed in the infantry role and I was to dictate and coordinate their patrol programme in conjunction with the armoured and helicopter-borne patrols across the southern GOSP area. Almost my own private army, I quietly thought to myself. Most importantly, at least for me personally as later events would prove, was the unexpected arrival of George (not his real name), an ex-Special Forces SNCO, who had spent a large chunk of his adult life as an undercover soldier "across the water" as Northern Ireland was commonly referred to by the older guys. His plain clothes unit, "the Det" as it was then known, had been chiefly responsible, along with its RUC equivalent and a handful of other clandestine units, in forcing an informer-riddled and almost impotent Provisional IRA to the bargaining table, in the form of their Sinn Fein colleagues. He was an extremely capable, proactive and utterly reliable soldier who became in all respects my right-hand man in the months to come during our time in Iraq, not to mention a friend for life into the bargain.

George had, along with Keith, been originally attached to the Pathfinders, but taking their farmer's Land Rover deep behind Iraqi lines was just a leap of faith too far, so they had been redeployed to work with the Paras. They had been briefed to meet the Paras at one of the smaller bridges which crossed the North Hammar Canal, except no one actually told the Paras about this arrangement. Instead, they spent the night alone on an isolated bridge and the only visitors they had was a blue and white Volkswagen camper van at the far side of the bridge, which disgorged several heavily armed men in traditional Arab dress and a Mexican standoff promptly ensued for the rest of the long, dark night. George had picked up a bug of some kind, so spent a lot of the night vomiting as the two sides nervously eyeballed each other across the darkened and deserted bridge, before the mysterious VW Camper and its passengers finally left just before the arrival of first light.

After this potentially quite messy incident, which could have gone disastrously wrong for two isolated British soldiers in light of recent tragic events, various recriminations flew around in a very heated manner. Eventually Keith and George were quietly reassigned to different duties and any and all possible mistakes were vehemently denied by our HQ staff, including the very existence of the VW camper. Strangely enough, one of our Lynx aircraft then spotted a blue and white VW van parked in a fairly odd location for a camper van in an active war zone. As they duly flew over to investigate, they were promptly shot at by RPGs and AK 47s, all of which luckily missed after some rapid evasive manoeuvring by a rather surprised Lynx crew, which proved to most of us that the camper van did really exist. Nevertheless George came to join my team as part of the "Camper van incident reshuffle".

As the FP empire expanded, Mike suddenly took it upon himself to re-lay the office floor in his limited off duty time, which was composed of literally thousands of small one-inch-square coloured tiles. I was astonished that he had decided on this self-imposed mission: his explanation was simply, "It helps pass the time in this place". the result being that all his spare time was spent patiently working on a massive jigsaw puzzle and his personal quest to make the FP Office look more presentable. The RSM thought this was highly commendable and promptly took a sympathetic sledge hammer to the ornate fountain as it had suddenly become a health and safety hazard, which seemed a bit strange in light of our surroundings and the stated activities we were here to conduct. Nevertheless, he seemed to feel much better for destroying it singlehanded, even if the troops were rather miffed by its total destruction for extremely debatable reasons. But the Army traditionally does things which seem illogical on a very regular basis and soldiers simply accept this as par for the course so the fountain was soon forgotten by all concerned and more important matters occupied our collective minds, along with the normal routine of life in a conflict zone.

As we began to establish a patrol routine around our oil fields a captain named Gerry (not his real name) just appeared one day in the office. He was from one of our more discreet intelligence gathering organisations and an ex-ranker like myself. In a quiet and discreet conversation, he explained he needed to "talent spot" amongst the local Marsh Arabs with a view towards recruiting agents for post war activities in Iraq in support of UK Plc. Agent handling to gather "HUMINT" (Human Intelligence) as this is known, is one of the few military activities left in which the UK are market leaders, due chiefly to our experience of decades of discreet practice in Northern Ireland. This wasn't new to me and it was refreshing to see someone was looking beyond the actual war-fighting stage. George was the ideal partner for him with his own background, so we quietly rearranged our armoured patrols accordingly and gave Gerry a seat as an "observer". Agents (or "Touts" as the Irish Republican movement called them) tended to be motivated by one or more personal drivers: money (a time-honoured favourite over the millennia); a simple desire for revenge; patriotism (a rather quaint notion in the 21st Century for a lot of UK citizens); a wish to be on the winning side and good old-fashioned blackmail: again a perennial crowd-pleasing favourite from the days of the lengthy Irish "troubles".

The obvious recruiting logic was that Saddam Hussein had been the arch Nemesis of the Marsh Arabs in recent decades, especially after the first Gulf War, so UK Plc figured they would be a fertile breeding ground for a small legion of willing agents, essentially for reasons of simple revenge (and perhaps some money thrown in on the side). "The enemy of my enemy is my friend" is a hugely popular and eternal saying within the Arab world for very good historical reasons. In hindsight, I now realise that I never actually formally asked the CO if Gerry's activities had been authorised by him, but no one seemed put out by his presence in the slightest, so we just carried on regardless.

The RTR crews of the FUCHS were more than happy to explore the Marsh Arab area, Armoured Corps soldiers thrive on mobile warfare and unlike their RAF Regiment colleagues in the then Joint NBC Regiment, who were trained primarily to defend large fixed installation such as airfields; the Army guys in contrast simply detested static guard duty operations and were more than happy to conduct mobile patrols. So, we planned and conducted a mixture of mobile, foot and helicopter-borne patrols, all coordinated with other units in the oil fields. If nothing else these were all very good means of deterrence: as a standard operating practice we assumed that everything we did was being observed by someone, somewhere, looking for any and all forms of weak spots that they could exploit or attack at a time and place of their choosing. This was an activity we later found the Taliban to be absolutely past masters at in conducting, being possessed of an almost infinite amount of patience, or so it seemed to us at times.

However, our little "Marsh Arab" campaign was disrupted by the strange case of the missing red Humvee almost at the outset. The CO suddenly announced that a US General was verging on the incandescent due to an unknown Marsh Arab stealing a US military Humvee which had broken down within our AO and then been abandoned by its crew. Not content with this "present" from the American forces, he had then painted it bright red (we were all baffled as to exactly where the average Marsh Arab found lots of bright red paint in the desert, but no one had the moral courage to actually ask that question) and was now, allegedly, driving it around the local villages in a direct affront to American military dignity. Again no comment from any of us. The CO gave firm direction that we had to find and recover this Humvee ASAP before the coalition became somewhat of a laughing stock amongst the local populace Accordingly a number of assets, including helicopters, were tasked to find the red Humvee in the middle of a war. Again, no comment from any of us, mainly I think because we were trying to work out when April Fool's day was due. This was however a serious matter from the perspective of our joint hierarchies, so we spent a couple of fruitless days looking for the absent Humvee which no one, at least from our side, ever saw and of which not a trace was ever found. Our best guess was that Mr Marsh Arab suddenly realised that the Coalition may not actually have found the entire affair too amusing and he probably had no fuel to keep it running either, so it was quietly buried or just disassembled to its smallest component parts in some remote part of the AO. In private, we had a sneaking admiration for this cheeky individual and we were secretly pleased that he never got caught. Eventually more pressing events took over and the mysterious case of the red Humvee was discreetly dropped from our "to do" list.

Following this, George came back from a patrol one long hot day and said abruptly, "There aren't any."

Baffled, I asked, "There aren't any what?"

"Any fucking Marsh Arabs," he said.

"Marsh Arabs?"?I replied. This was becoming a quite baffling conversation and very quickly too, I thought. The nub of his comment was that instead of the estimated 20,000 plus Marsh Arabs we had expected to find in the neighbourhood, we had found a mere 2-3,000, all widely scattered and living in small and quite isolated villages. Our agent recruiting pool was therefore significantly smaller than anticipated and moreover they simply didn't trust us or our intentions in the slightest. During George and Gerry's travels (unsurprisingly, Gerry spoke quite good Arabic) they met a similar tale time and time again. After the last Gulf War of 1991, they fully expected to be promptly liberated by the West and had made their feelings forcibly, often violently, known towards the local Regime members and their overriding dislike for Saddam in particular and the Ba'ath Party in general. Unfortunately, the West never actually came, so Saddam systematically drained their ancient marshland homeland, arrested and murdered hundreds of people and forcibly internally deported tens of thousands more. We now dealt with some of the embittered remnants of these people, who simply didn't trust us and merely wanted to be left alone by anyone and everyone in relative peace. No amount of flattery, cajoling or plain old-fashioned bribery would, it seemed, induce any of them to help us in any respect whatsoever, and so ended our cunning scheme to quickly and easily enhance our Humint capability in the marshlands of Southern Iraq.

Gerry simply took it in his stride and decided to therefore cut his losses and concentrate on the nearby city of Basra in his quest to recruit some other Iraqis, who he was convinced would appreciate the offer of extra money and new opportunities once the entire Iraqi banking system and the national currency collapsed post conflict, which it duly and rapidly did, along with most other aspects of Iraqi society and the bulk of its infrastructure and several accepted social norms. Accordingly, he quietly wandered off to make lots of new friends on behalf of our nation and we never saw him again. No doubt he was very successful in recruiting his embryonic agent network: empty pockets, bitter tribal rivalries and ancient religious hatred, fear and a hungry family are all far stronger drivers than most of us can ever possibly begin to comprehend within the UK, securely wrapped up as we all are in the socially overarching joint blanket of the welfare state and the NHS.

I received an unusual request from the Troop Sergeant, Sandy to his pals, of the Air Defenders shortly afterwards. On a routine patrol into the local desert, they had discovered an "MTLB". This was a Soviet made tracked and lightly armoured vehicle, designed to tow an artillery piece but used by the Iraqi Army as an armoured personnel carrier, as the Republican Guard got all the best and more modern equipment. This particular MTLB looked like Swiss cheese apparently, courtesy of the US Marine Corps and their varied weapon systems. The guys had inspected the burnt-out vehicle and were amazed to find the Iraqi machine gunner still at his post, although very dead and badly burnt he was still "covering his arc" as soldiers say. Around his feet were numerous empty cartridge cases and belted machine gun ammunition link: he had gone down fighting, whoever he was, against no doubt overwhelmingly impossible odds. This was something any and all professional soldiers can both respect and identify with, the ultimate "bottom line" for any soldier and no doubt the defining moment of your military career when you suddenly realise with startling clarity that your time to die has now arrived.

In this, by Western standards, remarkably cramped tracked vehicle, the gunner has to stand within a small enclosed machine gun turret. The patrol's view was that he had stayed at his post to allow his crew mates a chance to escape safely on foot from their immobilised vehicle. No other bodies were found in or anywhere near to the destroyed vehicle or the surrounding area. They respectfully asked to "borrow the padre" in order to give him a fitting burial. I was very moved by their request and agreed immediately, going to see the padre straight away. He, by denomination a Roman Catholic priest and also a highly-accomplished combat barber, agreed wholeheartedly and was also very familiar with Muslim burial practices. The following day, early in the morning to avoid the inevitable desert heat, the padre and his Airborne Air Defenders escort drove to the place of the unknown gallant Iraqi soldier's last stand to reverently lay him to rest, wrapped in a makeshift white shroud within his deep and lonely grave, marked only by a solitary wooden post. (It simply goes without saying that any form of cross would have been both totally inappropriate and hugely insulting towards this anonymous and courageous Muslim soldier).

Only Iraqi officers carried leather identification discs, Iraqi soldiers or "Jundi" as rank-and-file soldiers are known in most Arab armies, simply weren't deemed worthy of any formal means of identification, so all we could do was report the dates concerned, location and vehicle type, with any possible unit markings on the vehicle, which hopefully provided some clues to the long-gone crew's identities to the Red Cross, in the vague hope that his family could be somehow be traced post conflict. Our, probably vain, hope was that eventually they could somehow be informed of his lonely and gallant demise in the empty southern desert.

Personally, I think that highly unlikely at best. However, at least he was laid to rest with dignity, respect and reverence as a very brave soldier by fellow soldiers, albeit by his erstwhile enemies and foreign "non-believers". Like ourselves, he had been simply striving to do his duty for his comrades, his people and his nation, and we could all quietly and wholeheartedly identify with that.

The combination of air, foot and mobile patrols worked superbly well in deterring any would-be saboteurs from tinkering with our newly owned oil fields, to the extent that I was able to visit LSA (Logistic Support Area) "VIPER", a large USMC facility with the aim of both gaining and sharing intelligence regarding our respective operations in our neighbouring areas. I managed to tag on to a platoon of Paras, led by their company commander who were conducting some training for the US Marines. At this stage of our various wars, the Americans still regarded us as the counter insurgency experts and were keen to pick our brains accordingly. Equally we (and our egos) were very keen to be their willing mentors. It was very pleasing to be perceived in such a role by our lavishly supplied and well-equipped allies and went a long way in (quietly) confirming our own self-perceived superiority.

On arrival at this large, sprawling tented complex, the Paras duly went off to teach the US Marines about such heady stuff as vehicle check points, IED awareness, building up the "Pattern of Life" routine in your area of operations and other bread-and-butter stuff from our lengthy Northern Ireland experience. The aim of the exercise was primarily to better enable the Marines to protect a large and highly vulnerable fuel pipeline they had simply built as they advanced relentlessly into Iraq. No one on earth does logistics like them, after all, and they had literally thousands of ravenously fuel-hungry armoured vehicles to supply daily. In effect fuel was their sole Achilles' heel and the pipeline therefore required effective security: not a particularly thrilling task, but one which was critical to the success of their mission. Large-scale war requires logistics to match and successful armies are the ones who plan accordingly to enable (and far more importantly, sustain) the dramatic stuff so beloved of television companies.

I met my USMC counterpart who took me directly into their HQ, which to me, was like a scene from the *Star Trek* TV series in comparison to our own HQ. All their Command tents were linked together by enclosed canvas corridors and plastic walkways. Computers abounded, along with chilled water machines: air conditioning and electrical lighting was everywhere, most of which was a distant fantasy for us Brits, only a mere hour's drive away physically but at least a decade away technologically. The entire TOC (Tactical Operations Centre) was dominated by 3 large screens, onto each of which were shown the exact and current "Blue Force Tracker" icons (all American fighting vehicles electronically emitted their location and other information constantly by encrypted means), with a detailed electronic air overlay (American aircraft had a similar system on board), all suspected and known Iraqi positions, along with all major geographical features completed the display. We, by comparison, had two wooden trestle tables pushed together and covered by a large map in our headquarters. I decided not to mention that to these ultra-helpful and highly professional Marines as they held us in obvious respect, if not a slight element of awe. I didn't wish to disillusion them and I was personally far too embarrassed to admit any of our Stone Age command and control methodology to them.

Eventually, in Helmand, we caught up with them in technological terms, but in the process lost a large proportion of our formidable reputation in the eyes of most senior American officers following our embarrassingly hasty withdrawal from Basra. This was gradually accompanied by the loss of an awfully big chunk of our war fighting equipment and therefore capability, along with some 20,000 soldiers who became quickly unemployed to "balance the books" in the aftermath of two very expensive campaigns in fiscal terms. The human cost was also extremely expensive, to say the least.

We swopped intelligence (known as "Int" in British and "Intel" in American, classic two nations divided by a common language stuff). The Americans had very recently had a large logistics convoy ambushed in Nasirayah and well over a dozen American soldiers were killed or captured, due in essence to them simply taking a wrong turn and driving straight into a heavily armed bunch of Fedayeen. The American troops, confined in large and bulky logistics vehicles within a confusing maze of narrow streets, were simply a gift to the enemy and one they gratefully accepted. Mistakes in war are costly: of all mankind's assorted activities it does not forgive human error and "fighting fair" is simply not one of its concerns and to pretend otherwise is simple naïve 21st Century folly. All the American male prisoners were reportedly executed apart from a lone female soldier who was spared for blatant propaganda reasons, I'm very unsure of the accuracy of this report now, but then it was a stark reminder to us all that the Geneva Convention was hardly proving to be a popular document amongst our enemies. The Americans had faced a ferocious battle in Nasirayah, it was not a mere speed bump and unbeknown to all of us, a small PF patrol had literally fought for its life far to the north of this disputed city (much to the utter amazement of the US Marines) in a gallant but unsuccessful attempt to secure a desert airfield for a British helicopter-borne assault deep behind Iraqi lines.

It appeared to me that American and British soldiers alike seemed to be exempted of their human rights (allegedly one elite US Marine "Recon" soldier had been crucified alive: this was almost certainly just another military rumour, but the US Marines themselves took it very seriously), quite an anachronism considering our society's ever-growing obsession with this topic. Surprisingly to us, the Americans gave us an unconfirmed report of a small Republican Guard Special Forces Team observing and reporting on coalition movements and reputedly attempting to rally the local populace into action against us in our own area of operations (AO), but mainly failing, it seemed, due to the total lack of interest of the various villagers in our area, at least. However, we didn't take their report particularly seriously as it was our patch after all and we had heard nothing of this enemy presence whatsoever. Otherwise, we both had the usual problem with Bedu stealing anything that wasn't bolted down. We Brits just took their activities as a matter of course for this part of the world, but the American Military hierarchy viewed it as a portent to possible more serious action against them. Our advice was to just move them on, rather than start shooting them and accept them for what they were, rather than make them our enemies: we had enough of those already. I wasn't ever made aware of any Bedu being shot, so I rather hope they took our advice. Either way, in a very short span of time Iraq would have lots of people for the coalition to shoot at, and on a regular basis, as it transpired once Saddam's regime fell, rather dramatically, from grace.

The Paras had a rather good day teaching the US Marines some good old-fashioned "Northern Ireland" stuff. Over ten years later the tables have rather turned somewhat in terms of counter insurgency capability. Americans are, by their very nature, remarkably fast learners and tend to think outside the box far more easily and more often than the British Establishment seems able to do (and sack senior officers far more readily than we ever dream of: Americans seem to also lack the old-boy network that still discreetly pervades the upper echelons of UK society). We, of course, utterly resent that idea, but coupled with the savings-driven decimation of the UK's Armed Forces after the Coalition came to power, our place on the world's military stage has waned rather considerably, as both our enemies and allies alike have noticed. The truth can hurt at times and robust and aggressive statements by yet another bellicose British politician has zero effect on any potential enemy on a distant battlefield or conflict zone without the actual physical means to back those words up, should military action prove necessary. But that appears to be of little consequence to a generation of professional politicians with little or no experience of the real world and, as always, there are no votes to be gained from "defending the realm" any more. To be fair, the British public rightly expects someone else to protect them, be that the police or the armed forces, but the actual "how" it isn't a topic they worry about really, they expect it to somehow happen as part of both their birthright. Ultimately, very few people protested loudly about large scale cuts to the numbers and capability of either the police or the armed forces.

On our arrival back at our location I was briefed that we had an important escort task tomorrow: some American contractors, all oil men from Texas (where else, I thought?) together with a small US military escort, would be crossing the border at a prominent border village called Safwan and conducting an estimate as to exactly when they could get the southern Iraqi oil fields producing on a large scale again. My job was simply to ensure they were met at the border crossing and escorted to the oil fields safely. It would be awfully embarrassing to get some American civilians killed, after all. I duly tasked our Air Defenders to meet and greet them: mainly airborne qualified troops, after all and extremely well trained, they were utterly reliable, well-motivated and guaranteed to give the right first impression to our guests. We were, after all, America's most important ally and the British Army is, by definition, an immensely proud organisation.

George and I went to meet our guests the next day at an empty house we had recently commandeered for them to use as an office and base. To say we received somewhat of a surprise is an understatement. Our American "roughnecks" (they hailed from the famous Red Adair's company in Texas) dwarfed their 20-man escort with 15 immaculate, white 4x4 civilian vehicles, all with shiny Kuwaiti licence plates, each sporting large antennas and packed with cool boxes, electrical fans,

Gatorade energy drinks and various types of civilian and military equipment. I meet their leader, a confident and gregarious individual, who explained he had 30 roughnecks and 20 US Military personnel, ranging from US Air Force bomb disposal (just in case the USAF had left any unexploded "presents" lying around), US Army Explosive Ordnance (to deal with Iraqi booby traps and the like) and some rather large, taciturn US Marines for "general security stuff". It was quite an impressive mixture to behold. He explained they would commute from Kuwait City daily and would like to link up with his British escort at 0600 daily at the Safwan border crossing. As much as I wasn't too pleased at my best troops being tied down with this, I agreed: my brief was, after all, to give them "whatever they need and immediately". Once I agreed to that, he casually mentioned he would need them all day, every day to look after his guys, as we Brits had agreed weeks ago, apparently. I now felt totally gazumped.

I asked him how long he and his team had been waiting to get into the oil fields, expecting an answer of 2 or 3 days. It transpired they had all been sitting in a five-star hotel in Kuwait City for over 6 weeks, which had pleased his own Texan guys immensely, it being well equipped with an varied assortment of both eager Eastern European hookers (not the Rugby-playing variety) and generously-stocked bar facilities, whilst his military guys, Spartan types all, had made maximum use of its well-equipped gym and swimming pool to get "combat ready". Slightly different from our own experience in Camp Eagle, I thought. I was quite taken aback at this news, especially as this had apparently all been arranged several months ago between our respective governments. One of my NCOs loudly voiced our thoughts and said, "So this isn't about oil then?" Cynical, perhaps, but this was not a duty I had anticipated to undertake during the "liberation" of Iraq and these guys, unlike ourselves, were all exceptionally well prepared, superbly equipped and fully briefed for their task ahead. This obviously wasn't a spur of the moment, last minute deployment for them, by any stretch of the imagination.

The Americans quickly became part of our daily routine. In terms of meeting and escorting, they seemed quite professional at what they did and our soldiers didn't overly mind as the Americans gave them various titbits every day: magazines, iced drinks, the eternal US gifts of chewing gum, candy and so on. Apart from a couple of incidents when they felt a powerful and immediate need to shoot some locally scavenging Bedu — which our guys politely stopped and merely moved the Bedu on elsewhere — we had no great conflicts of interest with them after all. I stopped getting involved and just kept a general eye on things from a distance. The boys were all over it and no soldier really likes an interfering officer, no matter what army they are serving in. Meanwhile the ponderously moving Iraqi T 55s had almost reached their designated "line in the sand" to launch their long-awaited attack, it had become blatantly obvious by now that they had chosen the lightly equipped Royal Marines as their target, no doubt hoping to inflict as many casualties as possible and then rapidly get back to the relative safety of the urban Basra sprawl.

Just in case they did manage some form of a breakthrough, our CO had been busy pestering people to engage them with our ageing, but still highly capable, Lynx anti-tank helicopters, or at least put us on immediate stand by to "go and get them". But lots of units were all chasing good "kill figures" and smashing up a whole bunch of enemy tanks was simply exceptionally good for both regimental publicity and promotion profiles after all, so the local competition was remarkably fierce for the opportunity to "neutralise" these particular Iraqis. Essentially a rather large queue was forming to kill them. Meanwhile they rumbled on unknowingly, towards a growing number of people patiently waiting to kill them with extreme prejudice and associated violence. Ignorance can be bliss, after all. I had grown a sneaking admiration for these faceless, but obviously determined, Iraqi tank crews, but they were all now simply a collection of moving targets in cold military terms. Nevertheless I felt they deserved my respect, a modest modern-day version of saluting those about to die.

Our American guests surprised me by their boss asking for a helicopter. He explained that he really needed to check out the main pipeline for any major damage, as the pipeline ran across into 7 Brigade's area of operations, who were meanwhile rather busy with their efforts to capture a city with one million inhabitants from a lot of very determined defenders. I had to decline and remind him that we were fighting a war here and I rather doubt if one can be released, I simply replied politely. He persisted and eventually I agreed to approach my CO over the matter, much against my better judgement, but I had given him my word and the concept of personal honour mattered greatly to me (and still does, an extremely old-fashioned concept I know). I duly approached the CO and, as expected, he gave me a resounding NO, part of the reason being the impending "breakout" by the Iraqi T55s, but mainly that we needed all our helicopters to find and, when possible, engage the Iraqi military. The Army's then doctrine was "Find, Fix and Strike": we had no UAVs (drones, as the media consistently refers to them), so manned reconnaissance helicopters were vital for the find function and our TOW missiles, being very accurate with a decent range of 3,750 metres, were a much sought-after weapon system to strike the enemy once found. Then again, we also had a lot more heavy equipment with which to actually strike the bad guys with back then.

I went back to the American oilmen's boss. After all, I thought, he's just a civilian. He must know he is pushing his luck, surely? I explained the reason behind the refusal, expecting him to merely say okay. On the contrary, he was furious and told me, "I'll make a phone call and get one given to us," and stormed off muttering things like, "One lousy helicopter for one lousy day." I thought it was just transatlantic sour grapes and reported back that "it hadn't really gone down too well as answers go". A couple of guys laughed and we immediately went back to the work of winning our little war.

Several hours later I was abruptly summoned to see an obviously quite angry CO, who informed me that "my American" could have his helicopter tomorrow morning and I would have to personally fetch him here to brief the pilot of his allocated Gazelle helicopter prior to the flight over his route, what exactly he needed to see and so forth. He was blatantly not in the mood for any questions from me and discussion was obviously not an option. I nodded, quite dumbfounded and rapidly left the CO's office, wondering who the fuck had he rung? I immediately drove to their location to be met immediately by a rather smug Texan wearing a beaming "I told you so" expression all over his face. He was obviously expecting me and his persona was now all pure sweetness and light. I asked him who he had rung. "The Embassy, of course," he replied in a matter-of-fact manner. It transpired a senior Embassy official had then promptly rung the Commander of the MEF, (who was the overall commander of all British troops after all), and then, as the saying goes "Shit runs downhill" until eventually our CO was bluntly ordered to give up a helicopter to the American civilians exactly as they had requested. Orders are orders, after all.

Accordingly, the next day he, with another civilian colleague, flew the length of the pipeline at a height of about 20 feet in one of our Gazelles and gave it a visual check over, whilst all around them the British Army continued its determined efforts to capture Basra from its now quite desperate defenders. Their leadership had recently been devastated by the first operational use of the RAF's "Storm Shadow" — basically an air launched cruise missile — when our SF in Basra had spotted a major gathering of Saddam's most faithful taking place, and called in a very effective air strike, with between 100-200 leaders of all levels apparently being killed or badly injured, a singularly massive blow to their leadership and command structure. Ironically, by now they were using their clearly marked civilian ambulances to resupply their positions and move reinforcements around, knowing full well that we would not attack ambulances, a clear breach of the Geneva Convention. However, then and for the rest of our long years of assorted wars, this and any other similar conventions seemed increasingly only to apply to us and our allies. Our Americans returned happy and full of praise for the pilot, amazed that our helicopters were totally unarmed. The Americans simply bolted weapons onto everything, which in the Balkans especially had amused us at the time. However, we too would shortly do exactly the same, albeit far more slowly as we discovered the bitter realities of increasingly vicious modern counter insurgency warfare in an assortment of harsh desert environments.

The long-awaited Iraqi "Armoured Thrust" finally came and went in the same period. The T 55s advanced, just after dawn, in the traditional "extended line" assault formation, only to find to their (quite brief) horror a complete squadron of Scotland's cavalry waiting for them in their 64-ton fighting machines, along with whatever anti-tank weapons the Marines could muster. All hope of achieving surprise now gone, the Iraqi tank crews now played their part to the bitter end by dying to a man, the lucky ones as supersonic 120mm projectiles punched with consummate ease through their elderly armour plate, while the unlucky ones just burned alive. Unbeknown to them, the previous evening, Royal Engineers had quietly and rapidly built a bridge, protected by the infantry, over the large water obstacle the Iraqis had firmly believed would prevent our tanks participating in the coming attack and the RSDGs had discreetly moved into their pre-designated fire positions based on a good intelligence-driven estimate. It was a classic example of "all arms co-operation", something the British Army excels at and which allows it to punch above its weight in comparison to similar-sized armies.

Sadly, this very quality, combined with a wholesale "can do" attitude by the UK Military would tempt our ego-driven politicians with their personal ambitions to be significant players on the world stage into ever more demanding and gruelling operations and almost take the Army to breaking point in 2006-09 when fighting two geographically separate, increasingly bitter, simultaneous wars against extremely determined and well-equipped insurgents in distant countries. Under-resourced and inadequately equipped in many ways, the result was several thousand casualties, our inglorious and very hasty exit from Iraq and ever deeper involvement in Helmand Province, when the vast majority of the very numerous wounded would mainly be unreported by either the media or MOD, with only the dead receiving full media coverage.

The armoured encounter itself was brief, brutal and totally one-sided. In theory a military clash of armour, it was, in sporting terms, akin to the 1st choice England International Rugby XV taking on a pub team of middle-aged amateur players who just turned up at Twickenham. In Europe with all its battlefield clutter of forests, hills and urban areas, a tank crew would typically engage its target at a range of 500-1500 metres, in the billiard table topography of the desert region engagement ranges of 2-3000+ metres were commonplace.

The Iraqi tanks never even got into firing range to respond, the 21st Century British Challenger 2s with vastly superior optical sights, a simply fearsome main armament and manned by crews with far superior training simply wiped them out in their 1960s vintage and poorly maintained tanks, with no survivors. The Marines joined in with some MILAN anti-tank missiles to complete the party and the Iraqi plan ended in total and utter disaster. The wider morale and pyschological effect on the defenders of Basra was huge, and they simply had no answer to British tanks, some of the worlds finest infantry and our intelligence-gathering capability. No one had any great sympathy for the Iraqi tank crews, after all their mission had been to kill British soldiers in as large a number as possible and they had tried their very best to achieve that. Respect for their determined efforts, yes, sympathy, no. It simply isn't an emotion that war tends to breed very much. Ironically this success by our tanks would be almost their last act. Unlike all our major allies in Afghanistan we didn't take any tanks to Helmand and if you don't use it you lose it, so they slowly became rusty and unserviceable due to lack of spares and trained crews. Now the Army is pushed to produce forty or so battle-ready tanks, a far cry from their domination of the Basra battlefield indeed.

Some days later a series of obviously reproduced, rather grainy photographs mysteriously appeared in our brigade area. These were essentially a variety of Royal Marines posing on the destroyed T 55s, some with massively burnt, charred and mummified Iraqi tank crewmen fully visible and centre stage, in effect side by side with the victorious Marines who had helped to kill them. It was basically a blatant (and rather successful) attempt by the Marines to wind our Paras up, who had played no part at all in this action: internal military "hearts and minds" in effect. A very dim view was taken of the photos and all were rapidly destroyed whilst the Paras gave the entire affair a damn good ignoring.

With the Americans inexorably closing in on Baghdad despite some desperate attempts to stop them, it was increasingly obvious that Baghdad would soon fail, and with it, the regime. Meanwhile in Basra, the city was tottering under the effects of a modern piece of siege warfare by the British Army, with aggressive tank raids being launched into the city almost with total impunity by 7 Brigade. It was blindingly obvious that the Iraqi regime couldn't hold on for too much longer, but they also didn't seem to be particularly short of men who were still quite happy to die for their leader. I rather hoped that wouldn't be a popular career choice for hundreds of thousands of Iraqi males of fighting age once the war was over, but I wasn't at all convinced that would prove to be the case.

Due to an enthusiastic and regime devoted Iraqi Army Sergeant becoming the first suicide bomber (or martyr bomber to some, as suicide is strongly defined as a sin under the teachings of Islam) to cause Coalition (American in this case) casualties in the Iraq War, we had made some minor alterations to the Walled Garden, just in case. As the Force Protection Officer, I really didn't want a visit from a human cruise missile on my watch. Only later did we find out that a surprising number of these bombers, in both Iraq and more particularly Afghan (no ex-soldier calls Afghanistan by its full name) had financial incentives to vaporise themselves and that not all of these bombers were actually volunteers. Indeed, many of these "martyrs" were young men who were forced to seek "redemption" following some social misdemeanour and, rather than lose their name and be exiled from their family and tribe, chose — or were persuaded to by the Taliban — a violent ending to their young lives. Later would come ISIS/Daesh with their eager volunteers for death, but that lay in the distant and frankly unimaginable future in 2003.

Our now fully integrated "donation" from a grateful Iraqi nation, the now sand-coloured, popular and very military-looking JCB digger, complete with its false, but very authentic-looking military plates, dug some rather deep and very wide ditches on either side of the approach road to our walled compound. We also used the significant amount of earth spoil to form a tight chicane system which would force any potential vehicle-borne martyr bomber to slow right down on his (I say "his" as we, the Coalition, had yet to encounter any female bombers, that particular aspect of Jihadist womens rights and equality also still lay in the distant future) approach, at which point we would (hopefully) rapidly and repeatedly shoot him numerous times, hopefully causing him to detonate prematurely, thereby thwarting his attack, admittedly rather violently ending his life in the process, but other options were and still are remarkably limited in dealing with this particularly challenging scenario. Suicide bombers, by definition, aren't overly renowned for their interests in logical debate, based on our modern Western democratic model of liberal values and intrinsic human rights as important tools in resolving modern conflict.

All of this sounds rather simple, but this was also in a period of relative military innocence and long before the Taliban developed the technique of using multiple vehicle-borne suicide bombers as a very effective means of blowing entry points to allow them mass access for an immediate follow-up attack, as demonstrated by the very successful mass jail break from Kandahar Citys main prison in 2008 when over 300 captured fighters escaped, and occasionally against UK patrols and bases in Helmand Province. This tactic later became one adopted by Islamic State in breaching the defences of both the Syrian and Iraqi armies. Like IEDs previously, we would soon discover that weapon systems such as these successfully migrated across borders with consummate ease, and like other Western Armies we in turn would be forced to rapidly change our training methods whilst simultaneously attempting to re-equip and re-organise to deal with new asymmetric threats such as these for the "post-Iraq" world.

Unbeknown to me and everyone else as we enthusiastically dug our primitive but highly effective defences, the Black Watch — who had just captured Basra's airport, along with the RSDGs in a purely Scottish affair — would have the dubious honour of becoming the very first British unit to be badly hit by a devastating suicide attack the following year during their hugely difficult and often highly lethal deployment towards the Baghdad area. Subsequently in Helmand Province, the Guards, Paras, Mercians and Rifles would all lose young soldiers to these human cruise missiles. Each of these occasions forcibly reminded me again of the prophetic words of a US Army Ranger Officer I had served with in Macedonia in 1999 prior to our Kosovo intervention; "You Brits are okay, but you are all just too wrapped up with Northern Ireland and you've never had to deal with huggers". The "hugger" (named after the face hugger creature in the *Alien* film series) referred to suicide bombers, which the Americans had met in both Vietnam and Lebanon whilst we, as an army, had been entrenched in Northern Ireland and firmly focused on Irish Republican bombers, who very (very) much definitely preferred life to a heros funeral.

At the time, I had firmly dismissed his words, partly due to overt national pride on my part and partly due to the fact he was a Somalia *Black Hawk Down* veteran, where the American Military had learnt some very hard lessons and the American Military overall was none too proud of the outcome of that little campaign, to the extent that it was widely considered as "unfinished business" to a degree. He also referred to Somalian fighters as "skinny-looking guys but tough fighters who don't particularly mind dying, which tends to even the odds a lot", another comment I dismissed in my naïveté. All these years later I am sure that rather a lot of British soldiers now have their own very similar words to say following our own lengthy experiences in the villages and districts of Helmand Province we were ultimately responsible for during that long campaign.

About the same time as we dug these defences, we received a water and ration resupply from Kuwait, delivered by the Royal Logistics Corps (the RLC: the "Really Large Corps" or simply "Loggies" as they are commonly known) in the form of two supply trucks which had brought us several pallets of bottled water, a couple of pallets of field rations and — surprise, surprise — a couple of hundred yogurts in a variety of flavours, very much a surprise delivery. However the well-meaning loggie who had added these luxuries to our supplies had obviously forgotten that yogurts don't perform too well in temperatures of approximately 40+ degrees (somewhat of a design flaw inherent in most yogurts, sadly), and as the trucks weren't remotely refrigerated or even covered by a tarpaulin to give any semblance of shade, all of them had had either simply gone off or in many cases just exploded during the long hot journey north, which gave the truck's interior the bizarre appearance of having been deeply involved in a large-scale and many-sided, multi-coloured paintball fight.

The young lance corporal in charge of the detail came by to "book in", so that his unit would know he had arrived safely, part of our function being to log and follow vehicle movement across the area. The chemical threat was long forgotten now, we all happily believed the infamous "chemical trip wire" was now Baghdad. Accordingly, the approaching Americans would get seriously slimed, therefore not our problem. Somewhat callous perhaps, but a truism across the entire division. However, our vehicles were taking the odd pot-shots here and there. Initially it was "spray and pray" stuff (essentially *spray* the air with bullets and *pray* that Allah will guide your bullets) from pro-Saddam loyalists. All Iraqi adult males seemed to have an AK 47 or two tucked away somewhere, as we were rapidly discovering. But it wasn't too coordinated at this stage, so while we didn't dismiss this resistance towards us, we didn't worry too much about it either.

After taking a lot of ribbing over the messy delivery of explosive yogurts, he had left his 3 soldiers to unload the vehicles. Even so, he was quite sheepish. Personally I thought it a sign of how stretched we were logistically that he had been sent north with such a small, ill-protected and vulnerable command. After we had booked in with his unit, he hung around with the classic symptoms of a young NCO who wanted to ask a grumpy ex-ranker officer" (and one from a strange regiment to boot) a question he felt important, but wasn't sure how to poise the question without possibly getting shouted at. (In 2003 the Army still actually shouted at people. It's highly frowned upon now as being somewhat non-PC in the post-Afghan British Army).

Eventually I broke the long deadlock by asking, "Is there anything else I can help you with, Corporal?" He explained that he, as the NCO in charge, had five rounds, but his soldiers (all privates) only had three each and he wondered if there was any chance we could spare him and his men a few bullets, please? I was simply flabbergasted. This was a military version of Oliver Twist asking for more food in the orphanage and they still had a long and exposed drive back to Kuwait awaiting them. I told him to wait there and asked Mike to make him a brew whilst I tried to rustle up some ammo. Sadly, all I could acquire was 200 rounds of machine gun ammunition, a different calibre round from those of our rifles, but useful in the, probably vain, hope they had a GPMG mounted on one of their vehicles. True to form for this war of liberation of ours, they didn't, so it was simply a well-meaning but useless gesture on my part. I sincerely apologised to him, quietly cursing all the growing legions of assorted incompetents back safe in UK who had sent our young soldiers into harm's way with so little means of self-defence. He just shrugged, smiled and just said, "Thanks for trying, sir." He was obviously used to disappointment, as indeed we all were by now.

I asked him what his plan was if he got ambushed en route to Kuwait. His laconic reply was, "Try and drive through it. If that fails abandon the wagons, just run like fuck and hope we don't get caught." I couldn't say much to that bleak plan of his, I just wished him well. I was utterly disgusted and speechless. After he and his soldiers left, I sat in a quiet fury, not wishing to engage in petty conversation. We were just blagging it and hoping the Iraqis didn't catch on to how ill-equipped we really were. I really and honestly just couldn't understand why bullets and body armour and medical kit et al — all pretty basic stuff for any modern European Army — was just so bloody difficult for the MOD to provide us with, verging on the impossible, it seemed. Were we just too inconsequential to all our combined government agencies for them to arrange the provision of these key supplies? This was a major land war after all, not another repetitive exercise on a wet Salisbury Plain against yet another fictional Redland invader with majorly aggressive designs on the good people of Devizes and Warminster.

Later that evening, when I was finally talking to people again, I was informed that a company of Paras would be arriving as our attached Aviation Company, essentially the military term then used for an Infantry Company tasked with guarding our helicopters against enemy ground attack. The penny had finally dropped in Brigade HQ that we provided mobility, speed of reaction and firepower, all things the Brigade badly lacked due to the ad hoc manner in which we had been so hastily dispatched from UK. My piece was to give their officers a briefing on the area of operations, possible threats and suchlike. This should be fun, I thought: the Paras basic and collective DNA was to attack things, it really didn't matter what or whom, and do so ultra-aggressively. They despised being tied down with such "Hat tasks" as defending key assets or resources from the bad guys, so I expected a bunch of very grumpy Paras when they eventually arrived sometime after dark. Deep joy all round.

The short but stocky major in command of the Para Company turned up with his platoon commanders (three young lieutenants) in tow whilst his men got themselves quietly sorted somewhere off in the darkness. Britain's paratroopers simply thrive in Spartan surroundings: after all their idea of a militarily perfect situation is a 360-degree fight with an enemy who both outnumbers them and surrounds them on all sides (far more targets for them to "brass up" to use a favourite phrase of the Paras for shooting at people). Love them or leave them, they are confident, competent, superbly fit and aggressive soldiers who are simply frightened of no-one. Every nation needs soldiers such as these, I would argue personally.

After we had done the standard military formalities piece, he asked where and when the Int Brief would be held. I pointed out our little building and agreed a time with him. He asked if his section commanders could come too, another 9 NCOs, which would make it very cramped but I could hardly say no to him. British Infantry Section Commanders are all fit, intelligent and very highly motivated young corporals essentially, and accordingly a key aspect to military success in all operations which involve British troops and the Army duly invests a lot of time, effort and money in their very intensive and demanding training.

So, at "dark o' clock", Mike and I squeezed 13 tired but warlike paratroopers into our small and now rather cosy Force Protection/Intelligence cell, Mike giving a brief, along with one of our clerks from the Adjutant General's Corps (the Army's HR people). Together they had painstakingly built up a localised "Who's Who" directory of Iraqis whom we believed to be "players" (disappointingly, no one else had bothered) in terms of their positions, function and likely influence in a basic attempt to unravel the complex web of tribal relationships in our area, which is central to simply everything in Iraqi society. This was dry stuff but also simply key to all our operations in many ways. The Paras were far more interested in where the weapons were, likely enemy sympathisers, etc and did any heads need cracking together perhaps?

The lean, muscular and serious-faced young corporals reminded me of a pack of impatient and hungry wolves just waiting to be unleashed on their unsuspecting human prey. Utterly professional soldiers to their core, they asked a long series of thoughtful and serious questions before retiring to re-join their company, composed by now mainly of sleeping troops, no doubt. These were very much the archetypal "rough men" that society required to stand guard over them on the city walls so that good citizens could sleep soundly in their beds. Liberty, democracy, security and freedom are not an automatic birthright, but pampered citizens often forget that. The bulk of Roman society probably never imagined the barbarian hordes eventually storming the gates over a millennium ago.

I wandered down to our darkened HQ to make sure nothing else was outstanding prior to catching up on some Zs myself, as the saying goes. All was quiet there and we made military small talk or just "talked bollocks" in soldier speak. War is much more about waiting than any other major human activity. One of the things we discussed was an attack on the previous night against 2 RTRs "echelon": an echelon is the military term for the logistics part of a combat unit of regimental size, responsible for ensuring the front-line companies or squadrons are resupplied with fuel, ammunition, food, water, clothing and absolutely everything else they require to live, fight and operate. Right on cue, the night sky outside our "Big Top" tent complex burst into brilliant luminance. Suddenly our location resembled Wembley Stadium during a night kick-off match, but without the thousands of chanting fans. Instead a broad variety of urgent-sounding voices yelled, "Stand to, stand to"! The parachute-borne "white light" illumination (there is now a black light variety invisible to the human eye but very useful in conjunction with night vision goggles, or NVG. This would become our preference by far in Helmand Province. After the government actually bought NVG in large amounts, we had precious few sets for the Iraq Invasion) This action normally precedes a pre-planned and sizeable night attack and we were lit up like the proverbial Christmas tree: a rather vulnerable sensation in a war zone, frankly.

The militarily perennial cry of, "Stand to" was rapidly taken up across the entire location: it's a command that can be given by anyone if or when a soldier (any soldier) believes an enemy attack is seconds or minutes away (due to its serious nature, not a command given lightly, but British soldiers are taught to always err on the side of caution as lives can literally be in the balance). Sleeping soldiers everywhere grabbed their weapons and equipment and sprinted towards their pre-designated "Stand To" position and prepared to fight, dressed mainly in varying combinations of shorts and T-shirts: speed of reaction, not fashion or personal comfort, makes the stark difference between success and survival or defeat followed by possible death or capture.

As I was already in my Stand To location at the HQ — admittedly totally by coincidence — plus I had my weapon and equipment with me, I therefore had the luxury of an opportunity to quickly assess the situation fairly calmly. I stepped outside, where I could view helmeted heads peering anxiously over their respective trench parapets, like lemmings guarding their burrows, the thought randomly occurred to me. I watched the later arrivals sprinting and diving into their JCB-dug trenches, semi-dressed and breathless with the race to cover their designated arc of fire and with the loud "encouragement" of the NCOs echoing in their ears, no doubt. Our perimeter wall did not seem to have been breached anywhere and absolutely no gunfire was being exchanged. To state the obvious, either activity would generate a very noticeable amount of noise, whilst the illumination rounds floating above us were slowly flickering into darkness one by one until the darkness finally regained control of the night again. What was going on here? I thought to myself and walked back into the command tent, where the signallers were busy sending and receiving a variety of reports and returns, when one of them shouted, "Message from the Paras. That was their mortars, they were just bedding the base plates in". We looked at each other. This was a classic case of the Paras thinking, "Let's wake all the hats up for a bit of fun", and once someone had realised the amount of activity/chaos this had caused, including lots of people running around in the dark with live ammunition during ongoing total confusion, suddenly thought, "Oh shit, maybe this isn't funny".

There was no point in getting any more excited, we all knew no one was going to own up to this little prank and a thousand and one excuses would doubtless rapidly be trotted out: poor communications, radio battery problems, signal interference and so on. In terms of relative pointlessness, it would be rather akin to any of our politicians admitting, over a dozen years later when Iraq was struggling to cope with the ISIS invasion, that perhaps the 2003 invasion of Iraq and the ensuing chaotic violence was a major factor in the birth and subsequent rise of ISIS; something that is never ever going to happen.

Accordingly, we got around to the business of telling everyone, "False alarm, stand down", either by field telephone or radio, until it came to the turn of the group of soldiers who manned our bulk fuel vehicles (not the best job in a war zone admittedly), colloquially known as the "Bowser Boys", when it suddenly dawned on us that we, the HQ element had absolutely no communications, at all, with them in their location. We later discovered this was good old-fashioned human error in the form of, "We meant to lay line, but then we forgot to" school of mistakes. Nonetheless we had a group of 20+ soldiers manning their trenches in the darkness, fully expecting a ground attack. You cannot blame soldiers for doing exactly what their training dictates, especially in rapidly changing circumstances. Even more so when they are tired and sometimes confused by a recent series of probably violent events. This could be emotional, we realised.

To make things even more "fun" their relatively distant position (no one wants ammunition or fuel vehicles very close by, for obvious reasons) had been very poorly sited by the Warrant Officer in charge of "local defence" and he had merely put the troops in a nice circle of trenches to give "all round defence", which sounds great in theory, except if they opened fire from two thirds of the trenches they would shoot directly into other friendly positions, including our HQ and various sleeping areas. What works well on Salisbury Plain with blank ammunition tends not to be overly brilliant on operations where shooting with live ammunition is predominantly of the "Two-way Range" variety, as thousands of British soldiers would discover over the long years of conflict.

After a long quiet pause the senior captain present finally said, "Someone is going to have to simply walk over and tell them." More silence. None of us particularly fancied approaching spooked young soldiers on a dark night. Several "Blue on Blue" fatalities had occurred on similarly dark nights in Northern Ireland exactly that way over the years. "We could just shout across," someone ventured.

"Or just leave them until daylight," another voice chipped in. I was just glad the Paras weren't around to witness this debate: they'd love this as entertainment went in the military. Most people agreed we couldn't leave them there and just hope that no one opened fire at what they may perceive as hostile movement and shouting was deemed quite unreliable (and amateurish, frankly). A brief impasse reigned as we decided on our best course of action.

One of the HQ Officers looked at me and suddenly blurted out, "They're your soldiers," to which I replied, "I thought they were Her Majesty's troops and therefore the Army's soldiers rather than mine personally."

"No, I meant they are mainly from your regiment", meaning augmentees for the duration of the Iraq Invasion. We were obviously going into a tactical comedy routine here and had the entire tent's attention completely now.

"Which means what exactly?" I replied, though I had already guessed the punch line.

"They know you and probably wouldn't shoot you if you went over there and told them to stand down."

Fucking probably? Thanks very much I thought to myself. Everyone seemed to be looking at me, cue pregnant pause. Sod it, I thought, the blokes will all die of boredom in the trenches at this rate.

"Okay then," I replied nonchalantly (which I did not feel in the slightest), "Wait here and if they do shoot me, you're on next as the senior bloke here. Are you okay with that?" He nodded ever so slightly and with that vague gesture I spun around and walked briskly outside, thinking to myself, what the fuck am I doing? However, I was past the point of no return in terms of personal pride, I was therefore committed, as the saying goes.

I took a deep breath and walked slowly towards their position, holding my rifle vertically in my left hand, hoping to appear non-aggressive and therefore not a threat (as threats inevitably get rapidly neutralised). It was a moonless night: people simply don't realise how dark and cold the desert really is at night, it was no tropical balmy evening, quite the opposite. The silence struck me and my footsteps sounded incredibly loud, or at least they did to me at that time and place. As I got closer I called out in their direction, "Lads, it's me, Captain Mac. Hold your fire and don't shoot," having no better idea appearing in my head and we were a bit past the password stage in excitement terms, I figured, so I continued to loudly repeat this several times.

As I got closer I could make out two or three helmeted soldiers pointing their rifles directly at me. I remember thinking to myself, "I hope no one gets twitchy fingers right now". I decided to stop at this point: trying to walk straight into their position would be tempting fate, I thought. I slowly knelt down onto one knee, rifle still held vertically trying hard to be "Mr absolutely no threat to you whatsoever".

"Lads, it's Captain McGee. The stand to was just a false alarm, so apply your safety catches everywhere. You can all stand down." No response at all, they still all determinedly pointed their rifles at me. Bloody great, I thought.

A broad Glaswegian accent suddenly rang out. "Lads, it's Captain McGee, don't shoot him!" I recognised the voice, it was Del, a fanatical Glasgow Rangers fan and a very capable young NCO from my own squadron back in Yorkshire. I've never been so glad to hear broad Glaswegian in my entire life!

"Hello, Del," I called out to him. "It's definitely me, so tell the boys to apply their safety catches everywhere and stand down, please. Who's with you?"

"Me, sir," called out yet another Scottish voice from the darkness. I immediately recognised it as a young soldier named Joe, "The man from Lockerbie" and a promising young soldier.

"Hello, Joe, nice to see you. I should have guessed you Jocks would both be sharing a trench well away from all us English bastards!" That brought a nervous laugh from the trenches, which eased the tension somewhat and I now felt brave enough to stand up.

"Guys, I want you all to apply your safety catches everywhere, get out of your trench and move back to your vehicles and wait there, you can all stand down. All NCOs to me now," I called out. The guys did exactly that. Once the NCOs assembled, in an amazing variety of dress states, but all with helmet, armour and the "fighting stuff" on them, I briefed them what had transpired with our Para "mortars" friends. Telling them to check out all their guys and ensure all weapons were made safe (that is fitted with a loaded magazine but no rounds physically in the chamber and therefore not immediately ready to fire) before the troops got their heads down for what was left of the night. We'd sort the communication and poor trench siting problems in the morning. I was personally relieved no one had shot me and we had all learnt a few more valuable lessons. Most importantly, no one had got hurt. To me at least, simply *nothing* was more important than my soldiers' lives. I was also slowly starting to quietly believe that neither Iraq nor the personal whims of my distant political masters were quite worth dying for either.

Events now began to pick up a considerable speed of their own as the Americans inexorably closed in on Baghdad, the epicentre of all aspects of the regime. Whilst we didn't have access to the ubiquitous Sky News version of events in glorious full colour, our intelligence updates painted a pretty good picture for us all in our own static little corner of the war. Our Para Company who were, to a man, very visibly miserable in their static defence role suddenly cheered up when they were warned off for potential clear-up operations in Basra against Fedayeen diehards who, we believed, probably wouldn't surrender. Even better from their perspective, it would be OBUA (Operations in Built Up Areas) or "FISH" as the boys tended to term it (which colloquially meant "Fighting in Some Fucker's House"), house to house fighting was, by definition, up close and very personal, which just so suited the Paras' collective and innate preference for speed, maximum violence and aggression down to a tee. Accordingly, now we had lots of happy little paratroopers everywhere, who simply couldn't leave quickly enough to do some "FISH" in Basra.

At the same time a small advance party arrived from the RAF Regiment. We discovered that a squadron of them would very shortly arrive to replace our company of Paras. The RAF Regiment are essentially specialist force protection troops whose main military function is to guard and defend static installations and RAF aircraft. In this respect they were much better suited to the task than our pet Rottweiler Paras. The RAF Regiment may look very much like infantry, but they are very insular by nature and lack the same level of combat experience as the infantry/Royal Marines and don't really fit in well with the Army's all-arms concept, much preferring small-scale squadron-sized operations. Ultimately, they are content to discreetly keep their distance from both the Army and Royal Marines, viewing themselves as the "military wing" of the RAF. They have found a distinct niche for themselves providing fairly well-armed ground security and defence for large operational desert airfields since 2003. Whilst the Army and Royal Marines are quite happy that the "Rock Apes" (as the RAF Regiment is widely referred to) like defending things, which means they can leave that rather undesirable task to them, and get on with much more aggressive, preferably offensive, operations of a far larger and more mobile nature and take the actual fight, in whatever manner is required, to the enemy.

One of my NCOs rather unkindly announced, "The war must be almost over if the Rock Apes have come this far forward"! But they tried hard to fully integrate with us, being well out of their usual comfort zone as they already were by being placed under Army command and totally reliant on our own, rather fragile, logistics to support them. By upbringing they were accustomed to their usual "home" taking the form of a large airfield with its extensive and normally quite luxurious infrastructure (by Army standards) as their standard operational area. We gave them our homemade data base of the local players and various briefings on the AO and their perceived role within the battle group. It was decided to give them their own patch to look after, rather than mix them up too closely with the Army. Their strange and, to the Army, unexplained habit of referring to their airmen as "gunners" had already annoyed our Royal Artillery soldiers — where gunner was an officially recognised rank and had been for several centuries or so, rather than some form of catchy nickname, as they had bluntly pointed out to any passing Rock Ape. Boys will be boys even in remote, distant and austere conditions and pride in "the cap badge" runs remarkably deep within the collective psyche of the British Army, even today with its greatly reduced size and limited capability, the cap badge is still a very powerful force and unique source of motivation within the remaining regiments and corps of the British Army.

Meanwhile our brigade had recently received a battery of AS90 self-propelled artillery pieces: massive and highly effective self-propelled guns ("Real artillery" as our own brigadier referred to them), which silenced the Iraqi artillery almost immediately. Their Iraqi opposite numbers knew very well that any more aggressive activity on their part would mean their rapid extinction by way of rapid and devastating counter battery fire from the huge AS90s, so they discreetly "chose life" in effect. Our own light guns were, and are, absolutely fine for dealing with very lightly armed insurgents, such as the Taliban, but were quite easily outranged by anyone with their own artillery and being towed guns, lacked mobility in comparison to modern self-propelled artillery. However, the AS90 was also in an utterly different league in sheer military terms of "weapons effect", associated lethality and "reach" in terms of engagement range. These too have now been largely discarded by the Army to satisfy the government's ongoing need to save defence money post the lengthy, costly and inconclusive Afghanistan campaign and also pay for the new and rather costly aircraft carriers. This was also a clear sign that Basra was fast approaching its inevitable capitulation if 7 Brigade felt they could spare us such a large chunk of their own artillery assets.

The numerous night-time tank raids into Basra, which had been carried out with relative ease and impunity by both our Challenger Regiments, had a major psychological effect on the beleaguered defenders that was very disproportionate to the actual military damage inflicted by these raids. Essentially, Iraqi morale had been eroded to the point of defeatism by 7 Brigade's steady attrition, constant pressure and precision attacks. Only the sheer fanaticism of the Fedayeen and some increasingly vicious punishments had kept the bulk of the Iraqi defenders fighting. With Baghdad on the verge of collapse, Basra's fall too was imminent.

Ironically, we had somewhat of a scare. With the end of hostilities imminent, one of our Gazelle reconnaissance helicopters, flying at ultra-low level, hit some power cables and crashed close to some Iraqi Army positions. Fortunately the Royal Irish (as ever) were nearby and brought the dazed crew swiftly to safety. We really didn't need captured soldiers to worry about with the end in sight, so to speak. Iraqis just (literally) threw up power lines anywhere that suited them, so precious few were marked on our maps. Planning permission and health and safety concerns simply don't feature in building terms in Iraq. Post invasion the British Army would finally buy unmanned UAVs: The Israelis had been using them for 20 years already, with widespread American use in the Balkans and Iraq also) The beauty of UAVs is that there are no captured aircrew (or corpses) to parade before the cameras and then discreetly torture for information. If they get shot down they are casualty free, but then we didn't have that option and our crew had been rather lucky to escape so lightly. The powers that be back in UK demanded an immediate investigation into this crash, despite the nearby presence of the Iraqi Army, complete with artillery and numerous tanks at the time, which perhaps shows how completely out of touch certain agencies in UK were regarding our daily activities.

We were receiving numerous reports of large scale desertions, dissent and widespread hardship amongst the large civilian population and discord between the Iraqi Army and the Fedayeen hard core fighters — modern day siege warfare was wearing them down piece by piece, along with keeping our own casualty bill minimal — but all that would change later in all too short a time. Puzzlingly, we had almost zero reports of the long-range artillery which we had been repeatedly briefed would "slime" us all those weeks earlier when we sat patiently in Kuwait. The options for them were rather limited: either they were amazingly well hidden in the urban sprawl, or they had somehow slipped out of Basra to head north to await an order to fire on the Americans, or they simply were never in Basra from the very beginning. The latter option was not one openly discussed, going directly against the grain of the WMD theme as it did, but post conflict no trace was found in Basra of either chemical munitions or the weapon systems supposedly earmarked to launch them against us.

As Basra tottered on the brink of collapse, one of our artillery patrols had a surprising encounter, a Land Rover-borne patrol spotted four uniformed and bearded men in an older model white Mercedes: an unusual choice of car in our area of operations. These guys were armed with American M16 Rifles or the "Armelite" as it was well known in IRA circles. As they drove towards them, the Mercedes sped off. Our two Land Rovers gave chase as best they could but it was a very unequal contest. Surprisingly, the car made directly for the main two-lane highway towards An Nasirayah. On reaching the highway the occupants were last observed by our soldiers calmly overtaking a massive American Logistics convoy in broad daylight and disappearing towards "An Nas", as the boys referred to that town. The mythical Republican Guard SF team actually did exist after all and had boldly chosen to "hide in plain sight" to make their escape north. George and I were rather impressed by this very ballsy move on their part. We duly reported this to the intelligence chain, which made no comment initially, but confirmed, some two days later, that an American officer had reported seeing a Brit SF Team driving north at high speed, they had even exchanged waves. Fortune favours the brave, irrespective of your nationality or religion, it seemed. Where they went and what they did when they reached their destination, we didn't have a clue and never heard of them again. No doubt they and their skills set later added value to the rapidly growing insurgency against the Americans further north, I later thought once back in the UK.

Meanwhile the Paras had regrouped for their imminent FISH expedition to Basra. We watched them drive their convoy past our location in their little 1-tonne Pinzgauer trucks, soldiers with standing room only, crammed together like human sardines, with weapons and ammunition stuffed into any and all available spaces. The Pinzgauer was yet another vehicle that would be cruelly and rapidly exposed in Helmand Province by the ever-present IED threat, along with the infamous Snatch Land Rovers which were morbidly awarded the nickname, "the mobile coffin", by the troops as first the Iraqi Insurgents and then the Taliban gleefully exploited its obvious vulnerability to deadly effect: from the British perspective, a baffling choice of vehicle against such an effective and sustained threat. The Paras, grim-faced but also happy to have finally found a decent scrap, slowly disappeared on the dusty road to Basra. Everything comes to he who waits, we thought as we watched them leave. We almost felt sorry for the Fedayeen, but not quite. We all fervently believed that their worst nightmares would come true when they met the Paras up close and personal.

This was quite austere expeditionary warfare in the early 21st Century and for numerous reasons: a mixture of technical, security and general isolation. We lacked the instant news facility so taken for granted by most the world's population, so all our information came from UK Military sources, accompanied by the ever-present and parallel unofficial "Rumour Control" network much beloved by British soldiers globally, so part of our job was to counter these rumours as they appeared, which ranged from the bizarre to the ridiculous in nature, especially regarding Mr Saddam Hussein himself, ranging from him flying directly to Russia and claiming sanctuary, to dramatic Fuhrer-style suicide in some dark bunker in Baghdad and almost daily cross-border escapes to a wide variety of Arab countries, with the odd Central American nation thrown in for effect, presumably. No doubt eventually the truth will out, we hoped, and in the mean time we continued to squash the regular outbreaks of assorted rumours concerning Saddam's welfare and whereabouts.

Our embedded reporters were becoming rather bored, which was very dangerous as bored reporters tend to embellish things and then add dramatic little touches, which transforms the often-mundane truth into a worthwhile (if not 100% accurate) story. Luckily we discovered a local bunch of Iraqi parents who had complained over poor school facilities a little too loudly to the regime and promptly had their left ears chopped off as an example to other disloyal parents. The journalists all loved this juicy titbit and left us alone once we'd given them the facts, going off to rewrite this little piece of human tragedy with happy gusto after our accompanying solemn promise that we'd get them into Basra as soon as it fell. As the old saying goes there are three sides to every story: "Yours, mine and the truth". Ironically, one of our patrols had discovered a mass grave containing some 40-plus bodies some weeks earlier, a rarity this far south in Iraq, and we believed part of the chaotic aftermath and associated reprisals conducted by the regime following the last Gulf War. The press would have truly loved that story, but we were robustly ordered to withhold it from them, which we obediently did. Quite why we withheld this information I never knew.

Suddenly and without warning — for us at least, not having any access to any form of global media — we heard that Baghdad had fallen to the Americans and Saddam had disappeared, along with most of his inner circle. Iraqi resistance had, in the main, suddenly ceased and the Iraqi Army, rather than surrender en masse to us, just "went home" (the vast majority taking their weapons with them which, amazingly, seemed to bother no one in a senior position at the time, even though this was well over 250,000 soldiers, a figure excluding the ultra-loyal and almost exclusively Sunni Republican Guard elite troops, the police and the assorted intelligence agencies). There was no great surrender, incredibly few prisoners of war were taken or any particularly dramatic incidents to mark the end of the conflict, it just all abruptly stopped in a quite surreal manner.

In Basra, one of our Lynx helicopters, flown by our American exchange pilot, appeared on Sky News by flying *under* the street lamps along one of Basra's main boulevards while 7 Brigade moved en masse into central Basra to assume control of the city and therefore its population of around one million people. We missed completely the famous scenes of overjoyed Iraqis pulling down Saddam's statue (albeit with the help of an American tank) and pelting it with shoes, a deeply serious insult in Iraq, but we did see our Paras come home looking very miserable and dejected indeed. Whilst they had beaten the Royal Marines into Basra, 7 Brigade politely decided they needed neither of these famous units and equally politely told them both to go home, so the much-anticipated FISH trip ultimately didn't happen after all.

In Basra some fanatics simply refused to accept the defeat of the regime. One Fedayeen fighter hid under a pile of Iraqi corpses to suddenly leap up and engage an Irish Guards section at point blank range, killing two Guardsmen before his own inevitable and rapid death at the hands of their nearby comrades. Another young man did the same but chose to go up alone against a massive Challenger tank at a range of less than thirty metres. His RPG round merely glanced off the armour before the crew replied with a 120mm main armament round into, and effortlessly straight through, his chest. He (obviously) died rather instantly. Over a year later I was at Basra Airport, awaiting a flight home to UK and an Infantry Senior NCO told me how they had wiped out one last "Banzai charge" of over a hundred Iraqis who ignored repeated warning shots and calls to surrender, preferring to die together for Saddam. The rearmost man was armed only with a large screwdriver, as they had discovered whilst checking the bodies for wounded survivors in the aftermath. I found that story both incredibly sad and futile in equal amounts, but also wondered what exactly motivates men to go to their own certain death so willingly? Charging a modern and heavily armed armoured fighting vehicle clutching only a screwdriver was beyond my comprehension: bravery is something soldiers understand and respect, but the British Army hadn't experienced this type of fanatical action since fighting the Imperial Japanese Army so long ago. But this was all prior to us becoming acquainted with the growing threat of suicide bombers both in Iraq and Afghanistan (and sadly now the UK itself) and now is just a relatively commonplace occurrence in Iraq so many years after our invasion to "liberate" the Iraqi people. Islamic State has now taken this to almost an art form as a standard military tactic in their efforts to re-establish a medieval caliphate, a completely unimaginable consequence of our actions at the time.

Our reporters promptly all dashed to Basra to get some decent pictures and stories as fast as possible, all quite green with envy at their colleagues who had made it to Baghdad for the main event. We never saw them again, they rapidly made their way to Baghdad, courtesy of the MOD, hoping apparently to get some decent pictures of the PM or some US political notables. We had now had our five minutes of fame, it seemed, but we had served our purpose in mollifying the media for a few weeks in the desert. Frankly most of us were relieved by their absence and felt they were one less thing to worry about in the very uncertain period yet to come in the aftermath of the regime's collapse.

Despite our militarily impressive success in capturing Basra in a very effective campaign, armies simply aren't designed to run a large city in terms of administration, the judiciary, law enforcement, social services, and other key infrastructure issues such as power provision or waste disposal, transport network and medical/health care, to name but a few functions. A decent army can defend, destroy or capture a major city but not really administer it efficiently. No one seemed to have given any thought at all to this, or made any provision for the physical running of a city with a million inhabitants on a day to day basis. In Kosovo the myriad assorted major charities and United Nations personnel who followed us, like modern day camp followers, into Pristina numbered literally thousands, with tons upon tons of assorted aid to deliver whilst they got the (in comparison very small) city rapidly back onto its feet post conflict. Ominously, at least to my way of thinking, these same agencies were very noticeable this time around by their total and absolute absence. "This could be interesting" a few of us thought quietly: quietly, as it was best not to raise these "non-military issues" too loudly as the Army, aided by the Royal Marines and their US Marine brethren admittedly, had done its allocated job exceedingly well, with relatively few casualties overall despite our breath-taking lack of equipment and key supplies: best not to mention that too loudly either really, at least not if you want a decent career in the Army afterwards.

Some of us also noted that the long awaited chemical trip wire, the singular dominant major "military non-event" of the invasion, as it turned out, had appeared to be a complete and rather large-scale bluff, but one of our very own making, it seemed. Not once had Saddam's regime even obliquely hinted at the possible use of WMD, so could he actually have been telling the truth in saying Iraq no longer possessed any such weapons, a few of us asked ourselves?

This was a very perturbing question for some of us, and one which was quietly discouraged as a discussion point by the more senior officers, but I began to be increasingly perplexed by this possibility. After all, the now infamous government dossier was simply adamant that WMD was in Saddam's possession and this was the much-vaunted Cause Belli for our invasion. If this well-publicised foundation stone for war wasn't actually true, I thought, then why are we doing this? Heresy incarnate for a career soldier like myself, but someone, somewhere perhaps wasn't telling anywhere near the whole truth to either us or our nation, which made me feel like a very, very small military pawn in a political game over which I had neither control or input. I just had to play my minute part in it, wherever the game's masters saw fit to lead us all. I was simply one of the "little people" in the grand scheme of things; the Army is never particularly short of captains and you are taught that from your first day to your very last day of service, ultimately in the Green Machine simply no one is irreplaceable. You may convince yourself otherwise occasionally, but the British Army has been around since the English Civil War and probably will continue to be so for quite a while yet, so individuals, no matter how talented, self-important or courageous are simply quickly replaced. It's just the way of things.

This plus the fact British soldiers had been, on a daily basis, putting their lives on the proverbial line, and would doubtless continue to do so, despite being so poorly equipped and with an utterly disgraceful lack of support in logistical terms caused me to think again in many respects. These issues combined to ensure that my previously innate trust and unfailing faith (of 28 years) in my democratically elected leaders began to dwindle, and I started to doubt some of the long-held personal beliefs I had grown up with as I progressed up the ranks. One of which firmly stated that our cause was ultimately "*just*", but I kept my personal doubts to myself, parked in a quiet and lonely place somewhere midway between limbo and oblivion within my head. It was both highly inappropriate and utterly unprofessional to voice doubts of such a nature, especially as we hadn't yet finished in Iraq, even if we didn't know exactly what was coming next. Whatever did come our way would require us all to remain professional and focused and an officer — any officer — openly questioning the government's wisdom would hardly inspire the troops, after all.

Ultimately, duty — the largest and heaviest four-letter word in the English language — ensured my personal silence, that and the ongoing need to fetch all my soldiers home in one piece from this desert adventure which we found ourselves involved in, wherever that may now lead us all. After all, we now appeared to have neither a concerted plan, or any form of resources, for the aftermath of our actions across this large and soon to be bitterly divided nation. It was simply a case of a large collective "Now what?" So, as soldiers do so well, we patiently awaited our orders and checked our equipment in preparation, as generations across the centuries had done before us: in effect, it was ever thus. Some core aspects of soldiering, like selfless courage, patriotism and devotion to duty are simply timeless and irrespective of technological advancements and a rapidly changing world.

Whilst 7 Brigade triumphantly moved into Basra and the Americans celebrated the capture of Baghdad and their comprehensive victory over Saddam's regime, all watched by the bulk of the world's press, or so it seemed to us in our little military backwater, we merely sat quietly waiting for orders and thinking "Where to next"? The oil fields were all quite secure: our very own Americans were happy beavering away and seemed reasonably close to restarting production of the all-important oil and the local tribes seemed happy to be rid of the regime, so we were all very curious as to what the Army would decide to do with us next. After, traditionally, all it was not for us to reason why.

One of the very first post-hostilities decisions was for the RAF to demand their 2 long-lost Pumas back to the light blue fold. We had grown to quite like our "pet crabs" and viewed them as a very useful part of our team within the wider Green Machine, so we were rather sad to lose them. They had been instrumental in moving our troops rapidly around the AO, enabling us to do snap vehicle checks and building searches and generally keep any potential insurgents off balance by their speed and flexibility, enabling us to be very unpredictable from any potential bad guy's perspective. We also viewed them as a key asset in our battle group for their part in the casualty evacuation mission in the aftermath of the clever Iraqi ambush and the tragic American air attack. RAF helicopters would come into their own in this critical role in a very short time, but again that lay in the future for all of us.

On the final day of Puma operations, the RAF boss came into see me for his final mission briefing for the very last Eagle Patrol before they went back to their squadron somewhere south of Basra. I just looked at him and said, "Just do what you want and enjoy it." Totally unprofessional on my part, admittedly, but they had done us proud and if he just wanted to beat up the desert at ultra-low level at our distant taxpayers' expense, then why not? Suffice it to say, they did exactly that and came back with big smiles all round, although some of our soldiers looked decidedly queasy, but at least no one had actually vomited in either of the aircraft: always a bonus really in a very hot climate in terms of maintaining aircraft husbandry and cleanliness.

Their courage in extracting the wounded under heavy and sustained Iraqi fire after the "Blue on Blue" incident had impressed us all and only the previous week they had been repeatedly shot at whilst landing one of our security patrols on the American Main Supply Route (MSR), by some over-enthusiastic American National Guard Reservists, all fearful of last-ditch Iraqi Kamikaze helicopter assault no doubt. One of our sergeant majors had to make a long and lonely walk down the MSR towards the Americans, with his hands in the air, aware that several machine guns and dozens of rifles, all manned by nervous and inexperienced reservists, were pointing at him as he approached them to explain that he and his men were actually Brits tasked with ensuring the MSR security for both the US Marines and the US Army. The American National Guard troops in question were, rather surprisingly, totally unaware that the Brits were in Iraq too and presumed it was a suicidal Iraqi attack upon their massive and well-armed convoy. The joys of coalition warfare can be manyfold at times, especially when you are, very much, the junior partner.

Reservists take time to mobilise and train, whilst taking significantly longer than regular troops to settle into faraway operations, and by their very nature of being a part time soldier tend to have large gaps in their collective skill set, whilst they unavoidably lack recent operational experience, physical fitness and unit cohesion in the main.

They might be a fiscally far more attractive option from a governmental view of overall wages bill and pension costs, but they are fundamentally designed to augment rather than replace regular troops in times of conflict, a key point which UK's current political players seem singularly determined to ignore in order to provide national defence on the cheap. The invasion of Iraq was itself essentially based on the financially-driven "just enough, just in time" principle, so UK's contingent of deployed reservists was, to say the least, minimalistic in number in comparison to the US model, but reserve service in America is very much a badge of honour and widely popular across all spectrums of American society, which hardly reflects the prevailing social attitude in the UK.

So, we all patiently waited for our orders, although the dominant rumour was a move to Al Amarah, a city we had never heard of (on investigation we discovered it was very close to the Iranian border and located on banks of the River Tigris). We prepared our vehicles and equipment for a major road move: large-scale mobile warfare was then still the Army's bread and butter, after all. The troops got on with all the dozens of associated tasks that constitute the organised movement of several hundred personnel with a couple of hundred vehicles in harsh climates several thousand miles from their home base. Aside from keeping them busy, they were glad to be moving, the Walled Garden had now served its purpose and Al Amarah would be something different from their perspective, though none of us really fancied going into Iran. We were quietly hoping both our own and the American Government would just settle for just conquering Iraq (we did have the odd doubt at the time). Iran would be fairly messy and very, very painful, was the general view held at our lowly level. Luckily even our politicians of the time drew the line there, quite possibly because, as one of our young officers exclaimed (he was commonly referred to as "the blond one". This was essentially because he was "cute but dumb", like a human golden retriever really, despite a very expensive public-school education), who declared "Well We now have Iran surrounded, between here and Afghanistan." Personally, I was quite sure the Iranians had already noticed this none-too-subtle geographical fact and probably had their own, rather differing views on the subject.

We knew Al Amarah was (or more likely had been: we fully expected any semblance of the Iraqi Military to have disappeared long ago by the time we arrived) the home of an Iraqi Army Infantry division, about 10,000 troops: one of the several Lorried Infantry Divisions in the Iraqi Army which were designed primarily for keeping civil order rather than fighting American armour. They would thereby quickly die in large numbers (the American Military after all contemptuously classed these formations as mere "speed bumps"), plus no doubt carrying out border security tasks along the long and highly porous border with Iran, which was only some 30 miles distant. The scars of that 8-year-long bitter war still dominated relations — or rather lack of — between the two countries: hardly surprising seeing approximately a million people died. Ironically, Saddam's regime, way back then a hugely important regional friend of the major Western nations, had been very heavily supported by several Western nations, including us and the Americans, to keep a resurgent and ultra-Islamic Iran in check.

One issue which troubled me, but no one else it seemed, was the basing of the Mujahidin e Khalq (MEK or the People's Mujahidin of Iran) formation in Al Amarah, believed to be a unit of between 600-1000 strong, all battle-hardened fighters and apparently very well equipped. At the time a proscribed terrorist organisation by the US Government (they had previously murdered several US officers and civilians in the Shah's Iran in the late 1970s); the 5,000-8,000-strong MEK were, in simple terms, Iranian (and therefore by definition 100% Shia) Islamic Marxists who had participated strongly in the overthrow of the Shah and then fallen out violently with the highly theological regime of the Ayatollahs which replaced him. The MEK had a very colourful recent history, including an unsuccessful invasion of Iran at the end of the Iran/Iraq war (during which they had fought *against* the Iranian Forces). Since then they had been allowed to remain in Iraq and had carried out repeated cross-border raids and some rather high-profile assassinations within Iran, all with Saddam's tacit approval. Now they had nowhere to go, rather similar to the French and Belgian Waffen SS "last ditch" defenders of Berlin in 1945, who had simply fought to the death, having no other options except either the gallows or a firing squad in their home lands, being classed as traitors and renegades as they were by their own people. I sincerely hoped they wouldn't follow suit. When I raised this troubling issue the answer was, "I'm sure someone has thought about it", which I found unconvincing based on the evidence of any thought — or rather lack of it — shown so far in our little military venture.

Another issue which we seemed utterly unconcerned about was the Badr Corps, the Iranian riposte to the MEK, Iraqi Shias in the main and a mixture of political exiles, refugees from Saddam's overwhelmingly Sunni-dominated regime and defectors turned prisoners of war (Badr had been the scene of the Prophet Mohammed's first major military victory against his pagan enemies: Mohammed was also a very accomplished military leader after all). They were Iranian officered, trained and equipped, had been in Iran for 20 years or so and fought against the Iraqi Forces during the Iran/Iraq war. They too had carried out cross-border operations, with discreet Iranian approval, into Iraq, being ruthlessly hunted by Saddam's secret police, who had also no doubt simply disappeared by now, along with all the border guards, leaving the field wide open for the Badr Corps, so would they now return in strength into Iraq with some form of Iranian-approved agenda? The answer to that question was the same as the MEK question: apparently, I should just be very pleased that we had won a war. I resigned myself to keeping quiet rather than run the risk of being sent home, and later took no satisfaction at all from the Badr Corps returning to haunt us in Basra over the coming years of our occupation there. We had ignored them and their covert Iranian backers to our cost sadly. Whilst later the American Military would use them to hunt down the Sunni resistance/insurgents in Baghdad, this plan rapidly just deteriorated into them becoming a large collection of extremely vicious and brutal death squads.

To our minor surprise, we were informed the Royal Marines would take over security duties for the oil fields. All Army units would, in the main, go north, while our newly arrived RAF Regiment Squadron would stay behind to augment the Marines. The RAF Regiment were none too pleased with this news: whilst working with the Army, it seemed, was bearable for them, they believed, quite strongly, that the Marines would just give them all the shit jobs. Personally, I felt they had a valid point, whilst the later Afghan campaign amply demonstrated that the Marines and the Army's better battalions were very much of the same calibre. Frankly, back then the Marines still had an air of aloofness, verging on arrogance at times about themselves in 2003. Helmand Province and indeed the wider Afghanistan was a harsh equaliser in many respects for a lot of foreign troops, as the Russians had painfully found out some 25 years earlier. The Taliban showed absolutely no respect for reputation, simply viewing the majority of our regiments, like those of America, Canada and our allies, as merely infidel soldiers, with the singular exception of our SF units of whom they were quite rightly terrified.

But we, the West, ignored the Russians Afghan experiences totally in much the same way as we all simply ignored Iraq's recent history, tribal complexities and religious dispositions and, more importantly, long-standing social divisions of the Sunni/Shia divide. Unlike us Brits, both they and the Afghan population passionately "do God". Liberal democratic Westerners, especially our eternally vote-conscious politicians, seem simply unable grasp this basic tenet of Islam and that it often trumps nationality, democracy and all laws made by man, so is it really any wonder why social integration and cohesion in certain parts of UK are at best difficult and in some cases an abject failure? Saddam had achieved his secular society only by the widespread and repeated use of violence on a scale totally unacceptable to Western nations and literally murderous suppression of religious leaders. We likewise seriously underestimated the power of the imams and the long simmering distrust between Sunni and Shia. Frankly, we simply didn't have a clue in that respect of the Iraqi people.

A small reconnaissance, or recce, party was dispatched to Al Amarah, which was currently being held by a US Marines "Recon" Battalion (a wheeled light armoured unit). We were told they were currently centred on an old and long deserted Iraqi Air Force airfield outside the city. Meanwhile we prepared various briefing packs and planned a handover presentation for the Royal Marines whilst the troops busily prepared for the move north, which was just as well as they were getting bored and bored troops inevitably cause problems of one variety or another. Most soldiers are, after all, young people in uniform and reflect the society from which they were recruited. They don't cease to be young people merely because they don a uniform, or transform into another life form which isn't subject to fear, hunger, stress, homesickness or the complete spectrum of human emotions. Keeping them busy also kept their mind off the fact we didn't have the faintest idea when we would return to UK or if our supply chain would ever improve (or indeed if anyone within HMG actually cared that the supply chain was so dreadful) and improve our rather austere quality of life.

The recce party returned after a long and uneventful drive to Al Amarah and back in one day. The US Marines, it seemed, had rapidly got bored with being on the outer fringes of all things military and moved onto towards An Nas or possibly Baghdad, we didn't really know which. But the simple fact was that no coalition presence existed for us to take over the local area from and neither, it seemed, was there any remnant of local governance. Due to our complete and total lack of intelligence on the area, or indeed Maysan Province in its entirety, the border situation with Iran or just about anything and everything really, it was decided to base most units on the large abandoned Iraqi Air Force airfield several miles to the west of the city itself. Ironically the Iraqis had abandoned it because it had been repeatedly (and quite accurately) bombed by just about everyone who had had a disagreement with Saddam since 1980, which was rather a lot of people over the decades, and its main use, we later found, was more of a very large and extremely well-stocked ammunition storage area rather than an operational base for any recent regime aviation activities.

The Marines duly arrived to receive our presentation prior to handing the AO over to them. Their CO only actually spoke to our colonel: it was either a "colonels only thing" or he was just extremely taciturn/very snobbish by nature. Frankly, we didn't care anyway. He brought along two young captains, both wearing Ray-Ban sunglasses, obviously a farewell present from their US Marines brothers in arms. The two captains were massively up themselves and constantly interrupted various aspects of the briefing to repeatedly say, "When we took the Al Faw", irrespective of its relevance to the topic in question. The longer the brief went on, the more of a joint pain they became: arrogance personified, basically. Accordingly, we sped up the brief, omitting less important information as we went — they preferred to talk about themselves whenever possible after all — and we'd had enough of these two prats. The only point of interest from my intelligence brief was the Iraqi SF team's dramatic daylight escape, which brought forth a reply of, "Good effort. Real Commando stuff!" Oh, fucking really, we all thought silently, trying to retain some form of military manners, particularly as they never mentioned either the large amount of American support, or the various Army Regiments serving alongside them in taking the now famous Al Faw Peninsula, we quietly noted: obviously a minor detail. Finally, it was over and with the exception of our CO and two other officers, we quickly left the room, preferring not to engage in small talk with our egotistical amphibious comrades. As one guy put it, "Look on the bright side, at least they aren't coming with us up north." He was right, we had quietly decided that, "Come back the Paras, all is forgiven", was a better judgement call all round.

We left early the next day, our large convoy travelling at a pace of 40 kilometres in the hour. It was going to be a long day indeed. As usual Nelly and Bird, yet again, went immediately into a serious sleeping competition. Mike and I settled down to following the vehicle in front for hours on end. We'd all played this game before, dozens of times and at least it was a daylight move this time. Our Rock Apes seemed sad to see us go and for probably the only time in my entire military career I actually felt rather sorry for the RAF Regiment, they were definitely earmarked for all the crap jobs the Marines could find for them and, no doubt, the Al Faw would be repeatedly mentioned on a very regular basis to them in the days to come.

Initially we drove through small Iraqi towns which until very recently had been a source of military contention. As we drove through these towns the populations reaction was mixed. The adult males just quietly stared at us with expressionless faces, the women either avoided eye contact and ignored us totally or briefly glanced furtively at us while the children waved and chased our vehicles, treating this as some new game and hoping we'd throw sweets or chocolate to them. The odd brave soul waved at us shyly but there weren't too many of those. It was all very reserved, polite enough, but hardly an ecstatic welcome for their liberators. Perhaps they'd doubted our staying power after the previous Gulf War or were wary of this incursion by infidel foreign troops, it was just impossible to judge accurately from a moving vehicle. Evidence of the Russian oil workers' long presence in this area was physically provided by a surprisingly large number of pale-skinned children with either ginger or blonde hair. Mike and I exchanged various comments on the theme that they would have to be very tough kids to survive a childhood in Iraq with pale white skin and blonde or red hair: equality and diversity policies were rather irrelevant in this part of the world.

We noted, discreetly tucked away, mainly in well populated side streets or sat close by to key road intersections — but well placed in the main to be difficult to spot from a distance (or height for that matter) — T55 tanks and MTLB armoured personnel carriers in ones and twos, plus the occasional well-camouflaged D 30 artillery piece or small-calibre anti-aircraft gun. All of them looked perfectly serviceable and all their attendant crews had seemingly just walked away and abandoned their equipment, presumably to go home, which seemed to be just the way of things by now. Certainly, we had taken precious few prisoners to speak of considering the literally hundreds of thousands of Iraqi males who had been wearing a military uniform until very recently. The Iraqi population treated all this military hardware as quite normal and paid them absolutely no attention, except for the children who had found some large toys to roam over and fight their own imaginary wars with, no doubt. Exactly who the kids were fighting against would have been an interesting cultural question to ask them, but we drove on by, someone else would eventually take over the town and tidy it up. It wasn't our problem, we had a timetable to adhere to, albeit one much farther north.

As we moved onto the major road leading towards Al Amarah and other Iraqi cities north of Basra and the oil fields, we received a minor shock from the sheer quality of Iraq's road network. Two-lane motorway-standard roads stretched, straight as a Roman road, as far as the eye could see towards a distant desert horizon. We were informed later, by an ex-Iraqi Army officer, that Saddam took a very keen personal interest in his highways and their maintenance as they were key to the quick and efficient movement of troops and tanks (especially the Republican Guard) to rapidly quell any outbreaks of dissidence amongst his people. This was particularly true for the Shia-dominated south, the heartland of dissent against his lengthy regime. Iraq had a far more advanced infrastructure than the almost medieval Afghanistan, as we later discovered, in simply every single aspect of nationhood, from roads and infrastructure to education and irrigation schemes. In many ways, it was on the cusp of joining the 21st century, but well-publicised sectarian strife and continuous violence have combined since then to ensure an almost nationwide regression.

Our drive was hot (air conditioning was unheard of in those pre-omnipresent IED threat days and the subsequent large-scale purchase of mine resistant ambush protected — MRAP — basically armoured truck vehicles by the fleet load) and a long monotonous one. We stopped just the once and the QM promptly pointed out to us that we had just driven past the Garden of Eden en route. Our soldiers were, without exception, singularly unmoved by this announcement, or indeed a subsequent explanation of the name Mesopotamia (the land between two rivers: modern day Iraq encompasses this ancient land). No doubt they would have opted en masse for a cheeseburger with fries and a chilled milk shake given the choice, they were 21st Century Western soldiers all. We were, however, very struck by the slide rule-flat topography of the landscape — a massive, sand-covered billiard table as far as we could see, in effect — which must have pleased the American Tank Divisions all day long, we thought. Ideal country for them to effect "shock and awe" in large and rapid amounts on their way to Baghdad. Anyone who took the Americans on in such open terrain would rapidly die in large numbers. Little did we know the Iraqi insurgency would prove to be rather more durable and innovative than the Iraqi Armed Forces in the years to come.

Well, I thought to myself, now we have done all that, we'll have to go and "play nice", starting tomorrow. It could be quite an interesting experience, no doubt we'd soon find out for ourselves just exactly what the Iraqi population really thought of our rather large-scale and uninvited visit to their country. I had previous experience of liberating a nation (admittedly a pretty small one), as we had left Macedonia. Thousands of displaced Kosovar refugees had given us a memorably ecstatic departure. The Iraqis were, to say the least, rather more reserved towards us. Their obvious reticence quietly bothered us. Few of us were aware that a British General had publicly declared to the population of Baghdad in 1918 that the British Army had come as Liberators not conquerors when the Ottoman Empire fell. Or that within two years the entire Iraqi nation had violently risen against the British "liberators" with large loss of life on both sides, including the massacre of over one hundred captured British and Indian (non-Muslim) soldiers by the Iraqi rebels of the 1920s. Unlike ourselves, the Iraqi people hadn't forgotten about our previous visit as self-proclaimed liberators, but perhaps this time it would be much easier for all concerned, or at least, we all hoped so.

As we finally got closer to the outskirts of Al Amarah, an exclusively Shia city of some 300,000 inhabitants, we passed under some large motorway flyovers which lead to other Iraqi cities and towns. Al Amarah was the main gateway to both nearby Iran and Baghdad in essence. Historically this was a vehemently anti-Saddam city which additionally controlled the main approaches to Baghdad and also An Nas, amongst other places. We knew the Paras, somewhere off to the east, had taken over from some SF guys in keeping a wary eye on the porous and lengthy border to detect and deter any possible incursions by whoever felt that way inclined from the nearby brooding mass of Iran.

We had little or no knowledge of Iranian intentions, or indeed that of any of their well-armed proxies, such as the Badr Corps or MEK. The flyovers themselves strangely reminded me of similar constructions on the outskirts of Skopje, the capital of Macedonia, where bored pro-Serb/anti-NATO teenagers had regularly clustered together to drop lots of large rocks on us as we drove (quickly) underneath. My unit alone had been "bricked" 45 times as we waited for months in Macedonia to advance into Kosovo. Lacking any issue riot grilles, we had resorted to "borrowing" (on a long-term basis) several large metal bread delivery baskets from an unsuspecting local baker to afford us some homemade windscreen protection — along with wearing helmet and body armour whilst driving underneath them — and we took (thankfully) no serious casualties. Our friends the local Macedonian authorities simply gave this anti-social practice a damn good ignoring and let the kids continue to amuse themselves at our expense. Somehow, I quietly doubted to myself, if we managed to piss off the long suffering and already war-hardened Iraqi population, that they'd merely limit themselves to throwing just bricks and insults at us.

As we edged closer to Al Amarah and also therefore the nearby Iranian border, we drove past literally mile after mile of huge and seemingly quite well-maintained earthwork defences, major interlinked trench systems, dozens of prepared fighting positions for tanks, large, wide and deep anti-tank ditches and so on, all relics of the bitterly fought 8-year war between the two nations. Oddly — to us at least — these fortifications appeared remarkably well maintained. We later realised that Saddam's Sunni-dominated Iraq had, despite being badly weakened by the 1991 war, remained as the regional counterbalance to Iran's larger ambitions, seen by many in the region as that of becoming a Shia Empire (as an Algerian Marine Brigadier I later worked for referred to Iran's machinations across the entire region) hence the ongoing border mistrust. We totally failed to realise in our 2003 euphoria that we had now totally and irrevocably removed this counter balance to Iran's ambitions from the strategic board totally, no doubt much to the quiet glee of the Iranian regime.

The Iranians had, during their own war against Iraq, made several major attempts to capture the city and failed. I could now understand exactly why, simply by looking at the sheer depth and complexity of the defences that had opposed them. It staggered the western mind to think of the thousands of man-hours, sheer number of labourers and equipment that must have been required to undertake this massive and seemingly never-ending "military landscaping". I could only assume this must have been a major and sustained national effort involving the bulk of the adult population. It was a modernist desert version of some old black and white newsreel footage from the desperate building of defences for Moscow or Berlin during World War Two, I really can't describe it in any other relatively recent terms.

As we neared the outskirts of Al Amarah — a singularly uninspiring city in pure Architectural terms — we saw a line of six or seven T 55 tanks, all with their turret hatches visibly open (which happily signified to us that they had been long since abandoned by their crews) stretching parallel to and across the left-hand side of the main road as we faced north. All of them had their barrels pointing at or directly down the road on which we now drove. As we got closer it became obvious this had been some kind of defensive line, probably against the recently departed US Marines. Some "strike marks" were visible where Iraqi Artillery rounds had impacted and as we got close to the T55s we could spot where the Americans had returned the favour, including a few inaccurate bomb craters from their seemingly ever-present air support, no doubt. We also spotted several empty infantry fighting trenches with scores of Iraqi helmets abandoned on and around the parapets, but, yet again, no weapons at all had been left behind. This had obviously been a location where the Iraqis had made a very spirited stand, and quite successfully, it seemed at first glance. Later, Mike, our Signals Officer, did some minor battlefield tourism (not something you could safely replicate later in Helmand or indeed, Iraq in a few months' time, but he seized the moment and got away with it). On closer inspection, none of the tanks had suffered any major damage: rather they had fired all their main armament ammunition and once they had just run out of any further means to fight with, the crews had discreetly left the battlefield, taking their supporting infantry with them, it seemed. It looked to me like the Americans had not had it all their own way in this relative backwater of the invasion. I mulled over the possible significance of this and our now-imminent arrival. We were also very aware that the Iraqi Army hadn't been paid for several months and having to placate several thousand well-armed, now unemployed and exceedingly disgruntled ex-soldiers wandering around the local area wasn't part of our plans at all.

My own experience of liberating oppressed people — in Kosovo — had been rather different from this. Then the Serbian Army had withdrawn in good order, intact and very well-disciplined as part of a joint agreement with NATO. The KLA fighters had promptly come down from the hills to exact a bloody revenge on whoever they perceived as traitors or collaborators, or just plain competition and we had to rapidly become protectors for the few remaining Serbs, mainly the elderly and infirm. But Kosovo was a very small country and that operation had been popular with both our own pre-"open borders" nation and the Kosovars themselves, plus large-scale organised crime, rather than armed resistance against NATO, had been the KLAs and their key supporters' overarching priority. Also, then, like the first Gulf War, the Army had done its given task and quickly returned home. However, this operation now had no obvious plan for us to follow. In soldier terms, we were making it up as we went along.

We, at the time, were utterly unaware that all Maysan Province and therefore the entire population of Al Amarah had very recently "liberated itself" from Saddam's regime (alone amongst all the Iraqi provinces in doing so), having suffered repeatedly over the decades for its rigid adherence to the Shia faith, close affiliation with Iran and ongoing resistance and general intransigence towards the Sunni-dominated Baghdad regime, all of which resulted in regular, violent and often massive reprisals. These people had both seen and been through more strife and violence than any Western Europeans born after 1945 could ever even dream of, but we were blissfully ignorant of any of these facts and, in effect, we were "going in blind". This seemed to be a recurring theme in our recent wars: one of the questions I asked myself, especially later in our fourth Afghanistan War, was, "If I can read history, as a northern bloke from Wigan, why can't any of our politicians?" I came to the rather cynical conclusion that all history before 1997 must have simply been deemed irrelevant and pointless by them all. When you hold a massively overwhelming majority in Parliament, (especially when it came to repeated and assorted nation-building and regime change efforts, which seems to be rooted in our politicians' DNA) it makes dispatching military forces into conflict a rather tempting and simultaneously very easy option to undertake. This presumably explains why modern British school children know next to nothing about our own national history, unlike their counterparts within the Iraqi and Afghan peoples who were very keenly aware of their own histories, including previous British involvement in their countries, and many of the adults had certainly not forgotten our little "visitations" either.

We turned off the main route towards the city before we came anywhere close to actually entering Al Amarah. It was now, in effect, a new, improved and much larger version of Royal Irish Town. As always, they had got there first, complete with their flamboyant CO emptying a pistol magazine into the ceiling of a bank to "encourage" looters to leave the building immediately: it worked. The airfield, "Sparrowhawk" as it later became known to subsequent British Garrisons, was unimpressive on first sight, run down, dismal and totally unprotected in security terms. The buildings tended to be of a single-storey construction, very well spread out, presumably to make life slightly less easy for some marauding fighter pilot to bomb them effectively, be they Iranian or American. It had a distinct overall air of both quiet desolation and ongoing decay everywhere. Home sweet home, we all thought.

As usual, guides showed us into our respective areas. The airfield was now "home" for several brigade units, with the notable exceptions of the Pathfinders, whom we hadn't seen since they went off to do their long range desert stuff "up north" of the American Marines and our lone Armoured Squadron, who had finished the conflict with only one serviceable CVR (T) remaining out of the dozen or so they had started with. The rest had been destroyed, battle-damaged or plain trashed by non-stop operations, being all the (light) armour we had. They had certainly earned their pay. Both units were, we believed, deservedly regrouping somewhere back in Kuwait. Each of the units here basically got one building each to use as its HQ and a chunk of real estate for vehicle parking, accommodation and the normal routine of life in the field. We also got a chunk of runway to park our helicopters — the ones that still worked at least — and conduct maintenance, refuelling and other aviation-based standard operational stuff.

As we dismounted from our vehicles after a long and tiresome drive, we were less than enthralled to discover large amounts of human excrement literally all around the exterior of our sole building. We couldn't blame the Iraqis for this, as also liberally lying around on the ground were dozens of discarded US MRE wrappers, which vindicated the locals totally. The US Marines before us, obviously knowing they weren't staying for a moment longer than they had to in this locale, had treated the whole site with obvious contempt and a total disregard for any form of basic hygiene and we, literally, had to clean this mess up. We were none too pleased at this prospect, to say the very least. As no one else was going to come forward and do it for us, we resignedly broke out the shovels and got on with completing this nauseating task whilst we still had some daylight left, aided and abetted by the standard armada of flies that just seem to appear out of nowhere in the desert. A good start to our collective occupancy it certainly was not.

As we came to the end of our clear up (it could have been worse, in Pristina, the departing Serbs had liberally covered all the walls, floors and ceilings of our nominated buildings with their human waste in a "welcome gesture" to us), I was called away for a briefing in HQ. It transpired that my team was being immediately disbanded. Nelly had been posted to Germany, so he had to get back to UK to move his family to Germany and it simply couldn't wait, apparently (though I failed to follow the urgency: as far as I knew Germany hadn't been invaded recently, but the Army had a post to fill and therefore it would be filled before things became untidy, Iraq invasion or no Iraq invasion). Bird's father back in Scotland was very seriously ill, so he had to get home as soon as possible. One thing the MOD does get 100% right is getting people home, as rapidly as is physically possible by the fastest means available, for all compassionate matters, to give them their due: which therefore leaves me and Mike, I thought, so what are the two of us expected to do? Capture Saddam or something similar? I was also told that from tomorrow I would be the CIMIC second in command (Civilian Military Cooperation: the "nice soldiers" doing the famous "hearts and minds" stuff essentially). Great, thought I, so what exactly does that entail then? That question was given a good ignoring, I noticed. I sensed a classic "cuff job" rapidly inbound to me personally, with little option other than to just say, "Yes, sir", and mentally salute and turn to the right. To that end, I'd be on a helicopter recce of our nominated area of operations first thing in the morning, with the classic military post script of "more detail to follow" which normally means we don't actually have a plan yet, as I had repeatedly learned over my long years in Her Majesty's Army.

I spoke to Nelly, who was obviously happy to leave as, in his words, "This next bit will be shit now. Last time was much easier, we just got Kuwait back and all went home". Plus he'd be far better paid in Germany with his Living Overseas Allowance. Accordingly, he went happily away to pack his kit prior to a drive back to Basra, ever the pragmatic Yorkshireman, but his blunt northern comment would prove to be exceedingly prophetic within a matter of months. Bird was obviously upset: he may have been a Scottish Giant, but your dad is your dad. We shared some quiet words and I thanked him sincerely for all his help and wished him and his father well. He too would be gone in the morning, but hopefully by helicopter. I briefed Mike, who quietly took it all in and said, "So it's just me and you, then, Boss?" I replied that hopefully we'd get some replacements. I think he, like me, found the thought of the two of us alone in our farmer's Land Rover driving aimlessly around Maysan Province trying to be "really, really nice" to several thousand, possibly quite angry, locals in possession of an awful lot of weapons, a bit too challenging of a task for the both of us.

We settled down to get some sleep. Most of us just slept on the floor, if you were lucky enough to find some spare floor space in our one and only building. George and I both were that lucky. Mike, however, preferred to stay with the vehicle, which was now, in effect "his wagon" in both ownership and maintenance terms. Most our soldiers slept in or by their vehicles, with a makeshift Operations Room being manned during the silent hours until we had the opportunity to spruce things up in the morning. It had been a long and uneventful day and we welcomed a chance to get some of the proverbial "Zs".

Around three in the morning we awoke to loud screaming from very close by, inside the building somewhere. George and I grabbed our rifles and ran towards the sound of the yelling, along with several other soldiers into, we discovered, the RSM's room, which at some (pre-looting by the Iraqi population) stage in its past had been a toilet/bathroom of some kind. The RSM was sat bolt upright in his sleeping bag, holding his rifle in one hand and busily throwing a broad and highly varied selection of loose objects at the far wall of his small abode with his other hand. We shone a torch in that direction to see a pair of deserts boots and a large pile of assorted military equipment scattered around it. "Rat!" The RSM said.

"Rat?" we replied in chorus.

"Yes, I woke up to find a fucking big rat sat on my fucking chest looking me straight in the eyes!"

"Must have been a Republican Guard Rat then, sir" said a voice immediately from the pitch darkness behind us, which started us all laughing loudly: it's all about timing, as they say.

"Who said that?" asked the RSM angrily. Utter silence was the unsurprising response from the pitch darkness. British soldiers might do some quite bizarre things at times, but they aren't stupid when it comes to dealing with very pissed off RSMs at close quarters.

The "Republican Guard Rat" had last been seen scurrying across the building as he made a rather rapid exit from the building, and passed close by to several soldiers roused from their slumber by the RSM's screams. He had obviously found the aroma of human excrement mixed with the scent of assorted American rations packs simply too appetising to resist and ended up sitting on the RSM's chest for reasons best known to himself. The troops themselves all found it a rather highly amusing scenario and were inordinately pleased indeed by the rat's very selective taste in British soldiers, whilst the RSM himself, his pride somewhat dented by the entire affair, quietly vowing to take it upon himself to launch his own personal "shock and awe"-based eradication campaign against all the local vermin. The fun now being over, we went back to our various sleeping sites, all quietly pleased the rat hadn't chosen us for his midnight visit if the truth be known. By all accounts he was of a significant size and totally unimpressed by the sight of numerous armed British soldiers. The story of the Republican Guard Rat and the RSM is still remembered and discussed over a quiet beer by those people who were present in Al Amarah at that period: not quite stuff of corps legend, but I'm sure the rat in question would be inordinately pleased to know he made such a memorable and lasting impact on several hundred British soldiers and, albeit briefly, raised their morale.

Following our memorable early-morning rat experience, we duly assembled at the flight line the next morning. I was amused to see that several of our Lynx had small but distinctive bright red TOW missile symbols adorning the noses of their fuselage in the same manner as World War 2 RAF bombers had recorded their successful night missions in incredibly hostile European skies, and why not? The guys had done an extremely good job on some very active two-way ranges with an almost obsolete and at times quite unreliable weapon system against a well-equipped enemy in his own back yard, and most importantly came home in one piece afterwards. I saw absolutely nothing wrong with having a sense of pride in any of that. As a nation we have an immense amount to be proud of for such a small country, and the military is but just one rather small facet of our society and its remarkable achievements as a small island nation over the centuries. But we now seem to prefer politically correct appeasement at times to displays of national pride or British identity,especially if it's remotely populist at the time or irritates any form of a highly vocal minority group. But for then it was (briefly) peaceful in Iraq, or at least in the very early days of the post-conflict stage, and we were off to survey the Iraqi people in a far more passive manner, hopefully without any nasty surprises. Most surprises in recent conflict areas tend to be mainly of the unpleasant nature, in my own personal experience at least. As most soldiers will testify to in bluntly colloquial terms, shit, when it happens, tend to happen very, very quickly indeed and it also tends to roll downhill.

All our aircraft were still painted in their grey and green camouflage schemes, designed purely for war in Europe, the much-promised batch of sand-coloured paint didn't arrive until long after we'd left, but it really didn't matter for now, or the fact that our vehicles were a rather shabby-looking fleet as the rushed application of sand-coloured paint in Kuwait was wearing off to show the drab green and black paint schemes underneath, together with some of the troops still being dressed in a mixture of sand and green uniforms (or in a few cases just plain green: they went home dressed in green eventually). All in all, I thought, we verged on resembling a military version of a bunch of armed tramps. Oh well, I thought, perhaps the "follow on force" — the troops who'd relieve us eventually — will be better equipped and even have matching uniforms all round. In the meanwhile, the Iraqi people would simply have to just take us as they found us.

We climbed into a Lynx, sitting on the floor with our feet on the skids, a canvas strap — named an Eagle harness — across our chests for security and safety. Due to 21st Century health and safety concerns the British military don't do this any more, but for quick entry and exit of the helicopter it was ideal when speed really mattered. Climbing to about two thousand feet we simply flew from village to village within our expected area of operations. It was early morning. Our aircraft, designed for operations in European temperatures as they all were, just didn't cope well as the temperatures rose during the day and the available engine power dropped off correspondingly, so the bulk of our flights were in the morning. In Afghanistan, we encountered the additional problem of height. Iraq may be mainly flat, but all of Afghanistan, even the lowland areas, is of a markedly higher altitude and we rediscovered this problem for the first few years at least, to the extent that our Lynx became almost useless outside of the winter months. But for once we were physically cool as we gazed down onto "our piece of desert", a welcome change from the demanding and steadily rising desert temperatures and quite refreshing to say the very least. At that moment, life was good. We were relaxed and content after all the frustrations of the hasty deployment and seemingly never-ending logistical disasters. Amazing how a small perk like your own, albeit briefly, personal flying taxi can make you forget the assorted and highly annoying crap that went before. We actually verged on the cusp of open enjoyment. Perhaps our political leaders were right and Iraq would, after all, simply turn out to be a far bigger and much warmer version of Kosovo and my own myriad quiet misgivings would simply prove very ill founded and misjudged. It wouldn't be the first time I had been wrong about major issues in my life, or the last, no doubt. I smiled as I gazed down on a peaceful-looking Maysan Province as I just made the most of the tranquil moment: carpe diem and all that.

As always it was a clear azure blue sky, with almost unlimited visibility in every direction. We flew in a large triangle basically, west initially then northeastwards and back southwards and thence to our new home via the banks of the legendary River Tigris, but avoiding Al Amarah itself, where the Royal Irish had made their HQ and central base inside the local football stadium and we were keen not to annoy them by infringing into "their" town at such an early stage of our occupation of the area. This route took in all the major villages, most of the minor ones and the key roads within our AO, together with major waterways (which soldiers automatically tend to view as obstacles) and bridges or crossing points over them (which soldiers tend to view as a means of "canalisation" which, by effectively dictating your movement options, makes you far more vulnerable in forcing you to use these choke points). No doubt some Iraqi military tactics manual somewhere used much the same terminology: their Officer Corps was well versed in the reality of war, even if they were currently in plain clothes and possibly with some of them looking back up at me from one of these villages.

As the man who, to some degree at least, would have to plan and lead what I imagined to be repeated and regular patrols into these various villages, the lack of roads and few bridges concerned me as it would make varying our route that much more difficult and also fairly predictable to anyone with a hankering towards killing us and possessing a modicum of patience. Downing Street might well have been sat basking in the reflected glory of victory and the PM's ongoing desire to reshape the Middle East, but some of us mere soldiers in the desert were already well aware that post-regime Iraq was awash with both weapons and hundreds of thousands of potentially disgruntled ex-soldiers who knew very well how to use them and who were also owed several months wages. What happened next was crucial to both Iraq's future and our own ability to operate in relative safety, I thought, so until someone, somewhere resolved the overarching question of "what next?", the only question that really mattered in essence. Personally speaking, I was going to take a much more pessimistic approach and err on the side of caution. After all, the single most important activity all human beings conduct individually is good old-fashioned breathing. Without this, everything else becomes simply irrelevant in an overriding and ultimately final manner. Since 2003, British soldiers tend not to take this activity for granted as much as they used to in pre-desert war(s) times.

Whilst airborne surveillance by UAVs/drones later became a key asset amongst the Intelligence/Surveillance/Reconnaissance (ISR) daily functions of the Army's ongoing counter insurgency campaign during its lengthy time in Helmand Province, Iraq mainly saw the use of manned platforms, purely as we had yet to invest in modern technology at that time, having lagged well behind both Israel and a lot of Western nations in this respect. But for our little flight around our corner of Maysan Province it was of no real consequence at the time, as UAVs may now be highly effective but they still cannot yet gauge opinions and feelings, the local mood or ambience, morale, beliefs and a few dozen other invisible aspects of human beings. Only good old-fashioned HUMINT or human intelligence can accurately provide these intangible gems of information which add so greatly to any timely and accurate intelligence picture, but the West tends to be blinded by shiny new technology at times, especially when fighting "low-tech" enemies. At least, as we flew around each village, we could wave at the people below us, hardly hi-tech, but a UAV cannot wave to people and by their very design can appear remote and very forbidding objects to those looking up curiously. What, exactly, the Iraqi people thought when a strange helicopter full of white Christians (Iraqis, like most Muslims, simply don't understand the twin alien concepts of either Atheism or Agnosticism, so we were just all Christians to them, period) appeared above them is open to anyone's guess, but we waved for all we were worth anyway.

The reactions differed greatly from village to village. In the smaller (and visually poorer) villages everyone waved back, with the children enthusiastically running and jumping as if we were some kind of saviours passing by. Even from a couple of thousand feet up we could see they lived an essentially subsistence life style. Perhaps these people hoped for some form of positive social change with our arrival, certainly the poorer the village the warmer the welcome we received, but social change was simply never ever going to be either within our remit or capability. The larger villages, blessed with such luxuries as power lines, a reliable water supply and a road of some description were more conservative with their responses. The men would often hold their gaze towards us and perhaps occasionally raise a hand to acknowledge us, or perhaps not, whilst the children were again visibly excited at this strange visitation and no doubt then asked their parents, "What is that/who are they?" As always, the women at best gave us a quick surreptitious glance, but mainly studiously avoided showing any form of interest in us.

In a group of apparently prosperous villages to the north we beheld a unanimously neutral reaction, indeed with a large proportion of the population studiously at pains to ignore us, which baffled us at that time. We later discovered that the more pro-Saddam a village was in this Shia-dominated region — in terms of its sympathies and support — the more "presents" it received from the Sunni-run regime in turn. This, as we later discovered, manifested itself in several ways, from concrete lined irrigation ditches, Vietnamese-supplied foodstuffs and Russian-made tractors at the high end, to a local school and access to some form of medical aid, down to simply nothing — literally "dirt poor" in effect — at the lower end of this socially unbalanced spectrum. The villages who had given us a damn good ignoring fell very much into the high-end category, we would later discover.

It was a refreshing start to the day and gave us some idea of the AO, its population size and dispositions, together with topography and infrastructure. For example, one utterly deserted village, of obviously very new construction, had a lone anti-aircraft gun squarely on top of its tallest building. The regime liked to protect its assets with these types of weapons, symbols of regime power to a degree, but they were also quite devastating in the ground-to-ground role (you see them a lot on the news lately, normally bolted to a Libyan/Syrian militia or an Islamic State pickup truck) and aside from "making a statement" of authority and importance to the surrounding local populace, this particular weapons location simply dominated the single main road throughout the area. We had made a note to check out this village at the earliest opportunity, its modern architecture smacked of the regime's favoured people and very much being some kind of "regime hub" in an otherwise very agrarian area.

As the helicopter's rotors slowly wound down after we landed back at the airfield, the ever-oppressive heat of Iraq rapidly again made its effects plain. We Brits were still relatively new to the climate and the relentless nature of its environment. The desert is totally unforgiving by its very nature and a harsh land inevitably makes for a hard people, as we would discover soon enough. Our flight, aside from being a refreshing change after the past few weeks, had been very useful in giving us a decent overview of our proposed operations area. We wouldn't really know the feelings and views of the local population until we "got amongst them", which was tomorrow's task, but at least we now had a rough idea of our priorities and the ground itself. Understanding the ground is always simply a key activity in its inherent and enduring effects on any army's planned operations, be it Europe or someone's piece of desert, which were to become the destiny of thousands of us in due course.

I reported to our Ops Room to give a quick de-brief on our little sightseeing tour. I was delighted to be informed that George would become my own second in command (the 2ic, as it is referred to in the Army) and that an Lancashire Infantry Officer named Dai (his nickname, he was very much an Englishman actually) would be taking over the CIMIC "lead" for us (which was very good as none of us had received any form of formal training on the subject). Dai was one of a number of officers who formed part of the Brigade CIMIC cell, who had little to do during the conflict phase, being the "nice people for afterwards" who didn't really get involved in the death and destruction piece essentially, so this was now their moment. So I left, both pleased and relieved, Dai was well known to us from our time in Kuwait. A very popular guy with the troops, bright, witty and personable, he was on detachment from his battalion who were at the time in Cyprus and additionally he came across as a very capable soldier, all of which boded extremely well for us, frankly.

George was a huge personal bonus for me as a 2ic, eminently well respected due to his extended time "across the water" in Northern Ireland, fit, very well experienced and resourceful. I now felt we were quickly assembling quite a capable team for the forthcoming task in hand. My conservative estimate for our AO was that we would be dealing with a population of somewhere between 5-10,000 people in several differing villages. In this I was wrong, it was actually rather closer to between 15,000-20,000, which doesn't sound much in UK terms but it's rather a lot when there are less than a dozen of you. Ultimately quantity has a quality all of its own, which tends to somewhat nullify our parsimonious "just enough, just in time" approach, I would personally argue. In both Iraq and later Helmand Province, one resource we were always short of was sheer numbers of troops. In both cases the British Army became responsible for very large areas of land and to dominate that land you need to maintain an effective presence, and for this you require "troop density". We only achieved that when the US Marines arrived in 2009/10. Before that we had first class troops trying their best to deal with very determined, innovative and well-armed opponents across large ungoverned areas, troops who were therefore often forced to be repeatedly reactive in nature, which as any soldier will tell you is not how you dominate the enemy and put him on the back foot.

Overall things were going well for now, we almost had a team assembled, had a rough idea of where to go and at least one guy, Dai, who had some idea of what to actually do when we met all these Iraqis. After all, most people tend to get a bit annoyed when you decide to suddenly up and invade their country. We were rather hoping the fact we had removed Saddam and his regime in the process would strongly mitigate against this. With the eternal gift of hindsight, it is pretty obvious our US/UK Coalition Governments had absolutely banked all on this just making everything all right with around twenty-six million or so fairly bemused Iraqi citizens. However, at our much lower level in the food chain, it was far more of a pressing concern and not something we could take afford to take for granted. On the intelligence side, we knew precisely zero about just about everything, which we had come to expect by now, frankly, as standard practice. But we did have some maps, which after our recent experiences in Kuwait was a small form of an early Christmas present really, so things had improved markedly, plus some more hand held GPS systems had suddenly emerged from our ever unpredictable and erratic stores system, all of a vivid bright yellow in colour, so they had obviously been purchased en masse off the shelf from a civilian source back in the UK somewhere, and hastily shipped out to the desert. Better late than never, we thought.

All we needed now was for Dai and his interpreter to arrive from brigade and, once we had formulated a plan and briefed everyone, we could venture out into the great unknown in effect, "Boldly going where no Brits had gone before" and our "Team Star Trek" moment, according to one of our younger soldiers. At least he was being enthusiastic over the pending mission. In the rather more mundane interim period, as soldiers always do, we prepared our personal kit, cleaned equipment, loaded and checked the vehicles, sorted out radio frequencies and call signs, resupplied ourselves with lots of bottled water and yet again tried (and yet again failed miserably) to get some more ammunition (as the conflict had finished this was now deemed quite unnecessary). Being a very old-fashioned soldier, I personally preferred to have as much ammunition as we could get our hands on along with all the rest of the preparation that is key to all forms of modern military operations.

Once all this was complete, we got some rest as tomorrow, we all believed, could be quite a long day and we really did not know exactly how the locals would react to us. Oh well, I thought to myself as I chilled in the shade, as a wiry Geordie and one of our sergeant majors (and good friend and highly professional soldier) was fond of telling the troops, "It's not a job, it's an adventure!" To give him his due, he was absolutely right on that score.

Shortly after dawn, we assembled our rather small convoy of two Land Rovers and one white civilian 4x4 to go and meet the locals. We'd rather have had a few more troops and vehicles to be frank, but this was all that was deemed necessary and more importantly, it was all that we had available for the task in hand. The main effort was undoubtedly (and very publicly) the neighbouring city of Al Amarah, but our approach to our own area of operations was, I personally felt, pretty minimalistic. Accordingly, we rather hoped the Iraqis would be pleased to see us. Either way, we were about to find out. It was that simple, really, in effect we'd all just go for a drive and meet the locals on the way. Not much of a plan as plans go, but at least it was uncomplicated.

Dai had a Kuwaiti officer with him by the name of Omar, a big, cheerful and very affable man, like most British soldiers at the time. I had yet to realise the simply crucial importance of a reliable interpreter.

In a very short time these key assets would become known as "the Terp" and universally referred to as such within military circles over the next decade of counter insurgency warfare, or "COIN" as the military commonly termed these bloody and complicated little wars. A good Terp was worth *at least* a platoon of soldiers, especially for the detailed cultural and social knowledge and awareness they brought with them to the party, which enhanced their already critically valuable language skills and enabled us in turn to grasp complex situations and often rapidly tribal dynamics so much more quickly and easily. Our enemies rapidly became aware of this also and the pressures brought to bear on Terps became, to say the very least, rather considerable and often life-threatening in both our desert wars. Omar explained that, if asked, we were to say — emphatically — that he was an Omani officer, as most Iraqis then viewed Kuwait as a "long lost province of Iraq" (courtesy of the British and French enthusiastically dividing up the defeated Ottoman Empire between them in the aftermath of the First World War: Mr Blair is by no means the first British PM to have a personal vision of "reshaping the Middle East"; both Kuwait and Iraq had been long since "designed" by previous British politicians with similar visions of world influence and national position). As always, unlike UK with our rather limited and very selectively PC take on history, most peoples other than ourselves knew their own national history extremely well, we readily agreed. If the locals discovered he was actually a Kuwaiti officer, not the most popular of races in Iraq even then, life could rapidly become "interesting" for all of us.

So, armed with our brand-new maps and precious little else in terms of local knowledge we drove west, towards our designated patch. En route we had to drive past the local Iraqi Infantry Divisional Barracks, which Dai (being our designated leader and CIMIC expert) wanted to have a good look at. This was a view which was keenly echoed by the various intelligence cells: after all this was the home (or had been until very recently) for around 10,000 Iraqi soldiers, which meant a lot of buildings, infrastructure and a wide variety of military equipment in what we anticipated to be rather significant amounts by anyone's standards.

We, the British, had only been in Al Amarah for less than 48 hours in reasonable strength and the city had been, at least as far as we were concerned, extremely quiet and most of our time had been spent establishing ourselves on the airfield. Some, mainly very young, Iraqis had peered shyly at us from a respectable distance. The locals were obviously unsure of all these foreigners with guns, which was both understandable and a very reasonable approach from their perspective. Our view was one of the "great unknown" in many ways towards the local population: I doubted if they had much idea of the outside world beyond the city limits and our knowledge of them was equally scant, including just what kind of reception to expect. One thing we did know was that all the Iraqi males we were about to meet, if over the age of eighteen, would have experienced some form of military service — and probably the odd war too — which made them, coupled with the tens of thousands of weapons floating around the country, to my mind at least, potentially many times more "challenging" than the average Northern Irish or Balkan crowd. Oddly enough, this view was deemed "rather pessimistic" within the brigade: yet again I was obviously thinking too much, but I personally couldn't shake the growing feeling that we were approaching this with a large degree of smug complacency and were taking rather a lot of things for granted.

Following the usual last minute brief and communication checks, our little team duly drove out to meet the Iraqi people. As always, it was early in the morning before the sun rose and around the airfield it was almost tranquil. It reminded me of a quiet Sunday morning back in the UK. As a team we were silent, our intelligence was verging on nil and once we "got outside the wire" we were quietly conscious that we were a very small patrol, which was lightly armed, lacked ammunition and our communications were notoriously unreliable, not a great combination. Hopefully the Iraqis would be in a good mood or at least merely curious about us.

We drove slowly towards the local barracks. Initially the roads and streets were very deserted, then we began to see abandoned Iraqi Army vehicles in ones and twos — small "Gaz" jeeps and large "Zil" trucks — both Russian-made and very sturdy by nature. They had all been stripped of their batteries and tyres, probably had their fuel tanks siphoned and most removable items, such as wing mirrors and seats, had been liberally removed by someone before us. We reported these sightings by radio, with a location for each vehicle: the grand plan now was that all Iraqi Army vehicles would be recovered by us and held for the "new" Iraqi Army to be equipped with, although we weren't too sure when or how this new army would be formed or who would train it, or even be in it. That was just mere detail really, unbeknown to us all, very much a sign of things to come over the next few years.

As we approached closer the Iraqi Divisional Barracks, the streets' population increased proportionally, rather akin to approaching an English premier league stadium for a big match. Aside from the odd glance, most people simply dismissed us, which surprised us slightly. As the barracks came into view, we were even more surprised to see several hundreds of people of all ages and both sexes milling around for entry into the abandoned military base, which itself was much larger than we had anticipated. We slowed down to walking pace — military cruising if you like — and peered towards the base, taking in the numerous and now empty sentry boxes atop a high wall and fence combination. We could see more abandoned vehicles, again all stripped of anything remotely removable and scores upon scores of Iraqis inside the camp. Opposite the main gates, we stopped and surveyed the scene, temporarily speechless as the scores of Iraqis had now become literally thousands, in the courtyard, on the roof, clambering over vehicles, smashing windows and passing the contents out through them. It was both anarchy and semi-organised chaos on a grand scale. It seemed like the entire population of Al Amarah was having a free shopping day at Saddam's expense.

Some of the Iraqis closest to the gates noticed us and quickly gauged our strength and capabilities and very rapidly, almost contemptuously, dismissed us as any form of threat to them and their large-scale looting activities. They numbered in their several thousands, we were less than ten in number: very much a no-brainer for both sides. Women trundled past us with all manner of bags laden with whatever they had grabbed, children of all ages dutifully following their mothers and elder sisters clutching lamps, plant pots, rugs and other "accommodation stores" as our Army would call these items. We burst out laughing at the sight of two small boys, seemingly without an adult minder, dragging a small tree between them: obviously, all that remained for them to steal. On looking further into the camp, we saw large and well-organised groups of adult males with assorted large wooden crates and metal boxes in sizeable numbers, all of which we recognised as ammunition containers of some kind. I noticed some Soviet armoured cars of the BRDM family, but disturbingly, I saw that the machine guns had been removed from all the vehicle turrets, when and by whom it was impossible to guess, but this barracks was a sheer treasure trove of arms and ammunition as all the Iraqi fighting age males we were now watching were obviously very well aware as they "asset stripped" with undisguised gusto and enthusiasm.

We radioed details of the scene into our HQ. Following a lengthy pause we were asked if we could do anything disperse the crowd. As we were outnumbered by approximately several hundred to one and all of us were firmly convinced that somewhere within this milling crowd were probably many more weapons than we jointly possessed, and definitely far more ammunition than we had been meagrely issued with, we politely suggested that this was much more of a task for at least a company of armoured infantry and their attention-getting and very potent Warrior armoured fighting vehicles (size definitely does matter at certain times in your life after all). To be fair, our HQ agreed to call out the armour immediately to quell the looting and as we could do little if anything to impact on the large-scale looting in particular and the situation in general, to be honest, we opted to discreetly move on and explore further away from the city. Our mission after all was to gain intelligence and an understanding of both the local area and its population. Although nothing was said between us, we all quietly understood that this was our very own "discretion is the better part of valour" moment.

We hadn't expected either the sheer scale of the looting or the total absence of any form of social order. The implications of the "Ba'ath Party Decree" were now blatantly obvious to us. Sadly this wouldn't sink in at the higher political level until far too late, and by then the damage was simply irrevocable across the breadth of Iraq, but that was far above our lowly pay band. So in true British military tradition we cracked on regardless. We opted to just head west, towards the major town of Al Maymunah. it was a large town and dominated both major road and river crossing sites towards An Nas and, judging by our maps (alone) a significant number of, mainly nameless, villages along the connecting road between the two towns.

Our arrival in the main street of Al Maymunah received a very subdued reception from the locals, almost a non-event really. People of all ages and sexes quietly observed us, most without stopping their business and absolutely no visible emotion. This was an eerily quiet atmosphere for us to behold: there was no pretence at all that we were either liberators or particularly welcome, rather just some foreign people with guns. We had spotted several T55 tanks and MTLB APCs discarded along the high street and down various side streets, all in seemingly good condition, which the locals seemed to find a very commonplace sight in their town centre. We opted to investigate these vehicles. On dismounting our vehicles, the local populace simply walked around us, with at best a curious glance or just plain ignorance of our existence. Even the ever-curious children were kept in check by the grownups from getting too close to us. There was absolutely no pretence of any semblance of a welcome by anyone. This again was not what we had anticipated. It was slowly dawning upon us that we were most definitely not perceived as their liberators by these particular Iraqis.

Despite the cool reception, no overt display of hostility was made towards us either, so we decided to split into two groups of three, leaving three guys to secure the vehicles, and literally wander around, albeit cautiously. Within months, if not weeks, such a random plan of action would have undoubtedly cost all of us our lives, but this was early days and we still, albeit naïvely perhaps, held the view that the average Iraqi would be glad of our presence. Three years later our arrival in Helmand Province with our heavily politicised and overly optimistic mission, militarily small in numbers and with a painfully lightweight capability alongside a number of vague, often conflicting agendas would prove very, very painful by comparison. The Pashtun-dominated Taliban made their feelings immediately plain, to say the least, and in a singularly violent manner.

The first point we noticed about all the T 55s was the lack of their heavy "Dushka" machine guns, normally mounted externally on the turret for defence against aircraft. This was disturbing as this was simply a beast of a machine gun, firing a rather large 12.7mm round which could amputate human limbs with consummate ease and these rounds could still easily kill you after travelling a couple of thousand metres, even with body armour being worn. This wasn't a good start, I thought quietly. The good news was that, on peering inside the turret (we didn't climb inside for fear of booby traps), all the main armament rounds were still present. Shells make superb IEDs after all, but the crews had, as always, taken their own personal weapons home to Mum with them. Strangely, most of them opting to leave their tanks very neatly parked. Obviously Iraqi tank crews took civic pride and road safety rather seriously, I mused to myself.

Unsurprisingly the machine guns were absent from the MTLBs also and all the vehicles had their engine batteries long since removed by the local populace, who were still walking by us as if we were some form of inconsequential hologram, a bizarre and almost surreal situation really. We found a couple of large Zil trucks, which really had been stripped with gusto and enthusiasm, tyres, seats and wing mirrors notwithstanding. One vehicle had broad daylight were its engine used to sit and the absent fuel caps denoted siphoned fuel tanks, no doubt, but otherwise all was remarkably quiet still. Having noted the exact quantity, location and types of vehicles we moved back to the rest of the group with the future re-equipping of the future Iraqi Army in mind, who latterly donated most of their equipment to rampant Islamic State fighters in their undue haste to get away from them, but back then we dutifully recovered these vehicles as per our orders.

Dai and Omar had been talking to various passers-by (adult males only, of course), our own military version of being stopped in the high street by enthusiastic charity fund raisers in UK. The locals, I was informed, were polite enough, if very aloof towards us, healthily disinclined to lengthy conversations with us and in the main, all seemed to hold and forcibly express the common view of, "Why are you here?" On being asked about the Iraqi Army/Police/Party officials the standard response was, "They left". When asked where they had gone the curt answer varied between, "Baghdad" and just, "Home", wherever that was in this rather large country. The only time the locals showed any real interest in us was on our discovery of a decidedly unmilitary looking building in the main street, which had its plate glass window shattered by a large street sign (complete with concrete base still attached) and the doors rather obviously and violently smashed in.

Curious as to the reason behind this selective-looking attack, we wandered inside, to discover a freshly emptied Bank of Iraq branch, the vault, safe and cashiers' boxes all remarkably devoid of any form of currency and all the furniture and fittings removed for good measure. A small crowd watched us with undisguised interest from a distance, probably concerned that we might ask for the return of the newly liberated money. All we found was a handful of small denomination notes on the bank floor, obviously literally loose change in looting terms. We were more amused than concerned, to be honest: Iraqi dinars were neither of any value or interest to us. As long as no one was trying too hard to kill us, they were more than welcome to Saddam's money was our view.

That incident aside, we seemed as popular as a visit by the bailiffs back home, I thought. Obviously, no one had actively informed them that we were their long-awaited liberators from their lengthy oppression by Saddam and his odious, totalitarian regime. I really didn't see any visible hint of either warmth or welcome towards us. This could be a far longer haul than our own politicians may care for, I thought as I looked around at the totally unresponsive and unwelcoming townsfolk, they were absolutely underwhelmed by the arrival of the British Army.

Unbeknown to us, their collective view seemed to be that they had comprehensively liberated themselves prior to the arrival of any form of very foreign troops, towards whom, rather than them feeling indebted to us for their long-awaited freedom, they deemed us a quite unnecessary and uninvited presence, and quietly had concerns over our long-term intentions. To say we all expected a bit more from the locals is something of an understatement really.

Somewhat chastened by our lukewarm reception, we drove west towards the nearest village, time was passing quickly and we decided to err on the side of caution in getting back to the airfield and its relative security by last light. The village itself proved to be a collection of windowless buildings, all made in the traditional "baked mud" method of construction, no electricity or telephones and devoid of any form of motor vehicles, but some highly valuable goats instead: very much a timeless desert village, but essentially leaning very strongly towards the primitive rather than the romantic side of desert life and visibly poorer than the towns nearby.

Unsure of our reception, we drove slowly towards what we guessed was the village centre and "debussed" (Army speak for getting out of a stationery vehicle) to a seemingly empty village, and then we simply waited patiently in a small, quiet group to make first contact with another section of Iraqi society. After a few minutes a lone man appeared. He was fairly old, dressed in traditional Arab robes and appeared both highly talkative and surprisingly friendly. At last, we thought, someone seems to actually like us. Omar translated for Dai and a highly animated conversation broke out. We listened attentively. I tried to glean what I could in terms of useful information, more of the social rather than military type. I was keenly aware that we knew next to nothing of these people in comparison to Northern Irish Catholics, Orthodox Serbs or Balkan Muslims, to say nothing of the language or numerous cultural differences and potential barriers. We soon discovered that these cultural issues were of a scale that we and our government had simply failed to comprehend and the Balkans and Northern Ireland were relatively simple affairs in nature by comparison.

Our new-found friend was, it transpired, the village elder, as we spoke, emboldened by his example, more men appeared. They had obviously realised we weren't going to either kill them all, steal their children or rape all their women, as Saddam's regime had informed them on repeated occasions. We learned that the only foreign troops he had previously seen were some American vehicles driving by in the distance several days ago, presumably en route to An Nas and the bulk of their comrades. Meanwhile the regime's forces had simply melted away en masse. He didn't know where they had gone to, presumably, as the stock answer always seemed to be either home, or Baghdad. He insisted on showing us the village school complex, two separate single-storey baked mud buildings, one for boys, one for girls whilst, very unlike the totally male-dominated and ultra-conservative Afghan society, the entire Iraqi people both demanded and practised education for all females without any exception, although they hadn't then gone as far as mixed schools at that time. The schools were in danger of flooding, no one was quite sure why and the assumption was that the irrigation scheme somewhere had malfunctioned, and he asked for our help, which we promised to give, but we couldn't say when, due to our lack of understanding of the area, which he accepted as quite a reasonable response.

By now several male children had appeared and we committed a small cultural faux pas by giving them sweets. The elder patiently, but firmly, explained to us that the correct etiquette was to give the adults the sweets, who would in turn ensure a fair share for all the children. We apologised profusely, which seemed to both bemuse and amuse the grownups in equal measure. The local Shia population, we later discovered, had previously equated a "visit from the authorities" (either the Iraqi military or the police) with a large amount of apprehension and sometimes a lot of pain and grief in equal measures.

Another social discovery was passed on to us by Omar discreetly. He had been quietly asked, "Why do the British have convicts in their Army?" To end our obvious puzzlement, he explained that Al Amarah was infamous for being a centre of large-scale and well-organised smuggling for centuries. In the local prisons convicted smugglers tattooed each other as a mark of both professional pride and clan membership. The local Iraqis therefore automatically connected tattoos with convicts, which made the numerous tribes who weren't part of the smuggling fraternity rather nervous, to say the least. Trying to explain to the local tribes that this was just a harmless and increasingly popular fashion statement by our young people was an utterly pointless exercise. Therefore, we quietly resolved to make the soldiers roll their sleeves down from now on. Luckily for us this was before the post-Afghanistan and recruit-desperate Army relaxed its ban on visible tattoos ie forearms, hands, neck, etc. As Westerners with our almost instinctive and seemingly ongoing lack of cultural awareness, it doesn't ever occur to us that in certain cultures this body art may lie somewhere between verging on the offensive or a highly visible mark of very low social standing. In hindsight, I was extremely grateful we didn't employ any professional football players, with their penchant for garish and almost whole-body tattoos: not that we could have possibly afforded their wages, or indeed, their volatile temperament.

We elected to call it a day and head back to the airfield and have a "hot debrief" once there. The elder and the village males gave us an enthusiastic farewell. They obviously didn't get many visitors was our view as we drove away and returned their waves with interest, a small heart and minds piece, but a start at last, I thought. As we passed through Al Maymunah we were again greeted with collective and studied indifference. I again felt rather like a rather unwelcome hologram in sandy-coloured uniform, frankly. The Iraqi Army Barracks was eerily deserted in stark contrast to the morning's almost biblical scale looting as we drove past. Either the Warriors had forced them to go home or they had just exhausted anything and everything that could be physically removed by determined human beings. I later found out the Warriors had arrived well after the peak of the frenzied redistribution of Saddam's assets by the local citizens, too late in effect. This concerned me rather a lot as that, I felt personally at least, left a remarkably large number of arms and ammunition with new owners across the city and its surrounding areas, whose personal and collective views towards us might possibly not quite match the eager hopes of our own distant political leaders. I robustly told myself they would probably warm to us very quickly, opting for the concept of the glass being half full rather than half empty. Nevertheless, the effective looting of a divisional barracks concerned me greatly; an Iraqi Army Division was 10,000 strong, which equated to rather a lot of weapons and ammunition by anyone's military standards.

On arrival, back inside the airfield we jointly discussed our first venture "outside the wire". On the plus side, no one had reacted violently towards us. However, we hadn't really set the "hearts and minds" world on fire either. One concern we all shared was that we had precious little to offer any of the Iraqis aside from old-fashioned goodwill and smiles all round until the various charities and whatever the government had planned back in UK in terms of national redevelopment and restoring the civic infrastructure arrived. We agreed that our self-perceived task was essentially a holding action, little more than keeping the Iraqis friendly and on good terms with us. As we had no other direction from anyone, we made that our core mission statement. As the saying goes in the Army, "It sounds like a plan": not quite active nation building, but everyone has to start somewhere.

Dai asked Omar for his views. He wasn't just our Terp after all, he was an integral team member and simply key to our success (or failure), quite an enlightened view for the time. We were after all "intervention virgins" back in 2003. Omar spoke hesitantly and politely, as if surprised to be asked to enlighten us, but he grew in confidence as he spoke. Firstly, he explained, Arab society revolves around the family and the tribe. Large tribes hold and jealously protect their power base, smaller tribes seek alliances to survive. In short, the tribe always comes first and we needed to understand that. Iraqis (unlike the various ethnic groups whom we, somewhat erroneously, referred to as "Afghans" as we would discover 3 years later) had quite a keen sense of nationhood and their lengthy history (of which they were extremely proud), plus a burning desire to finally join the global league of nations, while the religious schisms of over a millennium always remained a possible source of friction and extreme violence.

Saddam had repeatedly and very effectively violently supressed the imams and rigidly enforced a secular, if Sunni-dominated state. Essentially the imams either toed the party line, sought exile in Iran, or died. However, the Shias had suffered accordingly (interestingly, Omar never mentioned the repeated purges against the Kurds until we asked: they were after all non-Arab Muslims and he tended to rapidly dismiss them as such). At all costs we must not cause offence in religious terms. Surprisingly, to us at least, he explained that Iraqi women were very highly valued by their men, who basically placed them on pedestals. Just because you (as non-believers or Kufrs) don't ever actually see them up close doesn't mean they don't have great influence or strong opinions and so forth. Again the opposite to Afghanistan where women were, and remain, very much second-class citizens at best, at worst mere possessions. Lastly, he spoke of honour and respect. In the male Arab world honour was everything: without honour there was nothing. The Iraqis would probably forgive our lack of understanding and different ways if they perceived us as honourable men. It was, he emphasised, an all-important quality in this part of the world. Meanwhile respect appeared to be mainly a combination of manners and politeness on steroids in our casual Western terms and a question of considerate awareness in many ways. This was an informative and invaluable insight for all of us and, for me personally, proved to be a singularly large help in dealing with the various tribes and villages yet to come.

Years later I look at our own 21st Century liberal and populist society and see an almost total lack of any sense of personal honour or responsibility in the combined ranks of our senior leaders, whether they are political, NHS, Civil Service or military amongst others. Most of them seem to epitomise "do as I say" rather than "do as I do", a far cry from the "lead by example" ethos which permeated the Army in which I served at all levels. This extends across all walks of daily life, with dysfunctional families galore, all combined with the pervading attitude of, "It's not my fault, blame someone else or just society", in effect almost a cult of victimhood. I occasionally quietly wonder perhaps who got it right and who got it wrong. In some ways I can vaguely understand why certain, more radical, elements of the UK Muslim population tend to view us as a decadent race when they compare their devoutly pious, family centric relationships and conservative culture to our own liberal, often hedonistic society, though, conversely they tend to simultaneously eagerly accept all the social and economic benefits given to them by our generous welfare state and liberal democracy.

Dai went to HQ to submit our patrol report: all British Army patrols submit a report which goes into the overall intelligence picture along with all the other diverse intelligence assets and sources and helps towards obtaining and developing an accurate picture of the local population and its pattern of life, an essential requirement for any form of lengthy campaign in terms of understanding the locals, tasking assets and resources and (very importantly) helping towards minimising our own risks and therefore possible casualties. The Army may have become much more risk averse of late, in line with the rest of UK society, due to a combination of increasing political pressure and public sensitivity towards casualties. However, it is simply impossible to make military operations risk-free, especially ground operations, but commanders at all levels do their best to mitigate these risks as operations evolve and develop. But our recent, rather determined, enemies all have an irritating habit of consistently complicating things, utterly uncaring of casualties of any kind and possessed of a total belief in their moral superiority over all aspects of the contemptuous Western "Kufrs" life style, utter faith in God's will and therefore eventual victory.

Additionally, we didn't have anything remote approaching a cohesive casualty evacuation plan in place during this period or any military hospitals to receive them anyway. Our government had convinced itself the days of taking large-scale casualties were over, so they had all been closed to save money. This would slowly (very slowly) improve with time, but it would be 2008 until the UK's medical system finally became fully able to cope with the increasingly large numbers of wounded soldiers returning home at first in their dozens, then scores and later thousands for treatment. In fairness to our powers that be, none of us really expected the conflicts to become both so intense and enduring in nature. Nevertheless we were conscious that our patrol area was a large land mass with some significantly large pockets of (possibly hostile) population, few routes in and out, with no real support to call upon, so we would inevitably be isolated and outnumbered for most of our time on patrol. This in turn meant we had to accept a significant degree of risk to simply do our job. The general attitude was one of simple acceptance, we were Brits after all and unlike our allies, we specialised in "back of a fag packet" operations.

As we casually discussed, "Where to tomorrow?" amongst ourselves, Dai returned from HQ, looking thoughtful and in a rather quiet mood. He was normally quite laid back, cheerful and chatty by nature. We thought nothing of it, we were hardly living the dream in terms of our surroundings and general life style after all. Dai abruptly informed us that he had been recalled to his battalion, the now disbanded Queen's

Lancashire Regiment, who were then based in Cyprus. He would be leaving tomorrow morning and then returning to Iraq as part of the "follow on force" in several weeks' time. This was a definite conversation stopper. Dai was the only one of us with any formal training in "nice soldiering" and therefore some vague semblance of a coherent plan. Additionally, he was both an extremely high-quality officer and very popular with the troops, not an easy achievement in any army, let alone a small, uniquely tribal and highly professional one such as ours.

He, George and I had a quiet and rushed discussion. Essentially, I was to take command of the "CIMIC Team", as we were now known, and George would become the team's overall second in command. The CO would give me his intent tomorrow morning and Dai would leave Omar with us to carry on the vital interpretation piece, at least for the immediate future. Well, I thought later, this is obviously a done deal, so yet again I'd have to roll with it. Fortunately for me, I had some excellent men in my, albeit rather small, team. As the wider Army in Iraq too was currently operating in a perfect vacuum in terms of any form of political direction regarding what to do next with the remarkable absence of any post-hostilities governmental strategy (aside from "do some Army stuff") I had utterly no one to ask advice from, so we were pretty much on "self-drive". I, too, at my own lowly level had absolutely no idea of what we would do, or how long we would do whatever that was supposed to be in our capacity as freshly arrived liberators. We were strangers in a strange land, but strangers with a remarkably vague and ill-defined mission in an extremely foreign (but also exceedingly well armed) land which appeared to have absolutely no remaining semblance of any form of governance, judiciary, police force, public services or any other traditionally accepted aspect of organised society. This, I thought, could be, to say the very least, interesting, and possibly quite emotional.

Early the following day Dai left for the long drive south to Basra and thence onwards to Cyprus, pending his return on OP TELIC 2, when his parent battalion of Wiganers, Prestonians, and the broad assortment of proud young northerners from St Helens, Bolton and across various Lancashire towns. These young men would soon patrol the culturally vastly differing streets and narrow, potentially vicious alleyways of

Basra, which was basically all he knew, the rest was "just detail", as the common saying goes in the Army. We all were very sorry to see him go: the boys viewed him as a "switched on" officer and a nice guy, praise indeed. British soldiers are traditionally (and rightly) well known for being a difficult audience to please. Personally I rated him highly as a very sharp cookie and a pleasure to work with. I was quietly painfully aware that he would also be an extremely hard act to follow. I asked George to get the team ready for today's "mystery tour" and made my way to HQ, to see the CO for my operations brief. To say the least, I felt as if we were simply venturing into the unknown. Our detailed local knowledge was precisely zero and up-to-date intelligence even less, hardly a reassuring way to commence a very sensitive military operation against a complex tribal network and still lacking an end date or any form of clear post-conflict direction or indeed, any specific overarching aims. The feeling that we had just been told to "Go north and do some Army stuff", wasn't yet crossing my mind, but as time progressed, I couldn't help but wonder exactly who was formulating our national aims for Iraq or when they would actually communicate those aims to the troops on the ground.

Still, mine was not to reason why, so I tried (yet again) hard to avoid thinking too much and took consolation in the fact that at least it was permanently nice weather now, with the nights no longer being "Baltic" in temperature terms. Indeed, the evening temperatures were more Mediterranean summer in nature, but not quite Club Med in all other aspects of daily life. The CO was in quite good humour as he briefed us: we now had three teams involved; the Artillery Air Defenders, who would be our main reserve, but also regularly patrol the western bank of the Tigris, it being a densely-populated area with several major crossing points over the river. A small team from one of the flying squadrons would take a couple of small villages to the north of the main An Nas Road, led by the same redoubtable sergeant major who made the long and lonely walk to explain to the jittery American reservists that, "The Brits are here too". But as the CO explained, this would not be their main effort, as we needed to get the regiment's equipment in good order prior to our handover to our relief and to facilitate the return of the majority of our equipment back to UK, but also simultaneously support the brigade with aviation assets daily, which basically meant flying people between Al Amarah and the main UK Headquarters in Basra. Essentially "Hearts and Minds" came third out of a list of three missions (fourth if you included the daily demands for Force Protection). At least I know my place, I thought to myself.

Which left me and my small team to tackle the rest of the AO, roughly 55 x 45 kilometres of desert. Only about 2400 (approximately) square kilometres, I thought, looking at the map. I was tempted to ask, "So we only get 300 square kilometres per man then?" But I held my tongue, the British Army ethos is to punch above your weight and this was an exceedingly fine example of that, it just happened to be my very own and rather personal piece of punching. The population was then vaguely estimated to be somewhere between 4,000-7,000 (perhaps more), but we really didn't know and the tribal composition or relationships between them was anyone's guess. This I thought, could be a quite a "challenge" in MOD speak, or a bit more painful perhaps. My team would be the CIMIC "main effort" and was duly charged with dominating the ground and, in the process, ensuring good relationships with the tribal leaders, maintaining law and order, restoring civic infrastructure where possible, gaining any and all useful intelligence about the area dynamics, former regime members, together with traditional "hearts and minds" stuff plus, as an afterthought, any snippets about WMD would be very useful indeed. I thought this quite an ambitious shopping list but, if I'm honest, I kept that opinion firmly to myself, yet again old habits die hard.

After everyone had left, I quietly asked the CO if I was to use both my Land Rovers to achieve these multiple aims. He looked at me blankly. I explained that I didn't believe I could effectively "dominate the ground" with just two Land Rovers and a mere eight men (including me). We shared a difficult silence as he mulled that over. He promised to give me some more resources, but for now that would have to do. "Okay, sir," I replied, "could that include a medic please?" This was now almost military bartering, but I was very conscious that our personal medical equipment was poor to say the least (highly effective tourniquets, the superb "Israeli field dressing" and literally life-saving blood-clotting materials all lay several years in the future as personal issue first aid items for all British soldiers as the IEDs patiently and inexorably took their steadily rising toll of casualties) and with the RAF's prompt withdrawal of the Pumas, we also lacked any form of rapid casualty evacuation system in such a large expanse of desert and therefore, any possible rapid reinforcement also, I thought quietly.

To be fair, the CO was between a large rock and a very hard place, simultaneously having to plan an eventual withdrawal, but maintain operations whilst downsizing in accordance with the government's wishes, a juggling act with which we'd all become familiar in the next few years. As he considered my request, I quickly added that a medic would be a very useful social asset as we explored these unknown villages and met their various inhabitants. This was, after all, fundamentally a "hearts and minds" mission. He said he would raise it with the RMO (Regimental Medical Officer) as the medics came directly under his control. Accepting that this was as much as I'd achieve here and now, I thanked him and headed outside to brief my waiting team. The possibility that their reaction might not be too joyful actively crossed my mind as I went to meet them.

George and the team were patiently waiting outside on the "veranda" — the HQ building was raised above ground level with a large step surrounding the structure — I was informed that everything was "good to go", an Americanism picked up by the troops from our time in Kuwait. I briefed the guys on our task, emphasising that we would be reinforced (eventually) and omitting "dominating the ground", (British soldiers are many things, but they aren't stupid) inserting "show a presence" instead and try to help the Iraqis rebuild their shattered nation to the best of our ability: a twist, admittedly, but I felt voicing more realistic aims was required, especially as we were such a small "Band of Brothers" and I was asking rather a lot from such a "precious few". After a couple of questions, my answers only seemed to highlight our lack of knowledge and intelligence, so I summed up by stating we were "going in blind", so we needed to work for each other as British soldiers do so well and have done for centuries. For those who have never served in the

Army, you need to understand that British soldiers are "brought up" to firmly believe that they can do simply *anything*, and the vast majority of the time, they can and do exactly that. Minor miracles are a commonplace occurrence for soldiers such as these, which probably explains why they find "Civvy Street" so bewilderingly difficult and plain strange when their time comes to leave.

With that we tested our communications, a mission-critical requirement and one that was so often unreliable in Iraq, as we would soon be reminded during our travels and drove out to meet the people of our patch. As we drove to the guarded exit, we noticed three women working in the fields adjacent to the airfield, all identically dressed in the traditional black burqas. To our amazement, one of them shyly waved to us, after a brief pause we waved back and all three acknowledged our presence. This was a good omen, I felt. Hopefully the majority of the locals would feel equally friendly towards us. Well, we'd soon find out, after all, their menfolk had the monopoly over AK 47s, not them.

I had decided to give the army barracks a miss after the previous day's plague of locusts experience and Al Amarah itself was very much out of bounds to us, it now being a new and larger version of Royal Irish Town and by default, their private fiefdom. We drove to Al Maymunah and slowly toured the town centre, mainly to check that the several T55s and assorted Iraqi Army vehicles were still there: it would have been rather embarrassing if some enterprising Iraqi had stolen a couple of tanks overnight, not to mention the security nightmare that would cause us or any of our patrols. All the tanks were thankfully present and the locals seemed quite uninterested in them, having removed what they deigned attractive already and again showing even more of a minimal interest in us and certainly none too inclined for any lengthy conversations. We moved on westwards, across the local canal and towards the far smaller and hopefully much friendlier desert villages denoted on our maps, our sole source of information at that time.

As we crossed the canal bridge, a couple of young boys half-heartedly threw stones at us. It almost made us feel at home. "Just like West Belfast or Derry," one of the boys commented. Over the next few weeks this minor stoning would both increase in popularity and intensity with young Iraqi boys and become our unofficial local "toll charge" for crossing the canal by means of "their" bridge. We just ignored it, mainly as it obviously amused the locals and also we were very aware that by arresting their obviously bored offspring, we would hardly endear ourselves to the elder generation, plus it was a much better option than the irate adults then possibly bringing AK 47s, RPGs and eventually IEDs to the party after all.

As we couldn't easily pronounce the village names, and to avoid confusion between ourselves, we gave each village a unique nickname, which also gave rather low level security if we discussed locations over the radio. Whilst our vehicle-mounted radios were secure and encrypted, our personal radios were not and we routinely assumed the Iranians were diligently trying very hard to eavesdrop on all of our communications on a 24/7 basis. So, over the coming weeks we'd visit such sites as School Village, Village With no Name, River Village, Mosque Village and the Sheikh's Village, along with a northern triumvirate of Salaf Villages. Hardly stirring names of military lore but this was our patch and we'd get to know it, and its people, rather well over the coming months.

We drove past the small, almost utterly flooded earthen schools along the sole road west and discovered a surprisingly comprehensive irrigation system which seemed to link all the villages, ranging from a large canal which wouldn't have been out of place with a UK-style narrow boat serenely floating along between its sandy banks, to small channels which a child could easily stride over, but then the desert had been the perennial enemy of these people for millennia, so perhaps it was rather arrogant on our part to be surprised by their achievements. We stopped briefly at the village I had seen, albeit previously from the air, with the anti-aircraft gun mounted on the highest rooftop, which was still pointing forlornly into the brilliant blue sky. I made a mental note to somehow neutralise this potential threat: its vantage point could dominate the road for several kilometres in either direction and tear our vehicles, and their crews, to shreds in seconds with consummate ease. I believed we simply couldn't afford to leave such a quite potent, if relatively low-tech, weapon just lying around as an obvious temptation to any disgruntled individuals. I wasn't prepared to naïvely accept that the entire Iraqi nation had tamely decided to call it a day, the regime was very deeply ingrained in their society, after all.

To our amazement, we also discovered a row of several very modern buildings, houses of a rather obvious Western design, complete with sliding patio doors, unfurnished but clearly ready for occupation. Behind these we found an ultra-modern medical centre, as yet (surprisingly) unlooted and of an almost NHS standard in nature. This village was clearly meant for housing regime members. To reinforce this, in amongst the buildings lay dozens of discarded D30 Artillery shell cases, I took a quick compass bearing and realised their trajectory pointed directly towards the, now abandoned, T55 "rear guard" we had driven past en route to the airfield several days earlier. Clearly that sharp action against the Americans had been a well-coordinated "all arms" action. Where the Iraqi artillery had then withdrawn to following that little scrap, we had absolutely no idea, as the entire village was now eerily deserted. Meanwhile all the locals seemed to be giving this site a very wide berth, another sign of both regime power and the population's lingering local wariness towards the long arm of the Ba'ath Party, I thought.

Time was passing so we elected to head towards what appeared to be village centred around a large mosque. This, I reasoned, would contain local people of influence, given the well-known devoutness of the entire population. As we drove into this small village, dominated by a large but extremely well maintained and very ornate mosque, I noticed yet another extra-large mural of Saddam in military uniform. These murals were simply everywhere, despite this being a Shia heartland. Unlike others further south, this one hadn't yet been either defaced or destroyed, which slightly surprised us. We later discovered the population were simply hedging their bets, unsure of either our intentions or our long-term staying power. Iraqis are first and foremost pragmatic realists who are understandingly keen on surviving. Unlike us rather pampered Europeans, their values are much less shallow and rather more traditional in nature, just staying alive being the perennially overarching one.

We parked respectfully away from the mosque, to discover this particular village was overjoyed to see us. It seemed to us that the smaller the tribe numbered, the more they liked us. Simplistic but at that moment it was refreshingly nice to be popular with anyone. As the perceived village elder slowly approached us, Omar quietly pointed out that the mosque was a very old one (we didn't know how he knew, we just took his word for it), so this otherwise small and featureless village probably had a disproportionately large religious significance in the province. Snippets like this were invaluable "atmospherics" to us, we alone simply couldn't glean, or indeed comprehend these types of key facts easily or quickly without local knowledge of some form.

To our great surprise, a young man accompanying the old man we all took to be the village elder and therefore its leader, addressed us in excellent English. We were flabbergasted: the village consisted of little more than a dozen dwellings, a small (empty) market place and the ornate and imposing mosque. A rather young fluent English speaker wasn't what we expected for our welcoming. The young man, whom I'll call "P", as Iraqis have long (and occasionally exceedingly vicious) memories and I'd like to think he is still alive somewhere in the murderous chaos that is present-day Iraq. He slowly explained he had learned English at Baghdad University and had been an engineer in the oil fields by Basra, at least until the Russians left in somewhat of a hurry. He also spoke passable Russian and was now waiting for the oil fields to reopen, so in the meanwhile he had simply come home to his family and tribe. He was highly intelligent, honourable, honest and helpful towards us and would prove to be a discreet sounding board in terms of local attitudes and opinions, a rarity in our experience, to say the least.

We were given a village tour, except for entering the mosque. We may have been liberators, but we were still unbelievers after all, I thought quietly. But they were welcoming, if wary towards us. Yet again our staying power was discreetly in doubt, despite it being very early days. One thing we did learn about the rather grand mosque was that it had been built under an Imperial Ottoman Decree from the distant sultan during the early eighteenth century, which surprised us; the West tends to forget that the (Sunni and non-Arab) Ottoman Turks ruled almost all the Arab world for several centuries, but never fully subdued their Shia (and therefore heretic) subjects, let alone the neighbouring Iranians. History was never really too far away in Iraq, we would rediscover again and again. We left, promising to return soon and quietly pleased that we had made some new friends, also hoping their neighbours would prove as friendly.

The next day we drove to "Canal Village", which we had seen from a short distance as we drove past en route to the mosque previously. It was shielded from view partially by a lengthy berm so we were unsure of its actual size of number of inhabitants. Parking behind the berm, we slowly approached on foot and were amazed to hear the sound of loud female laughter and splashing water. As we moved through a break in the berm, we covertly gazed in flabbergasted silence at over a dozen Iraqi women, all fully covered by their black burqas and discreetly washing themselves, all of them up to their chests in the canal and cheerfully laughing and splashing water over each other. We were instantly massively unsure of the etiquette here, and with no Iraqi males in sight, we silently, but quickly, backtracked immediately and decided to enter the village further along the canal. I was hugely relieved that none of the women had noticed us, the indignant furore that could have arisen from this wasn't something I wished to dwell on. This was also one of the few occasions when we heard widespread female laughter. We hadn't yet fully realised that conservative Islam, in Western terms, is really quite puritanical in nature.

This was definitely a safe bet, I thought, from the option of a few dozen male relatives rapidly digging up their AK 47s in response to our inadvertent but undoubtedly unpopular intrusion. It would have been literally painfully difficult to explain this faux pas, and I very much doubt we would have had any real success in doing so. The troops were simultaneously bemused and amused by this unexpected event: it had shown the, previously unseen, very human side of Iraq to us, but we had almost — albeit inadvertently — blundered into a major "cultural incident", which had all the potential to swiftly snowball into a very violent situation. People being killed or injured in the name of female personal hygiene would be rather hard to both justify and explain to my chain of command, but luckily none of the women had noticed us and I decided therefore, (rightly or wrongly) to omit this small incident from my patrol report. We all have our pride and reputation to protect, after all. We all came to realise, albeit slowly, by Western standards, Islamic society tends to be so very different to nearly all our perceived norms. As one soldier commented later, "Where's the music?" Such useless "Haram" frivolity as music, dancing and even often just laughter were all very noticeably absent, a yawning cultural chasm in effect.

Rather chastened by our bathing experience, we stood on the canal bank and spotted a ramshackle foot bridge which led to the small village, which even by Iraqi standards was rather basic in nature. It was remarkably quiet, no villagers were in sight so we crossed the bridge and spread out into two groups to seek out the locals. Almost immediately several rather mangy dogs literally sprang into sight, barking and growling their heads off, obviously not too pleased to find intruders in the village.

As my group backed off — many of these dogs were possibly rabid after all — a single shot rang out from the other side of the building we were adjacent to. Immediately we ran towards the sound, speaking on our radios as we ran, trying to find out what exactly was going on. As we did, from nowhere yet also everywhere the villagers appeared seemingly en masse, all of whom seemed to be shouting at us irately. We had transcended from total silence to chaos in a matter of seconds, it seemed. We discovered the other team engaged in a Mexican standoff style "glaring competition" with another, but larger group of dogs, all of whom were snarling past themselves at these new outsiders. I noticed one of our guys had drawn his pistol (in fact he was the only pistol-armed soldier in the entire team, pistols would not become commonly issued "secondary" weapons for several years to come) which he was pointing directly at the canine pack, who gave the distinct impression they fully understood the power of firearms, despite their very low social placing.

He saw me and said, "The fucking thing tried to bite me, so I shot it!"

I replied, "But you missed at five yards then?"

He then quickly informed me that he only meant to frighten it off. I decided we could discuss the marksmanship principles later. An Iraqi male shouted something in Arabic at the pack of dogs, all of whom instantly calmed down and immediately started to drift away. He then berated us at length, with the crowd in obvious and noisy agreement. At length, Omar explained to them that we came in peace and meant no harm, the shooting being accidental. I agreed enthusiastically and apologised. As I did so I noticed a large group of women, all clad in damp burqas, suddenly appearing to join in the day's unexpected entertainment. I remember thinking, "Thank fuck they never saw us if they react like this to one of their numerous skinny dogs being threatened".

We never got any further into the village: the irate human wall in front of us was obviously in no mood to move. We eventually exchanged bland pleasantries, during which I was lectured, at length, by one of the elders about their dogs protecting them all from "Ali Babas in the night" and if we really wanted to be their friends, then don't shoot the dogs. It wasn't the best of starts to our new relationship. I decided to eat a piece of humble pie and accept the lengthy lecture with a smiley face (which probably came across as more of a grimace in hindsight) which seriously went against my personal grain. The boys however were more than glad to leave what they saw as "a miserable shithole of a poxy little village". Rather crude perhaps but they were entitled to an opinion too. After the vivid contrast in our welcomes to date, we were beginning to slowly learn that "the average village" didn't exist in this land of seemingly surprisingly complex and very fragmented social/tribal relationships. As we drove back to Al Amarah, the thought occurred to me that perhaps the war and overthrowing Saddam's regime had been the easy bit of this operation, and if that was so, then what would come our way next?

Having diligently studied our maps of the area, we opted to next pay a visit to the MEK Barracks, the anti-regime Iranians who had fought for Saddam against their own nation during the long and bloody war between these volatile neighbours. Since then they had conducted a spasmodic guerrilla war inside Iran, whilst the Tehran-backed, and exclusively Shia, Iranian-based Badr Corps had returned the favour inside Iraq, who would eventually become a serious, well organised and violent thorn in the side of future British plans in Basra, but for now both organisations were very much unknown quantities to us. We did however know that the MEK were both well-armed and utterly friendless in a post-Saddam Iraq: in effect they too were now strangers in a strange land, so it was in both our best interest and our military remit to attempt to discover their intentions, peaceful or otherwise.

The MEK Barracks had been earmarked to become our Brigade HQ, once they moved up from the southern oil fields in their entirety, and as it lay inside our patch, we accordingly drove down there to meet the exiled Iranians and gain a feel of their mood and their exact size, capability and intentions. Being both stateless and classed as traitors and therefore in urgent need of large-scale and prompt execution, in the views of their own people, I felt their options were somewhat limited and they may just appreciate some "friendly" faces now that Saddam's world had collapsed. I personally compared their situation to that of the Belgian and French Waffen SS last-ditch defenders of Berlin in 1945: they simply had no place to go. Hopefully they didn't wish to die fighting as those SS Troopers had chosen to do in the face of the overwhelming Red Army onslaught. As we approached the camp, it appeared singularly untouched by any major looting. This was very much a rarity in this part of the world as anarchy still reigned supreme: we learned later that the reason for this pristine condition was both old-fashioned and simple; when the looters had eagerly arrived, the MEK had bluntly told them, "Go away or we'll shoot you all", which, it appeared from the almost pristine condition of the barracks, had worked a treat. Political correctness and an overriding regard for human rights just don't really exist in any part of the Islamic world, after all.

On the main parade square, we discovered an abandoned British-made Chieftain main battle tank of 1980s vintage, supplied by the UK to the long-deposed Shah of Iran, only to fight for the Ayatollah and be captured on some long-forgotten battlefield by Iraqi forces, obviously then becoming a post-war trophy for Saddam's regime. Otherwise the camp appeared deserted, but in very good condition in comparison to the rest of the city. We parked on the main square, only to find a lone elderly Iraqi, complete with a tired and exceedingly miserable-looking donkey, slowly ambling across the deserted square. We approached him, exchanged the usual greetings and asked him, "Where were all the Iranians?" Our intelligence had suggested they were between 200-500 strong and very well-armed, so we didn't really want them wandering around at will. He instantly replied, "All gone with the Americans," which quite surprised us to say the least. Omar pressed for more details and it transpired the Americans had very recently been here and apparently offered the MEK some form of amnesty, or so one assumed, if they transferred their loyalty accordingly as part of the deal. Either way the MEK had left in a very well organised manner, the 60-ton Chieftain tank being the main remaining souvenir left behind. There was little else of any military value otherwise.

As we spoke, two white civilian 4x4 vehicles, both fitted with black tinted windows and large radio "whip" antennas drove onto the parade square and parked some way from us. Four well-built young men of blatantly non-Iraqi origin, all in civilian clothes, got out of the vehicles, two of them walking directly to a nearby building. George and I went to talk to the two men stood with the vehicles, one of them white, the other black. As we got closer, we noticed both men had earpieces of the type made famous by the American Secret Service, wore pistols and carried Heckler Koch machine pistols. Unsurprisingly they were also both very lean guys and visibly alert. They watched us with what appeared to be studied indifference. "Morning, guys," we said.

"How you doing?" came the reply from the white guy. The black guy just stared at us quietly and very intently.

"Nice day for it," said George. Typical British understatement, I thought.

"Yup," came the reply from the white guy. This could be become a boring and rather one-sided conversation at this rate, I thought to myself.

As we spoke, a lone middle-aged man, of obviously local ethnicity, but neatly dressed in Western-style clothes scurried out one of the buildings carrying a briefcase and clutching some bags, to hurriedly meet the other two Americans; they obviously all knew each other. All three then walked quickly back to the waiting vehicles. "You guys are leaving now, then?" we asked.

The white guy just nodded in response.

"Long way to Langley, pal," said George in reply: a blunt reference to the home of the CIA.

Food Drop Troops and Locals

Friendly Kids

Friendly Locals

Helicopters Arrive

It rains in the Desert

Landmine Stockpile

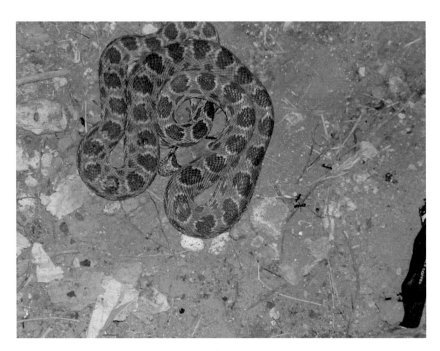

Local Pest

Local Transport

Me and My Shell scrape

Me, Mosque Village

Meal

Mosque Village (Ottoman)

New Village

Our Pumas

Road to Amara

Royal Marine Lynx

Take Cover

Uniform - NO

Welcome to Iraq

Women and Five Kids

Myself in Thought

"We're US Aid, just here to improve the lot of the Iraqi people," said the white guy immediately: the American equivalent of the Department of Foreign Investment and Development, or DFID, as we refer to it normally. We both thought, "Yeah whatever you say, mate". These guys just weren't the average bunch of civil servants having a quiet humanitarian day outing in Maysan Province. With that, all of them got back into their vehicles, the white guy at least pausing to wish us the traditional American, "You all have a nice day now," and with that they just drove off in a cloud of dust. Well, looking on the bright side, at least we now knew where all the MEK had gone. I immediately reported both that fact and that we'd just met the CIA to our Int Cell, who merely said, "There aren't any Americans in Al Amarah." I politely agreed that, yes, as they had all now left, and pointed out these people hadn't been a desert mirage and definitely weren't US Aid either, but no one seemed unduly interested in either them or the lack of all the MEK fighters, so George and I quietly admitted defeat and went back on patrol, rather quietly disappointed with our tacit and rather abrupt dismissal.

Following that very quiet day, we drove to the largest village in the area, which, we believed, had such rarities as electricity and the odd television, at least judging by pylons and the occasional aerial in or around the village. On parking our vehicles, we were amazed to see the entire (male) population pour out to greet us in an enthusiastic and noisy manner, and with the exception of the vehicle guards (otherwise at the very least large bits of the vehicles would rapidly go missing in our absence, Iraqis like to "collect" stuff) we were just enthusiastically mobbed, not something we'd expected or covered in our patrol briefing, or "orders" as the Army term this essential activity. The Army teaches its troops at all levels to plan for various "actions on": actions on being really popular is not something the Army routinely covers in its planning activities.

Without quickly realising it, I was surrounded by adult males, all smiles and laughing, talking noisily to each other, like a football crowd in tight proximity and as such I found I couldn't physically go against the flow. No matter, I thought, the troops are close by and with my PRR (personal role radio) I'm in instant communication with them. That sounds very complacent (which it undoubtedly was), but the locals were verging on the ecstatic and we were being treated like FA Cup winners. I noticed my "team" were inexorably drifting away from the village centre and I could see my own troops moving the opposite way, with their own group of "supporters" towards a large building. A dim alarm bell sounded in my head. I looked around and was horrified to discover I was the only British soldier in this new "team" of mine. Not good, I thought to myself, not good at all. I had a remote "Pressel" switch attached to my rifle stock: these enabled you to keep both hands on your rifle and operate your radio simultaneously. I pressed mine to transmit and was instantly seriously disappointed to hear absolutely nothing in my ear piece. Now I was thinking, "oh shit". I was both annoyed and embarrassed at this stage, this was a school boy error, being separated from my patrol. Being a soldier of the Northern Ireland generation, if I had done this in West Belfast or South Armagh, then my immediate survival would have been highly unlikely. Like all soldiers of my era, I well-remembered the gruesome fate of the two plain clothes soldiers who had blundered into a Republican funeral procession in West Belfast, and now I had done almost exactly that in Iraq. We veered left into what can best be described as a narrow back alley. The locals were all getting louder, I was literally hemmed in and going with the flow, as best I could tell I was with between 40 and 60 males, all of whom were travelling in absolutely the wrong direction from my perspective. I was now becoming growingly seriously concerned rather than merely annoyed or embarrassed: this was even less good I thought, it was becoming a bit emotional, really.

My helmet, in accordance with the declared British "soft hats" patrol approach was in the vehicle. My rifle, normally casually slung "muzzle down" over my shoulder (all to appear non-confrontational) was now being firmly both grasped by me and also pressed against me by the crowd around me. As we all jostled down the alley, I discreetly pushed the safety catch across to "F" (or fire) and slid the change lever to "A" — (automatic), this, I thought, was now my sole remaining insurance policy as I really didn't know where this was going. My (not very) cunning plan was that if and when someone tried to grab or "bag and tag me" I'd just raise my rifle horizontally, my overriding problem being that my rifle wasn't ready: I hadn't actually fed a round into the chamber of the barrel, as we were the "nice soldiers" and I hadn't remotely foreseen this situation. So, I sincerely hoped that I'd have both the time and physical space to do this, and thus be able to open fire at point blank range at waist height in a fairly shallow arc of fire across the alley's width. In doing so, should I have no remaining options, I'd attempt to get all my 30 rounds off rapidly as I doubted I'd have either room or time to aim properly. My best-case scenario was that I could then use the ensuing confusion to physically force my way out. I didn't intend to be quietly taken away to die in a ditch somewhere, recent events were very fresh in my memory. My worst case scenario was that I'd kill four or five of them before my magazine ran out and most probably get promptly beaten to death in fairly short order, as I probably wouldn't get the chance to do a "mag change". As I didn't have a third option really, I was, to put it politely, becoming increasingly concerned with my immediate future.

We appeared to be heading towards the bottom of the alley and I had now fatalistically accepted that I had committed a huge error of judgement, which the radio failure had turned into a rather worrying situation, over which I had absolutely no control presently. I wasn't going to start shooting until I absolutely had to, but this had now begun to look like a story with possibly quite a sad ending. I glanced at the brilliant blue sky and thought "What a glorious day", and idly wondered what both my sons were doing in UK. There wasn't much point in panicking, this was all out of my hands now, I remember thinking. Our enthusiastic mass jostle now began to slow down and the noise level also started to drop away. I paid great attention now, the next few minutes could, I felt, become quite interesting for me. I silently gave myself a bollocking for getting into this mess, I called myself a "soft bastard" and thought to myself, "If you do get killed here, what a bloody amateurish way to go". It's a matter of professional pride, a soldier thing if you will. Most British soldiers quietly hope they will die well, if the sobering time ever comes that they must do so, which rather differentiates professional soldiering from the average employment status in UK.

As if on cue, we all stopped and the noise died away abruptly, I glanced around, if I am honest, simply to try and identify the threat or in plain English, who to shoot first. Everyone suddenly moved away from me, which I found rather ominous and slightly worrying. By now I had my right hand on my pistol grip and my index finger firmly on the trigger: all I had to do now was feed a round into the chamber, raise the rifle and squeeze the trigger. Weapons don't ever (ever) just go off or open fire by accident, rather negligent people make them discharge ammunition as they are singularly designed to do. But no one made any attempt to move towards me, quite the opposite. So, I decided shooting two or three people probably wasn't too good an idea for now anyway, at least until I had a better idea of what the hell was going on here. All the males had now backed away from me, forming a rough semicircle around me, with a couple of metres' distance between them and myself as "the lone infidel". I found the new-found silence very disturbing: they all seemed to be waiting for something to happen, or perhaps someone, I thought. I noticed I was standing opposite a set of surprisingly well-maintained metal double gates, but the alley wasn't wide enough for any form of vehicle, so that baffled me slightly. On looking over the gates, I noticed the building was topped by a small green dome, which at the time meant nothing to me. Local architecture styles and decoration were then both rather low on my priorities list, frankly.

Silence reigned supreme for a few seconds which, to me at least, seemed far, far longer. All of us seemed to be staring at the gates, albeit for vastly differing reasons. Slowly one gate opened, then the second. I didn't move, but my mind now envisaged two or three burly men in balaclavas, all clutching AK 47s, rapidly emerging in a very unfriendly manner. Now it would probably be a variety of Western European Islamists, all of whom had been raised in a variety of very welcoming and rather benevolent and liberal democratic nations, and now returning all this childhood generosity and Western compassion by being rather keen on multiple murders and public beheadings for us "unbelievers": hardly an expression of gratitude towards Western generosity, welfare and education.

First one then the second gate slowly opened. Still no one moved or even spoke. I was trying to keep abreast of what was going on and frankly I was mentally somewhere between rather confused and very concerned. To my amazement a small boy, aged somewhere between ten and thirteen, stepped out and, looking directly at me, beckoned me inside with his hand. I didn't move. Instead I looked around me, to find everyone quietly staring at me but otherwise immobile. The boy quietly beckoned me again. Keeping a firm grip on my rifle, I slowly walked forward, mentally cursing both my PRR radio and my thoughtless hastiness at embracing our new-found popularity. I found myself in a small, well-kept garden. Behind me the boy diligently closed the gates, smiled shyly at me and quietly walked into the small house with the green domed roof. I rapidly scanned the garden for any lurking guys with AK 47s, relieved to find none and then did what professional soldiers seem to do best: namely, wait.

After what seemed like a small eternity, but what, in fact, was probably mere minutes at most, the boy reappeared with an elderly man behind him. We exchanged salaams and surveyed each other in silence. He was short, quite frail but had a serene air about him and a quiet confidence. He spoke to me slowly in Arabic, which I simply didn't understand. Where was Omar when I so badly needed him? I thought to myself bitterly. I didn't have any idea what he thought of me. I did my best to appear strong and confident, without, hopefully, giving off the air of a "foreign conqueror". I put the words "Saddam" and "Haram" close together, he smiled and nodded. Suddenly the penny dropped: he was the village imam (holy man) and this was his home, hence the green dome to mark the religious significance of the dwelling. The boy suddenly said in pidgin English, "We glad you here." Slightly shocked, I thanked him and told him we came in peace and hoped to help the Iraqi people. He just smiled: his English couldn't quite grasp that and my Arabic was minuscule. I discreetly re-applied my safety catch: negligently shooting a holy man, I thought, would probably end in me being rapidly (and literally) ripped apart and prove none too good for enduring UK/Iraqi relationships either.

The imam spoke again and at length in quiet soft tones. I nodded vigorously in what I hoped were the right places, saying, "Yes", or, "Thank you", in Arabic occasionally: not great, but the best I could do. The boy then produced, I don't know where from, a silver tray with an ornate dish of cold water and two glasses, into which he slowly poured the water as I watched. The imam then took a glass and offered it to me. I accepted then waited respectfully for him to pick up his glass. He moved sedately and eventually toasted me and, one presumes, the demise of Saddam's regime and their new-found freedoms.

At the end of his quiet soliloquy, we drank the water and he nodded to me. I nodded back solemnly, unsure as to the etiquette required on meeting holy men in Iraq. The boy politely indicated the gates. I nodded again and thanked the imam in Arabic, and he politely smiled, turned away and slowly walked back into his home. To my left the boy opened just one gate this time and I got a glimpse of my "friends" outside, still waiting patiently in the narrow alleyway.

I thanked the boy and moved back into the alley. As he closed the gate behind me, my new-found companions erupted into noise, all smiles and grins. I cracked a forced smile, thinking, "What the fuck was that about?" Conscious — very much so — that my real team had no idea where I was, I merely pointed towards the village centre and said, "Okay?" More smiles and grins, with some form of chanting breaking out to add sound effects to the proceedings, we quickly moved back towards the vehicles, my relief being palpable when they all hove into view and I saw our familiar uniforms. What a relief!

As I came back into the square, I noticed George, with a face like thunder, striding angrily towards me. Behind him I saw Omar, obvious by both his large build and uniquely patterned desert combats, deep in conversation and standing close by to what I (rightly) assumed to be the village school. I braced myself for an imminent impact: George was patently and very visibly unhappy. I presumed by my absence and lack of communications, this could be painful.

"Where the fuck have you been?" he demanded, followed by a rather sarcastic, "sir," after a suitable lengthy pause. I explained the radio failure, the "football match" effect and meeting the village imam as he held my gaze unblinkingly and allowed me to finish. After a long, long pause he said, "Don't ever, ever, fucking ever do that again, Boss. I was just about to rip this place apart." I was relieved our relationship had reverted to "Boss": we had an excellent relationship with neither the need or desire for any military bullshit piece and I was acutely aware that he would have, most definitely, ripped the place apart, house by house. This would have been very "emotional" for all concerned. Plus, our hearts and minds intent would have been thereafter stone dead in the water as a result.

For myself, I was both professionally acutely embarrassed and personally relieved that I was still in one piece. If push had come to shove I would have shot several of the locals in self-defence, but thankfully I had rolled with it and walked away, but purely because this was the honeymoon period for us in Iraq. However, I also fully realised that I had been outrageously lucky and I well knew this was a stunt I wouldn't get away with twice. George and I huddled together by the back of a vehicle and exchanged verbal notes. The sheikh who ran the tribe was away in either An Nas or Al Amarah "on important business", we didn't know with whom or doing what. His son had proudly shown George the empty school while Omar had repeatedly informed the villagers that, yes, Saddam and his regime really were history, that was true. The eldest son had asked that we come back in two or three days when the sheikh returned, it was very much the sheikh's tribe and personal fiefdom, we would discover in due course.

We all drove out of the sheikh's village to a rapturous farewell, but I was both quiet and deeply in thought. If one of my soldiers had "wandered off" in the manner I had, then I would have been furious and I had just screwed up big style. Fortunately George was discreet and my "street cred" recovered. However, I silently vowed to raise my game somewhat. If any British soldier had been this naïve in Helmand then his (or her) head would almost certainly have ended up impaled on a stake by the entrance to one of the scores of training camps in the northern border areas of Pakistan, but I'd walked away and my dented pride would eventually recover, plus I'd learnt some valuable lessons. I personally fervently believed that not all the Iraqis would be anywhere nearly as friendly as today's crowd, assuming they themselves stayed friendly toward us: the unknown sheikh would ultimately direct their loyalty. I was slowly beginning to understand Iraqi social "drivers", plus Saddam, no doubt, did still have numerous loyal followers somewhere around and we had yet to meet them in numbers.

The next few days were almost tranquil and for reasons we never quite understood, the Brigade Int Cell tasked us with locating, mapping and reporting on all the mosques in our area. Whether that had any connection to my "date with an imam", I really don't know to this day. I had promptly reported the meeting, which was deemed "significant", although I left out the more embarrassing details, to be totally honest. Why making a "mosque map" was important, we were never told and we spent a lot of time explaining to the obviously concerned locals that we had no evil intent towards their holy places, as our obvious interest quite clearly perturbed them and I must say I empathised with that. My personal best guess was that this mission was inspired by our long acquaintance with Belfast maps, which colour coded the city's population into Orange (Protestant) and Green (Catholic) areas and was a quick and clear depiction of that city's population demographic. However, this area was completely Shia in nature, or at least it had become post the rapid departure of Saddam's police and troops. Personally, I believed it simply made them nervous and slightly suspicious towards us and our possible future intentions. Saddam after all had ruthlessly crushed religion as any form of popular rallying cry against his lengthy dictatorial rule, his secular state was ultimately murderously enforced by the secret police and their torture chambers. The mosque map in question was never completed or produced, so we simply wasted several days and achieved precisely nothing in the process.

Once that pointless task was completed, we then received direction to do the same for all types of school in the area. Again, why we did this was something we never found out or indeed, where this direction originated from. So again, we engaged in this asymmetric mapping and again we caused the Iraqis to question our motives. However, this activity did give a lot of rather irate Iraqi parents the direct opportunity to loudly demand of us, "When will the teachers return?" This caused us a lot of embarrassment as the Iraqis were immensely proud of their education system and strongly blamed us (and the Americans) for the entire nation's teaching staff, in essence, simply running away as we advanced into Iraq, as in Saddam's Iraq it was a mandatory pre-requisite to be a card-carrying Ba'ath Party member or you would never, ever, ever become a teacher, it was that simple and stark a choice. (The exact same rule ran for doctors, nurses, all forms of "council workers", the civil service, judiciary, etc, etc and on it ran almost endlessly across a massively broad swathe of the complete fabric of Iraqi society). Our response of, "They will return very soon", didn't quite cut it with either the irate parents or much of an increasingly disenchanted population, but no one seemed to grasp this in our higher command structure. The truth was that seemingly mundane and domestic issues such as these, if not rapidly resolved, badly eroded our, albeit mainly self-perceived, credibility of being benevolent and generous liberators. But teachers, power station staff, rubbish collectors and doctors et al — or rather the lack of — simply didn't appear "sexy" enough to warrant the interest of either our politicians or generals, at least that is how it seemed to me at my lowly level.

All the schools of what we would consider a secondary level contained large wall murals in every possible location, all of which showed fairly graphic scenes, mainly of the ever-victorious Iraqi Army smashing the Iranians in a victorious and triumphal manner, but occasionally sometimes shooting down lots of American planes complete with captured pilots, (we Brits were very conspicuous by our total absence from any of these murals, which we supposed was a good thing, although it didn't boost our military egos much). The schools and (few) medical facilities we found were, along with the obvious and sacrosanct exception of mosques, were about the only buildings that hadn't suffered looting, everything and anything else being considered social "fair game", unless someone with guns told you to go away, it seemed.

The only break from our mundane mapping task was the discovery of a destroyed S60 type Iraqi towed anti-aircraft artillery piece, modelled on the WW2 Bofors Gun. We were initially curious how this had met its fate on an isolated stretch of road. On closer inspection, it had been destroyed by a British 94mm disposable anti-tank, known as a LAW (Light Anti-tank Weapon: the Army loves TLAs or Three Letter Abbreviations). We, in best Sherlock Holmes manner, discovered not one but two discarded weapons nearby: obviously the first one missed, we chuckled to ourselves. Our Paras obviously just felt the need to destroy something, simply because they could, I suppose. This rather demonstrated the differences within the Army's cap badge system very well: the REME would probably just have removed the breech block, the Royal Engineers would have cut away a very large chunk of the barrel, while the RLC Loggies would have put it on one of their numerous big trucks and moved it. We personally favoured using our Land Rovers to nudge it into a nearby canal, (my own corps enjoys being different) and the Royal Military Police would have noted down all available detail, but as always, the Paras simply attacked it, so the new Iraqi Army would have to do without this particular weapon. We figured the balance of power could withstand the loss and moved on, our very own CSI piece done for the day.

After our enforced "surveys" ended abruptly, which all of us felt had been a fairly pointless exercise, we decided to explore the outer fringes of our area and drove to the far more remote western (desert) area, in effect to explore our boundaries. En route we came across two young men, literally in the middle of nowhere, slowly walking in the intense and stifling midday heat towards An Nas, some 80 kilometres away, with nothing but sand ahead of them and a long, long perfectly straight road to nowhere. Finding this midway between highly curious and verging on clinical madness, we pulled over. Lacking Omar on this particular day, we'd just have to go for the time-honoured sign language option. Having established they were, crazily in our eyes, walking to An Nas, one of the guys suddenly noticed they both wore Iraqi-issue army boots under their traditional robes. They simultaneously realised we had seen their boots and went deathly pale, urgently looking around for something or someone non-British to appeal to for help, presumably. It suddenly dawned on me that they were now convinced we were just going to callously execute them, out here on the remote, empty road to nowhere. After all, we were probably the first ever Westerners they had met and the regime propaganda had repeatedly told them that we would just kill them. To say they went pale and exceedingly silent would be an understatement: no doubt at that moment they bitterly regretted not following the example of thousands of their countrymen in discarding their standard army issue footwear.

A few seconds later one of my soldiers voiced my thoughts by loudly blurting out, "They think we are going to slot them." ("Slot" being Army slang for shoot/kill: a blunt but factually singular action verb). To be fair, it was an excellent location for a quick and remote execution, almost geographically designed for such a sinister purpose and it would be exceedingly easy to then discreetly bury the bodies if you were that way inclined. But we were British soldiers, we had all sworn an oath (old-fashioned in modern Britain, but that's what our soldiers do) to both respect and enforce the rule of law, as dictated by a democratically elected government and not some random group of barbaric Islamic State fighters. A lengthy silence ensued as the two young Iraqis studiously avoided any possible form of eye contact with any of us. I spoke to the one closest to me, pointing at his boots and inquiring softly, "Jundi?" Jundi just means "soldier" in Arabic, a term normally associated with very low-ranking ones. He slowly nodded without looking up, both now appeared to be trembling despite the midday sun's heat. They were young men, somewhere around 18 or 19 years old and they obviously firmly believed that this was their day to die at the hands of the infidel invader.

"They just want to go home", I thought. Unarmed and lacking food and water, I personally just felt that their war was over and really couldn't see these two frightened young men changing the balance of power around here, or anywhere else for that matter. I looked around at my guys. They were either at best vaguely curious towards them or just plain bored: absolutely no significant feelings either way, towards these two former "enemies" of ours. For a few brief seconds, it occurred to me just how quietly seductive the naked power of absolute life or death can be, it is quite a powerful feeling, the real "dark side" in effect and also a ridiculously easy option in many ways. Essentially all you have to do is just dispense with your own morality for a singularly brief and very cold-blooded moment. In terms of human action when your potential victims are utterly defenceless, it is a brutally simple act to achieve, as regularly demonstrated by Islamic State, to brutally extinguish human life on the dubious grounds of religious racism justified by a hateful theological fascism, or perhaps just simple medieval-style and rather bloody entertainment for angry young men lacking direction and with little real purpose in their life and easily seduced by this "power".

This moment of dark thoughts passed and I turned to George, as always standing close by me. "Just give them some water and send them on their way," I said to him.

He simply nodded and replied, "Good call."

They almost cried with joy when they realised what our plans for them were, waving goodbye to us until they were small dots in the distance. Well, I thought to myself smugly, at least a couple of unknown mothers will get a pleasant surprise soon courtesy of the (nice) British Army. Of course, the question of their ongoing survival during the increasingly violent future that awaited all Iraqis was simply beyond our conception, but there and then we played nice and sent them home to their families. None of us know what the future really holds after all. I certainly didn't envisage the savage rise of Islamic State, as planned by former Iraqi Army commanders during their lengthy American captivity, or the arrival of Iranian boots on the ground deep inside Iraq to fight Daesh, a continuation of the seemingly eternal Sunni/Shia conflict amidst a nation's protracted and painful probable death throes.

We drove back along the northern route, which took us over the Tigris River and a very large irrigation canal by means of an impressively sturdy bridge, essentially the only way we could vary our route. It had been a long and unrewarding day, aside from the two jundi. We had driven to the imaginary boundary with American forces and found absolutely nothing. There were several villages north and south of the An Nas Road. I decided we'd visit them on another day, the desert was becoming one big microwave and our body armour merely trapped our body heat and added to discomfort and fatigue, so we were all quite tired and it had simply been a rather boring day overall.

We passed a "mini mosque", a little road side prayer room in classic mosque-style architecture and topped with the ubiquitous green dome, utterly in the middle of nowhere, but no doubt a great boon to weary faithful travellers. But to us unbelievers it was just a good navigational reference point, in military parlance. We treated these small holy places with due respect, although some of the troops were curious to enter, but they would have to remain curious, I told them, it wasn't worth any possible ill feeling if we were seen to enter this or any other mini mosque and respect for Islam was crucial to our continuing good relations with the Iraqi people. Close by was a single dwelling with a wooden table outside, atop which, rather surprisingly, was a small pyramid of Coca-Cola tins. Assuming this denoted a shop of some kind, on a whim I stopped our little convoy and told the guys to wait with the vehicles.

My plan was to treat the troops to a fizzy drink each, there and then. It would, I hoped, make a nice change from warm bottled water, essentially all we drank now. Maintaining morale is another one of the many invisible factors of military life that are vital to ensuring soldiers remain fully committed to the unit and the mission in hand. In demanding environments it's amazing how small gestures or minor items can make a very large difference to the attitude of the troops. British soldiers are stoical by nature, but the better officers and NCOs make time to look after their troops as best they are able to: respect, trust and loyalty are all two-way streets after all. The difference between good armies and poor ones is starkly simple, at its base level it breaks down to good leadership, excellent training (which the British Army excels at) and a common cause, which in the British Army is centred upon your cap badge and your mates. Anyone can look rather good in a posed photograph or look rather pretty on some parade ground: it doesn't mean they are a serious fighting force, or rather, as British soldiers often say of some of our erstwhile allies, troops with "all the gear and no idea".

I quietly walked into the dwelling to find a bare earth floor (the uniformly common floor covering across the entire area) and a large and very roughly built wooden counter with some fizzy drink cans adorned with Arabic labels and a very small boy on the dirt floor beside it, playing intensely with two empty cans and a small stick. He suddenly froze and looked at what, I assume, he saw through a child's eyes as an alien creature with pink skin, a crew cut, carrying a rifle and clad in body armour, towering over him. I gave him my best, "Salaam" and he promptly screamed loudly and then burst into even louder tears. Shit, I thought, this must be my nominated day for frightening Iraqis.

Suddenly, from what must have been a small room behind the counter, a young woman, barely old enough to be a mother herself by Western standards, came rushing into the room, only to come to a rapid halt on seeing me stood in the doorway and fully adorned in my war gear. She hurriedly covered her face, obviously hugely embarrassed by our surprise meeting. I averted my eyes and looked at the boy, who immediately screamed again, so I looked at my boots instead. She picked up the now quietly sobbing young boy and held him protectively, glancing guardedly at me and occasionally just glaring. No doubt she was hugely concerned about any combination of violent rape, possible murder and perhaps at least a major beating. I assumed her man was away at the war still as it was obvious that we were the only occupants of her rather Spartan shop.

To say the conversation within the room was now "forced" would be somewhat of an understatement. After a long and uneasy pause, I mumbled Salaam and thank you in Arabic, and literally threw a ten-dollar note on the counter, scooping up several of the Arab-style fizzy drinks from the counter — about half a dozen or so cans in total — and uttering another mumbled thank you, trying very hard not to look directly at her and add to her obvious and painful embarrassment. She pulled out a small tin box, obviously, her cash flow. I waved to indicate, "no change please", and quietly said "Laa" (no), at which point she said her first, last and only word to me, a softly spoken, "Shokran," (thank you). I nodded and walked out backwards with a (failed) attempt at a friendly and non-threatening smile, nodding all the way. I split the drinks between the vehicles (it turned out to be a rather sweet local Iraqi version of Sprite) and just told Mike to take us home. I didn't wish to share my shopping experience with the troops. I slumped wearily into my seat and reflected how totally different these people were to the Europeanised Balkan Muslims we were all very familiar with: in comparison they had been easy to deal with and far less complex to understand. In the Balkans, they regularly did lots of forbidden infidel things like drink alcohol, listen to pop music and dance, wear Western-style clothes, embrace the drugs trade and large-scale well-organised (clan based) crime to name but a few, and the ever-present love of football, of course. These people were so very different from those we'd encountered in our recent conflicts, I mused to myself.

A couple of days later, I bumped into some old friends of mine from the interrogation circuit in Brigade HQ, a Mancunian serving in an Irish regiment, named Simon and a reservist named Debs (reservists were always an extremely rare breed in Iraq), who spoke Arabic and several other languages fluently. They were also looking for agents on behalf of our intelligence community. I invited them to accompany us on some of our patrols so they could discreetly get to know the area and "talent spot". They had been largely ignored by our HQ so they accepted with alacrity. They had their own vehicles and driver, so it was a simple task for them to just tag along and it would give us three more sets of eyes and ears, as our promised reinforcements had yet to join our little band of brothers.

Pending them joining us we drove to New Village to revisit the modern buildings, somewhat of a curiosity in this part of the world and that anti-aircraft gun was bugging me, I felt it was a threat merely lying dormant for now, just waiting for an enterprising young Iraqi male to have a eureka moment either from patriotism, religious fervour or plain boredom. We pulled up at the front of the regime houses to find a small group of males checking out the houses already. As we parked up, three of them detached themselves and strode over to talk to us in a very confident manner. As they got closer, we could see one man, their leader as it transpired, had a very badly burnt face and neck. The boys immediately gave him the nickname of "Burnt Face": accurate if none too PC.

He wasted no time in asking us what our intentions were with these properties, which surely now should be donated to the Iraqi people, and when would we activate the medical centre? Before we could respond he launched into a short tirade about the missing teachers and lack of electricity since we had arrived. Burnt Face obviously wasn't the shy retiring type. My first impression of him was that he was an ex-officer of some kind, he had what the Americans would call "command presence" in large amounts, plus being tall and lean, his two quiet but burly comrades acted the part of loyal lieutenants very well and they too gave the impression of being ex-soldiers. Eventually we agreed it would be useful for all concerned to meet again to discuss his agenda at length with a few representatives from the small village adjacent to the regime buildings. He agreed and we agreed a date very cordially. As he walked away with his minders, George said, "He's trouble waiting to happen."

"Well put," I replied.

Whilst we had been chatting, Mike and some others had checked the buildings over for anything untoward. He now approached me with obvious urgency saying, "Boss, you need to see this now." We followed him, surprised to walk away from the houses, instead towards a nondescript single-storey dwelling, with the traditional walled compound around it. Having nothing to distinguish it from the other dwellings, we hadn't previously paid it any attention, but as we walked inside we were amazed to see literally tons of documents in the large main room, stacked to a height taller than me, somewhere in the region of 9 or 10 feet in height. Omar glanced at a few and immediately said, "These are police reports."

Mike interrupted and said, "Boss, this is fuck all, look at this," and led me to a small room with its door ajar. As I looked, I noticed it was ajar because a quite large anti-tank mine was acting as an improvised door stop. We didn't enter the room as its varied contents were clearly all the high explosive type and we were all allergic to and very wary of booby traps still. Assorted land mines of all types and sizes, mortar bombs, hand grenades, RPG rounds, wooden crates of "something" with Cyrillic markings, all just thrown haphazardly into a high explosive mess. The previous owners had obviously left in a hurry and have never passed the UK military's "safe storage of ammunition" exam either. We left the room alone, it was hugely untidy and it could just stay that way, from our perspective.

We had a quick team talk. The ammo room was a clear job for the EOD (Explosive Ordnance Disposal) team at Brigade HQ, but our

315

communications always died some five to ten kilometres short of our present location, so we couldn't talk to anyone other than ourselves, a perennial problem for us. It was getting close to last light and it was over an hour's drive back to camp, so did we secure this site or leave it and come back first thing tomorrow with the bomb disposal guys et al? I opted to cautiously grab the "sexiest" looking documents and leave. I had a "force" of eight men, including me, a lightly armed interpreter and no means of reliable communications and therefore no support, precious little ammo and this building would go bang very nicely and very quickly, I thought. No doubt I would take a bollocking for not securing a vast hoard of documents and lots of ammunition, but I wasn't prepared to do a possible British version of Custer's last stand with three or four men just to please some distant staff officer, whilst I sent a single "soft skin" vehicle to try and get some help, which would take several hours at least to arrange, no doubt. I felt the troops lives were all of far more value to me. No doubt some desk-bound strategist would disagree strongly, but I was the man on the ground and that was my decision, rightly or wrongly.

Once we got back, all was arranged for the next morning, a company of Warriors would secure and cordon off the village, EOD would remove and destroy the ammo and the intelligence gurus would sift through the documents pile, once it had all been checked for booby traps by EOD. We would guide the teams in and then step back. I did have to explain why I hadn't opted to stay on site overnight. Nothing was actually said to my face, but some people clearly felt I could have been more aggressive. I studiously ignored it and slept well.

Early the next morning, complete with EOD, Intelligence Corps and Military Police teams, we met the Infantry at the New Village. Their OC, a major, wasn't happy: the bridge at Al Maymunah couldn't take the weight of his bulky armoured vehicles, so he had to take a lengthy desert detour to get there. He later took his grumpiness out on me when I failed to call him "Sir". I explained that in my regiment, officers only called the colonel "Sir", otherwise it was first name terms all round. He countered that in his regiment (ever tribal, the British Army) even LE (meaning ex-ranker peasants like myself) officers would address him as, "Sir". As I detest snobs with a passion, I politely agreed to differ and decided to discreetly wander off to warn the villagers of all the forthcoming explosions. Once Omar had got the family heads together, I explained what we were doing, for their own safety, apologised for confining them to their houses and warned them that they would hear a lot of loud bangs. Omar duly translated and everyone immediately fell about laughing, to the extent that none of them could speak.

I patiently waited for them to recover and inquired exactly what had been so amusing to them. One of the men smiled broadly at me and said, "Captain Mike" (as I was now seemed to be universally known in the area), "We are Iraqi. We are very used to loud bangs in this country."

Fair comment, I thought. I made a mental note to self not to repeat that rather patronising comment and politely apologised. Luckily, they were too busy laughing to take any offence.

Having not had too much success with either our infantry or the Iraqi population so far, I asked Mike to come with me while I had another look at my favourite anti-aircraft gun on top of the house so I could work out how to remove it, leaving George and Omar to keep an eye on the villagers, who in turn seemed fascinated by the looming armoured presence of the green Warrior AFVs (the thinly and rapidly applied sand paint was peeling off everyone's vehicles by now).

As we approached the house, I was surprised to see the front door was wide open. Until now it had appeared deserted and locked. I remembered — being somewhat of a "weapons spotter", I recalled this weapon — a single-barrelled 14.5mm piece had a removable barrel, to aid cleaning and stop overheating and all that good military stuff. Russians do make simple, durable and utterly robust weapon systems after all.

"Okay, Mike, you and I are going in the house. We get on the roof and take the barrel off. That's the plan. Happy?" Mike just nodded. This was small-scale mission creep, which should please the Cabinet, I thought, they seemed to be doing that every day, after all, albeit on a much greater scale and with absolutely no shared military experience.

We got to the door, peeked inside and saw three young "fighting age" men were sitting in the room opposite, quietly talking, but had no obvious weapons, a good sign, I thought to myself, nodding to Mike we went through the door and rapidly headed for the stairs, shouting, "Salaam," towards the bemused men. Running up to the roof, weapons at the ready, we discovered the door to the small room atop the main roof was locked. Conscious we didn't have any idea exactly how many men — or indeed weapons — were in this house, speed was critical, so I gave Mike a lift onto the parapet and he hauled himself up, while I covered the access door from the house. As I watched, Mike heftily banged the barrel release catch and dropped the six-foot-long barrel down to me. I just heaved it off the roof to fall onto the sand two floors below us. Having quickly checked for any remaining ammunition (there was none), Mike jumped back down, both of us now grinning widely. We ran quickly downstairs past the still shocked young Iraqi men, shouting, "Goodbye, have a nice day!" They made no attempt to stop us, which is just as well, as we really weren't in the mood for being trapped in a strange house full of possibly Irate Iraqi males.

We took the barrel back to our little gang, another gift for the future Iraqi Army, I thought. Small things, however, can be so pleasing. Without a barrel, that gun was now just useless scrap metal. Simple plans are the best, after all. The EOD guys had a good day blowing things up, always a popular and fun activity for soldiers, while the intelligence guys and MPs found little of any significant intelligence interest amongst the pile of documents, but it got them out of the office for the day, while the infantry had a nice quiet and relaxing day out in the sun, so all in all a good day's work was had by all and, hopefully, we were also one day closer to going home, whenever that was destined to be.

We continued to explore our area of operations, trying to understand the often-complex tribal relationships and the "Who's who" of local power structures. Some villages were just literally dirt poor, others had some form of TV coverage with schools and limited access to the Iraqi version of the national power grid. It was, effectively, a human jigsaw puzzle. Brigade HQ meanwhile had its focus firmly on Al Amarah and was trying to form a "council of thirteen", a political/tribal coalition of sorts to hopefully run a city of over 300,000 people. Al Amarah after all dominated the approach to Baghdad from Iran, as well as being the provincial capital. It might have been in overall Iraqi national terms a relative backwater, but it was our very own backwater. Meanwhile the city dwellers looked down with disdain on the town dwellers, followed by the medium-sized villages passing on the favour to the smaller and more remote desert "subsistence" villages. The breakdown of all forms of governance, social infrastructure, law and order had been both total and national in scale. The Balkans in comparison had been quite well organised, or so it seemed from my personal perspective. Along with the rest of my team, we made notes for our "shopping list" to hand over to the various reconstruction elements we fully expected our government to send in very shortly and "kick-start" Iraqi society towards reconstruction as Iraq became a peaceful neighbour rather than a threat towards the region.

Our routine was occasionally interrupted by such amusements as returning to base to find everyone "stood to", as our neighbours (the Para Engineers) had just reported "contact wait out" over the radio net and were apparently under fire in their location. This transpired to be one of our very own overzealous warrant officers with a strong grudge against the local pack of feral dogs who leisurely roamed the airfield in search of any form of food. He had therefore "gone hunting" with his rifle. Sadly for all concerned, he both forgot to warn anyone of his intent and also didn't realise that a dog's very light skeleton doesn't much hinder a high velocity round in its supersonic travels, so his rounds merely relentlessly travelled on to crack over the heads of the very surprised Royal Engineers. Aside from the embarrassment to the individual concerned, it didn't endear us much to our neighbours, or deter the rather hardy dog pack one iota. Quite undeterred, the same soldier then tried to cull the pack with a pistol (at short ranges only, but unfortunately missed them all), followed by mini flares (very inaccurate pyrotechnics but we had lots of them and they were pretty to watch), clubbing (but the dogs were simply far too nimble and streetwise) and by running them over with a Land Rover, the" final solution" as it transpired, due to a late night vehicle crash into a long abandoned Iraqi trench, at which point the powers that be forcibly said, "Enough is enough. Forget about the dogs now". The dogs in question found it all a great sport to while away the day and never quite got the message that they were unwelcome.

Simon and Debs finally came along on a patrol with us, but found no one worth "recruiting" on our travels, but it gave them an idea of the local area away from Al Amarah. We returned via the bridge route and along the high embankment, which we crossed at high speed due to the fact we were skylined to the entire world (or so it felt to us), before dropping down to the Embankment Village and a nearby small oil refinery, to which we previously had paid precious little attention to during our local travels.

It was late in the afternoon, and it had been another long, hot and very boring day. To our huge surprise the refinery was surrounded by dozens of all kinds of vehicles, from Soviet-made tractors to locally-made copies of Nissan cars to mini buses and large ungainly Russian-made Zil lorries, with their occupants crowding the main entrance in what appeared to be a loud and unruly manner. What the hell, we thought, is going on here? On our envisaged nice quiet patrol, we hadn't anticipated some medium-scale civil disorder, which appeared to be on the verge of evolving into a minor riot. As usual by now, due to the singular lack of any functioning Iraqi agencies, this had immediately become our problem to resolve: anarchy does tend to show itself in many ways, after all.

As we debussed some way from the large and noisy altercation around the main gate entrance to, at close quarters, a surprisingly extensive refinery, we caught a glimpse of at least two armed men, openly carrying AK 47s and aggressively guarding the gate against the obviously agitated crowd surrounding them. This was an unwelcome surprise: while we had absolutely no doubt that Iraq was simply awash with weapons and ammunition, we also didn't expect such a brazen and public display of weaponry in broad daylight. I felt this was both a challenge and indeed a physical threat, intended or otherwise, to our newly-found authority, one I believed we had to tackle immediately. The ordinary citizens in countries such as Iraq and Afghanistan respect strength, power and money and little else, frankly. Unfortunately, liberal debate, human rights, the empowerment of women and all forms of democratic values come a very, very long way down the daily social values list (if they appear at all). That may not be a politically acceptable viewpoint in either Westminster or Brussels, but at street level that is the "realpolitik" of things.

As we approached, physically forcing our way through the crowd, the, now three in number, nervous gate guards seemed at a loss over what to do when confronted with foreigners with guns. Mao once famously said, "Real power comes from the end of a gun", which is true to an extent, but when the other guys have guns too, and outnumber you (for once we did and we were also far better trained and motivated), then it suddenly ceases to be quite that simple. The crowd parted like some kind of Wild West scene and quickly became rather silent, rapidly sensing a shift in the local dynamic. Via Omar, I told them to put their weapons on the floor, NOW. They didn't move. I repeated my request, rather more forcefully this time. After waiting a few seconds, I gave them a far straighter and blunt option: either put the weapons on the floor and step back or we will shoot you. I wasn't prepared to risk any one of these obviously nervous unknowns becoming either brave or stupid. I hadn't brought my troops all this way to die because some petty criminal or local thug wished to play up to his local crowd.

They looked at each other nervously. I told my guys not to fire without my personal order, and it was becoming all a bit serious now. The crowd watched expectantly. No doubt this was better than local TV, especially as they had had no electricity since our arrival. I was conscious that if any or all of them attempted to raise their weapons, especially at this short range of less than thirty metres, then they would, albeit regrettably, very quickly die in the very near future. We were all fast approaching the point of no return with this little Mexican standoff. Suddenly, without any preamble, the middle guy just dropped his AK on the sand and stepped backwards, keeping his eyes on us. After a slight pause, the other two did exactly the same. The crowd seemed quietly disappointed. Personally I was hugely relieved, although I didn't show it. I was very well aware if we had shot them, that in years to come, I'd very probably be on trial for manslaughter or something similar, but I'd decided to accept the advice of a wise old sergeant who once said to a far younger me in the then badlands of South Armagh, "It's far better to be judged by twelve men than carried by six". Sound advice that I never forgot during my lengthy Army service.

HM Government is not overly renowned for backing up its troops for too long. They are expendable in more ways than one, especially when it comes to legal judgement several years after the event. Armed police officers in UK seem to get a much more lenient hearing in comparison, but that goes with the (political) territory, I suppose. Recent events, be they formal police investigations based largely on the efforts of ambulance-chasing lawyers, trials or decades-old enquiries, in the case of Northern Ireland, have gone a long way to eroding soldiers' trust in that context. Whether that has impacted on soldiers' decision-making processes with regard to physically defending themselves in any future conflict is far harder to judge. But commanders at all levels are most certainly aware of this issue, including the recent efforts of the Iraq Historical Allegations Team and the Police Service of Northern Ireland's ongoing "legacy" investigations.

Having detained the three, now very sullen, guards I ascertained what was going on. In concise terms, it was basically a black-market petrol auction, petrol being much in demand for those Iraqis who owned generators due to the ongoing lack of mains electrical power. However, on arrival, it transpired all the petrol had been bought by "persons unknown" (presumably local movers and shakers) by a couple of agents, leaving no further petrol for sale. The Iraqis outside the gate became irate, at which point the armed guards appeared who, somewhat ironically, we were now protecting from their obviously and noisily angry countrymen. George informed me they had a nice selection of AKs between them: the traditional and iconic AK 47, an airborne version with a folding butt and a Romanian AKM (an AK 47 with a forward hand grip), which neatly demonstrated just how many types of weapons were in circulation around Iraq.

We found the owner in a small office, quite irate that we had arrested his guards and brandishing a piece of paper towards me. On reading it, to my surprise I discovered it appeared to be a handwritten note, from a British Infantry Officer giving him permission to both hold and use AK 47s to "guarantee the security of the refinery". I promptly called my HQ on the radio and asked them to contact the infantry to confirm this promise. I was, to say the least, very pissed off by this benign gesture: this was supposedly our AO and travelling grunts (as the infantry is colloquially known) giving out "get out of jail" chits regarding assault rifles without bothering to talk to us wasn't exactly "joined up warfare".

Now we had to take over the security of the refinery as the locals had sensed a chance to loot it, we went from hero to zero rapidly, but by now we weren't too surprised by this turn of events. As I watched the irate Iraqis Mike suddenly called, "Boss, I've found a machine gun." I walked over to a small mini bus and there was a loaded PKM belt-fed machine gun sat neatly on the back seat. I stormed back to the local boss and asked him for his "machine gun chit". He looked at me, bemused. "Right, pal, that's mine then," I said smiling politely. There was no way I was going to have a machine gun floating around the area. What next, I thought, a tank in the neighbour's barn?

Simon and Debs were enjoying the show, Mike was busy confiscating the machine gun, Omar was talking to the refinery boss and the troops were having minor physical scuffles on the gate, while George and another guy were searching our newly acquired prisoners. Busy troops are happy troops, as the saying goes. Emily, a young and attractive female officer was with the Land Rovers, talking to HQ. She had only come along to acquaint herself with the area and was enjoying a break from HQ. She informed me that the Iraqis did indeed have permission to carry AKs and I was to give them all their rifles back and let them go free. I was flabbergasted.

At this point four or five Iraqis broke through into the refinery and ran into the infrastructure, to do what, I didn't have a clue. Telling Emily to take over the crowd control operation, I ordered the reservist Military Policeman who was Simon and Debs' driver to follow me and ran after them: everyone else was busy enough. The Iraqis had disappeared into a maze of pipes and confined walkways, I caught a glimpse of one of them and ran after him, the MP close behind me, neither of us having the slightest clue where we were running to, or what to do when we got there.

After a short chase amongst the baffling network of pipes, we finally cornered two of them in a dead end in the centre of the refinery. They looked nervous, unsurprisingly. One of the made to climb the pipework. "Enough", I thought. Shouting loudly, I pointed my rifle at him and indicated for him to climb down. He did so and simultaneously the other three Iraqis just "appeared" from the pipes, all very "open Sesame" stuff. We lined them up and knelt them down. Yet again, it appeared they all expected a prompt execution by the pink soldiers and two of them started to quietly pray. Unbeknown to them, I just wanted to have a nice brew and soak my feet. Cold-blooded murder was definitely not on today's agenda.

The MP searched them and every single one of them yielded either a rather large, wicked-looking curved knife or a sturdy iron bar discreetly concealed beneath their clothes. Iraqi males didn't class these as weapons, rather they viewed them in the same manner as we view wrist watches, except they were vital assets for personal self-defence in a country overly prone to violence. We marched them back to the main gate area, all with their hands on heads and all looking visibly relieved we hadn't shot them. The MP seemed happy, it "beat driving the officers around", apparently. We just discussed trivia as we walked. I was curious to meet a reservist on operations, I later discovered he thought I was "fun", whatever that meant. Before we released them, I asked why they had run into the refinery. They simply replied, "Money. We could sell any petrol for a great profit." Human nature is a universal driver, it seems. I told them to go, but they stood their ground and politely, but firmly, asked for their knives and iron bars back. Why not? I thought. I had just been ordered to give the local hoods their rifles back, after all. I did so and the eldest man told me, via Omar, that I was an honourable man and they had enjoyed being arrested by me. I just said thank you. How do you respond to a statement like that?

The crowd had lost interest now: no gun battle, no petrol. Not the most entertaining of days for them, really, and they drifted slowly back towards the city, no doubt bemoaning the lack of petrol. George had given the guards their AKs back, who promptly disappeared, just in case we changed our minds, I suppose. The still irate manager loudly demanded his machine gun back. I again explained as he didn't have any permission for this, I was confiscating it and if he was unhappy with that, he could write to the commanding British General in Basra or a certain Mr T Blair in London and complain about me, okay? I'd had enough for one day. We bid Simon and Debs and their still-happy MP driver goodbye and returned to our respective bases. I duly handed in the PKM as a personal gift for the future Iraqi Army and gave my report to HQ. We quietly agreed between ourselves to keep an eye on the refinery, just in case the manager decided to quietly expand his little armed militia. Otherwise, Emily had enjoyed an interesting day out of the office and we'd convinced the infantry that it would be ever so nice if they gave us a list of exactly who they had given permission to bear arms in our area and this would also greatly help towards preventing us from shooting them, which would, no doubt, slightly annoy the locals.

Our poor communications continued to be a bone of contention and an operational concern. We had tried positioning a rebroadcast station on the main route to An Nas to extend our radio range, but we lacked both the troop numbers and such basics as ammunition (as always), machine guns or coils of razor wire to provide decent security, so Mike, our Signals Officer, had to reluctantly cease the attempt. A three-man static target was both vulnerable and attractive to the "bad guys", even at this early stage of the occupation. He did however promise me some of his better NCOs to augment our numbers, which would prove a welcome boost in time.

I had no option but to simply accept the risk of no communications in a third of my AO, we'd just have to carry on "cuffing it" in true British military tradition and hope for the best. The troops knew the risks and quietly carried on to the best of their ability. My great concern was the inability to call for any form of help if we got into trouble and/or took casualties beyond a particular grid line in the desert. I did wonder if our political masters had either knowledge of or any real interest in any of our myriad problems. Personally, I strongly doubted it, but I kept my doubts to myself.

Whilst back out amongst our villages, we learnt that the bazaar in Al Maymunah had reopened, a good sign on the resumption of normality so soon after our invasion. We decided to drive through and have a look.The next day, en route to the westernmost villages which we had yet to visit, we took a slight detour and drove past the long since looted bank into the market area. To our great surprise it was indeed bustling, with stalls a-plenty and we were reduced to walking pace as we crept through the pedestrian throng,— who were blatantly none too pleased to see us again. Suddenly Mike shouted, "Sir, look at this kid!" I had grown unaccustomed to being called Sir, having been called "Boss" for weeks now and all the troops being called by their first or nicknames, so this new-found formality got my attention. I looked across to Mike's window, to see a nine or ten-year-old boy pressing a Russian-made automatic pistol against the glass, literally inches from Mike's face, laughing aloud as he did so. Mike, understandably, was none too pleased at the very close proximity of a pistol to his head. I was both startled and slow to react at this boy and his childish but very potent threat. He laughed at us again and slowly drew his finger across his throat in a cutting motion and then turned to disappear into the crowd without ever saying a word to us. "Fucking hell," said Mike. I saw no point in trying to find the boy in this unfriendly and very crowded environment, so we quickly forced our way through the crowd and learned the lessons that the bazaar was both better patrolled on foot and very unfriendly with the now distinct possibility of a "close quarter" threat, including school children, it seemed.

Rather chastened by this, we drove in silence to the distant cluster of villages on the western fringe of the AO, choosing a village at random from the map to commence our, "Hello, we are the nice British Army", campaign. Turning off the road we approached the village, another subsistence village with no cars, electricity or other 21st Century niceties in sight. As we got closer we were surprised to see no human or animal activity at all. Not a good sign: why would they hide from us? I thought. We halted and debussed to find absolutely nothing. No people, no animals, all the buildings in an obvious state of disrepair and had been so for a rather long time, it seemed.

We searched the village. All we found was a single child's blue plastic sandal, some tattered rags and what appeared to be a rather forlorn lone teddy bear's arm. We drove on to three more villages and found the same result: not a trace of humanity, long-empty dwellings, almost like some kind of Hollywood trailer for a *Mad Max*-style post-apocalyptic movie. One thing that was common to all these villages was that every single water channel had been professionally and comprehensively dammed, by someone with obvious access to industrial-style support. Baffled, we drove to the Mosque Village: they were always open and friendly with us, plus P spoke excellent English. Why, we thought, in a nation which for millennia had fought the desert successfully, had someone gone to such extreme lengths to deny life to over a dozen villages?

When we asked the question, the answer was remarkably simple. These villages had expressed highly vocal dissent against the regime post the first Gulf War, including several acts of low-level violence against local officials. The regime's response had been swift and clinically effective: they had simply blocked all the water supplies to the villages and the army and police waited patiently on the main road. Eventually the villagers were forced to either walk out of their homes or die in them. The demoralised inhabitants had then been split into groups. The men were sent to work in Basra's factories, the children to become orphans of the state — either Fedayeen or domestic servants depending on gender — the women to An Nas to perform whatever tasks the state saw fit for them. This was simply systematic tribal and family destruction courtesy of the state: it made me think how fortunate UK's citizens are in a nation which so many of its inhabitants tend to denigrate on a regular basis, making loud and regular complaints which are often so utterly trivial in comparison.

The result was the utter destruction of the entire tribe and the village names were swiftly removed from all local maps and Iraqi history itself: actions both ruthlessly cost-effective and morally chilling in equal amounts. The neighbouring tribes, having helplessly watched this tragedy unfold, were all now suitably enthused to stick to the Party line, or quickly face extinction themselves. That said, after the Iraqi security forces had immediately looted the freshly abandoned villages in a literal sense of the old adage of "to the victor, the spoils". The neighbours then followed suit and lastly, as always, the Bedu picked the villages clean. Suffice it to say that we took this area off our "to do" list. Whilst it had been literally an eye-opener to the grim reality of Saddam's repeated and enduring ability to retain his power for so long, it was not one of our more fruitful days.

Some of the recurring questions I had asked my HQ were, "When will the charities arrive?" and "When will we turn the electricity back on?", along with other similar infrastructure-related issues. A constant complaint from the Iraqis that was prior to our arrival they had electricity for between ten and sixteen hours a day. Since we "liberated" them, nothing: some even openly saying at this very early stage of our occupation, "Saddam gave us more". This and the utter breakdown of their education, medical and utilities amongst other social services and key infrastructures was a growing source of increasingly verbosely expressed irritation. My own belief was if we didn't address these issues in the very near future, then we would simply lose the support and any possible good will of the vast majority of the Iraqi population. With the sheer volume of weapons across the length and breadth of this surprisingly large nation, the huge numbers of males with formal military training, added to the "disappearance" of almost the entire Iraqi Army and the Republican Guard, police, and various intelligence services we wouldn't be too short of a well-armed and trained resistance movement (or two) against us on a possibly national basis in a relatively short time.

We simply didn't have any realistic answers to these issues and to be fair, the British Army, or indeed any other professional army, simply isn't designed, trained or equipped to ensure the smooth running of a large post-conflict city such as Basra or even the much smaller, but still significant in sheer population terms, Al Amarah, let alone rebuild an entire society post national anarchy. But this seemed almost too basic a concept for our own political leaders to grasp, it seemed as if they just simply expected the entire Iraqi population to merely thank us graciously for rocking their world and then just quietly and gratefully get on with their lives, as if nothing significant had taken place.

Personally, I was very well aware of the huge effort and detailed planning that historical giants such as Churchill and Roosevelt had put into place in 1945, with the singular aim of ensuring post-Nazi Germany was efficiently governed and rapidly re-made into a functioning nation with absolutely no power vacuum or breakdown of law and social order. I suppose this yet again proved the saying that history is to politicians what sunlight is to vampires, so we stumbled along, simply trying to keep the lid on things. So, just like Helmand three years later we "did some army stuff", with an overarching lack of any realistic, let alone achievable national strategy or even just some clear and focused governmental direction, so we "guesstimated" what were good ideas or approximately the "right stuff" to do. One of the principles of war is to select and maintain the aim or aims. Without exception, all of our recent political leaders singularly failed to both understand and practise this. No doubt history will judge them accordingly regarding these repeated and cross-party failures, or at least I personally would hope so.

It was suddenly announced one day that the internationally-known Non-Governmental Organisation (NGO) of Medicins sans Frontieres (MSF) would visit us on a fact-finding mission the following day, with a view to possibly commencing operations in our area in the near future. This we fervently hoped would be the first of many such NGOs and would be exactly what we needed to get the local area and its society back on its feet. My team's attitude was simply one of "at last". Accordingly, our HQ planned a thorough brief for their English speaking representative, with the aim of convincing them to come and join us at the earliest possible opportunity. We felt this could be a great coup and significantly ease the pressure on us, whilst also pleasing the local population immensely.

We were very surprised when the MSF representative turned out to be a petite young French woman, attractive, intelligent and honest to the point of being painfully blunt. She, we quickly learned, was no one's fool. She listened patiently to the various aspects of the briefing, obviously both impervious to any attempts at charm and totally unimpressed with a room full of professional military men or by anyone's rank and she noticeably failed to take any notes. For my part I identified the regime medical centre in New Village as an excellent location for any MSF clinic, suggesting she bring her own security in order to stay neutral in the eyes of the Iraqi people and also visibly distant from us. She merely nodded.

Personally, I felt some of the presenters rather underestimated this pretty young lady and perhaps one or two were slightly patronising. She had remained almost totally silent throughout the procedure. After a summary by the CO, she looked at us all and announced that nothing she had heard today had convinced her that the presence of MSF would be of benefit to either Iraq or the overarching mission of MSF itself. She went on to explain that the invasion of Iraq, in both her own view and that of MSF in general, had been a politically driven war and MSF's presence would both damage its own credibility and possibly add credence to an illegal war. MSF, she further informed us, all would therefore not get involved in Iraq in any shape, form or manner, period. It was both a small bombshell and, to me at least, a huge disappointment: we badly needed such organisations to get Iraq back on to its feet and rather soon, I thought.

However, we merely thanked her and shrugged it off while she immediately returned to Kuwait, she literally couldn't wait to get away from us, but we were, after all, the British Army and therefore, as always, we'd just get on with things. It was a nice thought, but it was to a large degree wishful thinking on quite a large scale. We'd been sent here to fight and were trained and equipped accordingly — ignoring the ongoing logistics failures — and we had done our job accordingly.

So, we did what we have done best since 2003, held the line and waited for a distant and at times seemingly uninterested government to come up with a coherent strategy or at least a plan of some kind and hopefully allocate some worthwhile resources to us. After several years, the resources slowly came along (but ultimately the Army lost one fifth of its strength to pay for it), but the overarching national strategy never did arrive, it was all very much "gesture strategy", all very photogenic and with the right media sound bites such as women's rights, the drugs trade and other popular themes. But we were never going to "win" in the 1945 sense. As a nation we lacked the political commitment and determination for a long war so our wars were managed, financed and equipped for us to show a major presence, not to win.

Following this disappointment, we had our planned meeting with Burnt Face at the new village. I personally was still firmly convinced he was some form of ex-Iraqi military officer and very curious over his intentions. He obviously commanded a large amount of respect locally and had an unknown number of followers but both his agenda and political views were a complete mystery to me so, our meeting could possibly answer some of these questions. Without accurate and timely intelligence, all military operations are essentially just a broadsword aimlessly sweeping around. Therefore, one aspect of our job was to pick up any useful "low level" stuff, all of which went towards putting another piece into the "Int Jigsaw". So off we drove in our increasingly sorry-looking Land Rovers to the New Village, as our communications rebroadcast experiment was now officially over, therefore as usual we would be on our own for most of the day, once we drove past the limit of our radio range. By now we'd all given up on any possible improvements and just accepted it as another aspect of life in a green suit. Essentially the team ethos now was, "If shit happens, we'll just deal with it as best we can". Rather a crude concept of operations and utterly lacking military finesse, yes, very much so, but that was our best and indeed our only plan, it was that simple.

As usual, the sun rose like thunder and the temperatures shot up accordingly. We waved to the three women in the field. They waved back cheerily, ignorant of the fact that the troops were having increasingly lewd discussions about what they all wore under the burqa: it gave the guys a small distraction before we concentrated on today's task. At the main entrance gate, in the early mornings in particular, we often saw young Iraqis, normally young boys selling (now illegal) Iraqi dinars with Saddam's stern face adorning them and some form of Iraqi medals/militaria. The troops all knew they weren't permitted to buy them, but discreetly did so. We'd crack down on this every so often, but the Iraqis always came back: we had US dollars to spare, after all. I pretended not to notice any impending transactions: the average soldier's life was both extremely basic and pretty mundane plus we still had no end of tour date in sight. I also didn't feel a handful of worthless dinars as personal souvenirs would either bankrupt the world's financial system or fund any potential insurgency: after all, they already had at least several years' worth of weapons and ammunition stashed away.

We drove directly to New Village. It was another sweltering hot day, Al Maymunah was quiet, except for our now ritual minor stoning at the bridge, and we just waved and drove on as always. Mike and I made small talk. The word had got swiftly around the regiment that MSF had given us a "large sod off tablet", as the boys eloquently termed the totally negative results from our lengthy briefing, along with such traditional Anglo Saxon favourites as "What else can you expect from the French? They are still pissed off over Waterloo", or similar comments involving either cheese-eating or their rapid defeat and subsequent national surrender in 1940. The road was unsurprisingly deserted. People were visible in and around the villages we passed. Some looked up, most ignored us. Goats and crops were far more important than a handful of foreign troops in the grand scheme of things. This attitude was steadily growing as they still lacked electricity, teachers and so many other aspects of their daily lives and their impatience was becoming far more visible, too. Oh well, push on, I thought: a classic British Army expression if ever there was one.

As we approached the village, it quietly gave me some smug satisfaction to see the now impotent anti-aircraft gun silhouetted against the azure blue sky, and besides I still hadn't any idea on when — or how — we planned to physically remove it from the village. But as a potent and viable threat it was now neutralised, which was always a good thing from any soldier's perspective: dying after all is a relatively easy task to achieve in countries such as Iraq and Afghanistan for any British soldier; no point in increasing the risk further.

My smug mood was abruptly shattered as the little square by the modern houses came into view. Our friend Burnt Face and his usual two lieutenants stood silently waiting for us, along with approximately between two and three hundred or so other stern-faced and also silent Iraqi males. My first thought was simply "Shit". I told Mike to halt as I surveyed the scene. All of them simply stood, impassively and silently staring at our two Land Rovers, expressionless and looking annoyingly secure. I rapidly went through my options. The Army hammer it in to you that you *always* have options: they may not be great ones but it's up to you to choose the best (or least worst) one, and quickly.

George's calm voice came into my earpiece. "Boss, this could be interesting, what's the plan?" Succinct and to the point as always, SF guys do what it says on the tin. Best I make a decision then, I thought. The easiest option was simply to turn around and just drive off which would totally remove any and all risk in complete accordance with current 21st Century UK Nanny State doctrine. But then we'd lose both our credibility and with it any semblances of authority and never, ever, get that back in the eyes of the Iraqi population. Compassion, compromise and liberal values didn't form any part of Iraq's social values. Old-fashioned strength did, however.

Any loss of authority and related respect from any perceived weakness on our part would just result in more violence and therefore British casualties, inevitably, not to mention seriously hindering any progress in rebuilding this shattered nation. For me personally, as a British Officer, albeit one from humble origins, there was no way either my professional or personal pride could allow me to meekly walk away from this blatant and very public challenge to our authority, plus I'd never live it down. All men ultimately hold their reputation most dearly after all. Therefore I sincerely believed my personal options were rather few, to the point where I had no realistic choices.

"We'll go in and halt 50 metres from them and take it from there," I replied.

"Roger that, Boss." No fuss, no bother: a brilliant reply from my perspective. Mike looked at me and simply said, "Now, Boss?" I just nodded. This, I quietly thought could be a bit cheeky: eight of us (nine if you include Omar), so it's only about twenty-five to thirty to one. Thank fuck for the boys. No doubt they were thinking, "What the fuck?" But I knew they'd all come with me, with no questions asked, just young men doing their bit for their nation and the cap badge and, most importantly of all, each other.

"Okay, Mac" I said to myself, "Let's just get this done." I was, therefore, at that brief moment in time, an unelected formal representative of HM Government and also both my nation and my people, it was therefore time to earn my daily pay. It was that simple an equation.

We drove slowly onto the tarmac square, parking opposite our silent friends, ensuring we faced towards Al Amarah should a rapid "bug out" be necessary and parked parallel to them. Before we debussed, I told everyone to move immediately to place the vehicles between them and us. The absolute silence was rather deafening, at least to my ears. I moved out of sight behind my vehicle and lit a cigarette, rapidly attempting to weigh up my options, at least as I saw them. Burnt Face had outfoxed us and in doing so placed himself firmly on the front foot: the next few minutes would be critical, it was as simple as that. Perception is often much more important than reality after all, as all modern professional politicians know so very well. George positioned the guys as best he saw fit — I trusted him implicitly and my mind was elsewhere — then he walked over to me, Mike at my other side watching the crowd, two good men amongst a good team, just waiting for me to give some orders. No pressure then. The radios were currently useless (no change there then), the regiment may as well have been back in the UK, it was just my team and my call, we were to all intents and purposes utterly alone.

My mind was racing but essentially I knew I had only two realistic options: withdraw or deal with it. Withdrawal would give them a tremendous propaganda victory and utterly, possibly fatally, undermine our credibility, especially at this early stage of our occupation. In turn, this would boost their confidence hugely and make any and all future operations on our part much more difficult. So it was a blindingly simple choice: I would simply have to go into the crowd and call his bluff. Hopefully it was a bluff, or it would be a brief and one-way journey on my part. I didn't see the point of risking any more people to make this particular stroll any larger than I had to, so it would just be me and Omar. Hopefully he liked surprises, I mused. After my last lone adventure, I discreetly made my rifle ready to fire, just in case this didn't go well. I was determined, should that be the case, I wasn't going quietly.

George quietly said, "What next, then?"

I asked Joe — a young Scottish soldier from my own unit back in Yorkshire — to fetch Omar here immediately, please. The Army in reality is far from constantly barked harsh orders. He nodded and went the short distance to get him. I turned to Mike and George, speaking quietly. Not that our friends could hear us but old habits die hard and it was important to appear calm. Soldiers like calm officers: panic, like fear, is infectious after all. Burnt Face obviously wasn't going to come to me any time soon and asking him politely to do so would just add to his all-important "street cred" amongst his followers: plus, he knew very well that we didn't have anywhere near enough men to threaten such a large crowd in pure military terms, so I'd have to either demonstrate that we Brits were fully in charge and very confident, or meekly withdraw and thereby boost his standing amongst the locals immensely. I voiced my thoughts succinctly. "Mike, George, me and Omar are now going for a little walk. If it all goes pear-shaped in there, shoot if you have to, but above all, leave us and get the boys home, understood? I'll transmit as best I can, so you can keep up with things. Press once to say you understand and twice if I need to repeat anything. If it goes bad I'll just tell you to bug out now, the Iraqis probably won't understand that term. Happy with that?"

George protested. I cut him short. "If this doesn't work, I'll be dead before you get to me and we'll probably lose men in the process, so it's a pointless gesture so just do one, okay?"

Mike just looked at me and then said, "Are you sure about this, Boss?"

I nodded. "Mike, you get all the boys out, that's an order," and looked at George. "George, I'm the officer and therefore this is my job and mine alone. You know it makes sense, mate, don't you?" I said.

He looked at me and just said, "Take care, okay?"

I finished my cigarette and threw it on the floor, taking a quick peek at the crowd. Still there, still passive and unmoving.

Omar arrived. He was visibly nervous. "Yes, Mac?" he said to me questioningly, glancing across at the Iraqis, him watching them watching us watching them. Could be a cue for a song in better times.

"Omar, you and I are going for a little walk, okay, pal?" I said. He just looked at me blankly. "Okay, Omar?" I repeated.

"Now?" he replied.

"Now," I affirmed, nodding. He looked at me and nodded. "Stay close to me, Omar, really close, and translate whatever I say word for word, okay?" He just nodded quietly.

I stepped back from the vehicle a few paces in order to be able to see all of the guys. I quietly looked at them all and said, "Guys, I'm going for a quick chat. George is in command now, listen to him and do whatever he says. Any questions?" They looked at me and nodded as I made eye contact with all of them. "Okay, guys, just do your job and I'll see you all later." But I felt as if I was telling a lie, the pit of my stomach was incredibly tight and I was painfully conscious that several hundred eyes were also looking at me and not in an overly friendly manner. It was my time to go. I smiled at Omar. "Here we go, mate, come on then," and turned to make a rather long walk, or so it seemed despite the short distance involved. I stepped off and, as taught all those years ago as a young recruit in Catterick, pushed my neck back into my collar, pushed my chest out and pulled my shoulders back. I was, after all, a British Officer and the visible representative of my nation and my people. Admittedly both were so very different way back in 2003 and over three or four million immigrants ago in UKIP terms.

I didn't look left or right, merely forward, as I moved away from the vehicles. The crowd parted and Burnt Face, plus his sidekicks, moved slowly back into the centre of the massed and silent males. "Bastard", I thought, he really was making me — and therefore the British — come to him. I was on the back foot again. As I got closer the crowd closed ranks to face me. "OK I'll just keep walking and see what happens when I get there", I thought. It was so very, very tempting to look back at the vehicles and the reassuring friendly faces of my troops, but I badly needed the Iraqis to believe I was both utterly confident and totally unafraid. Image is everything, they say, so I had left my helmet in the vehicle and opted for being bare-headed, with my body armour left casually open. Anyway it wouldn't make the slightest of difference for me if this all turned nasty. The irony of this voluntary walk, following my recent experience didn't escape me. Hopefully I'd make this walk back, too.

Omar was so close to me now that we were on the verge of being the Army's first officially recognised gay couple. He had taken his instructions to heart, I remember thinking, along with, "oh well at least I'll have some company if it goes wrong". The silence was now totally oppressive. I looked at the expressions of the front rank of the Iraqis: hostile, blank and all focused on me, it seemed. The macabre thought crossed my mind, "I really hope they don't pluck out my eyeballs while I am still wearing them", but I was the officer and this was "officer country" and I was, like it or not, now the sole representative of my nation and fully committed, so I kept walking in what I hoped was a calm and unhurried manner.

As I approached the front of the crowd I made a bee line for Burnt Face, quietly hoping the locals would make way for me and assuming my "calm and confident face", looked them firmly in the eye. They slowly parted like a small version of the Red Sea, though I found the biblical comparison slightly incongruous given both the inland location and the local religion. As I moved towards the crowd's centre, they closed behind me, occasionally pushing into me, just so I could feel the outline of a large-bladed knife here and there. Mind games, I thought, but Omar by now was centimetres away from being intimate with me. He really was following my orders literally in staying close. I finally stood face to face with their leader. He had a slight smirk on his face and waited for complete silence before he spoke, obviously playing to the crowd. Well, he had chosen the where, when and how, something all professional soldiers would always choose to dictate rather than react to, but here I was anyway.

As always when talking with Iraqis, we spoke in circles, slowly edging towards the point in question, as is the traditional Arab way of doing business. Being blunt would be construed as both bad manners and highly insulting. Unlike the Afghans, who by our Western standards were rude, sometimes verging on arrogant as a matter of course, the Iraqis were essentially well-mannered and polite during formal meetings like this, so we exchanged small talk. Gradually he moved onto his key issues as the sun rose in front of me and Omar tried to get even closer, interpreting over my shoulder so I maintain direct eye contact with my new-found "friend". I quietly felt rather sorry for Omar, this wasn't his war after all and our Terps were the subjects of insults and constant intimidation, viewed as traitors at worst, with contempt at best by their countrymen: not a pleasant place to be really. They were all exceedingly brave men who deserved far more British Government recognition for their stoical efforts during all our years of desert wars.

Finally he declared that he and some of his followers would shortly be moving into the pristine, but empty houses to my right. I replied that was a matter for the Iraqi Government, not him, as all former regime property was rightfully theirs. The embryonic government was, he told me, composed entirely of rich cowards who had fled to the UK and US, leaving them to face the regime alone and as such wasn't recognised by him and his people (whoever they were exactly). As I was, in their eyes at least, speaking on behalf of the British nation, I replied that my Army disagreed and we would merely evict them, if necessary by force, which wasn't an ideal way for us to remain friends, I suggested sweetly. The subject abruptly changed to electricity, or rather the lack of, since we arrived: always a crowd pleaser, I thought. I replied that we were both actively looking for the former Iraqi power station employees and awaiting our own experts arrival from UK (both abjectly untrue, but sometimes we all have to tell little white lies in life) and we would greatly appreciate any help he, as a local leader of some note, could provide in finding the missing employees. He visibly enjoyed having his ego publicly noted by me, (effectively therefore recognition from the "British Army") and he accepted that answer, thankfully.

His two burly lieutenants merely gave me and Omar their best hard man stares for the complete duration of our discussion. In return I gave them a damn good ignoring, but Omar found it very unsettling, I tried to change the subject to a more neutral ground. "How did you get such injuries?" I asked him. He smiled and replied that in 1991 he had been a tank commander and his tank had been hit by an American M1 Abrams tank and both his face and the tank had caught fire. His honesty surprised me, he was even more confident than I had given him credit for, I thought. I tried to catch him out by asking what type of tank he

338

commanded. If he answered T55 it would mean the Iraqi Army, whilst a T 72 would indicate the elite Republican Guard.

He laughed and immediately replied, "An Iraqi one, of course!" This guy was sharp, I had to give him that. We then moved onto how this area would be governed and when. I replied that we had come here to give Iraq back to the Iraqi people, so a democratic process would be put in place at all levels to ensure Iraqis were governed by people of their own choice. I sensed that the crowd liked that (but I seriously doubted that they actually understood the term "democracy"), but he immediately asked what if the Iraqis don't want democracy? They weren't Westerners and laws, ultimately, were made by God, not man.

I replied that Iraq's laws were a matter solely for the Iraqi people. We fully understood that they were a pious and devout people and it was not for us to dictate such matters, whilst governance likewise was for them to decide, but it would take time, I said and we (the Coalition) would obviously require the help of the Iraqi people and then we would leave. A mistake on my part: he seized on this and demanded, "When will you leave Iraq then?" I shirked the issue by reminding him that I was a mere captain and — as he knew from his own time in the military — such decisions were for much more senior officers, but we aimed to leave at the earliest opportunity, having first ensured Iraq regained its predominant place in the global League of Nations. This seemed to appease both him and the crowd, thankfully.

I had lost track of time completely, I daren't check my watch and I had been discreetly pressing my rifle Pressel switch to keep George abreast of the nature of the conversation, occasionally receiving a reassuring single click in acknowledgment. Suddenly Burnt Face smiled broadly and asked me, "What if we just kill you, here and now?" This was a question I hadn't expected, or wanted, frankly. I briefly scanned the crowd's faces. They were blank and merely gazed back at me. I rather felt they would quite enjoy beating me to death. I paused for a second, keeping my head high. Here goes nothing, I thought, along with, this is a fucking long way from Wigan. The British Army traditionally expects its officers, if necessary, to die well. I was rather hoping that was one tradition I wouldn't need to strictly abide by.

I pressed "transmit" and spoke rather slowly. "If you decide to kill me, so be it. I will die here doing my duty and the day will be yours." Pause. I continued, "My men are under orders to not try and rescue me, so I will die here for my country while they will return to Al Amarah and if you try to stop them leaving, they will kill you and a lot of your men." He was listening intently, looking into my eyes. Arabs believe eyes are the window to your very soul, which is why I banned my men from wearing sunglasses and I was trying very, very hard not to blink. If I got this wrong, then I wouldn't be going home, ever. He continued to stare at me and I heard another single click. God bless you, George, I thought.

"But you need to know, if you do kill me today, and my friend," (Omar was physically shaking, I could feel him trembling against my back, poor sod), "Understand this. My Army will return, very soon, with tanks and planes and they will find you and kill you, then destroy your villages and smash your people, and the blood of your people will then be firmly on your hands." I decided to call his bluff — I had few options left anyway — fervently hoping that the 50/50 odds would fall in my favour. I continued in what I sincerely hoped was an utterly confident tone, "So if you wish to kill me, now is the time." Speech over, I thought. This time my safety catch had been off before I made my long walk and I had already decided that if this went wrong my singular aim was to try and take Burnt Face with me. I doubted if anything else was achievable, but it was worth a go at least and I certainly didn't intend to go to my maker quietly, or alone for that matter. British soldiers aren't designed to die meekly. I then just simply waited to discover my fate, looking directly into the eyes of Burnt Face. It was a long and silent wait and I could almost physically feel the scores of unfriendly eyes boring into me from the sullen and quiet crowd.

Suddenly he laughed. "My friend, Captain Mike, it's just a joke. we Iraqis love to joke!" he announced loudly.

Fucking really? I thought, how simply bloody hilarious. I nodded sagely. "Of course. How silly of me." So I played the "thick infidel" and cheerfully smiled and Omar, stoically behind me still, emitted a sigh of earth-shattering proportions. He wasn't having the best of days either. The atmosphere become suddenly rather more relaxed, I said I had to go soon, back to my headquarters. Another lie, just as the tanks and planes had been a lie: we had absolutely none of either, but they saw American jets high above them every day, saw us waving to the planes and pretending to talk to them on our radios, all part of our daily bluff, but they believed my lies , and I was currently simply so glad we'd waved at the planes, as stupid as we had felt doing so at the time.

Burnt Face said he understood my surprise over the "joke". I was now more than ever convinced he was ex-regime military in some form but I still had no real proof, annoyingly. On a whim, I pulled out my note book and asked him if I could write his name down, just for my own records, of course. He smiled and to my amazement, took my notebook off me and wrote his name down for me, in hesitant, but very legible English and as he returned the notebook he said, "For you, my very good friend," in clear if heavily accented English. You clever bastard, I thought as I politely smiled and thanked him. He had one last request: would I mind meeting a close friend of his soon? Absolutely, I said. I just wanted to leave now, extremely happy I still had all my dangly bits still firmly attached to my body.

With that I said my goodbye, slowly turned away and deliberately, sedately walked back to my team, hiding my overriding eagerness to get away. Omar was by my side, looking harassed and unhappy. I squeezed his shoulder, saying, "Omar, you did well. Thank you very much, my friend." He didn't respond.

George asked me, "How are you? You okay, Boss?" I replied I'd tell him back at the airfield as it was time to go. Waving a curt goodbye to my crowd, I jumped in the vehicle and told Mike to "just drive", lighting a cigarette as I finally looked at my watch.It transpired that I had been immersed in the crowd for three rather long hours. How time flies when you are having fun

I had bluffed my case yet again. I reminded myself that luck, like life itself, was finite and I had probably used my personal share for the decade already. I remained silent all the way back to the airfield, simply very grateful to be breathing still. The locals still hadn't fully realised what soft targets we were. If they ever did so, then I was sadly confident it would prove extremely painful, and possibly fatal for some, if not all of us in our small patrol.

We really were literally making this up as we went along on an almost daily basis. For a relatively small and highly professional army such as ours, surely someone somewhere must be aware of our shortages and the lack of any form of "joined up" strategy, I thought to myself. We may have recently won the war, but the small matter of winning the peace now seemed to me to be an entirely different matter, and if we weren't careful, we could rather quickly and very easily lose the goodwill of the Iraqi population, which would probably be quite emotional and physically costly for all concerned.

The very next morning brought a small bombshell. Omar had been to see our HQ and resigned. As a Kuwaiti Officer he was here voluntarily, in effect. We duly acquiesced immediately and arranged transport home for him. I was summoned to HQ to explain what I had done to Omar. I explained that he was a highly valued team member and we had treated him with the utmost respect and I didn't know why he was leaving (although I had my personal suspicions: he really hadn't enjoyed our little walk together in the slightest and I suspect he received some significant verbal grief from the locals). His transport back to Kuwait would leave from the nearby Brigade HQ, so we drove him there and he and I had a discreet chat whilst we waited for his lift home. In essence, he told me that I was a brave man (which flattered me immensely, I was only doing my duty as I saw it, no more) but he didn't want to repeat yesterday. It wasn't why he'd came here and he personally thought things could only get much worse in Iraq and very soon, so he didn't wish to be part of the chaos and violence he believed would surely follow. I told him I was grateful and fully understood his point of view (which I did, I had absolutely nothing but utter respect for him) and thanked him profusely. With that he shook my hand and went home. He was a very good man, but also a volunteer and he now chose to simply un-volunteer, as was his right.

Now Terpless, we carried on regardless, but in a far less effective manner. However, the RMO agreed to give us a medic on a daily basis. You win some, you lose some, I suppose. One of our team ambitions was to get a little Iraqi boy of about 4 years of age to some form of medical attention. When we had first arrived at the Village with No Name, we had been served chai, (the local very sugary tea with no milk) in the elder's home. This home was a mud hut basically. As we sat on the dirt floor drinking this local tea he only had one request to make of us: to help the little boy. Many of these villagers, whilst being literally dirt poor, were also very noble and extremely honest human beings, with honour and their tribe being the mainstays of their lives, in tandem with their fervent religious beliefs in their Shia faith. As we spoke, the rear wall of his small dwelling literally collapsed and several young boys fell through the wall and into our meeting. They had been eagerly eavesdropping, never having seen "pink people" before. This was hilarious and instantly broke the ice for all concerned, a highly comic moment which effortlessly crossed over our differing religions and cultures.

One of the boys was the young burns victim, clad only in ragged shorts and almost covered with disfigured, scarred and distorted skin, yet with all the trusting innocence of children of that age. He had fallen into a large open fire and seriously burned roughly a third of his body several months ago. The hospital in Al Amarah had been treating him, but now, as all the doctors, nurses and medical supplies had simply disappeared with our arrival, so had his treatment and medication. We agreed to help: he touched our hearts and the entire tribe, not to mention his parents, were obviously desperate for our help.

Unfortunately, we were promptly informed that our medical supplies were purely for us as (surprise, surprise) they were in short supply. So, on a daily/weekly basis, we quietly and relentlessly nagged both HQ and the medical staff for some help, explaining this was pure "hearts and minds" which would make us very popular with at least one small tribe in our area. Steve, our own CIMIC Man in Brigade HQ also kept up the pressure, until after several weeks it was eventually agreed he'd be picked up, with his parents, and taken for treatment. Thereafter they'd have to make their own way there (a 16-mile round trip. They duly walked and carried the little boy on their backs). Not perfect, but Steve made the arrangements and we had at least one promise that we kept: a small thing admittedly, but it gave us great satisfaction. However, we had to solemnly promise not to get personally involved in this manner again as we just didn't have the medical capability to look after the Iraqis in this manner and if word got round then they would all want some help. I quietly thought to myself, "MSF, please come back, all is forgiven".

On roughly the second patrol with a medic in the team, a male NCO on this occasion, we received a radio call from our artillery pals doing the rounds by the banks of the Tigris. They had a medical emergency with a local adult male and could we please assist ASAP? We did our best 999 impersonations (fewer blue lights and music obviously) and, luckily being fairly close by, sped to their aid, curious as to the exact nature of the emergency: they had been rather vague in detail over the radio net. Their patrol was halted across the narrow road, sat atop an embankment in a rather exposed location, as we approached we saw an unknown Iraqi male lying in the road, a cordon of troops around him, which separated him and two soldiers — giving the casualty first aid, I presumed — from what seemed to be the entire male population of the village, all of whom seemed to be very entertained by the ongoing situation.

The villages that lay directly across the (broad) width of the Tigris had a reputation for occasionally firing randomly across the river at passing Brits. It seemed to be more of a "fun" thing than any determinedly professional attempt to kill us, but "spray and pray" even in plain fun mode could be fatal, so we were all keen to move on. The gunners informed us that the man had just laid himself down in front of their vehicles as they approached, clutching his groin and then simply moaned non-stop, that was all we knew of his medical condition: not quite *Casualty* on a Saturday night. As the medic donned his surgical gloves and on seeing his Red Cross armband, a local volunteered to translate. He was, it transpired, a former English teacher. The young medic got to work, we gave him some space and kept the ever-curious crowd at bay. After a while the medic called me over and asked if we could form a human screen around him as he'd have to look at the guy's genitals. Okay, I said, this was a new one on me, so all my team formed an intimate (outward-facing) circle as the medic gingerly examined the casualty's wedding tackle. Our local chap now being all legs akimbo and his robes up over his waist behind us, we could hear the question-and-answer session via the teacher and our main tactical problem was now that of keeping our faces straight.

After a while, the local suddenly regained his health and vitality with a leap to his feet, looking like an Iraqi FA Cup winner, all smiles and grins now. The crowd cheered loudly at this "miracle" and we all thought, "What the fuck is this about?" The medic, shedding his gloves came to the point. "He's got a blobby nob, probably gonorrhoea. He's been shagging some prostitute in Al Amarah." We nodded, not quite expecting this particular diagnosis before lunch. He continued, "I gave him some placebos, told him to leave the wife alone for a couple of months and get some penicillin down him. Not much else I can do really." Okay, I said, I couldn't really follow that. Best we move on before the word got around and we'd have to open a Sexually Transmitted Diseases Clinic for all his mates. We smiled and waved. Our new best friend was waving past himself. "Don't envy his wife's job too much," said Mike out the side of his mouth as we drove past him. Indeed, I thought, well, the recruiting sergeant did say to me when I joined that the Army has loads of variety, I just never realised how much and now I also knew that the world's oldest profession was alive and well in the Middle East, even in this devout Shia heartland.

Later that day, when we drove into the sheikh's village, we received a personal invite to dinner with the sheikh, who had finished his business in Al Amarah. I thanked the sheikh — a tall imposing man, who gave the impression of being ruthless with a significant hint of arrogance — and suggested my commander would be a much more worthwhile guest than I. He agreed instantly, Iraqis love a formal hierarchy and senior tribal leaders roughly equate to our aristocracy of two or three centuries ago in terms of power and control over their people and they are all highly political animals. Just like our own political classes across the UK and the wider EU itself, they also loved and craved power, wealth and influence together with their significant egos being regularly massaged. We may be divided by a chasm of differing culture, religion and language, but in this respect the Muslim world is little different from the liberal and democratic (or corrupt and decadent if you have jihadist leanings) Western world.

The colonel was pleased, the sheikh (whose name was Adnan or "Lion") was a serious player, controlling a major tribe and de facto loyalty from several smaller tribes, and this was somewhat of a coup, he thought and proof that we were making inroads with the local populace. My personal viewpoint was slightly different: his people obviously feared him and family nepotism was rife. I strongly suspected this was much more a case of wanting to be pals with the winning side, for now at least. We duly made the arrangements, together with the security package. Losing soldiers is one thing, losing a colonel is quite another: it makes the wrong sort of headlines, never a good thing from the government's perspective.

A slight problem we had was a major scale outbreak of DNV:, Diarrhoea, Nausea and Vomiting, essentially caused by poor hygiene. Across the airfield, packed with troops and poor facilities, it was always a threat. Whilst in the desert, no one shared brews, everyone paid particular attention to cleaning their "diggers" (knife, fork and spoon), drinking mugs, etc, plus dug their own toilets and so forth. Being back in post-hostilities "civilisation" had taken the edge off these preventative measures and suddenly, within days, some 40% of the regiment was unavailable for everyday operations. Other units close by had very similar problems.

To top this off, we even had a minor dysentery outbreak, with those unfortunate soldiers quickly being placed in enforced isolation, looking very much like pathetic World War 2 Prisoners of War under harsh Japanese captivity. Additionally, our personal washing was limited to the odd Solar shower (we had been issued one between every 8-10 soldiers) but this relied on having the time to allow the sun to heat the water (obviously they didn't work at night) or simply getting possession of the shower in the first place. They were therefore preciously guarded items. Our only other option was a primitive strip wash utilising a plastic bowl. My team had one such bowl between every 4 of us, which we also used to do our laundry. We simply left our damp clothes on the camouflage net to dry during the day whilst out on patrol and improvised washing lines criss-crossed the entire location. Luckily we had each purchased our own personal stock of clothes pegs whilst in UK: small things are sometimes very important indeed towards your quality of life. It was therefore hardly surprising we had an outbreak of this nature, but nevertheless it was a major concern to have so many soldiers unavailable for duty for days at a time.

Galvanised by these disappointing events, the RSM promptly dug his personal pride and joy with a slightly press-ganged work force. Known in the Army as a "long drop latrine", some thirty feet deep and majestically completed by multiple wooden toilets, each wooden-walled and roofed in what the boys promptly dubbed this impressive construction, *"The Little House on the Prairie"*. It took the best part of several days' hard work, but it worked exceedingly well in its stated function. However in the meantime we had an enduring manpower shortage, so my promised reinforcements would have to wait a little while longer.

We took great pains to hide this outbreak from the Iraqis. The "no trading" rule was now robustly enforced with the local medal and dinar peddlers now being strictly "persona non grata" at the main gate and all locals kept at a very respectable distance until our DNV problems were fully resolved. Dinner with the sheikh therefore suddenly took up all our surplus manpower. The regiment had three enduring and concurrent operations ongoing: supporting the brigade with helicopters on a daily basis; preparing all our equipment for the return to UK and preparing to hand over key equipment to our relief, plus my little "CIMIC" piece of the pie; and finally the ever-present security, medical and other daily tasks all soldiers have to perform efficiently simply to make a unit function on military operations.

On the day in question, my team and I arrived early as the advance party and to perform a discreet security clearance of the location. The CO was also bringing along most of the regiment's hierarchy, a very tempting target for any ambitious "bad guys" indeed, so we took this task very seriously. As the sheikh's family and the villagers knew us by sight already and we knew the village pattern of life, we achieved this quite comfortably. We politely included "clearing" the sheikh's dining hall, a separate building from his home, easily identifiable as it was the only house with its own generator and a very large satellite dish. We never did get an invite inside there. In due course, after sending a code word to HQ (to confirm the village was clear), the convoy from HQ arrived. Essentially my guys were an inner cordon, whilst our gunners and re-employed soldiers formed an outer cordon as positioned by the RSM. So with 40 or 50 soldiers on guard outside, we sat down for dinner with the sheikh, his sons and the village elders.

We'd borrowed a Terp from the brigade. The CO sat close by the sheikh. The "dining table" was a garishly decorated and extremely large plastic sheet laid down the centre of the floor of this single-room building, the catering being done elsewhere by the ever-unseen female cooks. The sheikh dominated the conversation and was obviously well used to wheeling and dealing and political nuances. The CO responded on behalf of all the Army personnel present. I, George and a young soldier sat halfway down the plastic sheet, more than happy to just relax and eat, frankly: for once someone else could speak on behalf of the nation. Mike as always had opted to stay with the vehicle and given his place to the young soldier, a gesture typical of him. As we sat waiting to eat, purely with our hands, directly from the sheet, the young soldier commented on the large number of raisins on the rice pile facing us. George and I smiled at each other. George leant forward and waved his hand. Scores of flies rose from the rice immediately. "Flying raisins," said George, followed by, "enjoy."

The food centred on several chickens as the main dish, all very scrawny by UK standards, but a rare, much sought-after delicacy here, signifying the gravitas of the situation and the importance attached to our presence by the tribe. Sadly, a lot of our guys didn't quite comprehend that and had to be discreetly encouraged in eating everything in sight, as we really couldn't afford to insult the tribe by accident. Tea and bottled water were both very much in abundance, with fruit juice for the "Top Table" only, our waiters being exclusively male from lower ranking families.

The conversation was limited, mainly between the CO and a couple of HQ Officers and the sheikh, who occasionally allowed his eldest son to speak. We just chilled, frankly, enjoying the change of location and the culture change. The sheikh abruptly raised his voice. I paid attention. One of his less discreet statements (not a boast, but for him a mere statement of fact) was that he could raise up to 300 armed men within two or three hours. Personally I believed him and I didn't want my little band of brothers to meet them, frankly. I doubt if any UK bookmakers would have given us favourable odds. One snippet I picked up was that the sheikh was very aware and well informed of our dealings with Burnt Face and did not approve, but he failed to expand, though he admitted to coveting the former regime houses and facilities in the New Village, which we logged and gave a good ignoring. I really didn't want to get dragged into an Iraqi "bun fight" over property rights.

I was singularly conscious, as "P" from the Mosque Village had long since informed us, that the entire Iraqi Army (well in excess of a quarter of a million men) hadn't been paid for at least three months, and was currently "at home" anxiously awaiting a decision from the American administration in Baghdad regarding the payment of this missing back pay. Iraqi Army "Jundi" were only paid US$25 per month: a pittance to us, but a small fortune in terms of feeding their families. "P" had also told us many of them were becoming increasingly impatient and we were well aware that they had taken lots of weapons home with them, not to mention the mass looting of various abandoned barracks across the width of the entire country. I, at the time, found their reaction to us not paying them simply not worth contemplating. Personally I sincerely hoped we'd pay them, not just to avoid conflict, but also to ensure the swift return of law and order to this complex nation. I personally believed to achieve this we needed the Iraqi security forces in some form. Our well-advertised counter insurgency successes in Malaya and Northern Ireland had been achieved with the ongoing assistance of well trained and determined police forces with their detailed local knowledge and various intelligence sources. Accordingly it made sense to me to utilise at least some aspect of the Iraqi security forces rather than blunder around in an intelligence vacuum, but then again I wasn't very high on the food chain.

The point in question was Ba'ath Party membership. Someone (British) had made a disparaging remark over this topic. This provoked an immediate and quite heated response and the sheikh threw his own membership card onto the sheet. He then gave us all a lengthy monologue which essentially told us Brits what a naïve viewpoint this was: in order to be anything under Saddam you had to join the Party, or accept always being a social and political nothing. The politics of employment within the professions, advancement or sometimes plain survival were just that simple. He went on to show us his various travel permits. Without any permits you were fixed to your village and its surroundings. Party membership enabled you to travel in a far easier manner when dealing with the legions of Party officials who issued these vital documents.

I remember thinking, "He isn't frightened of us at all if he's admitting all this so publicly". A silence ensued. We all knew that, by the book, we should now arrest him following his confession to being a rather senior local party member. However, we all also realised that, apart from spoiling the dinner party somewhat, this would both cripple our relationships and immediately turn all the local tribes against us, possibly violently. The CO valiantly sought to build bridges and show understanding towards the imperative necessity of paying lip service to the Ba'ath Party under the extremes of rule under such a tyrant as Saddam Hussein. The sheikh merely nodded: he had made his point rather forcibly and quite put us Brits in our place. I just thought we'd had a brief insight into the street level political reality of Iraq. As always, I was thinking too much about "stuff".

Shortly afterwards the meal wound slowly to an end, photographs were taken as a matter of course and lots of hands were shaken. The HQ convoy drove back to the airfield, my team and I to move on towards the next village on our patrol programme and our normal daily routine. As we drove away, Mike calmly informed me that we'd been well and truly dicked whilst we were inside enjoying the sheikh's hospitality. "Dicking" is a Northern Ireland era soldier's term for patrols or bases being placed under low level, but through surveillance by the opposition looking for intelligence regarding our numbers, weapons, routine of habits, tactics, specialist equipment and so forth. We weren't surprised, it was inevitable, but I found it a rather large coincidence that the timing of this fairly comprehensive dicking had happened to coincide so neatly with the sheikh's invitation to dinner. The fact was that nothing happened on his patch without both his knowledge and tacit approval. The guy was, above all, a survivor first and foremost, I thought. He'd survived quite comfortably and appeared to have lived well under Saddam's long tenure in absolute power, so this is probably child's play for him in comparison, was my personal view. As the popular saying goes, there's no such thing as a free lunch.

One of the more interesting questions asked of me by one of the sheikh's younger sons, prior to the arrival of my HQ staff, was, "When would we remove the Iraqi Army from the fort?" Rather baffled by this, I asked him to please expand. He showed me on my map a large, seemingly innocuous, triangular earthwork to the north, at the junction of two major roads. This "earthwork", he explained, was actually a large Iraqi Army post, built to dominate the road junction and therefore all east/west movement. This was very understandable with the old arch enemy of Iran being so close by, I thought, not to mention the wide spread local penchant for large-scale cross-border smuggling. George and I had a quick discussion and agreed to clear this fort the following day, both of us quite annoyed to discover that this earthwork had a sizeable military significance and that we were blissfully unaware of its importance. Local knowledge is simply both invaluable and vital to success in this type of campaign, as Afghanistan would later reinforce to the majority of the British Army, but in spades.

Once I had explained this to our Operations Officer, he promptly agreed we needed to deal with this potential threat immediately. We duly managed to scrape together about twenty-five soldiers for the next day and we now had a new interpreter joining us, another ex-English teacher and a native of Al Maymunah, whom we will simply refer to as "T". Whilst a few more troops and a machine gun or two would have been really nice to have, a Terp was great news and until the DNV outbreak calmed down, I and my team would just have to make do with what we'd got: it's what British soldiers do far better than any and all of their NATO allies after all and have done so for generations. That said, a lot of soldiers, both serving and now retired, probably feel that we tried to punch above our weight once too often in Helmand Province, but future historians will, no doubt, eventually pass judgement about that lengthy, costly and ultimately rather fruitless campaign.

Explaining to our new interpreter what today's little job entailed as we drove, he came across as a highly intelligent man, with an impressive command of the English language, a surprisingly dry sense of humour and a man who appeared to welcome our presence in this troubled land. He made a very good first impression and he appeared to be a positive asset to the team, language skills and knowledge of the tribal dynamic was rapidly becoming invaluable to almost everything we attempted to achieve. On arrival at the earthwork, we were surprised by its sheer size, a three-sided "sand castle" with thick sloping walls, each of a length of approximately a hundred metres rising to a height of some ten to twelve metres and with a large "Sanger" (a fortified bunker) at each corner. This was, I thought, a company-sized location: roughly a hundred men, and here we were with a quarter of that. Hopefully they've all gone, I thought as I examined its wall through my pocket-sized binoculars (courtesy of a Christmas sale offer at the Dixons branch in Wigan, always a very reliable logistics supplier).

We opted to leave most of the guys to cover the location while four of us would scramble up the walls and explore it, hopefully gaining entry in the process. The classic black and white film *Beau Geste* sprang into my mind as we approached the seemingly deserted and eerily quiet sand fort. As we reached the foot of the walls, the steep gradient of the slope became apparent. Pausing to listen at the base of the wall, the silence was deafening. The boys looked at me as if to say, "Now what?" Recalling what a wise old Colour Sergeant once said to me when I was a young and overzealous corporal, namely, "Either lead, follow or just get out of the fucking way", I reverted to the old-fashioned way by quietly saying, "Follow me," and I scrambled up the sun-baked walls on all fours. Hardly an image from *Saving Private Ryan* but needs must. The boys followed close behind. Pausing at the top, we all gingerly stuck our heads over the wall like a bunch of cautious meerkats peeking out of their burrows and peered around. Absolutely nothing moved. We clambered over the wall and moved along the "battlements" to clear the Sangers one by one. These dark corners were slightly ominous and foreboding but also thankfully totally empty. We moved down into the courtyard to find a lone and rather forlorn Gaz 69 Russian Jeep, left with its bonnet up, exactly as it had been abandoned by its previous owners, obviously a nonstarter and a now merely a sand-blown relic of the long-departed garrison. Beside it were around approximately ninety discarded Iraqi Army uniforms, discarded as if in a parade formation almost. I could almost imagine their commander telling his men to go home and await further orders. The uniforms and helmets were untouched: obviously there wasn't much of a market in second-hand army militaria in post-Saddam Iraq. Ominously not a single weapon of any sort had been left behind and I suddenly realised where the two young men in army boots and so frightened of execution by us had appeared from: a small "Eureka" moment on my part.

Having checked the slightly ajar gates for booby traps, we summoned the remainder of the troops, waiting under George's command, to come and join us in our newly-acquired possession. We searched the Spartan accommodation buildings, command centre and the empty store room. Little remained of any value or interest, the Bedu had obviously been here before us, as always, it seemed. One of the guys suddenly loudly asked, "Can you hear a bell?"

"Fucking what?" came a rapid response from his mate, but we listened nevertheless and then we heard the faint ringing of a bell from outside the gate., Bemused at this incongruous noise, we gave up the fruitless search and wandered outside to where our vehicles were now parked.

Our bemusement turned instantly to amazement as we found roughly two hundred camels wandering slowly across the road, all dutifully following a very large camel with a bell fastened around its neck. "What on earth is going on?", was the unspoken collective thought. On cue a lone, wizened Arab appeared with another large camel, laden with bags and supplies obediently following behind him. On seeing us he halted, yelled aloud, at which point the camel with the bell just stopped in its tracks and stood quite still while the entire herd immediately came to a leisurely halt behind it.

Unlike us, he seemed to take everything in his stride and struck up a conversation with T and me immediately, beginning with, "What are you all doing here?" We replied something along the lines of the war against Saddam, to which he replied, "War? What war?" He was utterly and blissfully unaware of our invasion, living as he did in very deep and remote desert with his family and devoting his entire life to camel breeding. He was remarkably relaxed about us and nonchalantly explained that he was on his way to an annual camel market, as if meeting dozens of foreign soldiers was a daily occurrence. He was friendly enough and expanded on this to tell us he had been walking for ten days, with only eight more to go, then, God willing, he'd sell all his herd apart from two (the baggage and bell camels) then he would dutifully go home to his wife and son.

We were now unashamedly fascinated. The camels gave us a damn good ignoring and one of the NCOs asked him, "How do you navigate?"

He looked at us as if we were just plain stupid and replied, "By the sun, moon, stars and wind, of course." Silly us! Obviously satellite navigation and compasses were just not required by this guy, the troops accordingly thought him to be "Nails" (tough/rugged). After some small talk with us, he very politely said, "I have to go now, I have to go to market." He yelled aloud and the herd promptly moved forward again and off he serenely went, directly into the desert with his four-legged friends tamely preceding him. For him our presence, the war, Saddam's downfall and everything else was absolutely immaterial. His family had done this for generations and his son would continue to do so, the occasional war and the odd invading foreign army or two was of no consequence whatsoever in the grand scheme of things to him.

Following our surprise introduction to camel breeding, we now planned to push further north the next day and visit the "Salaf" Villages, three fairly large villages all sharing that name to some degree, adjacent to each other and arranged in an inverted V along what appeared to be a major waterway. Located on the outermost fringe of our AO, we had yet to visit these villages and little was known by us about them. The tribes we knew had little to tell us about them. It appeared they didn't mix much with other local tribes, which was unusual, slightly surprising and made us quite curious to know more about the inhabitants. Anyway, the episode of the fort had starkly reminded us that there still remained large areas about which we knew next to nothing and the Salaf Villages, on the map at least, appeared fairly substantial.

They were the most distant part of our AO and it was a long, boring drive to get there. En route we again passed the deserted sand fort, looming above the road like some kind of strange, brooding and now redundant monolith, with the desert leaving absolutely no trace of our friendly camel herder or his herd, as it has done for time eternal.

We approached the villages sedately, not wishing to alarm them and confident that they, unlike our camel herder friend, were well aware of recent events. As we entered the first of the three Salaf Villages, I received a big surprise. Everywhere I looked was evidence of relative prosperity: empty rice sacks from the Socialist People's Republic of Vietnam, a couple of Russian-made tractors, empty wooden packing crates marked "A gift from the workers of Cuba", together with power lines and numerous TV aerials. This was not a normal Iraqi village at all. The welcome, such as it was, was very muted indeed. People stood in their doorways and quietly stared at us, no one waved, the children it seemed had all been kept indoors, and it was an unusually silent atmosphere. We stopped in approximately the village centre. T spoke to me quietly. "These are Saddam's people. Look at that." He indicated a series of broad drainage ditches to me. Innocuous as that sounds, these ditches were deep, straight and made of concrete, obviously laid by engineers, not dug by hand with the sweat of the villagers. This was all new to us: no other village we had yet visited had any of these luxury items. We slowly walked up the road, towards the canal shown on the map as people slowly emerged from their well-maintained dwellings.

George pointed out two cars to me, a rare sight in desert villages, and adjacent to a large house which sported a satellite TV dish, a sure sign of the epicentre of local power. We stopped and waited for the elders to show themselves to us. Shortly a small group of men walked towards us in a brisk manner. They reminded me of senior Army officers or politicians, who tend to stride purposefully, in public at least, to visibly demonstrate (one presumes) their personal dynamism, keen intellect and associated highly advanced leadership qualities.

Facially, they all looked as if each of them had swallowed a wasp. It was blatantly obvious we were unwanted visitors, I doubted we would be offered tea and biscuits today somehow. They halted in line abreast, tellingly keeping just out of hand-shaking range. T made the introductions. The response, in terms of "Non Verbal Communication" (body language in other words) amply told us what they thought of T before he translated a single word. He turned to us, quite grim-faced and said "These are the village elders and they want to know why you are here and what do you want?" Hardly extended foreplay, I thought, more a "Wham bam" style really. I doubt your wife is a particularly fulfilled lady I thought, politely smiling to the man doing all the talking.

I explained that our Prime Minister and the British people had sent us, with our American friends, to liberate the good people of Iraq from the brutal oppression of Saddam Hussein and his regime and give them the chance to rebuild Iraq and elect the government of their choice. That was all I managed to say before the now increasingly obvious leader interrupted me at length.

T informed me that, according to the elder, neither Iraq nor any of its people wanted or indeed required democracy as that was a foreign, Western and utterly un-Islamic concept. Furthermore, Iraq simply required a strong man to lead it, and that man was rightfully Saddam, who they viewed as the father of the nation. What gave us the right to invade Iraq and kill Iraqis in their thousands? As his loyalties were fairly well known to us now, I counter-interrupted before this became a desert version of the Nuremberg Rallies: we have not and will not kill thousands of Iraqis, we have overthrown the regime in all its respects for the greater good of the Iraqi people and to enable Iraq to take its rightful place in the world. I admitted that, in self-defence only, we had been forced to kill members of the regime, such as Fedayeen, for example, but we had been compassionate and merciful wherever and whenever possible. He seized on this as proof of how loved Saddam was by his people, being their father and emphasised that Saddam would return soon and both the Americans and ourselves would eventually go home with our tails between our legs. He certainly wasn't hiding his views from us in the slightest, I had to give him credit for that.

He pointed to the Cuban, Vietnamese and Russian products around us, quoting the ongoing misery caused to the average Iraqi by the West's long sanctions and how Iraq's true friends had come to their aid. This could be a really long day, I thought. I noticed the troops had stayed close to the vehicles: they obviously had picked up the negative atmospherics too. As one of them told me later, "That place sucks". I couldn't really argue with such a pithy and focused summary.

Our conversation continued along that theme for quite a while. Their loyalty to the regime had blatantly brought them a rather superior life style, markedly different and almost luxurious in comparison to their southern counterparts. To break the repetition of our discussion, I asked where all the children were. He replied, indoors as you infidels frighten them and they will have nightmares because of you. I could hardly demand or order him to parade the children, so I pointed out that most of us too had our own children or younger brothers and sisters back home, plus we hadn't come all this way to frighten children, but rather protect them and hopefully improve their young lives in the process.

That got no response whatsoever, I decided we were getting nowhere and this was pointless. I thanked him for his time and patience, saying we would drop by regularly to ensure all was well and also protect them. He nodded, grim-faced to the end. Our reception from start to finish was rather akin to that of Margaret Thatcher suddenly appearing at an ex-Coal Miners' reunion dinner as a guest speaker, so we politely made our excuses and decided to move on.

We got back in our vehicles and drove on to the next two Salaf Villages. En route we stopped to inspect the main canal. It, too, was an advanced piece of civil engineering, providing a plentiful and guaranteed water supply to the satellite "designer" irrigation systems of all three villages, plus it was fully navigable by small boats and barges. This venue was midway between village number one and village number two: we used the privacy to have a cigarette and a quiet discussion. T told me, "This is a bad place, all of these are Saddam's people. We should leave." Quite a blunt but honest view of his fellow countrymen. George pointed out that the three villages had been almost designed to give each other supporting fire. I looked again: he was absolutely right; the place had even been built to provide mutual defensive support, not a popular architectural concept for the average housing estate in UK. However, it did demonstrate exactly what "toeing the Party line" could do for you to enhance your social wellbeing, that is, at least, until we arrived to violently burst the regime bubble anyway.

Both the other villages were exactly the same in attitude towards us, just less direct and more circumspect verbally. I strongly suspected they communicated by either some form of land line phone system or hand-held radios, we never discovered which. But it was an unpleasant experience during all our subsequent visits, which were very few, to be honest. Partly due to the distance, partly due to it being a lost cause from day one and also because their neighbours — all vehemently anti-regime — kept them securely "boxed in" effectively and frankly, with so few resources we had far better things to do.

From that patrol forth, we only returned in greater numbers, which really meant more than eight and less than twenty soldiers in reality. Their sentiments towards us never improved, they were predominantly hard-core Saddam supporters and appeared to be patiently waiting for the great day of his return to power. Occasionally someone in one of the villages would fire a few rounds in the air, albeit from a safe distance, just to say "we have guns too" in effect. It was a purely a noisy gesture of defiance as opposed to a serious threat: we took note and treated it with absolute indifference. We believed that any overly aggressive reaction was exactly what the elders seemed to want from us and we also suspected that not all of their people held Saddam in such high esteem. The reality was that unless we had the assets to maintain a permanent presence, which we certainly didn't possess and never would, then showing the occasional presence was the best we could manage. Accordingly we would never be able to either gain the trust of those people or provide any meaningful form of security, which served to be true for the vast majority of towns and villages around Al Amarah over the forthcoming years. It also served to remind us that not all Iraqis welcomed our arrival and Saddam did indeed have ultra-loyal supporters, even in this Shia heartland.

So the Status Quo was discreetly maintained and we kept our distance from each other, in an abstract way a precursor for us in effect to some parts of UK society now choosing to live "together apart" in terms of deliberate non-integration. Effectively, these particular villages were a lost cause, not a success story in the slightest sense, but also a self-contained entity and relatively quiet area from a military perspective. They feared their neighbours far more than us and revenge is definitely a dish best served cold in Iraq, and in very large slices. No doubt a charming bunch of people once you got to know them far better, but definitely not great fans of the British Army.

Just after we started our daily patrols, the word had come down from on high that we needed to "find something". What this "something" actually was never became defined in any precise detail, but the obvious inference, to us at least, was our old friend WMD. Our response was essentially a fairly cynical "whatever": with a massive number of remote desert areas to choose from our AO didn't seem a particularly likely choice, plus none of us could see Saddam hiding his most valuable goodies this close to the old enemy that was Iran, and in a fiercely proud Shia province that had been consistently hostile to his regime for decades. But we dutifully nodded our heads and quietly thought to ourselves that the government must be desperate to find some form of smoking gun as the fabled "chemical tripwire" had patently proved to be such a complete falsehood. If Saddam didn't actually have any "nasty stuff", I thought to myself (quietly of course: I rather liked being in the Army, after all), then that somewhat undercut the entire and overriding reason for our forcible liberation/invasion/regime change, depending on your own personal perspective, obviously.

We promptly parked that thought in some dim recess of our minds, our daily lives had more pressing matters to contemplate and if honest we viewed this as HMG's problem. We had all long ago written off the WMD Fairy, just like the mythical Ammunition Fairy, in essence we had ceased to "believe" and just got on with our daily routine. Some days later, we found ourselves along the northern of the two main access roads on a routine day out in Iraq, when George called over the radio, "What's that red thing to our right?" We stopped and scanned it using my Dixons binoculars. It appeared to be a "Grad", a Serbian-made Multi-Barrelled Rocket Launcher (MBRL) roughly the size of a large UK fire engine. This was quite a discovery as we didn't expect to find strategic level artillery anywhere near either the relative backwater of Al Amarah or this close to Iran, almost within reach of the old enemy. More importantly, this was one of the few Iraqi military systems that could launch CW with both a good degree of accuracy and in any substantial quantity in physical warhead terms. This impressive military capability was exactly why the Iraqis had protected them so jealously and we in turn had enthusiastically sought to destroy them during the hostilities phase.

The lone vehicle was about half a mile from the road, parked against a large berm and partially camouflaged, having been rather badly patch painted, or so it appeared, with Fire Engine Red paint, presumably as some form of urban camouflage: I had seen the Serbian Army do similar things in Kosovo. Then they had made many unorthodox, but often successful, attempts to confuse the NATO pilots trying to bomb accurately from 15,000 feet (both to avoid Serbian ground fire and also to minimise our own potential casualties). The access to it was across rough desert and a small irrigation channel, so progress was annoyingly slow. As we approached it my mind raced slightly. Could this be the "smoking gun" that our politicians were so utterly desperate to find? Surely not, not here, but there it was, nevertheless. Perhaps, I wondered idly, a hugely relieved Tony would make me "Sir Mac of Wigan" in a grand egalitarian gesture. It had a pleasing ring to it, well, at least I thought so.

We pulled alongside the MBRL or rather, what remained of it. It had been stripped to its bare bones from wing mirrors and seats to wheels and batteries and most things in between. The proverbial plague of locusts had paid it a very thorough visit. To our shared amazement, a long washing line had been hung from the vehicle cab and stretched to a large lump of metal some 20 or 30 feet away. Some obviously local clothing had been recently hung out to dry, so we assumed the owner(s) must be close by. George and I inspected the launch tubes which were still in the horizontal "park" position. None of them were loaded, in fact the tubes were almost pristine with no evidence of ever having been fired or perhaps even loaded recently. Oh well, who wants a knighthood anyway? I thought.

A lone Bedu abruptly appeared from seemingly nowhere on a small rise in the ground and spoke to us from a slightly elevated position, via T, but warily keeping a respectable distance between him and us. I felt that for him to actually talk to us must mean his family was close by and they needed time to rapidly pack up and move elsewhere. The Bedu viewed the entire Iraqi people as foreigners, let alone a group of white infidels and being an intensely private people, strange soldiers disturbing or searching his family wouldn't achieve much apart from earning the eternal enmity of each and every Bedu for literally miles around. We asked if he had spoken with or seen the MBRL crew, No, to both he replied. What happened to the vehicle? Don't know, he replied. How long had he been here and when did he first notice the vehicle? Can't remember. Had he taken anything from the vehicle? No, definitely not, it was someone else, but he had no idea who. Essentially he knew absolutely nothing about absolutely anything. I asked T what his personal opinion was: his view was surprisingly frank; the crew had possibly tried to make for Baghdad and then, realising the vehicle was just of far too great an interest to the Coalition, discreetly parked up and then had probably been murdered by the Bedu for whatever reason or cause, stripped of all possessions and buried, with the vehicle utterly ransacked immediately afterwards.

We simply didn't see the point of asking any further questions or aimlessly searching around the surrounding desert for the slim possibility of finding the shallow graves of people we never knew, so we bade farewell to the unreceptive Bedu and drove on. I was both glad and very relieved I hadn't made any excited radio calls on first sighting the MBRL: what an embarrassing anti-climax this could have been, I thought quietly.

We briefed the various Int Cells, who really had lost interest now, a classic case of going through the motions whilst waiting for the "freedom bird home", a malaise which was spreading slowly throughout the troops, the growing view amongst the rank and file being, "We won the war, so let's go home now". My reports were accordingly decreasing proportionally in both length and detail: I really didn't see the point unless it was either urgent or life threatening, as unprofessional as that may sound. No one seemed interested, after all. Essentially we were all just holding the line and waiting for our relief to arrive. Our next meeting with Burnt Face had been arranged: we had strongly insisted on a small affair this time, so yet again we drove to the New Village, slightly curious as to whom this "important person" actually was, but also prepared for some kind of trickery. Grudgingly, we found him a sharp, highly intelligent character and almost a likeable rogue in many ways.

On arrival we found just the two lieutenants, unsmiling as always, awaiting our arrival on the tarmac square. Politely they asked us to follow them into one of the plush and still abandoned regime houses. George made them wait as we posted a protective security cordon around the houses and ensured "rent-a-crowd" wasn't lurking anywhere: we were becoming quite allergic to surprises by now. We saw several other men around but all some distance away and they seemed to be working diligently on the irrigation ditches, a simply never-ending task in the desert if you wish to survive. They asked if just I and the Terp could go inside. I politely and firmly declined and insisted on George coming along, with my soldiers manning both the front and rear doors: a compromise between insulting their "hospitality" and our personal security, or at least I thought so. As if on cue, two of our Gazelle helicopters came roaring along, following the road at about 50-60 feet in height, obviously en route to An Nas and the Americans based there. On seeing our vehicles, they banked tightly right, did a circuit of the village, then flew past more sedately, waving as they did so. What superb, if fortuitous timing, we all thought. Accordingly we (very) casually waved back as if this was all prearranged, bluff was simply king from our point of view, it would be both disastrous and probably very painful too for my entire team if the Iraqis ever realised just how ill-equipped and poorly supported we were. To use a popular soldier's phrase, every day we simply "stuck our arses in the wind". I was only too painfully aware that this was a simply 100% accurate truism, we all knew that with communications being so poor and our ammunition so limited, hanging on for a couple of hours until the good guys (hopefully) arrived was most probably a both very naïve and a rather futile hope on our part.

After this little fly past, a minor display of British military power in effect, they instantly agreed to my request and made no attempt to go inside the building, merely nodding, escorting us to the door and quietly walking away. We slowly entered via the open front door, not sure what to expect and rather cautiously moved towards the living room. Burnt Face stood as we entered and to my great surprise they had found a three-piece leather suite from somewhere, together with a large coffee table placed neatly in the centre of the room. Home sweet home, I thought silently. We had yet to receive any "Lines to Take" (LTTs) from anyone in terms of the actual details of UK's policies or designs for the new Iraq, so each and every meeting was a "cuff job": basically I just tried to stress our good intentions and also not write any cheques that we undoubtedly couldn't cash. However, the longer this vacuum continued, the more difficult it was becoming to placate the increasingly impatient Iraqi people.

Three people awaited us: Burnt Face, a stern-looking character clad in black robes and headdress with a long silvery beard and another one of Burnt Face's associates whom we recognised vaguely. We started the usual circuitous discussion over the usual topics: the lack of electricity (again); when would the teachers and doctors return (again); what future did we and the Americans have in mind for Iraq and had we enjoyed our meal with the sheikh? The latter didn't surprise me: all the local factions seemed to have their own intelligence sources, with little love lost between any of them. As time wore on the guy in black just stared at us with a dour face like thunder. T seemed highly nervous while George (whom the locals now called "the quiet one who wears the vest": that was an assault vest, one of the few we had yet been issued) left all the talking to me. He sat expressionless but also very alertly with his rifle across his lap, facing towards the adjoining room and the stair well. For us to have searched the house would have been a major insult to their hospitality, hopefully the upstairs rooms were actually empty, a risk we simply had to accept.

Suddenly the guy in black burst loudly into life, demanding to know if the new Iraq's legal system would be based on Sharia Law. I replied that that was beyond my professional remit or indeed my authority, and a question for the new Iraqi Government under whatever constitution the Iraqi people chose to adopt for the future Iraq. He then abruptly denounced all forms of democracy as a Western and Christian folly, stating Iraq had no need for such a foreign concept and they should look to Iran for a shining example of a devout and highly successful Islamic Republic. The penny dropped with me then. P had told me of the Iraqi Intelligence Services during Saddam's reign ruthlessly hunting down Iraqi imams who had returned covertly from exile in Iran to "spread the word", eerily similar to the persecution of Catholic priests in England following the break from Rome and England's adoption of the Protestant faith. "He's an imam who has returned from exile in Iran and none too friendly", I suddenly realised. I fervently hoped he was blissfully unaware of one of our PM's closest advisors publicly declaring that "We don't do God", or it could possibly be a very long and painful conversation.

His long dialogue now decried us Christians for worshipping a lesser prophet (Jesus Christ) and our mistaken faith, reminded us that civilisation had begun in Iraq long before our people left their mud huts and also our support for the heretic that was Saddam during the long war against Iran. I had never encountered theological racism before, sadly now on the rise amongst some sections of the Muslim community across the region and even in UK. Our default social setting in UK seems to be that only white people can be racist. Racism is very much a multi-racial issue ultimately, in my own experience at least. Personally, I would argue this particular holy man proved the UK perception untrue. The imam firmly classed our religion as a second division faith and its associated Western "moral decadence", which included the complete concept of democracy and the naïve, corrupt stupidity of man-made laws (only God can make the law, as he repeatedly informed me). He was simply a firebrand and the complete opposite of the previous cleric I had met, albeit by naïve mistake on my part. The contrast took me by surprise, until I realised in hindsight that a cleric had to toe the Party line to literally survive under Saddam's regime, which reinforced my belief that this "man in black" had spent many years in Iran, just waiting for his time to return and spread the "true gospel" to his chosen flock.

I explained that we Europeans had long since decided that all laws were best made by man and applied to all equally and that religion had no significant place within our legal system, which merely reinforced his personal views, it seemed to me. He dismissed the entire reformation of the Christian faith as irrelevant to Islam as infidel religions were hugely imperfect in nature, unlike Islam, it seemed. I personally believed his overriding fear, probably like our own bishops of centuries ago, was the loss of power and status for clerics like him that any such reformation of Islam would bring with it, but I felt it best to keep that opinion to myself. That hugely unlikely event would rock his personal world to its core and was simply unthinkable to him, just as the Taliban were equally terrified by the prospect of universal education for girls. The prospect of Afghan women having opinions and thoughts of their own would rock their world also.

Western Europeans and democracy in general, in his point of view, was simply that we sat slightly above pagan heretics in the world's religious food chain and he simply didn't recognise any form of Hebrew faith, or its right to exist at all. This holy man was a shining example of religiously inspired bigotry, the simple facts that I was "pink", plus an infidel and that I had the utter cheek to express an opinion of my own obviously entitled him to speak to me in the manner befitting a lesser being. I could only imagine the content of his sermons to his faithful flock concerning Westerners and "Kufrs" globally. Any white — or black — guy speaking in this manner in UK would have been rapidly prosecuted (hopefully) as an utter racist. However, we don't seem to grasp the concept of racism based on theological beliefs in the UK, or perhaps we find it far easier to just ignore it, I'm not sure which. Muslims in UK do have a very concentrated and significant voting power after all and recent UK politics seems to have been centred upon power at all costs.

We then had a lengthy bout of verbal fencing as I defended Christianity and the right of people to choose what god they worshipped (or not) and their personal life style, I desperately tried to remember my long-gone Sunday School days to counter his "diktats" that there was only one true (Shia) faith, no god but Allah, Mohammed was his prophet and we Christians were simply misled fools who even believed in the monstrous heresy that was the scientific theory of mankind's evolution and so it went on. It was a long and bruising conversation to say the least. Throughout the duration, T was almost reverential towards the imam and I am quite sure he watered down much of what I said, including my point that both Christianity and Judaism pre-dated Islam by several centuries, before it came roaring out of the desert with fire and sword and, at least initially, a simple premise of "convert or die": probably a good idea that he omitted that, in hindsight. George merely kept a professional eye on our surroundings. My point on us all ultimately being "the sons of Abraham" was, I presume, definitely not translated across to him either.

Abruptly the imam declared he had to go and that the Iraqi people would now return to their rightful heritage and we infidels should quickly leave Iraq, as should all non-believers (then Iraq had approximately one million Christians in its population: it is less than a third of that figure now). This also included the entire Kurdish people, in his eyes, as they were both non-Arab Muslims and not of the Shia faith. I replied that we believed Iraq was a secular nation. He responded that secularism in Iraq had been a Ba'ath Party policy, which would now end with the demise of the regime and Iraq could now return to the true faith. There would be no remaining place for any unbelievers, especially for Sunni heretics (at least he hated us all equally, to be fair). The future, I thought gloomily, isn't too bright if this particular religious leader is anything to go by and I had the feeling he wasn't alone in his views.

Burnt Face had merely nodded for the duration. His colleagues' only input had been to serve chai and once they left, we never saw any of them again. I heard rumours the imam returned to Iran, no doubt having met the non-believers face to face he briefed someone accordingly over our viewpoints and aspirations. As for Burnt Face and his pals, we had absolutely no idea at all. Lots of people just disappeared in Iraq during this period and for a wide variety of reasons. I reported my belief that the Iranians were discreetly attempting to make serious inroads into the population, by virtue of the return of the exiled Iraqi imams. This was noted and that was it as far as I ever ascertained, no one seemed particularly interested. I spoke to our padre, a good listener and also a highly accomplished "Combat Barber". To my surprise he informed me that several padres had been to see a local council of imams and had a very similar experience, essentially being politely dismissed as second class holy men following a second class and very misguided religion. Whilst that didn't cheer me up in the slightest, it did make me feel better.

We went back to our circuit of the assorted villages. The question of electricity was being raised almost daily and by just about everyone except for the small population of the Mosque Village. P's grandfather, whose family had served as keepers of the mosque for almost two centuries, held the British in a fond regard, he remembered us from the 1930s and 40s when he was a young boy. Indeed, he remembered the Sunni uprising of 1941, German-inspired and with the Luftwaffe in action across Iraq's skies, a little-known piece of World War 2 history and now just a minor footnote in history. Ironically the uprising centred on the infamous "Sunni Triangle" and Fallujah, a town that would become well known to the US Marines in bitter house-to-house fighting in more than one vicious battle during the occupation years. The uprising of 1941 in turn led to the last Anglo-French war, when we invaded Syria and fought the Vichy French who had facilitated the German venture into Iraq, which in turn enabled the unsuccessful Sunni revolt against the British. Yet again, whilst we may have forgotten our history, others in the Middle East hadn't. Neither did anyone seem to want a large injection of Western Liberal Democracy, but our politicians seemed unable to grasp this and just ignored the views of millions of Iraqis by parachuting in a number of exiles who had been languishing in the West for several years in relative luxury. P quietly explained to me that all Iraqis would simply vote for whoever the elders or imams told them to vote for and that was the Iraqi way. He admired our noble ideas but politely thought us incredibly naïve and out of touch with the long-ingrained realities of Iraqi society.

The other growing concern was the rising water levels in the area where the Tigris met a major irrigation canal, home to several small villages and a large population. I went to inspect the canal, which was quite impressive in its construction, over 100 metres in width and several miles in length. The problem was obvious, the lock gates responsible for controlling the water level had been vandalised by looters and all the electrical wiring had been simply ripped out for its high copper content and subsequent resale value. As I examined the large but empty conduits, I looked along the main one and just saw daylight at the far end. This was a serious piece of electrical engineering, I thought, how am I going to sort this out? Whilst pondering this, a voice behind me said, "He lives over there." I turned round to see a tall, quite plump Iraqi male: being "well fed" is a mark of wealth, not obesity, in this part of the world.

"You speak good English," I said, surprised by this interlude.

"And Swedish too," he replied.

Swedish, in Iraq? I thought. "Who lives over there?" I asked.

"The chief lock keeper and his family." Quite a little nugget of information.

He introduced himself as Menshed Arab (a false name no doubt) and ex-member of the Mukbahrat, the Iraqi Secret Service. I nodded sagely, thinking "What?" He went on to tell me he had served in Sweden, tasked with "silencing" Saddam's exiled critics in Europe. I simply nodded in response, my only Swedish being Abba and Smorgasbord. After a pause, he simply stated, "I would like to work for the British. I can be of great use to you." Walk-ins, as they are known in terms of agent recruitments, are exceedingly rare, but his confidence, intelligence potential and obvious language skills were simply too good to ignore. I suggested we meet up in three days' time. Successful agent handling requires specialists. He agreed and insisted that T be kept in total ignorance, he didn't wish to risk his life unnecessarily. He had a good point.

After his departure we immediately visited the lock keeper's house, banging loudly on the door initially to no avail. Just as we prepared to force an entry, the door slowly opened to display a visibly frightened young woman with her children sheltering sheepishly behind her robes. Unsurprisingly, she told us that her man had left several days ago to destinations unknown. As I considered searching the house, we suddenly found ourselves surrounded by dozens of very irate and mainly male locals whilst older women formed a small protective circle around the lock keeper's wife. It rapidly transpired that we had committed the cardinal sin of visiting a house with no man inside and talking to an unaccompanied woman directly. Any form of search would now have obviously sparked a small riot, I realised. I gave the order to withdraw and apologised to all concerned, yet again giving my best (smiling) "stupid infidel" impersonation. Another reminder that Iraq was a cultural minefield and causing offence was indeed a very easy thing to achieve for pink soldiers.

Once we found a quiet piece of desert to park in, George and I had a quiet "team talk" over this surprise turn of events. We agreed it was best to keep this quiet and go straight to our local Agent Recruiting Team, namely Simon and Debs, which we promptly did. They were having little success in the area and appeared to be poorly supported in achieving their discreet mission and accepted our offer immediately. By sheer fluke, we had recently received a small consignment of portable radios, which were both solar and wind-up powered, ideal for Iraqi villagers lacking both batteries and electrical power. These we planned to issue at the rate of one per household. We had enough for three small villages only, so we included Bridge Village as one of these, purely as a cover to discreetly meet our potential employee.

So, come the day, my team distributed our much sought-after radios and broke up several "ownership" fights in the process, while George, Debs (who didn't actually admit to being a fluent Arabic speaker) and Simon quietly meet with Menshed to discuss his offer. My view was simple: we just make the introduction and walk away, as this type of sensitive activity was not part of our remit and frankly, way beyond our very limited capability. This initial meeting went well, apparently, with Menshed agreeing to go to Brigade HQ to further discuss his terms and conditions in becoming one of our agents. Simon and Debs were smugly pleased with their catch, we moved on to distribute the remainder of our small collection of radios and a good day was had by all.

However, sadly it all came to nought. Menshed duly appeared at the Brigade HQ in a quite indiscreet manner, announcing himself loudly at the main gate, much to the annoyance of the secrecy-obsessed agent handlers. Thereafter his personal demands were financially excessive, his entire motivation as it transpired was purely mercenary by nature and hugely unrealistic. With his manner increasingly self-important, verging on sheer arrogance, he abruptly stormed out of the meeting, loudly threatening to go and work for the Iranians. Like so many Iraqis over this turbulent period, following his volatile meeting with the Brits, he simply disappeared and was never seen again by any of us. I seemed to have developed an uncanny knack for meeting "interesting" Iraqi citizens who then seemed to have a common penchant for promptly disappearing. But in a country lacking just about every aspect of governance at all levels of society, all we could do was shrug our shoulders and say "whatever" and put it down to experience. That may sound cynical but it was simply an everyday reality, life in post-Saddam Iraq was simply a cheap commodity essentially and we had many other things to worry about.

Following our meeting with the angry imam, T became quite increasingly subdued. We never quite knew what insults or threats came the way of our Terps and therefore, perhaps, what doubts or fears these planted in their minds. The imam had essentially unnerved him. Although he wouldn't admit this to any of us, he was now almost a different man. The influence of the imams and their power could not be underestimated, but sadly, it often was at this stage of our occupation. A few days later T simply didn't turn up. After waiting around fruitlessly, we did our patrol without him, having asked HQ to find out from our security guys (who did the vetting) exactly where he lived. Again, on the next day he didn't arrive at the agreed time, so we took a drive to his home in Al Maymunah, having borrowed one of the few soldiers who spoke passable Arabic from our Brigade HQ Intelligence Cell, otherwise we'd just do aimless laps of the town.

Several hours later, courtesy of numerous question and answer sessions with several fairly surprised Iraqis, most of whom were overly defensive, to the extent we had to explain repeatedly that we were neither going to arrest or kill him, we found the large cul-de-sac in which T lived. That is a rather polite description: it was a large dirt-covered dead-end alley, overlooked by four floors of very squalid-looking flats, which effectively blocked the sunlight breaking into the open ground. As we parked, we could feel, rather than see, dozens of pairs of eyes peering at us from behind the various pairs of closed curtains overlooking us. The usual feral dogs barked loudly and we moved from floor to floor, flat to flat attempting to find T. This was turning out to be a surprisingly complex task and the troops were uneasy at being in such dark, confined spaces, with our vehicles also essentially boxed in. I agreed with them totally, this type of environment neutralises most of whatever advantages you hold and everything becomes a "close quarters" affair. All the flat's populations were uniformly sullen, unhelpful and just wanted us to leave and time was passing. The longer you remain static, the greater opportunity you provide to any local bad guys to do something violent in your direction, so we decided this just wasn't working and worked our way quickly back to the vehicles and therefore our means out of this vulnerable point.

As we got back into the daylight and conducted a head check to confirm we had everyone: being left behind on your own in a place like this is every British soldier's nightmare come true and brings with it a very good chance of dying alone very quickly and rather painfully. Surprisingly, an old man suddenly and curtly inquired what we were doing here. We explained who we were looking for and he gestured with his walking stick in a vague direction, spoke a few words and abruptly walked into one of the many doorways surrounding the alley, disappearing indoors and back to his world. I looked questioningly at our Arabic speaker.

"He says that T and his family all went to Baghdad two days ago."

Another one, I thought, plus we had now wasted the entire day and achieved the square root of fuck all, in the words of one of my soldiers. That said, we were all quite relieved to get back into the sunlight and back to having room to manoeuvre again, with no major incident having taken place. We wouldn't be doing any more "house calls" in that area, I decided.

On arriving back at the airfield, interest in T had increased amazingly in our absence. It transpired the Americans in Baghdad were keen for us to arrest him immediately and send him north to have a "little chat" with them. His brother, it transpired, was a senior colonel in Iraqi

Military Intelligence and had even made the infamous "deck of cards", while T himself had never really been an English teacher, it seemed: rather, he too was an ex-Iraqi Military Intelligence Officer and had been a fairly senior Ba'ath Party official locally, as well as serving as a reserve officer immediately prior to our arrival. Whilst rather embarrassing for our vetting section, my guys found it absolutely hilarious that we had employed the enemy as our patrol Terp and to be fair, we all thought he was an okay guy. Another small stitch in the rich tapestry of military life. We were asked some questions by the security guys about T's time with us. We explained we hadn't divulged any secrets that would compromise UK's national security and some report was filed somewhere by someone. We never did find out if T or his brother were captured (or killed) by the Americans, but to be honest it wasn't our problem and once we had all stopped laughing at the absurdity of it all, we rapidly forgot about him and got on with the job in hand.

Our HQ suddenly announced that we were "going to get some Americans tomorrow". The US Army had, for reasons no one quite understood, sent us a 4-man "PYSOPs" team (Psychological Operations) and apparently no one in the brigade quite knew what to do with them or how best to employ them (or in some cases even wanted them around, frankly). By default therefore they ended up with us. Whilst the Americans were an unknown quantity to us, they were also much needed reinforcements and had their own vehicle, (a Humvee: what else could it be?) supplies and equipment so I certainly wasn't going to complain.

At that time, we had quiet doubts about American soldiers whose venture to Somalia hadn't gone too well (or so we all thought in a typically very smug British manner). Meanwhile, we had defeated the IRA and brought peace to the Balkans, not to mention some successful and for the politicians, pleasingly brief (albeit it very small) operations in Sierra Leone. Over a decade later, now the Americans, having watched our embarrassingly rapid withdrawal from Iraq in sheer disbelief, then having been forced to send 20,000 US Marines into Helmand Province to prevent the impending failure of the UK's military mission in Southern Afghanistan, the British Army is now no longer viewed by them with anything like the same respect or trust it engendered in 2003. Indeed, we are now viewed by many American officers and soldiers alike as merely another middle-sized European army, albeit a proud, very professional and superbly well-trained one, but now with rather lesser capabilities in military terms. The Americans, however, do consider us blessed with some of the world's most outstanding Special Forces.

The American team, we discovered, were actually three mobilised reservists (National Guardsmen), volunteers to a man and an Iraqi-American named Ali, who had been captured in the first Gulf War and became a naturalised American, quite how and why was never fully explained to us. Ali was a DoD (US Department of Defence) employee and now a non-practising Muslim, who wore Army uniform and had volunteered to return to his homeland. He was by far and away the most effective and reliable Terp we ever had, he was simply head and shoulders above the rest. The Americans were led by Brian, an ever-cheerful Californian Staff Sergeant, with Gerry a pragmatic East Coast Sergeant, both ex regular soldiers and Gus, a young and naïve Private First Class from the Deep South, whose accent was as strange to us as our Scottish or Lancastrian dialects were to him. These were exactly the type of reservists the Army now urgently seeks to recruit to replace 20,000 regular troops made redundant to save money by the Coalition Government. They were self-disciplined, fit, enthusiastic, well-motivated and professionally capable soldiers, all quietly determined to serve America post 9/11, a pleasant surprise to us all. The bulk of our TA of the period just didn't really tick the majority of these boxes in our view.

Their Humvee was viewed by all of us as a great new toy, partly because of its huge twin loudspeakers mounted on the roof, but mainly the simple fact it also mounted an M60 machine gun— and they had lots of ammunition (unlike us). We finally had some firepower. It was rather a tonic: small things please soldiers at times. We initially re-discovered that, as Churchill once said, we were still "Two nations divided by a common language", but as time passed, we slowly found a common verbal ground.

We viewed the Americans as part of the team and they rapidly proved that they were indeed highly professional soldiers and enthusiastic partners. Initially they dressed in combat helmet and wraparound sunglasses, but rapidly adopted our "soft hat and no shades" approach. However, the next few years would violently force us to improve and upgrade our body armour, rifles, weapon sights and helmets several times over and provide every soldier with much needed first aid items, costing millions (and millions) of pounds in the process as various new pieces of equipment were repeatedly brought into service as the "soft hat approach" became a quickly forgotten historical episode. As the Army came to face with increasing and previously unthinkable levels of casualties and sustained daily violence, especially in Helmand, ironically it eventually came to virtually emulate the very Americans whom we thought were so "over the top" in Bosnia, Kosovo and the early stages of Iraq. The Iraqis viewed the Americans with open curiosity and Ali's presence in US uniform provoked mixed emotions, from naked hostility towards a traitor and turncoat to being welcomed as almost a prodigal cousin who returned to his homeland from America. That said, he quietly omitted to tell the locals that he no longer actively worshipped the one true God: a very wise and pragmatic diplomatic move, we all believed.

We had an interesting experience with regard to the sheer hold Saddam held over Iraq soon after the American arrival. We were exploring a cross-country desert track one day, purely to give us more movement options as we slowly sensed the mood change of most Iraqis as we continued to fail in the delivery of all our infrastructure promises. We came across an isolated house close to a fairly major irrigation canal but also quite hidden from view unless you were very close by. Thinking it deserted, we drove towards the house, only to see a young woman run inside and almost instantly a young man came frantically sprinting out of the house towards the open desert. Acting quickly, two of the soldiers immediately gave chase on foot, whilst the Humvee surged in front of him. Faced with an American machine gun in front of him and several British rifles behind him he rapidly ran out of options. Fortunately he saw sense and stopped, placing his hands on his head dejectedly; the young woman meanwhile anxiously watching the scene unfold from the doorway.

We approached him and explained we meant no harm and asked him, "Why did you run?" Initially he was silent and on edge, until we noticed that one of his ears was missing. It had been clumsily amputated. We made him reveal his ear to us fully; it was hardly the work of a skilled surgeon and had "healed" in a very ugly and disfigured manner. "Are you a deserter from the army?" we asked. He nodded, telling us that, just prior to our invasion, one of his officers had cut off his ear with a bayonet as his comrades looked on as he and several other young men were summarily disciplined for attempted desertion. We patiently explained that he had nothing further to fear as Saddam no longer held any power in Iraq, so no one was looking for him and he could just get on with his life now. He fervently refused to believe us. Saddam would never surrender, nor the Ba'ath Party quietly relinquish its stranglehold over absolute power in Iraq. We told him the Americans had captured Baghdad and Saddam himself was now a mere fugitive and on the run. He felt that was impossible. Just go and ask your family, we said. This brought no response and he looked at his feet miserably.

Ali then had a long and solemn discussion with him as we looked on from a discreet distance. After a lengthy exchange of words; Ali explained to us that he wasn't just hiding from the Iraqi Army or the regime. He and the young woman were from two tribes with a long history of friction between them: in essence they had eloped together and were trying to start a home together and therefore voluntarily lived in complete and splendid isolation. Playing desert matchmaker, even for the British Army, was well beyond our mission parameters. We solemnly gave our word to not mention the lovebirds to anyone and wished them well. I didn't envy them. As young couples go, they had just about all the odds stacked against them. If her father and brothers ever found them in their remote desert hideaway, then we felt his short life might just end quite abruptly and in a very violent manner.

By now, we just rolled with things, we had long since ceased to be surprised by anything in Iraq, and as long as no one tried too hard to kill us, then everything else was a bonus. We had absolutely no idea what was happening back in UK, our sole link to the world was our weekly 10-minute satellite phone call home and the mail, which was haphazard at best in delivery terms. We had finally given up on the idea that "the suits" were on their way from UK to help us any time soon: the essential people who could make a civic infrastructure function, from finance to hospitals to drainage, schools and electricity, which make a nation simply work. So we just aimed to try and keep the lid on things while our faraway government made some form of decision regarding Iraq's people. We did, after all, now own rather large chunks of it and along with it, several millions of its inhabitants.

We continued our rounds of the villages, encountering more and more singularly pointed questions about the ongoing electricity problems, closely followed by the still-deserted schools and hospitals. Us mentioning democracy, votes for women and the return of exiled Iraqi politicians was simply irrelevant and meaningless to them. Indeed, the exiled Iraqis were commonly viewed as a privileged bunch of cowardly rich people who had ran away from Saddam and had been living a corrupt and decadent life style in the West, so we stopped mentioning them quite rapidly. Alarmingly, one of our gunner patrols found a large arms cache close to one of the flyovers across the main road network: however, it wasn't the ubiquitous AK 47s but a significant amount of military grade explosives, complete with detonators and other items. This was not home-made stuff dumped by enthusiastic amateurs, but it showed someone had both violent plans and serious intentions for us and our occupation activities, plus the choice of location was telling. We seemed to be rapidly running out of Iraqi goodwill and patience, the honeymoon was gradually coming to an end, we all quietly agreed within the team.

As usual, we duly passed these combined atmospherics back up the chain of command. Whether anyone actually took note was at best fairly uncertain. To be fair, there were many other activities going on: catching up on the maintenance of a very large (and old) vehicle fleet; the Treasury now wanted everything possible back to UK, preparing to hand over the area to someone, some time in the form of another British unit and the ongoing political/tribal infighting with regard to trying to get Al Amarah functioning in a manner that could be portrayed as remotely effective. I was informed that some aid would soon be forthcoming from

Basra, so be patient, whilst the burning questions of electricity, education and a health service all received a deafening silence in response.

During our visits, when asked (as he always was) Ali told people he came from Baghdad. He actually originated from Basra. This and a false name were a means of trying to protect his family from any reprisals, he told us. I found this slightly ominous. He had been in America for 12 years, his family had disowned him long ago, so why, I asked him, was this necessary? His reply was brutally telling. "This is not the West. Iraqis will neither forget nor forgive, ever." Over a decade of carnage and conflict later, I have to admit he made an excellent point.

Some weeks later we took the same cross-country route across the AO. As we drove past the isolated house, a figure came running frantically towards us, waving his arms madly in the air. We pulled over to find it was our one-eared deserter friend, smiling broadly and he seemed genuinely pleased to see us again. It transpired that he had been to Baghdad, by the simple, if time-consuming, means of walking and hitch-hiking, purely to see if Saddam and his regime had really gone. He told us he had seen the toppled statue, famously shown on television screens around the globe and wandered, unchallenged and unhindered, around Baghdad with a complete lack of concern from anyone regarding his erstwhile deserter status. The utterly unthinkable and impossible had really happened from his perspective and his entire world had abruptly changed.

He thanked us all profusely. It was a pleasant change indeed for us to have a happy customer in our midst. We asked him his plans in the new Iraq: his reply was short and to the point. "To be happy and raise a family in safety." We couldn't argue with that sentiment, so we wished him luck and bade him farewell, we at least could leave him in peace to chase his dream. We weren't optimistic, but at least he now had an opportunity, however precarious. They moved soon afterwards to an unknown location. Why and where, yet again, we never knew. Hopefully they survived to pursue their dream in peace.

The much promised and long-awaited aid, we were informed, would finally arrive in the next day or two. Thereafter it would be "divvied up" between units and distributed accordingly. I was tasked to work out a plan for aid distribution in our AO. Whilst we weren't really sure what this aid consisted of, at least it was something with which to demonstrate our erstwhile good intent towards the Iraqi people. The larger overarching issues of electricity, education, medical services and all the other problems were apparently being dealt with at a higher level: who or where that level exactly was remained totally unclear to us, our job was purely to assure the locals that it was "in hand". George and I discussed the detail of where and how we'd distribute the aid, drawing in the rest of the team to ensure all our bases were covered.

As it transpired, we would have to distribute the aid over two days, due primarily to a lack of transport assets (we had very few big trucks, in plain English). The aid consisted primarily of cooking oil, flour, powdered milk, rice — all of which would be quite well received by the villagers — and bottled water in very large amounts. Providing water to a people who had successfully fought the desert for countless millennia and dug a huge number of irrigation ditches, associated systems and a very major canal system struck me as a rather patronising action by us. I questioned it, suggesting that perhaps baby items and basic school resources such as pencils, notebooks and suchlike might be better received, but essentially this was a case of, the government and its small legion of "experts" back in UK knew best. Orders are orders, so I dutifully nodded my head and planned accordingly.

Some good news was that Mike, our highly flexible Signals Officer, had released two of his best NCOs to join my team: Ben (the man who had waved to the Paras) and Sandy; both quality corporals who are still now serving as very high grade Warrant Officers, plus they came with a vehicle boosting the "CIMIC Empire" to a core of four vehicles and approximately 16 soldiers on a typical patrol. That doesn't sound very much at all now, but then this equated to a quantum leap combined with the American input. Our government had after all, seemed to smugly expect that the entire Iraqi nation would spontaneously welcome us warmly, with the apparent perception that the invasion itself would cause no significant associated interference to either their daily life or their nation's smooth running, so we still operated on something of a shoestring budget. Anyway, political naïveté and complacency notwithstanding, I was a very happy man to have amassed such military might finally.

The aid duly arrived from Basra, courtesy of the Royal Logistic Corps and the Ghurkha Transport Regiment (GTR) in a convoy of DROPS vehicles: a large truck with a hydraulic boom which simply lifted a massive pallet off the rear of the vehicle, which could be carrying anything from a shipping container to several tons of assorted stores as a load. Shortly before we departed to distribute the aid, we were given thousands of tabloid-style newsletters to hand out to the villagers. The antepenultimate rear page (bearing in mind Arabs read right to left, so it was from a Western view page 3: very apt, ironically) which was a full-page photograph of the popular American singer Britney Spears, in a rather low cut and "spray on" micro dress adopting a very raunchy pose, with the dress itself leaving extremely little to the imagination. I protested that this was tantamount to at best a cultural insult, at worst Western pornography, to these devout and highly conservative villagers. It was patiently explained to me that these news sheets had been written by long-term Iraqi exiles in London who aimed at bringing the local people on side to our invasion and forthcoming democracy by exposing them to liberal Western values, such as music and entertainment. Enter Britney Spears. Furthermore, the government wanted these distributed at the earliest opportunity, which was today. I suggested that, nevertheless, they may well find these newsletters rather offensive. My point was duly noted and I was directed to distribute them in conjunction with the aid, and it was not up for any further discussion. I accepted this directive with fairly obvious bad grace, but it wasn't actually a request and we both knew that. Essentially, I had had my say and lost. Hopefully it wouldn't cause me and my troops too much angst, I thought as I walked away from our HQ.

The plan was deliberately kept simple, we'd distribute firstly at the Mosque Village and then New Village, which meant we moved closer to home as the day passed and the Americans with their loudspeakers would meanwhile roam the area to inform the neighbouring villagers to congregate at these two points. I had about forty-five to fifty soldiers from several units and over a dozen vehicles of various sizes, so we could provide security fairly well, whilst aiming to spend no more than ninety minutes to two hours on site in order to minimise our exposure by being static and advertising this event in the process, which in soldier terms significantly increases your vulnerability to attack. The troops were in pre-nominated teams in terms of their allotted tasks and all the good old-fashioned military stuff such as "actions on". Our morale was high: young soldiers don't join the Army to sit around getting bored and this task seemed to be a worthwhile one, with quite a bit of variety from the normal routine.

We drove to the Mosque Village, as always receiving a friendly reception and the deep respect in which the village was held within the province, due to its centuries-old religious site, greatly aided the behaviour of any visitors. The Americans announced our intention by means of their massive loudspeakers and P explained to the village elders, who merely took it in their stride as if this was a daily occurrence. We laid out our stall under the watchful eyes of the elders in what passed for the village square while individuals and families from the neighbouring villages slowly appeared, openly curious as to what was on offer. When it came to the news sheets, the elders politely asked for a quiet word with me and explained that the images on them were very offensive in such a holy place and politely but firmly requested that we did not attempt to distribute them here. To be honest, I promptly caved in totally and just agreed to their request. I saw their point and empathised with them, this was similar to our giving out free girlie mags on the steps of a cathedral back home and I simply wasn't willing to ruin local relationships for the sake of some faceless and anonymous government PR guru who was safely back in the UK.

The CO arrived unexpectedly, a most unusual happening, to say the least, which took us somewhat by surprise. The troops had established security, we were ready to commence giving out aid and the elders played their part in gently coercing the villagers to form an orderly queue. Iraqis simply don't queue patiently, it is not in either their collective psyche or DNA. After viewing the activity, the CO suddenly decided we should "advance the programme" and conduct concurrent distribution at the new village also. I strongly disagreed, I really didn't want to split my small force in two and skimp on security, not to mention changing the plan that the troops had been briefed on, plus all their predetermined groupings and allotted tasks. Rank prevailed, as always, plus the CO was a product of one of England's finest public schools and a well-heeled Cavalry Regiment, whilst I hailed from Wigan and the ranks, so I was never going to win this little difference of opinion. To paraphrase Wellington, arguably Britain's finest ever general, this was a classic case of orders followed by counter orders, resulting in lots of disorder.

Accordingly, I summoned George and some of the NCOs explained the "fast ball" that HQ had suddenly dealt us. As he knew the ground and the locals, I asked him to control the new village site and gather the NCOs to quickly brief their guys on the new plan. I was very unhappy as I felt we were now just making things proportionally more difficult for ourselves for no logical military reason at all, but shit happens in the military, so you just deal with it. The bulk of the UK military now live in the age of the "long screwdriver" of regular high level distant political or senior officer direct interference with operations on the ground, whilst our opposition meanwhile don't seem to suffer from that particular problem. In contrast their aims are fixed, uncompromising and bear absolutely no heed to any form of populist public opinion or the vagaries of media commentary. In many ways they fight a much simpler (and far more ruthless) war than Western democratic Armies and they play to win at any cost.

The CO, having now viewed the operation, nodded his approval, summoned his escort and promptly drove back to the airfield and we reorganised ourselves accordingly, the troops thinking, no doubt, "We're cuffing it again". They weren't too far wrong, really. But it's a traditional military activity at which British soldiers are world class leaders: we have generations of experience to call upon, it's almost part of a British soldier's training. After ensuring the distribution by the mosque was under way, Mike and I drove the very short distance to New Village to find a rather less sedate scene. The leaflet distribution hadn't lasted long before the elders strongly objected to Western decadence and George was bearing the brunt of their verbal wrath, by the look of things.

Otherwise the GTR crew were offloading several large pallets of water and some foodstuffs, with the troops trying to get the increasing number of villagers to wait in a patient and orderly manner.

As George and I calmed down the elders and apologised for both our ignorance and any offence with regard to the images of Britney Spears, an old pickup truck slowly drove past with several young men in the cab and freight compartment. We noticed piles of our news sheets, literally hundreds of them, in the rear of the vehicle. As we watched, some older men literally threw themselves onto the moving truck, jumping onto the bonnet, the windscreen, opening the doors and fighting with the younger men, who in turn were trying to push them off, rendering us speechless at this rapid turn of events. Some iron bars and knives were promptly produced by both sides, at which point we intervened and physically separated the two sides. It transpired the young men intended to sell this "Western porn" for simple profit motives, whilst the older men physically objected to this blatant show of Western immorality. We now agreed to withdraw all copies immediately and not distribute them again in this area. This isn't going well I thought, surrounded by a couple of dozen angry and very irate Iraqi males.

The GTR, who weren't too pleased to be here and quite visibly showed it, had finally got all the bulky water pallets lined up and quickly withdrew back into the vehicle cab, closed the cab doors and opted for splendid isolation, preferring not to get involved in any dealings with a large mob of angry locals, so they decided not to play any more, in effect. A delegation of elders now abruptly informed us that they neither wanted nor needed our water, so we could just take it back, but the foodstuffs were acceptable to them. I was flabbergasted and quite angry. Our simple plan had unravelled rapidly, due to an eclectic mixture of higher level interference, cultural ignorance and tribal pride. I looked at the elders, hugely conscious of the watching crowd and told them we hadn't come all this way to help the Iraqi people merely to be sent away, so they could have the food and I'd just destroy the water here and now, as they obviously didn't want or need it. That proved to be a conversation stopper and after some heated debate the elders kindly agreed to take the water from us, purely as a favour to us Brits, obviously.

An uneasy peace settled over the village as we began the distribution, but rapidly it became apparent that no one was in the mood for orderly queues in the searing desert heat, and unlike the Mosque Village, the elders here now took a haughty distance from the proceedings. Some males decided to queue jump and help themselves. A scuffle promptly broke out within the queue and when two soldiers intervened to break that up everyone immediately turned on the soldiers. Within minutes my thin line of soldiers was all physically involved with scores of adult males and teenagers alike, some trying to isolate a soldier and presumably beat him senseless and acquire some new weaponry in the process. A couple of soldiers were desperately wrestling to maintain possession of their rifles. Loss of a weapon is a huge personal shame for any soldier, but especially a British one. Young (mainly Catholic) men had been trying to take our weapons from us in Northern Ireland for decades, and occasionally succeeding. As I watched this melee spread, one soldier used an old-fashioned and vigorous Anglo-Saxon head butt to deter a visibly culturally surprised male who was vigorously attempting to steal his rifle. Another soldier "butt swiped" a man with his rifle butt in the face, thereby winning the argument, frankly. This was all getting rather physical, it was a matter of time before someone became seriously injured amongst this fracas.

We were losing control of the situation rather quickly, I realised and the risk of a weapon being discharged in this close quarter melee, either by accident or design, was increasingly rapidly as more local males joined in the scuffle. Someone being shot at point blank range wouldn't be too good for our fragile "hearts and minds" campaign and neither did I want any weapons being lost and some of my men beaten to a pulp in the process as they clung desperately to their rifles. A couple of dead Iraqis would not endear us to anyone and the word would no doubt spread like wildfire around the whole province. We had no shields or batons with which to keep the crowd physically away from us, the nearest being somewhere in Cyprus, presumably, so this was very much an old-fashioned street fight between a small gang (us) and a much larger gang (them) rather than a controlled public order situation. This, I thought is definitely not "hearts and minds" any more and we'd only been here a matter of several weeks. I looked around and all along the line, every single one of my soldiers was involved in some form of grappling, pushing, pulling or jostling in some manner and both their sheer numbers and almost their intimately close proximity gave the Iraqi crowd increasing confidence, which in turn made them bolder and more aggressive. As looked, a young Iraqi male in his twenties ran towards me. I turned side on to him, giving him an old-fashioned rugby handoff and stepped closer towards him, shouting, "Now fuck off!" in my finest ex-RSM voice. He took this universal hint and promptly did so. Enough is enough, I thought.

George shouted to me, "Shall I fire some warning shots?"

I nodded immediately, saying, "Fire a burst in the air." He fired a short burst of rounds into the air. A few people close to us hesitated and looked across, but the huge majority merely continued. I suddenly remembered what a local had recently told me: "We Iraqis are used to loud bangs". The police in UK rely very heavily on the public being simply overawed by a Robo Cop image and the intimidating sight of armed officers openly carrying weapons, irrespective of their age or often physically rather portly size. However, Iraqis and Afghans alike aren't deferential by nature and don't afford you respect easily: violent men with guns are just commonplace in both societies and have been for decades, so that approach is an utter nonstarter. I now had only two options left: either escalate the level of violence by targeting some obvious leaders and selectively shooting a few people or withdraw before some of my own men became casualties. I looked at George and said, "They can have the fucking water, pull the guys out to the vehicles." I wasn't prepared to kill unarmed people, no matter how overtly hostile to us, just for my own or the unit's pride and few pallets of food and water with little real value and absolutely no military importance whatsoever. Sometimes not pulling the trigger is equally important, militarily speaking, as doing so, which is arguably a much simpler action. Killing people, especially unarmed ones, at very short ranges with modern high velocity weapons is relatively easy. "Unkilling" them, however, is a medical impossibility.

As the guys peeled off back to their vehicles I did a rapid head check. To my disgust I now discovered my three GTR soldiers had never even left the cab of their vehicle but simply sat and quietly watched the melee. Obviously not three of Joanna Lumley's finest. I later expressed my personal dissatisfaction to them in no uncertain terms. Once I was absolutely content that we weren't leaving anyone behind, we moved back to the Mosque Village to collect the rest of the team. On arrival they were just in the process of packing up: things had gone much more smoothly there. I had a few words with P, the elders had policed the event mainly and the people were quite pleased with our aid to them: one small victory for us after all, I thought. As I looked over his shoulder, a male suddenly grabbed a large sack of powdered milk and began to run away from the square. Some other locals caught him and started to immediately beat him. A couple of my guys broke it up. P asked for them to be permitted to deal with him. We needed to leave very soon, but I wasn't a fan of vigilantes either. "Why?" I asked pointedly.

"He has stolen from his own people, so now he must face punishment."

I assumed this meant some form of Sharia Law with the demise of Saddam. I asked him for his word that he would be neither killed nor seriously injured. I could easily take the man with us, but he'd still have to return to his tribe one day or become a social outcast for all time. He gave me his solemn word. I sincerely hoped their sense of honour would prevail. This was taking a gamble on my part, human rights lawyers are never too far away from the British Army's operations in the 21st Century, it is an extremely profitable activity after all, irrespective of actual witness credibility or physical evidence.

We drove back through the New Village, where all the women lined up and ululated incredibly loudly and proudly at the recent infidel failure. Sing when you're winning. Every male who was physically capable of doing so pelted us with hundreds of recently donated full bottles of water and the odd large piece of the wooden pallets they had been transported on, just for variety's sake. We couldn't understand any of the shouts, but it certainly wasn't, "Brits, we love you", and the loud, incessant jeering was of an instantly and internationally recognisable global language. No casualties were taken or any damage caused to any of our vehicles but the honeymoon, I thought, was now officially over. We had recognised many of the adult males from several of our villages. Previously all of them had been quite friendly towards us, but obviously their patience with foreign soldiers and invaders had now abruptly ran out. I was angry, embarrassed and rather subdued for the remainder of the long drive back to the airfield. Mike and George didn't seem too impressed by the day's fiasco either. This wasn't a moment for us to be proud of: militarily irrelevant in all respects, but to the Iraqi villagers a pleasing little victory over the invaders and a large psychological boost, no doubt.

During my "hot debrief" at HQ, it was patently obvious the CO was none too pleased, in particular that we had opened fire, albeit warning shots. Apparently I should have taken a "more robust stance" and much earlier. Whilst I quietly thought, "With what? The batons, shields and riot guns we didn't have?" I just nodded my head, there was absolutely no point in trying to dispute the party line and that would only become a more common occurrence as our desert wars expanded and dragged on as the Army was told to do ever more with ever less and the growing casualty figures were discreetly buried. I sat down and planned tomorrow's job, determined to dominate this time, choosing a spit of land between two large flood areas: very large ponds in effect, but like most desert dwellers, Iraqis, as a race of people, don't swim too well, if at all. By placing troops at either end, with the stores in between, I could control access far more easily, I believed.

I briefed the guys, including the recently arrived 4-man "TACP" (Tactical Air Control Party) from the RAF Regiment, a surprising addition to the team and, like the Americans, another bunch of waifs and strays for whom no one seemed to want ownership rights. I was rapidly becoming some kind of local military adoption society but equally the TACP had absolutely zero UK air power to control and more troops were always a bonus. I had a major role for Ali, who was taking more and more intimidation from the locals, so the Rock Apes would be his dedicated protection party, not a role they were overly pleased with, but Ali was simply vital to the success of our mission and Rock Apes stand their ground extremely well, to give them their due. I also made sure the

GTR drivers knew that on this day, they would definitely be getting out of their nice safe cab and joining in with all the Army stuff along with the rest of us.

On arrival at the site, ironically adjacent to the mud school where we had first met the Iraqis after viewing the mass looting, we set up the site. This time we wouldn't tell the Iraqis until we were ready and fully set up to receive them (and fully control them if honest). The Americans toured all the villages within five miles and broadcast our location with their loudspeakers and when we would be "open for business". Slowly they arrived to meet at least a reinforced section of troops each controlling a narrow access point, plus the water also served as a useful barrier for keeping different tribes apart, a bonus from both a security and crowd control perspective.

As the impatient crowds built up, I asked Staff Sergeant Brian, sat on top of his Humvee, if his loudspeakers could play music. "Sure, what would you like?" he replied.

"How about something American and rather loud?" I replied. He immediately smiled broadly, jumped into his Humvee and just a few moments later, ZZ Top blasted out of the loudspeakers at their absolute maximum volume. The Iraqis just stopped in their tracks with amazed looks on their faces, being hit by a literal, and to their ears, utterly foreign wall of noise. This was obviously a crowd control measure Saddam's troops had never thought of, to dominate the locals with. Music, like singing, clapping and dancing, is after all simply the work of Satan in pure Islamic terms, so this loud and unexpected "short cut to hell" made them physically stop in their tracks. I had to hide behind a vehicle to conceal my amused satisfaction: I simply wasn't accepting a re-run of the previous day's debacle. The Americans meanwhile seemed rather pleased to donate a liberal amount of pure American culture towards the operation too.

The troops also weren't in the mood for being mucked around today and must have given off the appropriate "vibes" as the locals, still shocked by the "music of Satan" now waited patiently to be called forward and given a family-sized ration of everything. Two young men jostled a couple of soldiers and suddenly found themselves in the water, which they discovered to their horror was too deep to stand in, floundering loudly in the process. After a short while of "letting them learn to swim", the troops pulled the bedraggled pair out of the water, sending them straight to the back of the queue, much to their youthful embarrassment. No one else jostled the troops, so I thought swimming lessons also worked well for crowd control in the right circumstances. Later, and to my quiet relief, I saw yesterday's milk powder thief, who had all the visible signs of quite a decent kicking, but no major injuries, so the tribe had maintained its local law and order, I thought. I was relieved that his punishment had been swift but minor: debating human rights didn't feature too highly on the average tribe's to do list. More importantly by far, they hadn't killed or maimed him, which pleased me immensely. He caught me looking at me and avoided my gaze, quietly shuffling away out of sight. I watched him go, idly wandering just what his personal opinion of us Brits was, but I'd never find out as I never met him again.

Just as we thought it was all going pretty well, an old white 4x4 vehicle came thundering towards those same troops. The crowd rapidly parted and a single shot rang out, the vehicle halting immediately. As I moved towards the vehicle, the driver was robustly hauled out, surrounded by very alert armed soldiers. I questioned him with Ali, noting a very neat little hole in the windscreen, very slightly above where his head had been seconds earlier and thought in passing, "An excellent piece of shooting". He was loudly belligerent and very hostile, claiming he'd had brake fade. I told him it was very strange how a bullet through his windscreen had totally cured his brake problem and if he didn't shut up I would arrest him immediately and also confiscate his vehicle. He promptly shut up. I congratulated a young bombardier on his outstanding marksmanship and making the right judgement call: as always, a split-second thing.

Now aware that a lot of males were listening, I told Ali to inform all of them loudly that the next time anyone tried to run any of my soldiers over my men would, from then on, shoot to kill without any prior verbal warning. I actually had no such authority whatsoever to give any such order, but the Iraqis didn't know that, it was just yet another piece of bluff on my part, but it protected my soldiers against any further such "accidents", so my conscience is totally clear. That message they clearly understood, but Ali needed his RAF Regiment protection team even more after passing that message. As always, the interpreters took the brunt of any bad feelings and insults, not to mention associated threats and intimidation. The Rock Apes, true to form, robustly stood their ground and gave at least as good as they received. They are after all the "military wing" of the RAF, from the Army's viewpoint at least.

Once we reached the predesignated cut-off time for our departure we split the remaining aid into two equal amounts and summoned the elders from both tribes, basically saying, "This is your share, take it away as you see fit". I wasn't having any lengthy discussions today and the troops weren't in the mood for debating things much either. Head check done, I gave the order to move out. Today no one was either throwing things at us or shouting insults. Professionally speaking, we felt much better, but the local mood had definitely changed towards us.

I gave a more positive and upbeat debrief at HQ, but my euphoria was shattered slightly when I had to justify opening fire again. I stated it was a totally necessary act of authorised self-defence and I supported the soldier's actions 100 per cent and it would almost definitely happen again, as we had, I personally believed, now lost the initiative with the local tribes. That didn't go down too well, the government likes to hear good news only when it comes to 21st Century military operations. Unfortunately, the bad guys insist on using their vote repeatedly and they have time on their side. Democracies become bored with conflict much easier than theologically-based fighters and insurgents and they also live for the fight, as it's all that they have got in very many cases.

Comparing possible talks or negotiations with either the Taliban or Islamic Jihadists with a beaten and weary IRA and the N Ireland Peace Process is a naïvely foolish and very inaccurate comparison. It took us over thirty years of attritional warfare, long term intelligence operations and ongoing political determination to eventually get them to the negotiating table. All of the Troubles in Northern Ireland happened in a very small geographical area where the sheer numbers of troops and police officers was overwhelmingly in our favour, not to mention a well-functioning judiciary and a robust penal system to facilitate the ongoing rule of law. Lastly, both ourselves and the various Republican and Loyalist terrorists had, to slightly differing degrees, a shared language, history and culture, all encompassed by some form of Christian faith in terms of upbringing, absolutely none of which we remotely share with 21st Century Jihadists. When we did finally get our newly found Republican friends to the negotiating table, we promptly played very soft, rather than hard ball with them in agreeing to the majority of their demands, covertly if not overtly. Like many ex-soldiers of that era, I wonder if (and no doubt former RUC Officers too), the motivation of our politicians, who seemed driven by the prospect of a legacy of being hailed as peace makers with a quick fix solution rather than totally ending Republican terrorism.

Additionally, they were essentially terrorists with European-based values, such as universal female education, equal rights for women and the right to work, not just a life of managing the home and breeding children. Our Irish Republican enemies also enjoyed a social life involving singing, dancing, alcohol and sex, including relationships outside marriage and a legal system made by humans, not God, to name a few differences. Unlike the average jihadist, IRA volunteers weren't, as a rule, too keen on "embracing death" either. Besides, you always sing when you're winning. You only talk when you start to lose, a truism of all guerrilla movements. Western politicians tend to forgot this all too easily when those insurgents are several thousand miles away and perhaps badly battered but still essentially unbeaten.

The conflict in Northern Ireland has few, if any, direct comparisons in terms of size, scale, ruthless extremism and sheer intensity with those in Iraq, Afghanistan and similar recent wars. Those British political figures who keep raising the "Peace Process" as the singular model for all to globally emulate do so, in my own view, for reasons primarily of personal ego and vanity. It's nice to go down in posterity as a peace maker, but to pretend this example will transfer across the globe with consummate ease is simply a naïve notion displaying an awful lot of ignorance regarding the sheer complexity of the players involved. The eternal Sunni/Shia schism, anti-West breeding grounds such as elements of Wahabism, Salafism and the historically anti-British Deobandi branch of Islam, together with the ongoing covert power struggle for control of Islam between Iran and Saudi Arabia, each with their various well-armed proxies, not to mention rampant tribalism all contrive to make this comparison rather wishful thinking. Yet another example of our ongoing inability to comprehend the wide diversity of Islam in the 21st Century. After all, the only democracy in the entire Middle East (even after the much vaunted Arab Spring) happens to be a Jewish state.

The following day, we discovered the RAF Regiment had been recalled back down south. We didn't know why and didn't even bother to ask, being just happy that we still "owned" the Americans. We drove out on patrol to our desert villages, back in our usual small team. The boys, as always, waved happily to our three ladies in the field. They didn't wave back this time, or indeed even deign to look at us. They never, ever did wave at us again during our remaining time in Iraq: this was proof positive that our honeymoon had now definitely ended. Personally, this small omission by those nameless and faceless Iraqi women quietly signified to me that we were now definitely and irrevocably strangers in a strange land.

Our welcomes in the local villages now became, at best, polite and reserved ranging through to blunt comments such as, "have you only come for our oil?", "when will you leave?" and "Iraq needs a strong man, like Saddam, not western puppets", to mention but a few. I duly passed these rather significant changes in the local atmospherics up the chain of command, but essentially, they were either filed away or quietly ignored: no one seemed overly concerned or even very interested. Our mindset seemed to be that we had, after all, won the war. Accordingly, we just carried on regardless and did our best to placate the locals and keep some form of peace across our area. The Americans had become an integral and very professional part of the team: we even managed to teach each other alternative versions of the English language for day to day conversation, although Scottish and Northern dialects still baffled them. Ali was suddenly transferred to another American unit much further north, which was a great loss for us and our team capability. He was replaced by another local man, who (apparently) had taught English, but we hadn't yet forgotten our very own Iraqi Intelligence Officer, so trust was an immediate issue. We'll call him "W", a narrow-faced man and very self-confident, slightly too much so for my liking, but beggars can't be choosers. However, we were very circumspect in what we discussed within earshot of him.

Interestingly, P, the young engineer at the Mosque Village distrusted him and hid his command of the English language from him, privately telling me he smelled of either the regime or Iran. P's own father and two of his uncles had died fighting the Iranians, serving in the Iraqi Army, so Iranians weren't top of his personal likes, unsurprisingly. I was well aware that Iran was discreetly conducting small-scale intelligence operations to find out our intentions and capability, but we only had hearsay rather than hard proof, but the border was very close by and highly porous in security terms while our local knowledge, compared to that of the Iraqi regime's intelligence capability was very, very poor in every respect. From personal experience from Macedonia (prior to the Kosovo liberation) I knew that Iran's Intelligence Agencies and their capability demanded professional respect, plus their conservative and highly theocratic regime had survived some traumatic decades, despite the very best efforts of both Saddam and various American Presidents, so I doubted my little team caused them any sleepless nights.

Some of the villagers in the canal area were becoming increasingly anxious over water levels as we still hadn't got the large lock gates operational, so they feared flooding and flagged us down on several occasions, begging us to do something. We assured them we had told our superiors, which was really all we could do and that help was on its way. Apparently our HQ informed brigade. From there we really didn't know who had been told, so we just carried on with our patrols attempting to "increase our footprint", but you can only do so much with four vehicles and sixteen soldiers in such a large area. In a way it was a microcosm of the British Army's future efforts in both Iraq and Afghanistan. Ultimately you need what soldiers refer to as "mass", which simply means numbers of troops. You can't "dominate the ground" without an actual physical presence, after all. In Northern Ireland, a relatively small area of land after all, we achieved that in the "difficult" areas in which we wished to have an enduring effect and then sustained that presence for decades. In both Iraq and Afghanistan we never did. Irrespective of good training, uncommon and repeated gallantry and the large technological gap between us and our enemies, if you cannot maintain your presence then you will never dominate the ground. That may sound rather old-fashioned and simplistic but sadly it's also militarily true, both then and now.

Most people no longer wished to talk to us voluntarily. The euphoria of our arrival had now long worn off and the same old topics repeatedly came up: electricity, schools and teachers, medical facilities and all the other usual suspects in daily conversational terms with the villagers. Our repeated assurances had by now lost all credibility and now caused either amusement and disbelief or scorn and anger in equal measure. Iraqis view words as cheap and meaningless without visible action to support them, which is fair enough really when you bear in mind their collective "upbringing" and recent history. We no longer got invited inside for endless cups of chai or dinner with the elders, the sole exception being the Mosque Village. Small actions, or indeed lack of any real interaction was obvious to both me and my small command, all of whom in turn were visibly less relaxed and far more distant towards the Iraqi people. Body language can speak volumes in overcoming the lack of any common spoken language.

On one occasion we came upon some kind of meeting in the desert, our attention being grabbed by a collection of large awnings under which sat a group of men. We discovered some elders we knew and many others who we didn't: obviously some form of political forum. Around the exterior were several silent and obviously muscular young men. They had even brought their own security detail with them, we thought quietly. W was respectful to the point of almost being deferential with these people and he told us it was "just a picnic to discuss local agricultural matters". I thought he was hedging his bets for the future and simply didn't want to piss these people off. Ali, I felt, would have far more forthright, but he was all we had. No one spoke to us unless spoken to and I had no valid reason to either detain or arrest anyone: for what, having a men-only picnic in the desert?

George pointed out two large Russian-made ZIL trucks, with civilian plates, each bearing a large colour photograph of the Grand Ayatollah of Iran on the windscreen. We asked what these were doing here. To carry the awnings, we were told. I personally felt that two 15-ton trucks seemed a somewhat excessive requirement for moving a couple of tents perhaps, but they stuck to their story and calling them liars would hardly endear us to them. Lots of tyre tracks led to and from the rear of the vehicles, but that was all. George suggested the Iranians were playing us at our own game and distributing aid. Highly plausible, but again we had no proof. I thanked them for their time and patience, these were very obviously local power brokers and unanimously looked none too impressed by our uninvited presence. We learned a few days later that it had indeed been a discreet aid distribution operation, but only to villages which weren't too friendly towards us. This never happened again, possibly because of our surprise and unwanted intrusion at the event, but it proved, to me at least, that we weren't the only players in the area.

Shortly after this we noticed a large man who had an uncanny knack of appearing in most of the villages we visited, bearing in mind the total lack of any form of public transport and the distances involved. He favoured a red shemagh, the scarf/headdress worn by a lot of Arab men, however, this was a very unusual colour in clothing terms amongst this part of Maysan Province. Once he came to our notice, we discreetly watched him watching us for a few days. He never got too close, didn't appear to mix with any locals and appeared to be purely interested in us and our activities. Eventually, having no real proof of evil intent or similar ambitions and therefore no reason to detain or arrest him, we just confronted him and questioned him, in essence saying, "Mate, we've rumbled you". He was a big man up close and surprisingly confident, avoiding our questions in a highly practised manner, to the point we bluntly told him that he wasn't too welcome and next time we'd arrest him: another complete bluff on our part as we had no real proof, but he didn't know that. He never reappeared and I quietly mentioned the episode to P for his personal opinion, who simply replied, "He's returned from exile in Iran. There are many others like him in Al Amarah."

All of this was passed upwards. In essence, the responses were that the meeting of elders was deemed plausible as a gathering of landowners merely discussing water rights, goat herds, crops and similar agricultural essentials, whilst the "Iranian Iraqi" who had been watching us was probably either us being overly paranoid or probably just a misunderstanding. I couldn't be bothered arguing. What's the point? I thought, just look after the guys and get home in one piece. This is all slowly going to rat shit and we've only been here a couple of months, while none of our military/political hierarchy back in UK seemed to have either any noteworthy ideas, or indeed plain old-fashioned interest in how to deal with a rather large and almost totally broken nation. Post invasion, it came to public light that one of the President's advisors had told him that if the Coalition invaded and thereby took control of Iraq, then the rule of, "If you break it you pay for it" would apply. It appeared to me (and still does) that this particular sentiment never made it across the Atlantic to our side of the Pond.

One day we came across a freshly dead donkey beside a fairly busy T-junction, with the local pedestrians walking blithely by, seemingly oblivious to its presence. I halted the patrol to look at the hapless animal from a close-up perspective. Not being much of an expert on donkeys, it was blindingly obvious that it was indeed freshly dead. Presumably it had simply dropped dead of exhaustion and its owner had moved on. By the attitude of the locals this was a fairly common occurrence. Animals existed purely for a given functional purpose, the concept of "pets" did not exist and animal welfare was an unknown concept to all Iraqis: indeed, to them it was simply another example of Western "softness". The next day the poor beast was still lying there but now visibly swollen by the heat. For reasons unknown, it flashed into my head that its now rather large stomach would be an ideal place to hid a quite large explosive device and some "shipyard confetti" (nails, bolts anything that has a very nasty effect on hitting the human body), if you didn't mind the messy job of first removing its innards and of course, stitching it all back up afterwards.

Again, I halted the patrol and checked my possible "dead donkey bomb" for any tell-tale signs of incisions or related sewing (I'm quite serious about this). Luckily none of the locals appeared to share my idea for the discreet placement of IEDs within large dead animals. Several days later we found its remnants still being fought over by feral dogs, as the locals continued to idly stroll by the remains of its now grisly skeleton. This certainly wasn't Europe in terms of civic health and I duly shared my dead donkey bomb theory to a polite audience, who appeared to think, "He's losing it". The troops duly referred to this road junction as Dead Donkey Corner for the remainder of our tour and I quickly forgot my bizarre idea of converting a donkey's corpse into a crude but effective weapon system.

That is, until 6 months later, when an American foot patrol on the outskirts of Baghdad was blown up by one of its distant and equally dead cousins. A stark example of asymmetric warfare at its best. Never in our wildest dreams had anyone considered dead donkey bombs or similar little unpleasant surprises. After all, the Iraqi insurgents in just over a year surpassed 30 years of the IRA's achievements in terms of Improvised Explosive Device (IED) development: not exactly a boost to humanity's cultural advancement, but a very impressive achievement nevertheless and one totally unforeseen by both ourselves and the Americans alike. Later the Pashtun tribesmen of the Taliban took IEDs to an almost industrial scale, adding their own refinements along the way: a good example of migration in action. In due course it would not be deemed too unusual for a British Infantry Battalion (@ 650 soldiers) to take 25 to 40% casualties during a tour of Helmand Province. "Do the maths", as they say.

A couple of days later each of our Americans received a large food parcel from the States, free of postal charges and quite well stocked with all American goodies. It would be years until we gained the same privilege. For any of our families to send a similar-sized parcel would have been expensive to say the least during the early years of our desert wars. One of the few positive points from our desert conflicts was the steady rise in popularity of the Army with the British public, aided by sombre images of Royal Wootton Basset for the final homecoming of hundreds of soldiers. This in turn drove various governments to slowly improve the lot of the armed forces on operations, like the much vaunted but still sadly fairly toothless Soldier's Covenant and the gradual (if slow) improvement in treatment for the thousands of wounded, which in all likelihood was driven by public opinion and the related drive for votes rather than any real political compassion or conscience. The Americans were quietly surprised that we had no equivalent and became quite sheepish. Eventually Brian suggested they'd like to share their parcels with the team, a very generous offer as we had been solely reliant on our operational ration packs for months by now.

Our daily routine started with Mike digging a small hole for a "Hexy" cooker (a small Army Hexamine solid fuel cooker) onto which he'd place the metal team kettle, which he had acquired from somewhere and was now a very precious team possession. We'd all then place our boil in a bag rations into this ,having first written our names on our choice of rations. Once the water boiled you'd remove the ration pack and eat it, having also made a coffee with the hot water. Like all soldiers, Mike firmly believed officers couldn't safely look after themselves, even ones who were ex-RSMs. You lose all your powers once commissioned, apparently, rather like Samson getting his hair cut.

The average day's ten-hours-plus patrol was spent drinking lots of warm water in the region of over a gallon each daily (it was a microwave environment to which our body armour, whilst essential equipment, merely enhanced personal dehydration) with the odd Army biscuit. We had neither the time, means nor inclination to stop and cook once on patrol. Once back in, a quick team debrief, a second hot meal, wash and then sleep. We had no potatoes, bread, fruit or vegetables of any kind for well over ten weeks, so the average weight loss in our battle group was thirty pounds per individual, a hugely successful (if unintended) mass dietary plan on behalf of the MOD. On several occasions I was reminded of the war stories I had been told long ago, as a young and inexperienced soldier, by my then NCOs, most of whom had served in the bitter Arabian campaigns of Aden and the Radfan. They too had required copious amounts of water merely to function, let alone fight. Ultimately, without this basic human need being fulfilled, all our technology was useless and our planning pointless. Back home expressing such a thought would be viewed as weird.

On one memorable occasion our ration resupply proved to be 14 days of the pork casserole menu (some lazy logistician back in Kuwait couldn't be bothered to provide us with a choice) which I didn't like personally and with the local population obviously being devout Muslims, we couldn't even give them away to the Iraqis, so day after day we ate pork casserole and "Biscuits Dead Fly", as the troops called Garibaldi biscuits. So when the Americans offered tinned fruit, flapjacks, assorted candy and suchlike, this was an absolute certainty to be well received by the troops. Brian and I resolved to discreetly facilitate a patrol which gave us an opportunity to taste this American hospitality.

Accordingly, I told the team we were going to check out the empty villages where Saddam had turned off the water back in the early nineties. The troops looked baffled and thought I'd lost it again, presumably, this was a classic pointless military exercise for all concerned. We drove the boring and featureless route there and after a slow drive through an area we hadn't visited, I picked a deserted village at random and we parked next to a line of long-abandoned, now crumbling dwellings. I gathered the team and briefed them that actually, we were now going to have a desert picnic, courtesy of the US Army and just chill for once. On my part this was unprofessional to say the least, but I felt that team morale needed a boost. The guys had consistently done me proud and I firmly believed they deserved it. You can't be an effective leader in the Army and simultaneously expect to be popular, but you can and should look after your soldiers and their welfare as best you are able to, so this, I personally felt anyway, was exactly, that, plus W had asked for a day off to visit a sick relative, which was extremely useful for this particular day.

Brian and his team shared out the goodies from America. George and Gerry organised driver training: we drove the Humvee and the Americans drove a Land Rover, the guys explored the modern ruins of a major village and took lots of team "happy snaps", reminders of Iraq for all of us. I found a piece of shade and caught up on writing letters home. Around me the Humvee and a Land Rover drove around a de facto driving circuit the boys had selected and a small touch rugby game took place, using a water bottle in lieu of a ball. Trying to explain the rules of rugby to our Americans proved an impossible task, as was their equally vain attempt to decipher American Football's complicated rules to us Brits.

One bunch of NCOs, three lance corporals and a British Army version of the Three Amigos asked if they could take a vehicle and visit another ruined village very close by. I agreed as other than us, the nearest person was at least thirty or forty miles away. They reappeared an hour or so later, looking pleased with themselves. I asked them what they had found. The answer was, "Nothing, sir, but we took some great photos."

"Of what?" I asked. Silence was the deafening reply. After some minor badgering from me, it transpired they had taken some "Naked Romeo" happy snaps, a parody of our designated "Dress States" for chemical defence. In essence they had worn boots and gas masks (respirators by their proper name) with rifles and nothing else. Well, a great, if fairly unique, family heirloom to show the grandkids, I thought. I was sure the future Iraqi nation could live with this, as long as we didn't actually tell them.

We concluded the day by the younger soldiers firing the M60 machine gun mounted atop the Humvee, essentially demolishing a wall in the process. We couldn't return the favour with our rifles as, unlike the Americans, we didn't have very much ammunition and we had to account for every single round we fired. They were unconcerned: we were, after all, their closest allies and the debacle that proved to be Iraq for the UK's national involvement was ultimately yet to unfold. We drove back to the airfield in high spirits and I told HQ that we had had an uneventful day's patrol in the AO, which was, after all, very true. To any former soldier who, no doubt, finds this all unprofessional, yes, I agree totally. Do I apologise? No, not in the slightest, it was my call and I felt my soldiers fully deserved such a very minor "perk". They did a stoical job on a daily basis, lacking support, equipment, ammunition, direction and to a large degree, even interest from higher up the command chain, so a few hours relaxing in the remote desert is not something I feel obliged to seek absolution for. Maintenance of morale is after all one of the keystones of effective command within the military lexicon.

Shortly afterwards, as our medic rotated, a female NCO joined us, a feisty Glaswegian girl and a high quality CMT (Combat Medical Technician). Whilst we personally had absolutely no qualms over this, we were curious on how the Iraqis would receive her. Iraqi society, unlike that of Afghanistan, as we would soon discover (Afghan wives are little more than another possession in male terms), put their women on a minor pedestal in many ways, but they were still very conservative in nature. To our surprise, obvious curiosity aside at seeing a Western woman in uniform, they simply weren't too bothered at seeing an armed woman in our midst. Iraqi women, it transpired, held a far greater social position than we had assumed and as a medical person, her profession greatly engendered respect. One aspect of village life this opened was both far more access to children — albeit always with the mother or an elder sister in attendance — and therefore active dialogue with Iraqi women, a taboo subject for us until now.

As she explained to us once, she had been brought up in Glasgow with four brothers. She learned to stand her own corner very early in life and she did not take any lip from our male soldiers either, she was very much an equal partner within the team. She rapidly became a very important member of our patrols and proved adept at gauging the mood or opinions of the locals, sometimes reinforcing, often confirming our own beliefs or views. One example was the presence of Al Qaeda. When we raised this with the male population, their response ranged from "Who?", to hilarious laughter: the very idea of AQ being active in Iraq at that time was something they found both absolutely ludicrous and totally absurd, which in turn was viewed with suspicion by our own intelligence cells. She discreetly raised this issue, in the form of "foreigner fighters with guns" within the female population. Their response was unequivocal. You mean the Iranians of MEK in Al Amarah?" They patiently explained that under Saddam, foreigners only came to Iraq if the regime expressly gave its permission. All the borders were tightly controlled, as was all internal movement within the country, so anything else was just a fanciful notion.

AQ, to be fair, did flock to Iraq in large numbers, but *after* our invasion had opened the borders and with the express purpose of fighting the infidel invaders. We soon became, in effect, a rallying call for AQ and their erstwhile followers, exclusively in the Sunni areas, which was therefore mainly an American problem (with the exception of our SF who rather vigorously took the fight to AQ around the greater Baghdad area). We Brits would have enough of our own issues with the Shia militias and the Badr Corps around Basra as time moved on and Iraq quickly fractured along age-old religious fault lines.

One day, to our mutual amazement, the senior elder of the Mosque Village casually informed us that his wife would like to invite our Glaswegian Lady CMT to high tea with other villagers' wives: no one else, just her. Taken aback, I asked her would she like to go for chai with the village "wives' club". Her response was immediate: "Absolutely!" We agreed to come back in two days and I asked the RMO for his permission, she was after all under his command ultimately. If I ensured security then okay, was his response. George and I sat down to plan security for a wives' club tea party, not a job we had banked upon doing, but this was a rare offer and a mark of respect on the part of the Iraqis concerned. Similarly, for us to refuse would have been both very insulting to the elder, his wife and indeed the whole village itself, plus it would ensure that this invite would never, ever, ever again be extended to any British troops.

So, come the day, having borrowed a second female soldier for the occasion (mutual support in effect) and ensuring both ladies had functional personal radios, ammunition and a good briefing with regards to "actions on", just in case. We trusted the villagers and hospitality was sacrosanct to them. They would, I honestly believed, literally die to protect a guest within their home, but this was Iraq, after all. We put a cordon around the elder's house (as always the largest in the village) and escorted the excited "girlies" to the entrance. The elder and the other husbands met us and explained the women held their tea mornings upstairs and suggested we wait downstairs. They fully understood that we wished to protect our women, and gave us their solemn word that they would be totally safe and secure. To ask to check out the rooms would have been a mark of extreme bad faith and deeply insulting, so I had no choice but to roll with things. Having one last minute brief with the girls, off they went for afternoon tea. Modern war, I thought as they disappeared from my view.

George, Mike, I and another couple of soldiers plus W sat down for chai. I asked if W would be required upstairs to translate. To my great surprise the answer was that two wives had brought their eldest daughters along, both of whom spoke English, having been language students at university prior to the outbreak of hostilities. "Never judge a book by its cover", I thought. Sadly, unlike society in modern UK where appearance, ego and spin tends to consistently win over against knowledge, experience and ability. We waited, rotated the troops in and out of the sun, changed positions, drank some more chai and patiently waited, occasionally faintly hearing girlish laughter above us. Islam is after all very much a man's world and not renowned for either its feminist movement or showing much concern for women's rights, so this was one of our more surprising experiences. I for one couldn't envisage this being repeated too often, if ever, frankly. After a quarter of a century of being a professional soldier in the "world's finest small Army" this was not a task I had ever anticipated in my wildest dreams. then we waited some more. Fortunately, waiting is a skill that all professional soldiers are well acquainted with and even more practised at, so we did this task very well.

Finally, our ladies reappeared, all smiles and good cheer. they assured us that they had both had a great laugh. Their Iraqi counterparts had (literally) apparently let their hair down with the utter absence of males, the food had been plentiful, along with endless chai and the two daughters spoke good English and enjoyed the opportunity to practise their English language skills. In brief, the women had discussed the rising food prices, the difficulties of raising children post invasion, the stupidity and impatience of men (a universal topic for all female discussions, no doubt) and great anxiety about the future, including the demise of secularism in Iraq and impending violent strife between Sunni and Shia. They found our desire to give them democracy and women's rights baffling, it seemed: they already had rights a-plenty, they felt and very few Iraqi men took more than one wife, so why did they need Western Democracy anyway? Some very candid and surprising points, all in all. I felt it gave some invaluable insight to what the locals discussed behind closed doors. On a trivial note, they also confirmed to me the total lack of books in Iraqi homes, apart from the Koran. Perhaps they had them in the larger towns and cities but not here. I found this absence of books startling in a country which seemed so keen on universal education. I'm not sure what the Int guys thought of this event, as they never got back to me, but personally, I thought the girls did a simply tremendous job on behalf of UK PLC.

Eventually the Army did, quite successfully, adopt "Female engagement teams" in Helmand Province, but not for several years and only when our mission there was almost over. In addition our mission had by then been drastically changed several times in tune with our political turnover and, along the way, we'd quietly lost our "lead nation" status and (like it or not) been discreetly rescued by the US Marines due to the strongly-held joint American/Afghan belief that the Brits were on the verge of a catastrophic mission failure in Helmand Province. Ironically we had, as an Army, gone into Helmand determined to make up for our failure/defeat in Iraq. With the singular exception, perhaps, of the most junior officers and soldiers, few soldiers really believed that Iraq had been anything other than an embarrassing failure whilst the word "defeat" itself was studiously avoided.

All these years later, I still find it difficult to accept this major change of military fortunes would take a mere four or five years to enact, ably reinforced by an overarching lack of either political will or vision, any realistic or enduring strategic direction and the Treasury's ongoing reluctance to fund these foreign ventures. It takes centuries to build a tradition of military success and decades to gain a reputation as the world's finest professional Army, but it sadly takes rather a lot less to end one and severely damage the other.

Following the wives' tea party, we discovered that most locals had two major concerns, with their priority depending on precisely where they lived: the first was imminent flooding due to the still-unrepaired lock gates, or at least a widespread and growing concern with the ominously steady rise in water levels and the possible effect on their lives. Yet again I reported this to HQ with my strong opinion that we really needed to make this a very high priority. This was noted, but not,

I personally believed with too much in the way of enthusiasm. Hopefully someone somewhere would realise we needed to be singularly proactive in dealing with this particular issue. For the locals this was a huge concern, their families and essentially all they owned in the world. I believed this to be of an urgent nature, but we had passed this onwards and upwards and now we carried on with our daily patrolling and awaited a response.

The other major concern of all the villagers remained our ongoing inability to deliver regarding any or all of the now missing civil foundations of electricity, education and medical services. We now faced on a daily basis heated questions over these perennial topics. Yet again, the increasingly common question of "Did you come here for us or our oil?", along with the regularly restated belief that Iraq didn't need the rich exiles to return from their Western homes to govern the nation, rather it needed a home-grown strong man like Saddam (but a much nicer version obviously) to restore the nation (in a similar vein many Afghans referred to Mr Karzai disparagingly as the "Halfghan", having been plucked from his restaurant in America to become President of Afghanistan, despite being almost unknown in his home country). The fact was that, under Saddam's regime, electricity was normally available for between 12-16 hours on a daily basis in most towns, not to mention schools, hospitals et al and conversely, since the demise of the regime (which obviously coincided rather nicely with our arrival) all of these essentials of life had simply ceased and were therefore social hot topics.

I suspected that someone unknown was "stirring the pot" as all, these themes and comments were all remarkably similar in manner. Indeed, they seemed quite coordinated. All this despite the obvious distances involved for an essentially pedestrian populace who distinctly lacked both mobile phones and any means of public transport. Iraqi patience had now reached its limits, it seemed, and in an increasingly irate manner. As this was a Shia stronghold we could hardly blame any remnants of the long-departed Sunni-dominated regime. I suspected the returning exiles from Iran, but again, personal opinions and hard evidence were two rather different issues. Western media was firmly concentrated in Baghdad so this slow-burning dissent was to all intents and purposes invisible to them: Maysan Province simply wasn't "sexy" in journalistic terms, it wasn't even on the media radar.

Our local prime candidate was a suspected black marketeer named Mohamed. We had visited a small water filtration plant some weeks earlier and quickly found some poorly-hidden AK 47s which (unsurprisingly) no one at the plant claimed as their personal property. The workers' collective excuse was much along the lines of "A big boy must have just dumped them there and then ran away", essentially. It transpired Mohamed ran the plant with some local hoods as security. He was visibly none too pleased when we took the weapons away, probably because it would cost him money to replace them. They were quite lucky, the Americans would have been far less kind than us with very robust rules of engagement, and visibly armed men were shot on sight in their area, or at the very least promptly arrested, but mainly shot. While we Brits "had a chat" and (eventually) disarmed them at this stage of the campaign, our rules of engagement had basically reverted to the default setting of Northern Ireland, except this was definitely neither Belfast nor Armagh.

Mohamed was a large man, about 6'3" in height and very well built. Iraq's class system was similar to ours in many respects and the higher your social position, then the better fed you were and you could see the results in terms of purely physical stature differences across the social classes. Mohamed seemed to have lots of fingers in lots of pies and was confident to the point of arrogance, he also resented our attempts to both maintain order and freely give away fresh water and assorted foodstuffs to the villagers, which his "helpers" already discreetly sold to the locals, amongst other things, no doubt with a significant profit margin. As usual, we couldn't prove anything and the Iraqis certainly weren't going to give us any information about a large and almost certainly rather violent bully with his own presumably well-armed sizeable gang.

He also had access to a number of cars, very much a rarity in this area and also a highly visible indication of his wealth, which enabled him to appear at will, with some followers and add his anti-British, anti-invader rhetoric, which grew increasingly in volume as time passed. To say he became a royal pain in the arse is an understatement. Any attempt to find out more about him and his background met with an uneasy silence, it immediately reminded me of the fearful silence that surrounded IRA hard men in Belfast or KLA thugs in Pristina. He was a forceful rabble-rouser who focused on our failures and unfulfilled promises but all we had were suspicions, not proof. He had refined his intimidation techniques to a fine art, which we had briefly witnessed several times, but W also seemed frightened of him, which made his translations dubious at times, to say the least. In turn any villagers were reticent to engage in any form of discussion with us regarding Mohammed, a vicious circle of silence in effect.

Unlike the Americans, our rules of engagement and detention were both unrealistic and ineffective. Our masters back in UK were keen to apply liberal Western European guidelines to what in reality was more like the Wild West, so in turn we appeared quite weak to people like Mohamed and the pro-Iranian supporters in the area, which rapidly added to their growing confidence. While Western liberals consistently ignore the fact that Israel is the only functioning democracy in the Middle East, in most other countries it's simply power, strength and occasionally the widespread application of violence that matters and Iraq was certainly no exception to that unpalatable fact. A period of growing frustration was quietly endured by us, especially as our perceived inaction regarding electricity and other key services gave them and their grievances, in their eyes at least, more substance and fast-growing credence across the local populace. Any trust or feelings of goodwill towards us were almost tangibly eroding on a daily basis and we seemed unable to regain the initiative. Put bluntly, the locals wanted more than our smiles and ongoing promises.

Finally, during one large-scale and very heated public debate in which Mohamed was prominent, we got a break. Mike had cast a discreet eye over Mohamed's car and called me over by radio. When I arrived he pointed out the folding butt of an airborne version of the AK 47 literally peeking out from under the passenger seat of Mohamed's car. I asked Mohamed for a private chat by his car, just me him and W to interpret. He agreed without hesitation, a sure sign of his confidence. As we stood by his car, pointing at the poorly concealed AK 47 I asked him if he had permission for the weapon. He, unsurprisingly, had no knowledge of the weapon as it was a friend's car that he had borrowed. We searched the car and found a further two AKs in the boot, of which he (obviously) knew nothing either.

I informed him that he was under arrest for possessing illegal firearms and would be taken to Al Amarah for further questioning. He asked me what I would do if he refused to get into our vehicle in a very belligerent manner. I really didn't need a scene and possibly find the rest of the local males piling in to either prevent his arrest or a muscular gang attempting to rescue him, so I offered him two straightforward options. One, quietly get in the Land Rover with my soldiers or option two, as I considered him a rather dangerous man, I'd shoot him in the femur, purely in self-defence on my part, obviously. I further informed him that whilst he'd recover, it would certainly make his eyes water and he would more than likely walk with a significant limp for the rest of his natural life. To emphasise the seriousness of my offer I casually pointed my rifle at his lower body from a quite intimate range of less than two metres. He grasped my point rather quickly and decided, albeit very ungraciously, to accept a lift from the British Army. This was, yet again, a complete and total bluff on my part, but it worked and his feelings weren't too high on my list of personal concerns, whilst shooting him did have a certain appeal, I have to admit.

We discreetly cuffed him, placed him in a Land Rover and drove him to Al Amarah, the crowd not noticing his absence until he was well out of the way and I returned to discuss civic issues with the crowd which, lacking Mohamed's noisy aberrations, was much calmer. Several hours later, on returning to my HQ, I asked for an update about him, only to find he had been released after explaining that the car was borrowed and his friend had failed to mention the rifles- he was merely an innocent trader (who had an unfortunate knack for being around concealed AK 47s) just attempting to make ends meet, only to find himself mistakenly arrested by a totally unreasonable British Officer. I was utterly furious but unable to do anything about this hasty and incredibly naïve decision. I immediately tried to find him and re-arrest him as soon as possible, only to be told, yet again, that he had gone to Baghdad. We never saw or heard of him again, but at least he was no longer our resident pain in the arse.

Just when we thought we had returned the AO to an acceptable level of peace and quiet, we awoke one morning to discover that not one but two canals had flooded the surrounding area, forcing a number of villages to rapidly evacuate their homes, miserably clutching what possessions they could manhandle to higher ground, or at least, what passed for that in Maysan Province. Initially all we could do was tour the area and conduct a damage assessment and offer our sympathies to the bedraggled locals, who were hoping for something rather more tangible from us.

As we drove down a levee we found our path blocked by a ramshackle dwelling made of wood and cardboard. As we slowed an old woman, followed by a small tribe of young children, appeared to quietly glare at us. She suddenly and very loudly demanded that we move her "house" to slightly higher ground. We were trying to assess the flood damage and politely said so. Her response was to tell her children to sit down across the track, in effect a very juvenile sit-down protest and thereby barring our path very effectively. Negotiation failed miserably, so eventually both Brits and Americans moved her "house", supervised by this formidable lady who was actually probably only in her late 30s to early 40s: life is hard on a single mother in the desert. Finally she was content and allowed us to continue. We all thanked the fact that she had never been one of Saddam's generals, or the recent war would have been both far more difficult and much lengthier in nature for all concerned.

Luckily for us, a consignment of "family boxes", each designed to feed a family of 6 for 24 hrs, arrived from Basra, along with powdered milk, flour and cooking oil. It was completely coincidental rather than good planning, but rather fortuitous for all concerned. Accordingly, on the very next day we set out at dawn to assist as many affected villagers as we possibly could and generally provide as much assistance as was humanly possible. The family boxes went down famously with all the locals we encountered that day, but our newly regained popularity would only last until the waters receded. You do what you can with what you have, ultimately. After learning lessons from our previous attempts, we now cut open any sacks containing foodstuffs and used a metal mug to share out the contents, that way it can't be stolen and you can then hand over the ration distribution to the elders rather easily and very quickly. We made a point of going back to the formidable lady: we suspected her man had simply deserted her (but none of us had the actual courage to ask her) and gave her several boxes. To our surprise she thanked us profusely. In a quiet way we were all moved by this plucky, if volatile woman and her determined efforts to just keep her family together and alive.

The following day, as if to reinforce this lone woman's determination, we were stunned when, impatient with both our own and the male elders' apparently inefficient distribution efforts, some villagers' wives abruptly and forcefully took over from us. We had never been physically so very close to Iraqi women and it made us all surprisingly uncomfortable to a major degree. We were terrified at the prospect of any of them talking to us directly and all of us were trying hard to look away from these women. It was surprisingly unsettling for us, although the women seemed unaware of their effect. I remember trying remarkably hard not to stare when I was amazed to discover the woman next to me, in lieu of make-up, had tattooed dark ink onto both her lips and eyelids in a form of a permanent make-over, complete with permanent ear rings tattooed onto her ear lobes.

We simply gave in gracefully and left the ladies to complete our task. Frankly we were speechless at this unexpected turn of events, it was a unique event but it did give us a glimpse into the hitherto "invisible" human side of the Iraqi people. One other aspect we discovered was that when Ben suddenly appeared carrying a pickaxe handle, everyone just ran away from us immediately. Ben occasionally carried it after our recent street fight (we never were issued any batons) purely "just in case" of any further minor riots. We later discovered that during Saddam's regime, the police routinely used camel whips to provide an urgent emphasis to their orders, and neither men, women or children were exempt a few lashes and with absolutely no human rights lawyers or sympathetic media on call, it was rather a one-sided issue. We ceased carrying pickaxe handles immediately, but it gave us an insight into life under the regime nevertheless and Iraqis have extraordinarily long memories. Westerners in comparison have an extremely short-term view of history and consistently fail to grasp the sheer depth of distrust and fear following the long centuries of hatred that dominates this troubled region.

Belatedly, once the full extent of the flooding was realised by our senior commanders, we were re-tasked to carry on with this work for several more days. The team enjoyed this work, we felt that it was positive and worthwhile and for once, the locals were glad to see us. I had a huge degree of independence, which was personally refreshing and the rumour of our relief being imminent was now floating around the regimental bazaars, so it seemed to me that having now escaped the recent doldrums, we might just finish on a high. My soldiers accepted the myriad equipment, ammunition and planning shortfalls stoically, but everyone needed to understand why are were doing this and this had been a quietly growing issue at times, once we all realised that Saddam's much publicised WMD and the infamous dossier was a best a myth, at worst an absolute spin-based political falsehood. I don't believe in lying to people who are prepared to put their lives on the line on behalf of a nameless suit or some shameless politicians several thousand miles away. However, conducting flood relief operations (not at all why we came here admittedly) did give them all a positive sense of purpose above and well beyond merely obeying orders because "that's what we do".

One day we were approached by a huge man, whose right arm hung uselessly by his side. I was struck by the air of melancholy that just surrounded this man, but coupled with a stoical dignity and quiet pride at the same time. He politely explained that he and his young son needed food, pointing at a small packing crate construction nearby which was currently his home. We gave him several boxes and then with some embarrassment realised he couldn't carry them all with only one working arm. Two of us accompanied him to his dwelling, to find a little boy who immediately hid as he saw us approaching. His father reassured him in Arabic and we deposited the boxes and quickly left. I felt sorry for this small family and idly wandered how they had come to be in such dire straits, even by the standards of Maysan Province.

Two days later, as the waters began to recede — nothing at all to do with our efforts, we still hadn't repaired the lock gates and electricity was still a distant aspiration at best on our part — we were touring the area to confirm the fall in water levels and therefore our requirement to continue distributing aid. Our feisty Iraqi lady had moved on, where to we never found out: hopefully she and her children found somewhere safe to rebuild their lives. Meanwhile the people were resignedly getting on with their lives and now again treated us as just another part of the landscape. I saw the big man with one arm again and he waved at us in recognition, his small son literally hiding behind him and peeking around his dad at the strange foreigners with guns. On a whim, I stopped the vehicles and taking W with me, walked over to him.

We made some small talk, neither of us was in a rush to go anywhere, after all. His son seemed openly fascinated by the pink bloke talking to his father. I innocently asked him about the rest of his family. He explained his wife had died in childbirth, the baby being stillborn, whilst his other son had died of some undefined fever. To cap that, he added, his brothers had been killed in first Iran and then Kuwait fighting Saddam's wars and his parents were dead also. Essentially, he was a man alone, it seemed. A long and uncomfortable silence ensued as I struggled to follow that. I asked him if he had been injured in the war also, meaning his useless arm. He replied that he had survived his war (he didn't specify which one and I didn't ask) and came home intact, but then had been dragged out of his bed by the secret police and then tortured and questioned for several days. He never knew what his supposed offence was, he was just stripped naked, beaten, covered in water and repeatedly electrocuted along with some other men he didn't know. Somewhere during this process his arm had been brutally smashed with a hammer, he told me in an emotionless voice. Eventually he had been released without explanation. He was just grateful to be alive. He never saw the other men again and just presumed they all died in some manner. Apparently there was a rather broad variety of ways to die in the hands of the Mukbahrat. You just didn't ask any questions, he explained, just thanked God you were still alive. Here, I thought, is a man who really has had his human rights abused and no one would ever fight his particular corner for any form of compensation.

I gestured towards his remaining son and replied that at least now, he could safely grow into manhood without the fear of being dragged from his bed and severely beaten for no reason. Now Saddam had gone, surely the future for Iraq could only get better, I said. He looked me directly in the eye and simply replied, "Inshallah," God willing, essentially. Over a decade later and following the rapid and often barbarically violent rise of the Islamic State, coupled with the abject failure of the multi-billion dollar new Iraqi Army to counter its meteoric rise, which thankfully is now being forcibly countered, I often reflect on that quiet conversation, not very far from the banks of the river Tigris, with such a stoical and dignified man and how totally and absolutely wrong I was. I also shudder to contemplate what he now thinks of me personally, the British Army in general and its distant government after our quiet conversation of so many years ago. I personally suspect (if he or his son remains alive) that he reflects fairly bitterly on both our unfulfilled promises and all the cheques we wrote to his people, which we never, ever did cash in so many ways.

The end to our daily desert sojourns came surprisingly rapidly. We returned to the airfield one day following a mundane day's patrolling, the main event being a very visible outbreak of anti-British posters in Maymunah: bed sheets draped high in the streets, proclaiming in both Arabic and English such sentiments as, *"We are not wanting military in our peaceful town"* or the now boringly familiar, *"Is it us you came for or our oil?"* Several quite large towns — Maymunah, Marjah and others — seemed to have little or no British presence, in effect almost small republics as we concentrated almost all our efforts on Al Amarah. Whilst we ourselves drove through Maymunah on a regular basis it was not really our "patch" and I never felt we actually controlled the town, quite the contrary, really. I got the distinct impression that as long as we Brits didn't actually stop and try to do anything in their town, they were simply content for us to drive through en route to somewhere else.

As we reported yet another "combat indicator" of our slipping grasp over the new Iraq, the response was basically, "Yeah, whatever, we're leaving in 5 days". The decision had been made to withdraw the brigade and leave a single battalion behind: unsurprisingly, the Paras. A squadron of tanks would also soon arrive from Basra, along with some Warriors to back them up so we'd finally have some armour but, even so, we were down-sizing dramatically. Meanwhile the overall UK contribution would shrink from a division to a brigade, a reduction of two thirds essentially but we simply couldn't maintain our troop levels for very long and unlike the Americans, we didn't have either too many regular soldiers or very many reservists who particularly wanted to be mobilised. The Americans meanwhile just opted to keep their troops there for a year. Unlike us, they weren't obsessed with keeping it all as cheap as possible. Al Amarah controlled the approaches to Baghdad from the Iranian border, so the Brits could, to a significant degree, minimise the flow into Baghdad of IED components, weapons and ammunition sourced from the Revolutionary Guard and Badr Corps, amongst other roles. When the Brits suddenly withdrew from Al Amarah as the bitter fighting in Helmand Province took our government by total surprise and that rapidly became "the war" for the British Army, the incidence of IEDs against the Americans in Baghdad rose by over 100%, as did American casualties. As always, the Americans were too polite to complain and eventually had to retake control of Maysan Province from the inadequate Iraqi Security Forces.

I was briefed to plan a hand over to a Para Company, who had been providing border security. Our Americans would just return to their army and most of my troops to normal duties. George, Mike and I had a last coffee with our American friends, who were genuinely sad to leave us. Europeans simply love to criticise the Americans, but the reality is that without them our joint European global influence and capabilities are remarkably limited. Even our own armed forces are now in essence superbly well trained and highly self-motivated minor players following the recent Coalition's SDSR and its relentless aftermath of much-reduced forces with some glaring gaps in overall capability, a "hollow force" in many respects. Despite the current claims of various European politicians regarding the EU, it never kept the peace in Europe, rather NATO did and we still ultimately rely on the Americans for the security of Europe, unpalatable as that may be in the increasingly volatile 21st[t] Century. Political rhetoric simply doesn't replace thousands of redundant troops and an embarrassing lack of fighter bombers, maritime patrol aircraft, armoured fighting vehicles and a broad range of key equipment to people who wish to do us harm on a large-scale basis.

That night I took my turn to call home on my weekly satellite phone call. Electing for some privacy I went outside. As I walked around a corner, I came face to face with a fairly large camel spider which seemed far less surprised than I was by our evening encounter. I stopped abruptly and so did it, but far less abruptly. We stared at each other for a short while and I realised it wasn't prepared to move, instead it just appeared to watch me from about 4 metres away, presumably eyeing me up as possible prey. Following another period of mutual watching I thought, "Don't be stupid, you're six foot tall and he's only two inches high", so I slowly walked towards him. He/she/it then appeared to slowly rock back on its hind legs and suddenly it leapt forward and upwards, shooting rapidly past my right ear and disappearing instantly into the pitch darkness of the desert night behind me. It was a classic "what the fuck" moment, Iraq is never that boring for a pink bloke.

The following day W went back to the brigade pool of interpreters. We were glad to see him go, he wasn't a man we believed that we could trust to any degree and we felt he had his own agenda. It was also a definite sign that we were now officially yesterday's soldiers. Lacking a Terp and any real role any more, we basically went for a final drive just to check that all was quiet in our AO. We were back down to two Land Rovers and 6 soldiers so our capability had now gone full circle, déjà vu in many ways. It was a mundane and very quiet, if singularly hot day and we were extremely subdued. I showed a distinct lack of moral courage by choosing not to stop and talk to the friendlier villagers as they waved as we passed them by. I personally felt that we had let them down by failing to help them in any worthwhile or enduring manner and in some ways we had simply made their daily life more difficult by rocking their world with an utter absence of any coherent national post-conflict strategy on our part. Their collective future seemed very unsure indeed, words after all are an extremely cheap currency when you live a very basic life in such a harsh, often violent and eternally unforgiving land. So here I was, about to depart along with all my comrades, except I was personally both embarrassed and saddened by our repeated failures, and as such I didn't expect them to remember any of us particularly kindly.

Later, on another whim we drove to the Iraqi Army Barracks where we had impotently watched the mass looting shortly after our arrival. Ironically, whilst we had driven past it on an almost daily basis, it was the first time we had actually gone back inside the now long-deserted complex. All the Iraqi Army vehicles were now long gone, recovered for the future "new" Iraqi Army and as we toured the buildings we were struck by the absolute emptiness of them all. Unless it was bolted down (and in some cases that hadn't stopped the looters), nothing was left with the notable exception of numerous, albeit smashed, portraits of Saddam and torn-down propaganda posters. We were just about to leave when we heard the unmistakable sound of children's laughter from inside a large storage building. Bemused, we walked over to investigate. This was hardly the archetypal western idea of a playground. Walking through some wide open and thickly armoured blast doors, we could hear the echo of laughter. Rounding the corner of a wide corridor, we were amazed to find several young boys, each of about ten years of age.

Even more amazing was the fact they were playing some form of hopscotch, but using artillery shell fuses instead of pebbles. These fuses contain a small, but effective, explosive charge that makes the shell go "bang" at the far end of its trajectory, enough to kill or main any adult stupid enough to play or tamper with it, let alone a small boy. They stopped their game when they saw us, surrounded by dozens and dozens of fuses all over the floor as they were: a lot of explosive when viewed collectively. Lacking a Terp to fully explain the threat to life they faced, we confiscated the fuses they held and tried to explain the danger involved. They just looked at us blankly, openly full of distrust, so we shooed them outside to safety. Once outside, they merely waited until we got back into our vehicles and promptly ran back inside to continue their game. We gave up, we were mere foreign killjoys and the bright shiny metal objects inside were both fun and interesting. All we could do was request the EOD guys to visit and dispose of this hazard. I really don't know if they ever did so, as shortly afterwards their fathers, uncles and elder brothers enthusiastically started blowing British soldiers up on a regular basis, which obviously concentrated quite a few minds on our part, especially the bomb disposal teams.

In a way this small incident was a metaphor for all our efforts over the previous months. We meant well and came full of good intent, but offered little in practical or physical terms from the Iraqi people's perspective, didn't understand their social structure, vastly differing culture and related values whilst we, they felt, disrupted their daily lives, the national infrastructure and any and all business. But most of all, we just didn't have any realistic form of a tangible plan. Admittedly a rather simplistic view but at the time and place it struck us as ironic in its own small way, to say the least. We drove back to the airfield fairly slowly and rather quietly. It had finally dawned on us that it was almost our time to go home, back to the real world.

On arriving back at the airfield we were rather jealous when we discovered that almost everyone, it seemed, had a piece of fruit or two, some bread and a chocolate bar, except us. We were very unimpressed: now even our own side now seemed to view us as yesterday's soldiers. Having seen none of these luxury items for months, some fairly irate questioning ensued along the lines of, "Where are our fucking goodies, then?", we were informed that our rations were on the veranda. We promptly discovered that some kind soul had put our "bag rations" on the floor, thereby allowing access to hundreds of Iraq's finest ants to infest everything. This single thoughtless act by an unknown comrade, quite trivial in the overall grand scheme of things, had the greatest single impact on our morale by far, courtesy of our own regiment. It somehow seemed to epitomise the planning and execution of the entire invasion.

The Paras had earmarked a small platoon to take over the AO. They obviously didn't relish the task, at least on the Iranian border they had a possible chance to at least "swop a few rounds" with someone. Here, that was decidedly unlikely, which seemed to disappoint them somewhat. However, they would soon find their "day of days" in Helmand Province, where they became known as the "men with squares" to the Taliban, a reference to their DZ (Drop Zone) flashes. Each Para Battalion wears a different-coloured square in order to "rally" on the DZ. They engendered both lasting respect and a wary caution amongst the Taliban as being fierce and "full on" warriors, a quite rare commodity during our long campaign in southern Afghanistan: the Taliban are not overly impressed by reputation. Then they had to settle for more mundane tasks, until Iraq "kicked off" at least. I admire the Paras immensely: not great table partners for tea with your grandmother, but all democracies ultimately require "Rough men to stand guard on the city walls in order for good citizens to sleep safe abed at night", and they are those men without a doubt. (But just don't expect too many deep and meaningful philosophical discussions). In an era where less than 30% of young Britons would actually fight to defend their nation and Islamic State have regularly out-recruited the Army reserve in UK, soldiers such as these are becoming an increasingly rare commodity in the UK.

With the exceptions of the oil refinery — always a good prospect for an illegal weapons search — and the sheikh's village, which warranted their OC's presence, a muscular major showing his face to appease local expectations (as the sheikh was both a shrewd political survivor and a "mover and a shaker" on a local scale, so worth some humble pie from our perspective to pander to his undoubted ego), the local villages disappointed our new arrivals. Otherwise the Paras didn't take too kindly to their new role. Oh well, you win some, you lose some, we thought without too much sympathy. After all, we and they were ultimately different military tribes, albeit on the same side. The sheikh dropped us with shameless alacrity, he was a truly political beast, worthy of a Westminster seat from my humble perspective. However, it was time for us to go and therefore let go as it simply wasn't either our concern or our mission any more.

I decided it was probably best for the Iraqis to get to know the Paras and their uniquely robust attitude towards life themselves and we had the strange experience of a day off. With no defined job and not much else to do, we visited some of the numerous warehouses and bunkers dotted around the airfield. The sheer scale and quantity of the diverse contents amazed us: hundreds, in some cases literally thousands of Italian and French mines of all sizes; American TOW missiles (exactly the same type we had used against their armour a few months earlier) and artillery shells of American, British and European manufacture; not to mention several nations' bullets in their tens and possibly hundreds of thousands. This was a military Aladdin's cave, all supplied to Saddam in the days when the West strongly backed his war against Iran and now being saved for issue to the "new" Iraqi Army, it seemed. Whilst we had been starved of ammunition and most things needed in war-fighting requirements by old-fashioned incompetence and dreadful planning by our own ultra-complacent hierarchy back in the UK, the Iraqi Military had been almost literally awash with military ordnance, it seemed to us, even after thousands of future insurgents had finished their "post-invasion shopping" in the national anarchy following Saddam's downfall.

All of this was no longer our concern, so we jogged around the airfield — a small piece of rest and recreation and our first opportunity since leaving Kuwait — safe in the knowledge that the Mobile Baths and Showers Unit (I am not making this up, it was then a TA unit) had arrived, so we could pamper ourselves with a hot shower. Sadly, when we duly turned up, each of us clutching our Army green towels and our issue soap, we were informed the water had just run out. The Morale Police it seemed had returned with a vengeance. Back to strip washes and sharing the team plastic bowl it was then.

Just to emphasise that our role was over, I was placed on duty for my last night in Iraq. We had been excused duties when patrolling every day, so I was the duty officer in a very Spartan Operations Room. We had packed most of the communications equipment away in preparation for our drive back to Kuwait. In the centre of the room was a large map board, mainly for show now that we were leaving and the radios were silent, so this was very much a boring evening for all concerned, we thought. Shortly after midnight, one of the NCOs cried out, "Look at that!" We turned to find a rather large camel spider, sitting motionless in the middle of the map and eyeing us all malevolently. It had either been attracted by the warmth or was just hungry, we couldn't decide which. The guys tried to make it "shoo". It ignored us completely. So we ganged up on it, five soldiers against one spider. It just refused to budge. We waved papers, banged on the table and shouted loudly. It simply stood its ground motionlessly and eyeballed us. Eventually we decided to take drastic measures. Four of us distracted it while a huge NCO (aptly nicknamed "Horse") sneakily crept up behind it with a large shovel. Amazingly, the blow just stunned it. Several blows later we jointly pronounced it dead and agreed we all really needed to go home soon.

The next day, having paraded at "early o'clock" we lined our vehicles up for the long-awaited drive to Kuwait, to be loudly informed that, before we left Al Amarah, we all had to return our ammunition. We were speechless at first and then laughed aloud, thinking, "That's a good one, we nearly fell for that!" As the laughter died down we were solemnly informed that this was not a joke, we were to hand all our ammunition in now. This was not well received by the troops, including myself. Loud questions were asked along the lines of, "What if we get ambushed?" The response was that the first and last vehicles would have ammunition and they would deal with it. Anyway, the war was over and there was no threat, period. I could not believe my ears. We had violently invaded this country, overthrown its government and seen nationwide anarchy and looting, only for some idiot to decide this was akin to driving from Colchester to Salisbury Plain back in UK. I quietly questioned the wisdom of this policy. Apparently it was necessary to ensure "good accounting". I turned away and gave up in disgust.

So with empty magazines fitted to our rifles (against orders admittedly, but at least the Iraqis might think we had some bullets) we drove south towards an eventual freedom bird to UK. Along the way we saw that some of our tanks had finally arrived from Basra, little knowing how crucial they would become to just maintaining our presence here as Al Amarah soon became a major magnet for insurgents and the scene of bitter and prolonged fighting, as I would discover on a visit to Iraq some 18 months later when the garrison had been engaged in prolonged and vicious fighting. Indeed, a large part of our national and military response to the Al Amarah fighting would be essentially a news blackout, just like Helmand in 2006 when the outnumbered Para Battle Group would have to fight for its sheer survival on an almost daily basis. Ironically, HMG had sent two female officials from DFID, escorted by locally hired Pashtun Gunmen (some of whom were undoubtedly "off duty" Taliban), to test the water prior to the Paras' imminent arrival to tour Helmand and show the flabbergasted desert-dwelling Helmandis the BBC *Blue Planet* series. The illiterate villagers duly watched the series in stunned silence. Even the simple concept of an ocean, let alone strange sea-dwelling creatures, was simply beyond them.

On the basis of this stunned reception to two unarmed females (who, being merely women weren't construed as a threat in this male-dominated land), we were later briefed in Oman, on the final pre-deployment training, that the locals are friendly. You really can't make this up: our politicians deciding to send a small and underequipped force on a naïvely perceived "reconstruction mission" on the basis of two women showing a BBC TV series, which aptly demonstrates the slipshod manner in which we drifted into a second bitter and bloody desert campaign where 19-year-old infantry soldiers would see far more action in a single 6 months tour than an armed police officer would ever experience, or even dream of during their entire career and our superb Special Forces would repeatedly go into the very "heart of darkness" on an almost nightly basis.

By chance we encountered our American pals who waved goodbye as they passed us in their Humvee. Unlike us, they were still well armed, which was the singular highlight of a long and (thankfully) boring drive south, but the IEDs were yet to come and for that we were very thankful. We were too aware of how vulnerable our vehicles were to anything above a medium-sized stone. Someone actually showed a modicum of common sense and we pulled in at the first roadside shop inside Kuwait, a typical petrol station and mini-market. We wandered around, all with lots of dollars burning holes in our wallets like the proverbial kids in a sweet shop faced with Pringles, Coca Cola, Sprite et all. We really didn't know what to buy first or how many. George resolved the issue by buying me a Coke, saying, "Mac, we did it. We're alive." A sobering comment which brought home to me just how much we had relied on sheer bluff on a daily basis. I thanked him and cherished it for quite a while before drinking it, which promptly gave me hiccups for most of the day. We were all quite accustomed to mainly drinking warm water by now.

On arrival at Ali Al Salam, our new home until we left Kuwait, we re-joined our circus style tents, put our weapons in the armoury and thought, "What now?" One novel concept was that we now had chefs and a canteen to feed us. We all trekked to the evening meal, like lemmings towards a cliff. We just wanted to go home and restart our lives, such as they were, back in UK. The chefs, who had been left behind in Kuwait, hadn't seen us for months and they put on the mother of all meals to welcome us back to civilisation. It literally stopped us in our tracks: various roasts, several types of potato, lasagne, ice cream, the ever-popular sight of chips, a salad bar and so on. After a long pause the troops got stuck in, as always the junior ranks first and the senior ranks and officers last. I got a large salad with an assortment of bread and some cheese, Mike attacked the ice cream and George made some baguettes, while the cold drinks bar was under siege. None of us could actually face the hot foods, our stomachs had shrunk significantly over the last few months, but the younger troops heaped a bit of everything on their plates around us. "It will all end in tears," George remarked. Mike and I sagely nodded our agreement. Sure enough, within a few hours dozens of soldiers found that their digestive systems rejected this rich food in a quite dramatic and prolonged fashion.

Our days now centred on meal times, reading and lying on our camp cots, waiting for something to happen. Very traditional really, we could have easily been Wellington's troops waiting for the French to arrive in some ways. Time dragged but we were going home and hopefully someone would tell us something, preferably about a plane home. Eventually we all lined up to be searched by the RAF Police before we finally got on the plane home, mainly it seemed for now worthless Iraqi dinars, portraits of Saddam or Iraqi flags. It seemed we could kill Iraqis in large numbers, but the UK Government didn't want us being "triumphalist" in doing so. Our politicians both then and now seem convinced that you can somehow wage a "very nice" war. This naïveté is an utter contradiction in terms, especially when our current enemies routinely behead people (sometimes en masse) and wage a medieval and ruthless form of warfare. After all, this is an enemy who detests every single aspect of our "Haram" culture and views all and every "nonbeliever" as legitimate targets worthy of death by whatever means possible. Ironically, the discreet masterminds behind this so called "Sunni awakening" would be disgruntled former Iraqi Army Officers and all ardent followers of Saddam. Revenge, it seems, is indeed a dish best served cold.

After our eventual defeat in Iraq, regime change became politically attractive again somehow, but our intervention in Libya is no longer mentioned in political circles, despite us somehow expanding a UN approved "no fly zone" into a rather lengthy air campaign to forcibly eject Mr Gadaffi from power. Yet again no one considered the aftermath, so we succeeded in utterly de-stabilising the country and making it a very popular terrorist arsenal in the Middle East, followed by the usual power struggle by opposing tribal factions. But back then, we were all going home, "job done" and optimistic that surely a huge number of lessons would be learned by all concerned after this large-scale sandy-coloured bluff we had all participated in, or so we all rather naïvely believed. How wrong we all were, as events over the next few years would prove. It rather appears that few, if any, significant lessons were learned from Iraq in terms of military intervention.

Ultimately, we never gave this much thought. We had done our job and just wanted to go home, it was up to the politicians to sort out Iraq's future: that was after all their side of the fence to deal with as they saw fit. The British Military are simply just another tool set for political use and individuals are mere commodities, but conversely, such is the very nature of small professional armies within a democracy and the contract of service is understood by all. But British soldiers are all volunteers, old-fashioned patriots, well trained and well led, ever stoical and exceedingly courageous. It "was ever thus" in effect. Personally speaking, my service gave me the repeated opportunity to walk with giants and irrespective of the vague and often diametrically changing political direction, the Army held the line under incredibly difficult and hostile circumstances and in doing so fully paid the blood price that one of our PMs spoke of prior to the commencement of our desert wars.

The Army will continue to do its duty for the nation, irrespective of its now greatly reduced capability and all the bombast and ongoing rhetoric of professional politicians. I'm sure the Roman Legions quietly had very similar thoughts towards their Senate. At the risk of being rather unkind, the average Roman General seems to have had far more success than the majority of British Generals in recent years, but in their defence, unlike modern British Commanders, Roman Generals never had to deal with such incessant and large-scale political interference from distant politicians and were largely left alone to actually fight their wars.

Our actual homecoming was remarkably low key. After landing at Brize Norton we drove to East Anglia, collected our kit, and following a brief and remarkably succinct "thank you" from the CO, we immediately boarded a coach for our own regiment in North Yorkshire. That was it in a nutshell, the Army prefers the minimalist approach. Our own regiment gave us a warm welcome, significant amounts of alcohol (we didn't need much) and sent us all on leave at the earliest opportunity. My own home leave was awkward. Whilst it was tremendous to be reunited with my sons, frankly I was very irritable and lacked patience with my wife, had problems sleeping and after months in the open desert, found town centres claustrophobic and overwhelmingly noisy. To say my wife was bemused is probably an understatement. It wasn't the joyous homecoming either of us imagined. I feel secure in surmising that several thousand British soldiers can identify with that situation fully.

Shortly after returning to UK, the shocking news that a Royal Military Police Patrol (RMP) from our brigade had been massacred in Marjah, very close to Al Amarah. This for me was a case of, "There but for the Grace of God go I". They, too, had been a small isolated patrol and just like my own team, lacked ammunition and decent weaponry with the same ever-unreliable communications, but unlike us, their bluff had been called with tragic results. Some of the RMP soldiers were captured, and promptly executed in cold blood by the mob. We vaguely knew some of them: 16 Bde is a tight-knit formation and we were simply stunned by the news. This could easily have been any one of several units, tragically for the RMP personnel concerned, fate conspired towards their small patrol. Like so many soldiers of this era, I could easily picture the scene and I personally have no doubt they well knew in their last moments on

Earth that absolutely no one would be coming to their rescue and there was only one possible ending.

The resulting enquiry was inconclusive and despite the strident calls of solemn-looking politicians, the RMPs' killers were never fully brought to justice. Like many soldiers in the Army at the time I felt the entire incident was both tragically inevitable, yet also very avoidable. The perennial ammunition shortages and radio issues combined with collective complacency had simply come home to roost with murderous effect. Within weeks of this came the further stunning news that Dai — the bright, affable and talented Infantry Officer — our former CIMIC guru, had also been killed in Basra. He lost his life in a manner utterly typical of him: he was killed while shielding one of his wounded soldiers with his own body in an IED blast against a clearly marked ambulance. Dai was accompanying the already wounded soldier to hospital and the Red Cross symbol meant nothing to the insurgents. Now it was pretty obvious our control of Iraq was slipping away fairly rapidly.

Eighteen months later the situation had deteriorated in Al Amarah sufficiently for the UK to consider sending its brand new Apache attack helicopters to enhance the garrison's capabilities, so I found myself back in Maysan Province once more. In order to resupply CIMIC House (our main post in the city centre), a tank escort had been necessary to fight their way in. I was amazed to hear how British tanks, for the first time since the Korean War, had to machine gun each other to remove insurgents who had "swarmed" the tanks, actually climbing onto them as they slowly moved along the streets of Al Amarah. They were emboldened by our ultra-restrictive rules of engagement: unlike our American allies, we couldn't engage insurgents openly carrying weapons until they actually opened fire on us, and if we did, once they turned their back on us and therefore technically ceased to be a threat, we had to cease firing. In effect the Brits were routinely fielding a seven-a-side team for a Premier League match and giving the opposition the ball as well.

On returning to Basra I had a coffee with a young Infantry Officer, fresh from Sandhurst, who had personally led three bayonet charges in one day to clear insurgents from their urban ambush positions. He had rapidly matured into a battle-hardened young man. Meanwhile the insurgent leaders were offering $25,000 for any British soldier captured alive, preferably a female one (DVDs of captured American soldiers being slowly tortured to death or the beheading of Westerners always sold exceedingly well in the markets of Baghdad). Currently the Army intends to employ young women in the infantry and will accordingly no doubt discreetly lower its physical standards to enable this, in effect a "quota rather than merit" process driven by political populism. Future battlefields will ultimately prove, or not, the wisdom of this decision. It remains to be seen how the British public will then react should any of these female soldiers then be either gang raped or beheaded (or both) on social media, as has recently happened to female Kurdish fighters.

Further north the Black Watch had been badly hit by a suicide car bomber and a young NCO who hailed from the Caribbean had been recommended for the Victoria Cross for displaying amazing courage in Al Amarah. I really couldn't help but think we were slowly creeping towards national failure unless our government paid some serious attention to Iraq and finally produced a workable strategy. In a mere 18 months the situation had transformed beyond all expectations and not in any way remotely to our advantage. It never crossed my mind that the Army would eventually have to negotiate our ultimate safe withdrawal from Basra with these very Shia militias, but that too lay in the future and no British soldier would have actually believed that suggestion at that time.

The Army, aided by the other services (the Royal Marines in particular) would repeatedly display uncommon valour, tenacity, stoicism and old-fashioned loyalty in huge amounts on a daily basis over the next 12 years. But the nation itself was never at war in anything but name, British industry never worked extra shifts of weekends to support the military and it was a hugely pointless exercise to attempt to try and contact the MOD or other government agencies on Saturday, Sunday or Bank Holiday when you were deployed on operations and fighting a 24/7 war. Rather the nation's military went to war while the nation went shopping or watched Premier League football and vacuous TV programmes about "our war" such as *Our Girl*, *Bluestone 42* or similar, which just cheapened the sacrifices made by the "Afghan Generation" of young servicemen and women during a decade plus of bitter desert fighting thousands of miles from home.

The Apaches never went to Iraq, mainly as their deployment could have delayed our planned deployment to Afghanistan in 2006 into some then unknown, distant and barren place called Helmand, a remote and backward province almost the size of England. The Treasury capped the initial force at 3,300 troops with ill-suited equipment primarily designed for either Belfast or German forests. I would argue that any Chief Constable who suggested he could police an area almost the size of England with so few officers would probably be immediately laughed out of office. The rest, as they say, is history. British soldiers never lost a single firefight, but they didn't win the war either. Uncommon valour and dedication to duty ultimately would never make up for the lack of numbers and equipment shortfalls. On my last military trip to Afghanistan in 2011, I idly discussed with some Army and RAF officers the question of, what could we have done differently? We all agreed that the error of arriving with too few in number, too little military clout and unachievable aims had laid the foundation for us Brits being constantly being reactive rather than proactive, a deadly game of catch-up in effect.

The decision to fight two concurrent wars had forced the services to divide these wars into "types". The RAF sent their Tornado bombers and Merlin helicopters to support operations in Iraq, with the Chinook helicopter fleet and the now American-owned joint RAF/RN Harrier ground attack jets went to Afghanistan. Meanwhile the Army sent its Armoured Brigades to Iraq and the "Light" Brigades to Afghanistan, which meant 6 months of war with roughly an 18-month gap until the next operational tour for the soldiers in these units. Repeated tours simply meant the odds of probability for being wounded or killed inevitably shortened against you. The simply enormous growth in the use of IEDs sharply exacerbated these odds. In Northern Ireland the IRA placed them in ones and twos, in Iraq this became fives and tens, in Helmand this became twenties and forties: even more so than suicide bombers, this was a major game changer.

In blunt terms we had nothing else to send anywhere. To sustain operations you require at the absolute very least 4 complete manpower cohorts: the one actually deployed, the one that has just come back from their tour and the final one training to deploy on its forthcoming tour whilst the fourth cohort picks up all "non-war related" tasking. This ongoing rotation soon eats into your available units, not to mention equipment availability and all the other logistical demands hidden away in the background. Both wars were manfully supported by the RAF ageing transport fleet as best it could and the Navy mainly looked on. With the exception of the Fleet Air Arm and Royal Marines, there really isn't much use for a navy in a desert war.

Once we abandoned Iraq the tour gap became much easier for the troops, but the heavy artillery and tanks weren't sent to Helmand as Whitehall apparently believed this would "send the wrong message" in media terms. Our Canadian, Danish and American allies didn't share these concerns, but the Brits quietly did without these key assets and got on with it, as our troops always do. By the time our Afghan campaign finally ended it wasn't unusual for a soldier to have deployed on 6 or more operational tours in both wars, essentially 2, 3 or even 4 years purely spent at war. Specialist troops (such as Bomb Disposal, IED search teams, SF or similar units, always in short supply) tended to do more in desperate attempts to plug key manning gaps and to fill the inevitable gaps caused by a steadily growing and very under-reported casualty list.

I finally left Camp Bastion in late 2014, now as a civilian contractor supporting UK Military Operations (ironically with Russian-made helicopters, flown by Ukrainians and South Africans, maintained by Russians), when our national priority had simply become "get the kit home", a military mission now run by uniformed storekeepers and distant accountants. Camp Bastion was essentially stripped clean, much to the chagrin of the Afghan National Army (ANA), except for several hundred tons of ammunition, which the British Army diligently spent weeks blowing up, apparently as it "was cheaper than sending it home" and for reasons unspoken we didn't wish to donate it to our ANA allies. One of my Russian pilots observed that we and the Americans certainly hadn't achieved any more, and possibly significantly less, than his own Army had in the 1980s. Sadly, I thought he had a very good point.

Very much a far cry from both our optimistic and determined entry in 2006 and the enthusiastic naïveté we had all shown for the Iraq invasion of 2003. Ironically the Army was determined to make up for its failure in Iraq by ensuring success in Helmand Province, myself included. Along the way the mission had changed on an almost annual basis in Afghanistan, whilst our rapid exit from Iraq was professionally embarrassing and badly damaged our national credibility with our key allies, a 21st Century version of the Suez debacle almost. But very unlike Suez, no one resigned. Like many retired soldiers I am totally unsure what, if any, positive legacy we left behind or indeed why we went there with no clearly defined national aims or a coherent long-term strategy. In Iraq you could argue we opened Pandora's Box and from it sprang a virulent strain of imperialist and extremist Islam (in terms of a 21st Century caliphate) operating along medieval lines, but one equipped with modern weaponry and thousands of European fighters counted amongst their ranks. Hardly a positive advert for liberal multi-culturalism and cohesive social integration in the 21st Century and recent events have shown this threat can reach Europe quite easily.

I don't really discuss either campaign except with other ex-soldiers. The Premier League and numerous celebrity game shows coupled with the perilous state of the NHS and the ongoing social impact of years of uncontrolled immigration are very hard topics to compete with in conversational terms. A Labour Party activist told me a while ago, there are only two rules in politics: rule one, gain power; rule two, stay in power. There are no more rules. Apparently this explains why Mr Blair was allowed to freely engage UK in so many wars: he won lots of elections after all, so the odd little war was a small price to pay in return. At the end of over a decade of desert wars, the Army is almost unrecognisable in shape and size whilst the politicians steadfastly refuse to accept the enormous damage inflicted on the nation's ability to defend the realm, but there are no votes in defence.

I personally quite like the analogy of the Emperor and the Senate in the latter stages of ancient Rome, who entertained the mob with gladiatorial games and gave them bread, thereby ensuring their own popularity and therefore power and influence, while foreign workers flocked to Rome to do the menial jobs Roman citizens no longer wished to involve themselves with. These foreign workers brought with them aggressive new religions that would one day replace all the Gods of Rome. Meanwhile the legions were slowly disbanded in order to pay for the games, imperial opulence and the bread issues. Deals were cut with barbarians and payments made in return for peace, as the legions were no longer the feared force of the Glory Days and defeat followed defeat until the Empire finally fell. A liberal, prosperous and democratic lifestyle has to be defended, even in the 21st Century, as the barbarians haven't really gone away and PC-driven appeasement is doomed to ultimate failure, as history has proven so often in the past.

The one bright spot from my uninvited visit to Iraq occurred two or three years ago when, after a Christmas drinks session in Liverpool, the last train home was replaced by a coach, unexpectedly driven by an Middle Eastern-looking man wearing an Everton football top. I greeted him with "Salaam Alaykum" on boarding the bus. He seemed slightly surprised. Later, on leaving the bus he asked me, complete with Scouse accent, "Are you a soldier?"

"Used to be," I replied.

"Basra?" he asked.

"No, Al Amarah," I responded.

He paused, the other passengers now becoming quite irritable by this strange conversation and the resulting delay. "I am Basrawi, but I live here now and life is good."

I smiled and said, "Good for you, mate. I'm glad you're happy."

He looked at me and said, "Thank you for invading my country or I would still be in Basra."

I really couldn't follow that sentiment, so I just said, "Shokran, Inshallah," and walked home in the winter rain, chuckling all the way. At least we had one happy customer to show for it all, I thought to myself and that really, to me personally, sums it all up very nicely.

Well over a decade after our invasion of Iraq, that once proud country continues to implode with Kurds, government forces, Islamic State and Iranian-reinforced Shia militias, all bitterly fighting for control of various areas. Meanwhile the air forces of several nations, including a small RAF element and the Iranian Air Force, add their combined weight to this bitter struggle and somewhere in the midst of this Western Special Forces are no doubt quietly doing "their thing". History has taught us that all wars must end one day, but it's hard to envisage Iraq surviving the aftermath of all this lengthy and vicious turmoil as a state in its current form. Meanwhile an even more complex war has erupted in neighbouring Syria, complete with a resurgent Russian Military. Certainly, one of the aspects I never remotely considered before the invasion was the radical change in the regional balance of power that would follow in its aftermath. As one of our PMs once remarked, "The kaleidoscope has been shaken and the pieces are in flux", ironically a very apt piece of fortune-telling as it transpired for Iraq and many of its neighbours.

No one pretends that Saddam Hussein was a benevolent human being, but even now the lack of planning and thought from our political and military leaders for "after the war" is simply breath-taking in both in its smug complacency and almost unbelievable incompetence, as indeed is the collective lack of responsibility for this and numerous other failures, not least of which was the lack of ammunition and other basic requirements to go to war with. Only pure blind luck kept the British casualty list down during that stage of our occupation, initially at least. Under Saddam and his obnoxious regime, his badly weakened armed forces, whilst all instruments of a massively unpleasant regime, were ultimately not a "clear and present danger" to either the region or Western civilisation. Like many veterans (as all ex-soldiers are now called, it seems, irrespective of length of service or operational tours, etc) I still await someone to honestly explain the infamous "dossier" or why the previously successful combination of sanctions and bombing was no longer deemed adequate to contain that thoroughly odious regime, but hindsight is a wonderful thing and regime change was then firmly on the political agenda.

Meanwhile hundreds of serving and former British soldiers are looking over their shoulder as British Human Rights lawyers, the Ministry of Defence (in the form of the Iraq Historical Allegations Team) and latterly the Police Service of Northern Ireland almost vied with each other for legal action against soldiers who simply tried their best to carry out their duty in demanding, complex, confusing and ultimately highly dangerous circumstances which simply defy any meaningful comparison with normal human experiences in UK society. One organisation does so for significant financial gain and two others for reasons of political correctness presumably, a fitting finale in some ways to the very nature of the invasion and yet another landmark in the ongoing sad decline in fortunes of the Army I proudly served in for some many years. No doubt many former Taliban fighters will watch the outcome of these events in UK with keen interest: after all, it is highly unlikely the American Military will ever offer them any form of financial payouts based on vague and quite possibly spurious claims.

Do I personally regret the invasion? My answer on a personal basis has to be a "reserved no". I participated enthusiastically and initially I believed we could be, just like in Kosovo previously, a "force for good", albeit on a much larger scale, in essence the very physical embodiment of our PM's concept of liberal intervention. Once in Kuwait and later Iraq I endeavoured to do my perceived duty to the best of my ability, like all the countless generations of British soldiers before me. Sadly, somewhere along the way I lost my personal belief in "the cause" as the fabled dossier proved to be, in old-fashioned Army terms merely, "Stating a falsehood" and the total lack of post-war planning slowly became more obvious and our unique and fleeting opportunity to be a force for good rapidly evaporated as our politicians both failed to grasp the ramifications of their decisions and policies or take any meaningful actions as Iraq descended into (well-armed) anarchy along its religious and ethnic fault lines, whilst various external "players" quickly entered into the resultant long and bitter insurgency to support their proxies.

Thereafter I did my duty purely for my soldiers, my cap badge and indeed the Army itself, but I found the aftermath of our invasion immensely frustrating. I never imagined being forced to repeatedly lie on behalf of my nation, or rely on utter bluff as a routine military tactic to safeguard my soldiers' lives, but I had no viable options and that particular regret will stay with me until I finally depart this existence. But neither do I remotely subscribe to the belief that Western Foreign Policy alone is totally and singularly to blame for the ongoing rise in violent

Jihadism: that's a very comfortable and simplistic supposition, but also ignores completely many difficult issues within the Muslim community globally in a remarkably convenient manner.

Both our soldiers and the Iraqi people were, to put it mildly, badly let down by our politicians and policy makers, albeit in vastly differing ways, but no one will ever, it seems, be held to account or accept any form of responsibility for their actions, or lack of action, as the case may be. Such is life in the era of spin, image and populist politics, but the ramifications of our invasion are manifold and seem destined to impact on our world for years to come in such a variety of ways. We briefly had a "once only" window of opportunity regarding the Iraqi people and our intentions, a honeymoon period in effect, when we could, perhaps, have shaped Iraq in a rather positive manner, but that moment passed by far too briefly and Western complacency and inaction proved fatal in many ways.

De-Ba'athification of Iraq sounded a very logical step, but it was poorly and ineffectively communicated across Iraqi society and even more badly conducted in practice. The ensuing effects were totally underestimated, as was the decision not to pay the Iraqi Army its outstanding, and rather meagre wages, or utilise any aspect of its manpower in the post-conflict anarchy. The rest, as they say, is history. Public interest in the failures of both the Iraq War and the Afghanistan campaign is slight and that doesn't surprise me. The Armed Forces are now exceedingly small in number and both wars were fought far away by a small number of professional soldiers and conducted relatively out of sight of the media and therefore the UK public. The impact of either failure is very minimal to the man in the street and the true cost of both wars has been very well obscured by various governments whilst the "new", much reduced British Army has numerous fresh challenges to meet with very limited capabilities, which won't be aided by dwelling on our recent failures.

Personally, I would like to think we have learned some valuable lessons from our various interventions, but I am far from convinced. As one female American Colonel recently commented on hearing of the destruction of Iraq's oldest Christian monastery (which had been guarded and refurbished by the American Military) by IS/Daesh was simply, "So what was it all for?" Similarly, I doubt if any brief epitaph such as, "Really sorry, but we meant well," will be of much consolation to either the Iraqi people, UK and American widows, wounded veterans or future historians passing judgement, or indeed, the one-armed torture victim I stood with by the Tigris River all those years ago as he shook my hand and simply said, "Inshallah".